Paper Bridges

Kadya Molodowsky, around 1938, in the United States

פּאַפּירענע בריקן

געקליבענע לידער פֿון

קאַדיע מאָלאָדאָווסקי

Paper Bridges

Selected Poems of

Kadya Molodowsky

Translated, Edited, and Introduced by

Kathryn Hellerstein

Wayne State University Press

Detroit

Library of Congress Cataloging-in-Publication Data

Molodowsky, Kadia, 1894–1975.
[Poems. English & Yiddish. Selections]
Paper bridges : selected poems of Kadya Molodowsky / translated, edited, and introduced by Kathryn Hellerstein.
p. cm.
Includes bibliographical references.
ISBN 0-8143-2846-6 (alk. paper)
ISBN 0-8143-2718-4 (pbk. : alk. paper)
1. Molodowsky, Kadia, 1894–1975—Translations into English, 2. Holocaust, Jewish (1939–1945)—Poetry. I. Hellerstein, Kathryn. II. Title.
PJ5129.M7A25 1999
839′.113—dc21 98-15479
HE

Some of the English translations that appear here have been previously published in earlier versions and sometimes in the context of scholarly articles in the following journals and anthologies:

AJS Review 13, nos. 1–2 (1988): 47–79. ("Women-Poems/Songs of Women I–VIII")

Bridges 2, no. 1 (spring 1991): 53–61. ("Dzshike Street," "Chronicle," "My Paper Bridge," and "Letters from the Ghetto")

Borders, Boundaries and Frames: Cultural Criticism and Cultural Studies, edited by Mae G. Henderson, 64–106. New York: Routledge, 1995.

Four Centuries of Jewish Women's Spirituality: A Sourcebook, edited by Ellen M. Umansky and Dianne Ashton, 154–55. Boston: Beacon Press, 1992. ("Prayers I, II, III" and "Songs of Women VI")

Grove, no. 6 (spring 1982): 36–37. ("Women-Poems/Songs of Women VI")

Handbook of American-Jewish Literature: An Analytical Guide to Topics, Themes, and Sources, edited by Lewis Fried, 195–237. New York: Greenwood, 1988. ("Songs of Women/Women-Poems VI and VIII" and "Fallen Leaves")

Imagine 1, no. 1 (summer 1984): 74–75. ("Women-Poems/Songs of Women VIII")

Parable and Story in Judaism and Christianity, edited by Clemens Thoma and Michael Wyschogrod, 205–36. New York: Paulist Press, 1989. ("Fallen Leaves II" and "Prayers I, II, and III")

Present Tense 8, no. 3 (spring 1981): 50.

The Uses of Adversity: Failure and Accommodation in Reader Response, edited by Ellen Spolsky, 143–52. Lewisburg: Bucknell, and London and Toronto: Associated University Presses, 1990.

Two Lines: The Stanford Translation Journal (spring 1995), issue on "Tracks" ("My Father's Fur Coat")

Women in Praise of the Sacred: Forty-three Centuries of Spiritual Poetry by Women, edited by Jane Hirshfield, 238. New York: HarperCollins, 1994. ("Prayers I")

Yiddish 7, nos. 2–3 (1988): 182–87, 192–94. ("Songs of Women I–VIII" and "Prayers I–III")

TO
DAVID STERN

תּוכן

Contents

Acknowledgments

This book has been long in the making, and I am indebted to a number of organizations and individuals for support and advice over the years. I am extremely grateful to the Lucius N. Littauer Foundation and to the University of Pennsylvania Research Foundation for their grants to subvent the publication of this book. A fellowship at the University of Pennsylvania Center for Judaic Studies, formerly the Annenberg Research Institute, in 1989, gave me the opportunity to begin revising the translations of the poems. The Marie Syrkin Fellowship, under the auspices of *The New Republic*, granted me a month of writing time at Mishkenot Sha'ananim in Jerusalem, in August 1991. Fellowships from the Ratner, Miller, Shafran Foundation, the Fox Fund and the William and Gertrude Lipman Foundation, all of Cleveland, Ohio, helped support this project in its early stages.

The librarians and archivists at the YIVO Institute for Jewish Research in New York City and at the Jewish National Library in Jerusalem were as always helpful in locating texts and sources.

I have been extremely fortunate to have had many readers of the translations and the introduction in draft. These patient friends and colleagues have offered me comments and suggestions that helped enormously in my revisions. I am especially grateful to John Felstiner, Gella Schweid Fishman, and Irving Massey, and to a host of others who also read the manuscript or responded to individual translations. If I have forgotten anybody's name, I beg forgiveness. My gratitude extends to Chana Bloch, Andrew Firestone, Amira Goma, David Kenosian, Irena Klepfisz, the late M. Littvin, Allen Mandelbaum, Helen Nakdimen, Anita Norich, Avraham Nowersztern, Adrienne Rich, Chava Rosenfarb, David Roskies, Sheila Segal, Sara Sfatman, Vera Soloman, Carol Troen, Josh Waletzky, Miriam Waddington, my Yiddish literature and language students at the University of Pennsylvania, and the Philadelphia Women's Writers Group. I thank Itzik Gottesman, David Guralnik, Mikhl Herzog, Sol Katz, Mordkhe Schaechter, and Dov Noy for sharing their expertise in the Yiddish language with me. With all this help, I nonetheless take full responsibility for whatever errors or infelicities may mar my rendering of Molodowsky's poetry.

Other colleagues helped me with background information: Darra Goldstein provided information on Lermontov and the legendary Tamara. Mendele listservice subscribers, especially Paul Pascal of Toronto and Gaston L. Schmir, gave me geographical details on Otwock and Bereza Kartuska. Michael Steinlauf advised me on Polish details. Dovid Fishman alerted me to materials on Molodowsky. Haya Bar-Itzhak and Dan Ben-Amos advised me on details of folklore.

Kadya Molodowsky's friends and family have been extremely helpful. Elain Drost Friedman generously gave or lent me copies of Molodowsky's books, manuscripts, letters, photographs from the collection of her parents Yosel and Bessie Drost, and shared with me her personal recollections. Kadya Molodowsky's niece and nephew, Edith Litman Schwarz and Ben Litman, were also extremely generous with their own memories and their aunt's family photographs. Michael Silver of Victoria, Australia, granted me an informative interview about Molodowsky when she taught him in Warsaw. Naomi Zuckerman and Mordechai Tsanin gave me insight into Molodowksy's years in Israel. My delightful conversations with David Rosenthal over the years have helped fill in my sense of Molodowsky as a person and provided crucial details about Warsaw in the 1930s.

I also thank Arthur Evans and Janet Witalec at Wayne State University Press for their rigor and support in the production of this publication.

I am grateful to my mother Dr. Mary F. Hellerstein and my late father Dr. Herman K. Hellerstein for their encouragement and support. I thank my children Rebecca and Jonah Stern, who, listening repeatedly to my translations of Kadya's children's poems, have offered questions, comments, and interpretations. Their babysitters Catherine Felton and Elisha Williams gave me the gift of time.

Finally, I thank my husband, colleague, and fellow translator, David Stern, for his advice, support, and faith in me and this project from its very beginnings. I dedicate this book with love to him.

Introduction

Major Themes and Conflicts

Kadya Molodowsky (1894–1975) published six major books of poetry in Yiddish, including the children's poems for which she is best known today, as well as fiction, plays, and essays. She participated in nearly every aspect of Yiddish literary culture that existed in her lifetime, first in Poland, where she lived until 1935, when she emigrated, and then in America, where she lived until her death. Before her emigration, Molodowsky taught young children in the Yiddish schools of Warsaw. In New York City, she supported herself by writing for the Yiddish press and founded a literary journal, *Svive* (Surroundings), which she edited for nearly thirty years. In 1971, she was awarded the Itzik Manger Prize, the most prestigious award in the world of Yiddish letters, for her achievement in poetry.

Molodowsky was one of the few Yiddish women poets able to sustain and develop her writing throughout her life. She published continuously from 1927 until 1974. All her books, both poetry and prose, reflect the cultural and historical changes that their author experienced. But the poetry in particular evinces the often contradictory influences of the cultures among which Molodowsky lived—the Russian symbolists, the Yiddish modernists (and through them, modern American and European poetry), the Hebrew Bible, rabbinic writings, Yiddish prayers for women, social protest poetry, modern drama, and world folk- and classical lore. Although the distinctive voice that emerged from this confluence of cultures addressed the same social issues that concerned her contemporaries, it was given its particular force by Molodowsky's immediate and intense focus on women's lives and works. Because of this focus, Molodowsky's poems reshape the questions that pervaded modern Yiddish poetry: questions about the poet's political responsibility, national identity, religious belief, aestheticism, and individualism. The themes of her poems are often polemical, but the poems themselves rarely slip into easy ideological slots. Rather, they bring the compressed intensity of the lyric to the expansive forms of the meditation, the narrative, and the poetic sequence. Molodowsky's poems play constantly yet unexpectedly upon the Yiddish language—its musicality, emotional complexity, and mélange of dictions. They also encompass the folk idioms, the learned rabbinic phrases, crass Americanisms and neologisms, political clichés, and literary affectations. As a result, the poems have a deliberate self-consciousness that exposes the poet to her own merciless gaze.

As Molodowsky developed, her poetry came to embody the conflicts within her life. A woman with modernist sensibilities, a Jew thrown into crisis by secularism, an intellectual enraged by social injustice but wary of ideology, Molodowsky wrote in a tradition that was not always sympathetic to her sexual identity, her religious feelings, or her poetic politics.

Early Life

By her own account, in the autobiography she wrote and serialized in *Svive* during the final decade of her life, from March 1965 through April 1974, Molodowsky's childhood was not, in its details, typical for an Eastern European Jewish girl. Writing this account after the Second World War, Molodowsky believed that the shape of her life was representative of the Jewish people's fate.

Molodowsky's autobiography, "Mayn elterzeydns yerushe" ("My Great-Grandfather's Legacy") is a problematic text, selectively shaped by Molodowsky's sensibility as a storyteller and her sense of mission. Despite the abundance of details about people and places, Molodowsky provides very few dates, omits many crucial facts, and of the facts she does present, many are difficult or impossible to corroborate. Writing from her post-Holocaust perspective, in the wake of her losses and in her support for the State of Israel, Molodowsky presents in the autobiography a vision of her life as representative of Eastern European Jews. In essence, she intends to preserve through her particular story an entire culture that has been lost. Yet her poems reveal a different kind of truth. The account of Molodowsky's life and poetry that follows reads the poems against the autobiography and the autobiography against the poems while verifying facts from other sources.

Kadya Molodowsky was born on May 10, 1894,[1] in Bereza Kartuska, a shtetl or small town in the part of the Pale of Settlement called White Russia, located within the czarist Russian province of Grodno (now the Belarus Oblast' of Brest), some sixty miles northeast of Brest-Litovsk and fifty-six miles west northwest of Pinsk.[2] The second of four children, Kadya had an older sister, Lena, and two younger siblings, a sister, Dora (or Dobe), and a brother, Leybl. Her father, Isaac, a traditionally learned Jew who taught Hebrew and Gemara to young boys in *kheder*,[3] was also an adherent of the Enlightenment and an admirer of Sir Moses Montefiore, the nineteenth-century Jewish philanthropist, and Theodore Herzl, the founder of modern political Zionism. As a sign of that apparent paradox, Molodowsky recalled that in her childhood home, a portrait of Herzl hung next to a picture of the great eighteenth-century rabbi, the Vilna Gaon.[4] Molodowsky's mother, Itke[5] (the daughter of Kadish Katz/Kaplan, for whom Kadya was named)[6] ran a dry-goods shop. Later, she opened a factory for the making of the mild, fermented beverage rye kvass.[7]

Molodowsky's first teacher, whom she called her *rebetsn*,[8] was her paternal grandmother, Bobe Shifre, who taught her the alphabet, how to recite the prayers, and first exposed her to the Megillah (the Scroll of Esther) in Yiddish.[9] Her father instructed Kadya in the study of Khumash (the Five Books of Moses)[10] and also hired various Russian tutors, including one young woman, to teach her Russian language, geography, philosophy, and world history,[11] all in preparation for the high school graduation exams given in the regional city of Libave.[12] Such an education, especially the instruction in Hebrew, was not at all typical for a young girl in the shtetl, and Kadya was better educated than either of her sisters.[13]

At the age of seventeen, Kadya passed the exams. She tutored students in Bereza until her eighteenth birthday, when she was permitted to obtain a teaching certificate. Her first post was in a private Jewish school for girls in the Polish town of Sherpetz (probably 1911–12).[14] After that, she took a year's appointment in Bialystok (probably 1912–13), where her mother's sister lived and where she joined a Hebrew-language revivalist group. In 1913, she went to Warsaw to take courses with Yehiel Halperin to qualify her officially to teach children Hebrew.[15]

1914 was a crucial year for Molodowsky. In the spring, when she was home in Bereza for Passover, the First World War broke out, and her shtetl was flooded with Jewish refugees from the front.[16] This was also the year when advances were made in Jewish education: Educators in Warsaw, Lublin, Lodz, Brest-Litovsk, and other Jewish centers opened Hebrew kindergartens, of which Molodowsky and her peers in the Warsaw Hebrew courses were enthusiastic proponents.

As the war brought homelessness and dire poverty to many Jewish communities, however, it temporarily destroyed further developments in Jewish education. When Molodowsky returned to Warsaw, she worked in a day home for homeless Jewish children, sponsored by Halperin. When Halperin decided to move his courses to Odessa, farther from the war front, Molodowsky returned to her parents in Bereza for a brief stay. Because Bereza itself was very close to the front, this was to be the last time Molodowsky saw or even communicated with her parents until after the end of the war. She spent the next year and a half shuttling between teaching and day-home jobs in different towns (such as Poltave) and cities (such as Romny and the freezing Saratov on the Volga River), until Halperin finally invited her to Odessa, and she accepted the invitation.

Molodowsky arrived in Odessa—a sunny city rich in diverse Jewish cultures—in the summer of 1916. There, she taught in Halperin's model kindergarten, helped produce a journal of children's literature in Hebrew, and took the third year of Halperin's Hebrew course work in elementary education.[17] In 1917, the chaotic political situation resulting from the Bolshevik Revolution forced Halperin to move his Hebrew course yet again. This time, Molodowsky did not follow him. She attempted to return to her parents in Bereza, which was under German occupation, but got no farther than Kiev. There, she found work, first, with a baker's family as tutor for his children,[18] and then in a home for children driven from their *shtetlekh* around Kiev by the nationalist pogroms in the Ukraine. In 1920, having survived the Kiev pogrom herself, she made her literary debut.

MOLODOWSKY'S POETRY IN THE CONTEXT OF HER LIFE

Although Molodowsky had been writing poems privately since childhood, she had never thought of herself as a poet.[19] In 1920, as Molodowsky recounts in her autobiography, she was "discovered" by the well-known Kiev writers David Bergelson, Yehezikel Dobrushin, and Der Nister (pseudonym for Pinchas Kahanowitch), who published two of her poems in *Eygns* (Authenticity), an anthology of local authors.[20] Publishing her poems alongside works by the up-and-coming writers Lev Kvitko, David Hofshteyn, and Peretz Markish, as well as her conversations with Bergelson, transformed Molodowsky's sense of her poetry. Bergelson taught her the difference between a strong and a weak line of poetry, and he shepherded her through her first poetry reading. The example of his own prose taught her that writing—in its imaginative act and in its language—is rooted in deeply felt experience and heritage. Realizing that her poems were now a part of a public discourse, Molodowsky developed standards for judging and revising her own work.[21]

Throughout these terrible times of political unrest, violence, and hunger, Molodowsky continued to write poems. In Kiev, she met Simche Lev, a young scholar and teacher originally from the shtetl of Lekhevitsh, four train stations away from her hometown.[22] They married during the lean winter of 1921. After celebrating the occasion with the purchase of new shoes for Kadya, the young couple began a difficult journey home to Lekhevitsh and Bereza to see their families. Stopping in the city of Minsk, they managed to obtain the papers necessary for their repatriation to their hometowns in the regions of what was now Russian territory, near the Polish border. After their wedding visit to Simche's family in Lekhevitsh and to Kadya's in Bereza, where they stayed for two months, the couple went to live in Warsaw,[23] which became their home until 1935, except for a period, around 1923, when they worked at a children's home sponsored by the Joint Distribution Committee in Brest-Litovsk.[24]

In Warsaw, Molodowsky earned her living as a teacher in two schools: by day, in the elementary school of the Central Yiddish

Schools Organization (known by its acronym TSHISHO) and in the evenings, at a Jewish community school. She was also active in the Yiddish Writers' Union located at Tlomatske Street 13. There, she became acquainted with the Warsaw figures Israel Joshua Singer, his younger brother Isaac Bashevis Singer, Melekh Ravitsh, Peretz Markish, and Nakhman Mayzel, the editor of the weekly literary journal *Literarishe bleter*, as well as with Moyshe Kulbak from Vilna, Rokhl Korn from Pshemishl, and such famous visitors from America as Sholem Asch and Halper Leyvik.

***Kheshvndike nekht* (Nights of Heshvan)**

In 1927, Molodowsky published her first book of poetry, *Kheshvndike nekht* (Nights of Heshvan), under the imprint of a prestigious Vilna and Warsaw Yiddish publisher, B. Kletskin. Some forty-five years later, in her autobiography, Molodowsky characterized the poems of this first book as "sad poems, as if sung out from the abyss, prayers of a dejected mood,"[25] and attributed this mood to her having witnessed the poverty and persecution of the Jewish people:

> Working in the kindergarten, I saw and spoke with the children's parents. I took to heart the poverty of the Jewish population in Warsaw: unemployment, businesses so small that there was nothing to trade on but advice. The poems that I wrote at this time are almost entirely an enactment of a difficult, sorrowful Jewish world. I was unable to free myself from this mood. Whenever I took pen in hand, right before my eyes there appeared women in twisted shoes hawking bagels on the street, children lugging around pencils to sell, children pulling carts full of apples and pears, begging the passersby to buy. Before my eyes, there arose a Jewish community in such need that I was overwhelmed. I published my first book of poems in Warsaw in 1927. Although I was still young, I could not think of another name, so I called it "Nights of Heshvan"—the Jewish street is dark and rain-drenched, there is no sun to be seen, not a drop of light to warm the heart. "Nights of Heshvan," autumn nights. On the Jewish street, it is the month of Heshvan, and an autumnal mood lingers in these poems.[26]

More than monochromatic mood pieces, though, the poems in *Nights of Heshvan* are characterized by of a sensibility that has been informed by the experiences of different kinds of Jews—from young, irreverent modern women, to poor people, to the most devout figures. Each of the book's twelve poetic sequences consists of lyric poems that are linked by an underlying narrative. The speaker in these sequences places herself in "the early middle-age of a woman,"[27] but as she moves through the landscape of Jewish Eastern Europe, she assumes a variety of roles: a teacher, a traveler, a lover, and an empathetic observer of "all impoverished women who scour burnt pots."[28] Throughout the book, the narrator continues to contrast her modernity with the roles decreed by Jewish tradition for women, either halakhically, that is, by Jewish law, or by custom and history.

The sequence "Froyen-lider" ("Women-Poems") poses the central question of Molodowsky's early poetry: How can a woman writer reconcile her art with the culturally dictated, specifically Jewish precepts of womanhood? Molodowsky found a unique way to formulate this conflict through the peculiarly Jewish intertextual struggle of these poems. The closing lines of "Women-Poems I" make explicit a metaphor of life and text:

> And why should this blood without blemish
> Be my conscience, like a silken thread
> Bound upon my brain,
> And my life, a page plucked from a holy book,
> The first line torn?

Earlier in the poem, the narrator's dream vision of "the women of our family," who have carried to her "a pure blood across generations" like kosher wine, and of the *agune*, the abandoned wife who obediently renounces her sexuality, has evoked the sacred texts of prayer and law that govern the ritually correct way of living. From the simile of women's pure blood as a binding thread (like the straps of the phylacteries, two small leather boxes containing prayers, worn by observant men during prayer), the speaker challenges with her metaphorical question at the end of the poem the way women's lives have been bound into the Book of the Law. Such intertextuality continues throughout the sequence. In "Women-Poems VI," the poet tells of the compassion of the Matriarchs for poor, humble, and barren women and calls to mind a *tkhine* of the Matriarchs, a type of supplicatory prayer in Yiddish, recited by women who were assumed to be illiterate in *Loshn koydesh*, the sacred tongue of Hebrew and Aramaic. By narrating rather than expressing the substance found within the traditional prayer, however, "Women-Poems VI" calls into ironic question the very efficacy of praying. The last poem of the sequence,

"Women-Poems VIII," set in a night of insomnia, offers an angry gloss of the *Kri'at shema 'al hamittah*, the prayer affirming the fundamentals of Jewish faith that an observant Jew recites just before falling asleep.

Molodowsky's experiences of death, loss, and poverty inform the other poems in *Nights of Heshvan*. Her mother's death at the age of fifty-four from pneumonia is commemorated in the 1923 sequence "A matseyve" ("A Gravestone").[29] A short time later, Kadya herself was diagnosed with a spot on her lung and ordered to recuperate for several months at the tuberculosis sanatorium in the resort town of Otwock, near Warsaw. There she wrote a sequence of poems that she named after that town.[30] By that time, both of Kadya's sisters, Lena and Dora, had emigrated to the United States.[31] When her younger brother Leybl moved to Warsaw, her father was left alone in the shtetl Bereza Kartuska. Molodowsky wrote about returning to the shtetl deserted by its young:

> And when sometimes I travel home
> Neighbors stand around me in a circle
> And weigh me with their heads like a set of old scales,
> And they haven't brought me greetings from anyone,
> And I am silent, too, opposite them.
> Afterwards, I spin about in the market place
> Like a lost sheep
> For a day or two,
> Then I wind a veil around my hat,
> And at daybreak, a rickety wagon drives me rocking away,
> My father stays, planted near the balcony.
> And a gray dew settles on his head.[32]

Having lost her mother, the poet feels mothered by the earth:

> I breathed heavily . . . and rose
> Like a water-leaf
> Stretching, stretching, stretching upward
> Out of the marshy mother-lap.
> . . .
> [Now] I return
> To the brown plain,
> To the lowly lap,
> Shaking the dust from my clothes.[33]

Yet the maternal image of the land also emphasizes the determinism of a woman's life cycle. Throughout these poems runs a subliminal anxiety about barrenness and childbearing. When, in the sequence "Oreme vayber" ("Poor Women"), a sense of social injustice emerges, the message is couched in the terms of the individual psyche:

> In my dream-filled nights
> I am in a dim house
> Among women, exhausted and collapsed on the ground,
> And their hands are hands well-known to me,
> With nails notched from years of drudgery.[34]

The depiction of women and women's problems is deeply personal, internal, and individualistic here, as the speaker within *Nights of Heshvan* struggles to define herself as a woman and a poet through other prototypes of womanhood.

Mayselekh (Tales)[35]

Although Molodowsky never became a mother, children were an important presence in her life and poetry. As a teacher in Poland, she had worked closely with children. Later, in the United States and Israel, she continued her educational activities and maintained close ties with her niece and nephews in Philadelphia. But in Europe, in particular, Molodowsky's pervasive awareness of the poverty in which Jewish children often lived and studied helps us to appreciate the children's poems she published in Warsaw around 1930.

According to her autobiography, Molodowsky began writing for children after she "failed" to fulfill adequately an assignment she received during her teacher training in Kiev in 1913—the year, she points out, in which Mendel Bailis was exonerated from the famous blood libel accusation.[36] Her instructor, Halperin, had asked his students to write a story about a horse—plowing the fields, twitching its ears, eating hay—as a pedagogical tool to teach kindergarten children about spring. Instead, Molodowsky wrote her first children's story:

> Once there was a boy who wanted to ride a horse, but his father, who was not a wagon driver, didn't have any horses. So the boy grabbed hold of a goat, climbed on top, and, straddling her shouted, "Run, horsey, run, horsey!" The goat jumped straight up in the air, threw

> off her rider and ran away. The little boy's hat fell off. His face and hands were smeared with dirt. He came home in tears and told his mother what had happened. His mother said, "So, now you know. Horses are for riding, but a goat gives milk. She doesn't want anyone to ride her."[37]

From this little tale and a sense of responsibility for her students in Warsaw, Molodowsky wrote the children's poems that appeared in *Mayselekh* (Tales), a collection she refers to in her autobiography as *Geyen shikhlekh avek* (Little Shoes Go Away). Ostensibly published in 1931 in Warsaw, later reprinted many times in Yiddish in Warsaw and New York, and translated into Hebrew by Lea Goldberg, Natan Alterman, and other notable Hebrew poets, these poems made Molodowsky famous. For children growing up in Palestine and Israel in the 1940s, 1950s, and 1960s, the Hebrew translations of these poems were considered such classics of children's literature that some readers did not even realize that they were originally written in Yiddish.[38]

In her autobiography, Molodowsky described how writing poems for her students in Warsaw provided relief for the children and herself from the grinding poverty:

> My tales and poems for children . . . saved me from dejection. I wrote one poem about how a poor family passed a coat from one child to the next. Theirs was the ultimate poverty. When I read that tale to the children in my class, they enjoyed it very much and clapped their little hands. Aha! As the coat was passed from child to child, each of my students wanted to wear that coat! Without intending to, I felt, the children taught me something that made sense: Don't be upset if you have to wear an old coat. . . . The children taught me how to survive in difficult times. I sensed the miracle of life. Although I was their teacher, they taught me much more than I taught them. They managed to squeeze a drop of joy out of life. When I was extremely discouraged, I wrote many of my poems for children. These tales would uplift me.[39]

According to one of Molodowsky's students from the TSHISHO school at Twarda Street 22 from 1932 through 1934, these poems were uplifting to the children, as well. "Teacher Kadya," soft-spoken and dressed in "a sweater, often the same sweater, handsome, very tired, used-up," wearing shoes with heels that "needed attention," would read her poems to her class, occasionally from a handwritten page. A teacher who gave her students confidence in their own minds and voices, Molodowsky taught these children the great Yiddish writers I. L. Peretz, Sholem Aleichem, Sh. Anski, Winshevski, and the contemporaries Joseph Opatoshu and Mani Leyb.[40]

The poems in *Tales*—a selection of which are included in this book, as well as two poems from *Afn barg* (On the Mountain, New York, 1938), an expanded edition of *Tales*—are about children who, though deprived of food, money, clothing, and love, possess the imagination to survive and the language to articulate their struggles. One of the best known of these poems, "Olke," tells the story of "Olke / mit der bloyer parasolke" ("Olke and her blue parasol").[41] The six-year-old girl lives in the back streets of Warsaw, "at the end of desire," in a yard filled with mud, beneath a half-fallen roof, where a swallow has built its nest. Summoned by her father, a blacksmith, and her mother to do housework, she is scolded by them in a recurring refrain:

> Potatoes need peeling,
> Stories need telling.
>
> A little to read,
> A little to write—
> Remember, I'll drive you out of the house tonight!

In these enigmatic lines, stories require telling in the same way that potatoes need peeling. Olke's stories are functional; they fit into the drudgery of daily living; their purpose is to quiet her baby brother, perhaps, or to provide a kind of basic nourishment like potatoes.

Yet Olke, through these stories, through her imagination, reshapes her environment. She observes things as they are in the muddy yard—geese and ganders, birds on the wing and an airplane, buttons spilling from the sewing basket, and then, when she opens her imaginary blue parasol, she creates a special place for herself. Olke's parasol, an accessory intended to protect a feminine complexion from the elements, is the color of the sky. It both encompasses Olke's world and enables her to remake it in her own terms, as if she were the possessor of the blue sky that umbrellas everyone's world. "A little reading / A little writing," the acts in which the poem's reader and its author are both engaged, stand in opposition to the parents' harangue against the little girl. They fight against the mundane, time-consuming tasks of woman's work thrust on a girl before her time. The poem ends climactically as Olke escapes on a train made of buttons that have rebelled against their duty to hold together clothes and decency. Buttons, the tiny implements of women's work, become the machinery of a technological world in which women drive trains. The tasks of the home provide the means for Olke's escape, and home itself now becomes a portable blue umbrella, omnipresent as the sky, beneath which the girl is free to read and write. If the blue umbrella of the imagination becomes a portable home, then wherever the imagination is free to open up, Olke is at home.

In Molodowsky's other children's poems, the powers of language and of imagination transform the grimmest facts of life. "A mayse mit a balye" ("The Tale of a Washtub") evokes the spontaneous self-invention of a modern washing machine from an old-fashioned, wooden kneading trough. With this device, all the Jewish housewives in the Warsaw tenements are freed from doing their weekly laundry. "Der taykh" ("The River") tells a Jewish version of "The Sorcerer's Apprentice" through the figure of a golem, the legendary clay mannikin brought to life by a holy rabbi who employs the Ineffable Name of God. In "Shikhelekh" ("Little Shoes"), the magic of animated things, a pair of shoes that go wherever their cobbler sends them, is stopped short by the spectacle of a child suffering, "all alone, / Barefoot, naked, on a stone." "Di gril" ("The Cricket") asserts the irrepressible and mysterious nature of art: "Nobody knows what she eats," "Nobody knows where she lives," yet every night the cricket makes her music. The poem "Efnt dem toyer" ("Open the Gate") celebrates the golden chain of Jewish tradition and ends with an image of delicacies—"A pear / And an apple, / A cup filled with honey, / And a yellow ginger cake / Sitting upon a golden plate"—as though the poem were intended to provide the food that its child readers actually lacked.

Soon after the publication of Molodowsky's children's poems, the Jewish Community of Warsaw and the Yiddish Pen Club awarded her a cash prize of two hundred zlotes. Although she was grateful for the money, then a considerable sum, Molodowsky confessed in her autobiography that she felt disappointed that her children's poems, her "writerly frolics," had received this recognition while her book of serious poems, *Nights of Heshvan*, had not been given any comparable acknowledgment.[42] Even so, Molodowsky's *Nights of Heshvan* was reviewed some twenty times in the Yiddish press. Nearly all the reviews were laudatory, including one by the distinguished critic and scholar Sh. Niger. Even if she was not entirely happy with how her career developed, Molodowsky had established herself in the Yiddish literary world.

***Dzshike gas* (Dzshike Street)**

In contrast to the reception of these two earlier books, however, Molodowsky's third book of poems, *Dzshike gas* (Dzshike Street), published in 1933 by the press of the leading Warsaw literary journal, *Literarishe bleter*, received a mixed welcome. Of four contemporary reviews in Warsaw and New York, three offer praise. Rokhl Korn, writing from Pshemishl, most likely for a Warsaw paper, cites Molodowsky's *Dzshike Street* as a book that steps out of the margins of existence to which women have conventionally been assigned, and addresses the central issues of Jewish life in Poland after the Great War. She concludes by lauding Molodowsky as one of the "women writers" by nature "closest to reality," for her portrayal of the "true," "brilliant joy" waiting to be revealed beneath the hunger and need of Dzshike Street.[43] The review by Nakhman Mayzel, editor of *Literarishe bleter* from 1925–38, praises Molodowsky, whom he calls an "absolutely subjective" poet, for producing poems empowered by the "objective fact" of Warsaw Jewish poverty.[44] Writing in the New York paper *Der tog* on a Sunday in early February, 1933, Niger evaluates *Dzshike Street* in light of Molodowsky's previous works. He asserts that, as *Nights of Heshvan*, although rooted in Jewishness and about women, raised Molodowsky above the categories of a "yidishkayt dikhterin" and "fartaytsherin fun spetsieler froyendikhtung" ("a poetess of Jewishness" and an "interpreter of specialized women's poetry"), so, too, the "social motif" of her new poems does not entrap her in the category of a socialist versifier, but rather gives her the ground to present the difficulties of being a "an emeser poet" ("a true poet") who is socially aware.[45]

However, the review, by H. S. Kazdan, which appeared in the Bundist *Vokhnshrift far literatur, kunst, un kultur* (Weekly for Literature, Art, and Culture), gives a negative assessment of the book.[46] The reviewer condemns Molodowsky's poems, and especially those in the title section, on political rather than literary grounds. Complaining that the book is too "aesthetic," Kazdan argues that its poems deal inadequately with poverty because the poet "is in love with life." That her strength as a poet was her "pure lyricism," struck this reviewer as a liability; he could not understand how a lyrical strength could coexist with the poet's professed distaste for the poverty of the Jewish street.[47]

Kazdan, wearing the political blinders of his day, exemplified the ferocious disagreements among the Jewish socialists and communists in Poland at the time. In reality, Molodowsky's precise political sentiments are not clear from her poems, and this obscurity may have fueled the critic's objections. But a lack of explicit partisanship continued even in Molodowsky's autobiography, written in the 1960s and 1970s. There, too, Molodowsky purposely obscured her political positions and interactions in Warsaw during the 1930s. Her departure from Poland for the United States in 1935 may well have been precipitated by some political activity, but Molodowsky never admitted this.[48] Even so, Kazdan, while condemning Molodowsky's political inconsistencies, failed to see, as Niger in America had seen, how the poems in *Dzshike Street* worked out the struggle in which Molodowsky was passionately engaged, namely the struggle between the aesthetic and the political responsibilities of the Yiddish poet in times of economic, social, and political hardship.

Molodowsky's attempts to resolve that struggle differ from the pragmatism of the more politically acceptable Yiddish poets of contemporary Warsaw, whose models seemed to be the popular, turn-of-the-century Labor Poets. In the United States, for example, such poets as Dovid Edelstat (1866–92), Morris Winchevsky (1856–1932), and Morris Rosenfeld (1862–1923) identified themselves as spokesmen for the Jewish working class and readily put their poems into "the people's" service. But the ability of a really good poet to write such unambiguous and doctrinal poems for the masses had come and gone. Although a strain of political poetry in Yiddish persisted well into the 1950s, by the 1920s the best Yiddish poets had been touched by one form or another of modernism. During her years in Warsaw, Molodowsky also absorbed the lessons of the modernists, especially of the American poets known as the *Yunge*, whose guiding principle was that poetry spoke only for the individual sensibility. She was particularly influenced by two poets once associated with the *Yunge:* Moyshe-Leyb Halpern, who wrote acerbic, ironic lyrics and whose 1919 book *In nyu york* (In New York) was reissued in Warsaw in 1927, and H. Leyvik, a visionary writer whom she met when he visited the Writer's Union in Warsaw, probably around 1930.[49] In the poems of *Dzshike Street*, Molodowsky worked out a resolution between her various allegiances to the rigors of art, to her own life as a Jewish woman, and to the suffering of the people around her. The poetry she created sought to find a common ground for the inner and outer worlds of a poet.

In Warsaw, Molodowsky and her husband Simche Lev lived in an apartment on Dzshike Street.[50] One of the poorest streets in the Jewish section of the city, Dzshike Street was infamous for the Pawiak, a terrible prison where political dissidents were held.[51] Molodowsky set her poem "A mame" ("A Mother"), outside the walls of the Pawiak. In her autobiography, Molodowsky described her encounter with a child on Dzshike Street:

> In the streets of Warsaw, one often met children selling shoelaces, buttons, pencils, bagels, bottles of kvass, and other poor merchandise. These children were helping their parents supplement their meager livelihoods. One rainy evening, as I was walking on Dzshike Street, I passed a ten-year-old boy, who stood by a cart, selling kvass. Hardly anyone was on the street. The boy shouted out praise for his merchandise: "Buy, people! Buy!" When I saw this small vendor standing in the rain, hawking his wares, all my teacherly feelings awoke. I wanted desperately to cheer him up. Approaching him, I asked him for three bottles of kvass. "Three bottles?" he asked joyously, as if the sun had risen right then and there. His face lit up. He handed me the bag filled with my purchases and assured me in a happy voice, "You will enjoy this kvass. It's sweet as sugar. Drink it in good health." I did, indeed, enjoy that kvass very much.[52]

Molodowsky, ever the teacher but never a mother, described her feelings for the child as "lererishe gefiln" ("teacherly") rather than maternal.

Whereas the poems in *Nights of Heshvan* were set in the town and the countryside, the poems of *Dzshike Street* are urban. They convey a sense of the crush of people, the "street" as a collective entity. Thus, even though the title poem, "Dzshike Street," is lyrical when describing the mildness of the spring month Iyar, it vibrates with a hyperawareness of the poverty and political vulnerability of Jewish city life. The poem itself explicitly dramatizes the vocation of the poet who is accused by her subjects, the people in the street, of being irrelevant, beside the point, even exploitative:

> There she is—the lady singer,
> The devil take her mother,—
> She hangs around here all the time

And braids our misery into rhymes.
Yesterday, she should have gone into the street with us and
seen
The twenty-year-old man flogged to death
In Dzshike Number Ten.

In her earlier book, the poet dramatized her lack of a place as a modern woman in the social and religious aspects of traditional Jewish life. The poems in *Dzshike Street*, however, confront the poet's dilemma in a time of political crisis: How can she write poetry that speaks simultaneously for the poet's "blood" (in "Marsh" ["Marching"] she writes, "I try / to find a word for my blood") and for her people? The poems address this question by focusing on the work of the imagination.

No poem in the book better shows just how the poet's imagination works at such a moment of crisis than "Mayn papirene brik" ("My Paper Bridge"). According to Jewish legend, when the Messiah comes, the Jews will cross into Paradise over a paper bridge. In this poem, Molodowsky changes the legendary paper bridge into a symbol of private, personal desires. The speaker of the poem builds her paper bridge to reach into a mild and innocent time, when all the world around her would be beautiful and harmonious. But her dreams of a husband, a child, a home, and adventures evaporate when she comes face-to-face on her paper bridge with a sixty-year-old woman, barefoot, frostbitten, starving, who lacks the necessities to survive the present moment, a winter day. The old woman makes the poet realize that she, too, "has nowhere to go." The presence of this old woman within the poem and upon the paper bridge changes the poet's sense of her poetry, which, written on paper, is itself a kind of paper bridge.

In *Dzshike Street*, Molodowsky also explored her literary relationship to other Yiddish writers. This exploration is important because it shows her growing confidence in herself as a poet and in her relationship to other more established, more famous, male writers. Thus, she dedicated "Dzshike Street" to Joseph Opatoshu (1886–1954), the American Yiddish novelist whose realist works depicted the gritty underside of shtetl life. And she dedicated "My Paper Bridge" to her early mentor, David Bergelson (1884–1952), the innovator of the impressionist style in Yiddish fiction between 1905 and 1917 who, after the Bolshevik Revolution, abruptly made his work conform to socialist realism. In Kiev, Bergelson had taught her the dialectic between life and art that invigorates *Dzshike Street:* "The substance of a poem is rooted in experiences that break through the musical line."[53]

Another poem, "Halo, mayn harts" ("Hello, My Heart!"), shows the influence on Molodowsky of the American Yiddish poet Moyshe-Leyb Halpern, who died in 1932, the year this poem was composed. As a tribute to Halpern, Molodowsky's rough-hewn, ironic diction and imagery echo Halpern's famous 1915 elegy for I. L. Peretz. Poems in *Nights of Heshvan* had also shown Halpern's influence, as in the image of the fly trembling at the window pane (in "Tfiles I" ["Prayers I"]) and the modernist folk legend of the seven spinning women ("In bloyen baginen" ["At Blue Dawn IX"]). By acknowledging other writers in *Dzshike Street,* Molodowsky found a way to move beyond their influence and make her poetry her own.

Molodowsky's insistence on her individuality as a poet during this period also influenced her view of other women poets. In "Bagegenishn" ("Encounters"), an article from *Literarishe bleter* of January, 1930, Molodowsky satirically protested the literary category of "froyen-dikhtung" ("women's poetry") and empty generalizations about how women write, quoting "a prominent Yiddish poet," who characterized the work of one woman poet in this way: "She writes, in general, like all Yiddish women poets."[54] Such clichés were in the air, especially after Ezra Korman published his collection of women poets, *Yidishe dikhterins: antologye* (Yiddish Women Poets: Anthology) in Chicago, in 1928. Although Molodowsky had contributed nine poems to this volume, she protested the critical response to Korman's anthology.[55] She voiced her objections to one critic's dismissive comments on poetry by women in her 1927 article, "Meydlekh, froyen, vayber, un . . . nevue" ("Girls, Women, Wives, and . . . Prophecy"), a lively response to a piece by the poet Melekh Ravitsh that had trivialized and mocked the work of women poets.[56]

In her 1930 article "Encounters," Molodowsky satirized the arbitrary groupings of women poets by critics, newspaper editors, and anthologizers through a series of imagined encounters by women poets whom she regarded as opposites—the urbane modernist Anna Margolin with Rokhl Korn, whose poems celebrated country life; Miriam Ulinover, whose poems depicted the archaic piety of a shtetl grandmother, with Esther Shumiatsher, who used images from Christianity and Islam; Sarah Reyzen, a poet of conventional domesticity, with the sensualist Celia Dropkin; and Kadya Molodowsky herself with Hannah Levin, a Leninist revolutionary.[57] Indeed, by identifying each poet through images and phrases typical to her poetry—Margolin's mask and lily-dress; Korn's bare feet, linen garb, damp earth, and cow's milk; Ulinover's old-fashioned, high-buttoned jacket; Shumiatsher's litany of God's name (here, Allah)—Molodowsky parodied the works of these writers. Yet she had a purpose in this exercise: Submitting even her own poetry to this reduction, she sought to distinguish it from that by other women and especially from poetry written from the communist point of view, whether by men or women:

> I myself met up with Hannah Levin on one page of a newspaper. We both, by chance, came out with relics in our hands. From between my fingers poured torn, holy pages from an old prayerbook, and the wind drove them about me. Hannah Levin piously carried Lenin in one hand and in the other, a gun.
>
> Lenin and a gun.
>
> I was a little bit frightened. Lenin, I soon realized, was a photograph. But a gun?
>
> "Tell me, Hannah Levin," I asked her, "does the gun really shoot?"
>
> "It shoots."
>
> "Really?"
>
> "Yes, yes."
>
> She shot it off. Indeed, the gun gave a bang. And Hannah Levin began to look around to see if it had shot someone.
>
> After that, with her characteristic great sincerity and feeling, Hannah Levin said, "See, all of us have guns. One must have a gun!" She began to count on her fingers all those who had guns: Khashtshevatsski has a gun. Fefer has a gun . . . Suddenly she remembered that I was carrying an enemy relic and threatened me with her gun. The Book of Exodus, still in my hand, fanned out its pages and set down between us a white, paper path.[58]

Even in the context of this spoof, the pathway formed by the unbound torn pages of holy books strewn on the ground between the two women poets—one of misguided political idealism and the other of the broken tradition of Judaism—connotes the paper bridge that recurs in Molodowsky's poems. There is a double message within this image, for although this paper path is formed by an unbinding of Jewish tradition—as the torn pages fall out of the holy book—and although the article argues for the unbridgeable differences between women writers, in fact, the paper pathway links the two women, Levin and Molodowsky.

The enigmatic concluding poem in *Dzshike Street*, "Shloyminke der shmid" ("Shloyminke the Blacksmith"), spoken with a self-conscious skepticism, throws all the preceding poems into a new light and reshapes the reader's perception of the apparent "sincerity" of the poet's endeavor in *Dzshike Street*. Here, Molodowsky questions the integrity of poems that exploit the oral tradition of folk stories to fulfill the demands of the contemporary literary world. The poet confesses her own pretensions—she has reworked the "golden treasure" of the tall tales she heard as a girl from Shloyminke the Blacksmith into a "mirror" of herself in order to try to please a literary critic, identified as one M——— ske. The problem, raised in the title poem, of the poet's sense of dual responsibility to social issues and aestheticism is answered in "Shloyminke the Blacksmith" with the poet's merciless exposure of her own artful vanity.

***Freydke* (Freydke)**

Two years after *Dzshike Street*, Molodowsky published her fourth book, *Freydke*, more than half of which consists of the title poem, a sixteen-part *poeme* or narrative sequence, from which sections I, II, IV, and V appear in this selection. Freydke is the poem's heroine, a Jewish woman who, by peddling eggs door-to-door in Warsaw, supports herself and her young daughter, Reyzl. Although her name means "joy," Freydke is the archetype of grim Jewish survival amid poverty. Capable, strong, intelligent, Freydke, the poet tells us in "Freydke I," could have been a sailor, an astronomer, a builder, but, caught up daily among "Hundreds of thousands and thousands of steps, / Uncounted, / Uncautious, / Spilling onto the street," she is bound to her basket of fragile eggs and to her tattered wallet with its few copper pennies. Although the wallet, "A legacy passing from father to children," represents the communal poverty, it is also a disgraceful mark of identity, "Like the medieval patches of yellow," and thus an emblem of Jewish exile and endless geographical displacements. Freydke herself, though, goes no farther than the street, where she sells eggs door-to-door and encounters the gamut of Jewish religious and political pieties within Warsaw.

Writing this poem in a didactic mode, Molodowsky used Freydke as an example to expose the marginality and despair of young, working-class Jews, and especially women. Although its program is more subtle than most political poetry of the day, "Freydke" calls out for political and social reform.

Molodowsky may have been inspired to write this *poeme* of near-epic proportion in reaction to Kazdan's stinging review of *Dzshike Street* which charged her poems were "sweetly charming, daintily feminine love-songs."[59] This politically correct*ed* poem, which makes two working-class women the heroines, both victims of their class and times, and which includes a paean to the 1934–35 strikes by French Jewish garment workers,[60] may also conceal a portrait of the poet as a woman writing in "mame-loshn," a woman deliberately "braiding rhymes" in a context where rhymes should be forged. If Freydke and Sheyndl Kanerey (the strike leader forced to flee to France, whose name means "Pretty Canary") together represent the poet, then this poem is about how the woman poet, like the egg peddler and the singing fugitive, has been sent into a kind of "cultural exile," a radical homelessness, a state *between* being expelled from her own voice and being coerced by a male mode of writing. Molodowsky makes her homelessness productive by finding in exile a fertile ground for creating the kind of new poem epitomized by "Freydke," which at once conforms by teaching the correct politics and mirrors its own author's exile within Yiddish poetry.

In addition to its title poem, the book contains lyric poems, such as "Mayn shlep-shif" ("My Tow-Boat"), "Mayn tog" ("My Day"), and "Den tatns pelts" ("My Father's Fur Coat") as well as satirical, folk-like poems that draw on "exotic" motifs of China and Japan, which Molodowsky may well have gleaned from Bernard Witt's 1930 Yiddish translation of Lafcadio Hearn's *Some Chinese Ghosts.*[61]

In land fun mayn gebeyn (In the Country of My Bones)

As she recounts the story of her emigration in her autobiography—which, as it has been said, is a less than entirely frank document—Molodowsky tells us that she decided to leave Poland almost on a whim. Holding down two teaching jobs in Warsaw, in a Yiddish school by day and in a Hebrew school by night, Molodowsky had grown very depressed by her constant exposure to the poverty, disease, and helplessness of her students. One day in

1935, she met a visitor from New York City, Lipe Lehrer, director of Farlag Matones, the publishing house of the Sholem Aleichem Folk-Institute, who almost casually invited her to "come visit us in America." He assured her that because her four books of poems were selling there, she wouldn't feel like a foreigner in the New World.[62] Members of her family had already emigrated: her father and her two sisters with their families lived in Philadelphia, her Uncle Benye's children were in Washington, D.C., her mother's sisters in Boston. She wrote, "I had wandered considerably throughout various cities in Russia and Poland, and to take a stroll to America seemed to me like a hop, skip, and a jump."[63]

Molodowsky departed for the United States in 1935, leaving behind her husband, Simche Lev. Lev was able to join her only in 1938, after an ordeal in acquiring a visa.[64] Although she had planned to settle near her sisters and father in Philadelphia, two weeks after her arrival, Molodowsky visited New York City. In New York, she was greeted warmly by the Yiddish literary world. On Friday, October 11, 1935, the poet H. Leyvik welcomed Molodowsky to New York at a reception with a speech published that same day in the newspaper *Fraye arbeter shtime* (Free Workers' Voice). In this speech, Leyvik hails her depiction of Dzshike Street as "Dzshike Street, wild street, . . . sorrow street, impoverished street, Kadya Molodowsky's street, our street."[65] Feeling more at home among the Yiddish writers, who included both old friends from Warsaw and new acquaintances, she decided to live in New York.

Soon after making this decision, Molodowsky was invited to give a tour of poetry readings and lectures in Chicago, Detroit, and Cleveland. In her autobiography, she describes this trip in detail. At least initially, she writes, the trip was a very positive experience. She relates how her hosts and audiences in these Midwestern Jewish communities "were *heymish* people" who made her "feel at home." But by the time she reached Cleveland, Molodowsky's feelings had begun to change. For all her complimentary words about her hosts, the Drosts, and their Yiddish-speaking children, Molodowsky had fallen into a state of despair. The source of this feeling, at least in part, was her perception that in America, as she writes, "Yiddish is but a small corner, true a warm corner, but certainly no more than a small corner."[66]

Indeed, from the very beginning of her arrival in America, she had felt not only foreign, but fragmented:

> I sensed that in Jewish America there were very many mirrors reflecting all the different corners, each corner with its distinct image—old-fashioned, American, of the great world, of the small shtetl—its secularism and its *yidishkayt* mixed up together in the same pocket.[67]

Later, speaking with the writer Menachem Boraisha and the poet H. Leyvik, each of whom had been in the United States for nearly twenty-five years, Molodowsky continued to perceive the fragmentation of American Jewish identity. She told Boraisha:

> In America I feel that I am traveling away from one *yidishkayt* to another kind of *yidishkayt*, a fragmented type of *yidishkayt*. As American as you may be, beneath your American clothes, you carry memories of a past life with its study house, its customs, its prayers. Whether or not you are pious, the past lives on, concealed. You hide it, wanting to appear American.[68]

Of Leivick, she said,

> Standing with him at the top of the Empire State Building, I sensed his life in two worlds, in the noisy world of New York and in the distant past of Jewish longing and prayerful yearning for redemption.[69]

This sense of fragmentation and the despair it caused Molodowsky suggest the emotional background against which she wrote the poems in her fifth book, *In land fun mayn gebeyn* (In the Country of My Bones), published in Chicago, in 1937:

> In my wanderings, I saw the Jews of Kiev, of Minsk after the Russian Revolution, beaten away from their livelihoods. I saw the helplessness of the Jews in Poland, their poverty, their struggle for a piece of bread in the country of Polish oppression. I traveled through Germany in the beginning of Hitler's reign and sensed the mute fear that lay over the Jews of Germany. I came to America sated with different exiles. A perilous storm drifts above Jewish roofs. I gave this book the name "In the Country of My Bones." The poems in this book bring out the sorrow that lay in my bones. L. M. Stein told me that he would buy new type so that the book would be published nicely. The book appeared in the year 1937.[70]

This passage is typical of the autobiography. From sentences that stunningly reveal the writer's feelings, like "ongezapt mit farsheydene golesn" ("I came to America sated with different exiles"), the narrator abruptly turns to the most mundane details—her publisher's promise to buy a new font for the publication of her book.

The poems in *In the Country of My Bones* are lyrical, obscurely symbolic, intensely private. They represent an internalization of exile, as the poet, who observed the alienation of Freydke with dispassion and compassion, now is compelled to confront her own several exiles—from her geographical homes in Lithuania and Warsaw; from her language, Yiddish; and from her very self.

In the Country of My Bones, the very title of the collection, suggests the ambiguity at the heart of the book. Where—or more accurately, what—is "the *country* of my bones," from which the poet speaks? Is it her birthplace, the land where her bones were formed? Or is it the country of *my* bones, that is, her own body, which is all that she now has as a homeland? Or is it the land in which she will be buried, that is, the land where her skeleton will lie? The ambiguity in the title signals the book's central concern: How does one find and recover a place in the world?

In the end, it is within the very poems in the book that Molodowsky finds her true footing in America. Thus, in "Mayn artsibiografye" ("My Ultimate Biography"), the poet seeks the essence of her own being and a justification for her writing by reinventing the story of her life. The poem's allusive, even obscure, language, its sudden shifts of voice and imagery, make its reader struggle to understand how the European Yiddish poet is transforming herself into an American poet right before our very eyes. For example, the word *artsibiografye* in the title does not exist in the dictionaries; a neologism, it seems to denote an arch-biography that is more intense, more essential than the standard *oytobiografye*, autobiography. And so, in her *artsibiografye*, the speaker in the poem assumes various dramatic roles for herself. She is a homeless wanderer and a peddler of "bundles of culture," rather than of dry goods. A music maker, she likens herself to her own mother, who peddled "ringing" bottles of kvass. She rides in the cart of Yezepke, a peasant driver, and engages in a dialogue between two children who at first play horse-and-wagon and then take parts in a Purim drama. She recalls listening to Shloyminke the Blacksmith (who had appeared in *Dzshike Street*) and the schoolteacher of the town Sorok tell their fantastic tall tales, which strike her as more valuable than all the high culture of New York City. And, finally, she even ridicules the idea of knowing her own identity, when someone asks her the quintessentially American question of when her birthday is. The Singer sewing machine that this persona operates in the sweatshop where she works, with its squeaking, rusty pedals that turn wheels going nowhere, becomes the ultimate symbol for another type of singer: the Yiddish poet in America.

The conflict between America and the Old World recurs throughout this book. In the title poem, the poet, after immigrating to New York City, comes to terms with her new residence by seeking her old homeland within her very bones. What she finds there, though, is, comically, a fierce debate between a shtetl cottage and the Empire State Building.

Another poem, "Bay mir in hant tsvey federn fun a fazan" ("In My Hand Two Feathers from a Pheasant"), presents a variant vision of a homeland—a kind of imagined national homeland like the Soviet Birobidzshan, which turns out, in the end, to be located in the realm of pure language. "Oysyes" ("Alphabet Letters") focuses directly on the individual letters of the Yiddish and English alphabets that appear on business signs and Boy Scout uniforms as literal signposts of the familiar and the alien. Finally, in "Yerushe" ("Legacy"), the poet finds her heritage in the state of exile, signified by the letters of the Hebrew alphabet that exist solely for their own sake. What one sees here, then, is a progression from autobiographical narration to a kind of semiotic system in which inscribed letters become signs of the only stability that the poet can find for herself within the instability of exile.

Der melekh dovid aleyn iz geblibn (Only King David Remained)

Following the publication of *In the Country of My Bones*, Molodowsky's literary endeavors branched out in several directions. In 1938, she published a book of children's poems, *Afn barg* (On the Mountain). In 1942, she published *Fun lublin biz nyu-york: togbukh fun rivke zilberg* (From Lublin to New York: Diary of Rivke Zilberg), a novel about a young immigrant woman.[71] According to Melekh Ravitsh, parts of this novel were broadcast on the radio.[72] Around this time, Molodowsky also wrote a series of columns on "Great Jewish Women" for the Yiddish daily *Forverts* (Forward), using Rivke Zilberg, the name of the novel's protagonist as her own pseudonym.[73] But mainly these years, from 1937 to 1946—the years during which, as we now know, Europe's Jews and their culture were destroyed by the Nazis—were for Molodowsky, as for most Jews in America, years of anxious waiting, of partial knowledge, and finally, of horrifying revelations.[74]

Writing her autobiography in 1973, Kadya Molodowsky described how, in 1941, in New York, she sensed the pending destruction:

> This was the time when dark clouds hung over the Jews in Poland. No details were yet known, but there was the feeling that a storm was brewing over Jewish heads and the clouds stretched across every happy encounter.[75]

But only in 1943, when she learned about an unspecified event in Poland, perhaps the uprising and the subsequent liquidation of the Warsaw Ghetto by the Nazis on April 19 of that year, did the terrible knowledge of the events in Europe really take hold:

> The bitter news about ***khurbm poyln*** (the Destruction of Poland) began to arrive. In agitation, I began to tear at the fingers of my hands. One finger became so badly infected that it required surgery.[76]

Lacerating her fingers must have been an especially symbolic act of grief for a writer. With her fingers crippled, how could she write? Indeed, Molodowsky herself wrote that she was "too upset to occupy [her]self with the literary journal,"[77] *Svive*, which she had helped to found earlier that year.[78] Putting aside her editorial responsibilities, and despite her injuries, she began to write the poems of her postwar collection, *Der melekh dovid aleyn iz geblibn* (Only King David Remained), which finally appeared in 1946.[79]

It is no accident that the publisher of this book bore the symbolic name Farlag Papirene Brik (Paper Bridge Press), a phrase connoting miraculous redemption that Molodowsky had chosen as the title of a central poem in the 1933 book *Dzshike Street*.[80] And, indeed, in *Only King David Remained*, a poem entitled "A lid tsu der papirener brik" ("A Poem to the Paper Bridge") does express her hope for messianic redemption.

Molodowsky's description of the book and of how she chose the title is worth quoting in full:

> I saw in succession before my eyes a Jewish world that had been destroyed, Jewish cities, destruction and pain. I gave this book the name *Only King David Remained*, in order to say that the Jewish people was no more, all that remained was King David alone with his sorrow-crown on his head. The book begins with the poem, "Eyl khanun" ("Merciful God"):

Merciful God,
Choose another people,
Elect another.
We are tired of death and dying,
We have no more prayers.
Choose another people,
Elect another.
We have no more blood
To be a sacrifice.

> All the poems in this book are *khurbm-lider,* (holocaust/destruction poems), lament and crying. . . . This book seemed to me like a tombstone for a life that had vanished. Often my breath would simply stop; it felt like I was being choked.[81]

Molodowsky depicts her own bereavement with the phrase, "King David alone with his sorrow-crown," an allusion to the account in 2 Samuel (18:29–19:5), which relates how the king, after he learns that his rebellious son Absalom has been killed, mourns him with the words, "O my son Absalom, my son, my son Absalom! Would I have died instead of thee . . ." (2 Samuel 19:1). The figure of King David at this terrible moment comes to symbolize the absolute, bereft isolation of the survivor. In the passage just quoted from her autobiography, Molodowsky describes her own loss of breath as she succumbed to a grief as inconsolable as King David's. This second, perhaps psychosomatic, symptom of her response to the knowledge that the Jewish world had been destroyed further dramatizes the difficulties she overcame to write these poems. Both the breathless, choking sensation she experienced and the wounds she inflicted on her fingers impaired the two parts of the body the poet most needs to write—her voice and her hands.

The poems in *Only King David Remained* are primarily *khurbm-lider,* poems lamenting the destruction.[82] The Yiddish word *khurbm* derives from the Hebrew *ḥurban,* a term that originally referred to the Destruction of the Second Temple, but which, in Yiddish, subsequently became the generic name for all catastrophes in Jewish historical experience. As the scholar Alan Mintz has stated, a catastrophe in Jewish terms does not connote solely loss of life or possessions or dwellings, but a crisis of spirit that arises because the catastrophic event seems to overwhelm and confound all explanations for its occurrence: The classical example in Judaism for such an explanation is the covenantal notion found in the Bible that suffering is punishment for sin.[83] The history of this covenantal paradigm, as both Mintz and David Roskies have argued, essentially created a vast and continuous literature in Hebrew and in Yiddish, beginning with responses to the Destructions of the First and Second Temples in ancient Jerusalem, and continuing into the present era, which elaborated, revised, and transformed the biblical notion in accordance with the changed historical and religious development of the Jews.

Molodowsky's poem "Merciful God" draws directly upon this tradition of response, and it does so in the form of what Roskies calls a "sacred parody," in this case, of a prayer.[84] Although prayers normally confirm the covenantal relationship between Israel and God, Molodowsky's poem subverts this confirmation by appealing to the merciful God of traditional prayer to negate His Covenant with the Jewish people and to bestow this blessing, now perceived as a curse, upon the enemies of the Jews. Molodowsky thus responds to the destruction of European Jewry with her own act of annihilation. Paradoxically, though, the poem affirms even as it subverts. Although the prayer darkens into a curse of the deity to whom it is addressed, it confirms, albeit with much ambivalence, a yearning and desire to believe in God as a presence who can still be addressed. For all its anger at God, the poem never completely severs the link between the poet and the subject she addresses.

Several other poems in the collection are sacred parodies—"Di nisht dertseylte blat" ("The Unrecounted Page"), "Shir hamayles" ("Psalm of Ascents"), "Badekns" ("Veiling"), "Toyter shabes" ("Dead Sabbath"), "Havdole" ("Havdalah"), and "A tfile" ("A Prayer")—but the book also contains a second kind of *khurbm-lid*, one that I call the poem of unravelling. Many of these poems were written during the early years of the war, the period of partial knowledge of the catastrophe, and they express the poet's feelings of powerlessness and anxiety through the imagery of scripting—pens, paper, words, syllables, and the letters of the alphabet. Not that this was the first time such imagery recurs in Molodowsky's poems. In her first collection, *Nights of Heshvan*, the imagery of scripting was used to signal a modern woman's confrontation with traditional Judaism. In *Dzshike Street* and *Freydke*, these images indicated the conflict between the aesthetic and political obligations of the poet. In *In the Country of My Bones*, they pointed to the immigrant's cultural crisis. But throughout the wartime poems in *Only King David Remained*, the imagery of scripting calls into question the very efficacy of words, of any and all words—the words of prayers and poems, but even of postcards, to describe the terrible events that have occurred. Here, the disintegration or unravelling of written Jewish language became a figurative enactment of the destruction of the Jewish people, a means by which the poet herself could work out both the futility and the necessity of her own act of writing.

For example, in the 1941 poem, "Briv fun geto" ("Letters from the Ghetto"), the poet receives postcards from friends and family in the Warsaw Ghetto, in which the silences speak louder than the words actually written down. The poem develops a tone of rage that calls for divine revenge. In the 1943 poem, "Gezegenung" ("Leavetaking"), Molodowsky turned the metaphor of scripting inward to refer to her own writing of a poem. As it narrates the disruption of its making, this poem comments on the historical events of the Holocaust through a description of the decay of its own words and letters until, finally, the speaker forgets the very alphabet in which she writes.

Although some eighteen of the eighty-one poems in *Only King David Remained* deal explicitly with or allude to the destruction of the Jews, all the poems in the book are suffused with a weariness, a despair, an anger that comes out of the historical moment in which they were written. In "Mayne kinder" ("My Children"), the poet confronts another kind of loss, where the speaker's own unborn offspring, aborted or miscarried, speak to her about their lost future. The poet's confirmation of her craft can be seen only as ironic in a group of poems about the pettiness of the literary world—"Di kleyne fukselekh—shoelim ktonim" ("The Little Foxes, Little Foxes"), "Kines sofrim tarbe khokhme" ("The Rivalry of Writers Increases Wisdom"), "Mayn geshpan" ("My Harness"), and "In shtal fun lebn" ("In the Stable of Life").

Even a poem such as "Khad Gadya," which seems simply to tell the story of a character that the writer has dreamed up and then discarded, can be read as a poem of sacred parody. By refusing to let its creator alone, the poet's invention reenacts the paradox of the prayer that subverts the God to whom it is addressed and the poem whose language crumbles in the course of its poetic composition. In this paradoxical, self-contradictory pattern of creations that enact their own destruction, we see that writing poems in Yiddish was Molodowsky's way of witnessing the unthinkable events in Europe.

The guilt of survival is played out in poems with a Biblical theme, such as "Der dude-shpiler fun sdom" ("The Fife-Player of Sodom"), "Der melekh dovid aleyn iz geblibn" ("Only King David Remained"), and "Der bal-tkie" ("The Shofar Blower"). The fife-player, who is a witness to destruction, whose own body is "burn layered upon burn," asks God why he must, in his agony, continue "To sing this Hallelujah-song for You." Almost in response, the despairing, emblematic figures of King David and the man who blows the ram's horn affirm the continuity of Jewish tradition in the face of utter destruction. Reconnecting to this tradition gives the poet her strength to keep on writing and living.

***Likht fun dornboym* (Light of the Thorn Bush)**

Following the appearance of *Only King David Remained*, nineteen years passed before Molodowsky published her last book of poems, *Light of the Thorn Bush*. For Molodowsky personally, these were full, productive years. In 1945, another edition of her children's poems, *Yidishe kinder* (Jewish Children), was published in New York, and her children's poems, translated into Hebrew by the leading poets, were published in Tel Aviv. She published a long poem, "Donna Gracia Mendes"; two plays, *Nokhn got fun midbar* (After the God of the Desert) (New York, 1949), which was produced in Chicago and in Israel, and *A hoyz af grand strit* (A House on Grand Street) (New York, 1953), which was produced in New York;[85] a chapbook of poems, *In yerushalayim kumen malokhim* (In Jerusalem, Angels Come) (New York, 1952); a book of essays, *Af di vegn fun tsion* (On the Roads of Zion); and a collection of short stories, *A shtub mit zibn fentster* (A House with Seven Windows), both of which appeared in New York, in 1957. She also edited an anthology, *Lider fun khurbm* (Poems of the Holocaust) (Tel Aviv, 1962). In 1960, she revived the quarterly journal for literature and criticism, *Svive* (Surroundings), which she had helped found in 1943 and publish for seven issues through 1944.[86] She now served as its editor, fundraiser, publicity department, and salesperson.

In 1949, Molodowsky and her husband Simche Lev went to Israel. They bought an apartment in Tel Aviv and lived there until 1952.[87] Molodowsky traveled extensively throughout Israel and became involved in Yiddish cultural and literary life there, although she returned to the United States several times during this period. She edited the journal *Heym* (Home), which portrayed life in Israel and was distributed to all members of the Pioneer Women

Organization.[88] The years in Israel were unsettling, as a sampling of letters from Molodowsky to her friends, Yosel and Bessie Drost in Cleveland, reveals. In one letter, postmarked Tel Aviv, June 21, 1949, Molodowsky exclaims how impressed she is by the new nation Israel's cities and villages and by the Jewish culture that includes Yiddish, although not officially. In a letter to the Drosts from Tel Aviv on January 11, 1951, Molodowsky writes of the most recent issue of her journal *Heym*, complaining that the "fiery Yiddishists" in New York were ignoring it. On December 5, 1951, she writes the Drosts a note from her sister's home in Philadelphia, in which she tells how exhausted she is from laboring over *Heym*. A month later, on January 2, 1952, Molodowsky writes the Drosts that she and Lev have just returned to their apartment in Tel Aviv.[89] She writes to the Drosts again, from New York, on December 2, 1952, to announce that she has resigned the editorship of *Heym*.

Mordechai Tsanin, a Tel Aviv Yiddish writer who knew Molodowsky well, spoke in negative terms of Molodowsky's time in Israel.[90] He said that the reason why they left Israel was because Lev, "a communist," had decided that the couple would not stay there, even though Molodowsky had received more attention in Israel than any other Yiddish poet. Her work was quickly translated into Hebrew, and she received wide coverage in the Hebrew press.[91] Tsanin emphasized that Molodowsky was an ardent, outspoken Zionist. He pointed out that, although she did not speak Hebrew, Molodowsky chose to "ingratiate" herself with the Zionists by speaking in Yiddish against the Yiddish language and in support of Hebrew, arguing that Yiddish was not necessary in Israel. Tsanin ended the interview ironically: "She was a great patriot, and then she packed her bags and left."[92]

During her time in Israel, Molodowsky also began work on a novel, *Baym toyer: roman fun dem lebn in yisroel* (At the Gate: Novel about Life in Israel), which was eventually published in New York, in 1967. At the end of this period, she began to write her autobiography, "Mayn elterzeydns yerushe" ("My Great-Grandfather's Legacy"). Unfortunately, Molodowsky did not complete her autobiography—the last installment, published in *Svive* 41, in April, 1974, chronicles the period she and Simche lived in Israel, and so we have no account of the last twenty-four years of her life, or even of the making of her final book of poems.

Published in Buenos Aires in 1965, Molodowsky's *Light of the Thorn Bush* consists of 204 pages of closely printed poems, including a lengthy *poeme* "Der shteynhaker fun rishon" ("The Stonecutter from Rishon") (which I was unable to include in this selection), as well as lyric poems of various types.

The most powerful works in *Light of the Thorn Bush* are the dramatic monologues. Some are spoken by (or to) legendary personae, such as Diogenes ("Dos lid fun diogenus" ["The Song of Diogenes"]) or Jonah ("Yoyne" ["Jonah"]). Other personae are modern characters who combine legend with whimsy ("Mayn shif fun pimsnholts" ["My Ship of Gopher Wood"]) or with surrealism ("Ayzerner kholem" ["Iron Dream"]). In "The Sabbath Song," the speaker is a heroic woman who battles "With the emperors / Of the six days of the week," until the Sabbath Queen appears and the Sabbath candles bring all the forces of nature under the domain of the Sabbath.

Other dramatic personae are versions of the artist who is preoccupied with language, music, and storytelling as tropes that empower her to continue believing and creating in a hostile world. The speaker in "Mayn shprakh" ("My Language") calls forth an unspoken and unwritten "pure language" of the soul that will, when "I am dead," "unseal the stifled words" of inarticulate life. In "Ikh bin a viderkol" ("I Am an Echo"), the persona claims that her voice is "an echo / Of a vanished symphony," whose fiddler miraculously appears to her and prophesies a second, revenging victory at the walls of Jericho. In "Der vint iz alt gevorn" ("The Wind Has Grown Old"), the speaker tells that although she has been transformed into "a beggar woman in the valley" by the wind with its gloomy stories, its frightening, hollow melodies, and its deadly secrets, she refuses to "believe the old wind" and its negation of all that is humane. In "Bletlekh" ("Pages"), a poet struggles unsuccessfully to discard her unfinished poems.

Some monologues are prayers. The speaker approaches her father's graveside in "Dos likht fun dayn tish" ("The Light of Your Table"), where she addresses her dead father in a vein reminiscent of the *tkhines,* Yiddish supplicatory prayers, that women used to recite at their parents' graves, importuning the dead to intervene on their behalf in the world-to-come. "Bahalt mikh in a blat" ("Shelter Me in a Leaf") beseeches God for protection, returning to the tone and imagery of the sequence "Prayers" from her first book, *Nights of Heshvan.*

A lighter tone—self-parodying, comic, and ironic—is found in "Mabl" ("Flood"), where the speaker's exhaustion and despair are masked with a joke about a talking cat and the flowers decorating a hat. "Fun midkayt kh'varf arop di shikh un zokn" ("I Kick Off My Shoes and Socks in Exhaustion") begins in this tone, too, as the poet argues against the harangue of her sore feet, her ears, and her hands. However, the self-irony darkens into a deeper alienation from the self, as the poet, looking in her own mirror, confronts her body's relentless aging:

> For protection from my faithful eyes, I looked in my mirror.
> But there stood a stranger, an unknown face.
> He gazed at me, as if in deep disgrace:
> "How does a stranger come to *me* in the mirror?"

The strangeness of her own image, made male by age, reverses reality, casting a darker shadow on the sense of exile seen in earlier poems.

Indeed, the ruin of growing old colors many of the best poems in this book. In "Untergang stam" ("Random Sinking"), a senile ship captain has a momentary flicker of memory, in which he is annihilated. "Af der papirener brik" ("On the Paper Bridge") is the final variation on the legendary trope of messianic redemption, which Molodowsky used earlier in *Dzshike Street* and *Only King David Remained.* In this version, she takes on the persona of a wanderer who, seeking employment in the homes of the Patriarch Abraham, King David, and the Matriarch Rachel, cannot find a job. Linking this world and the world-to-come with the paper bridge, Molodowsky dramatizes the feelings of uselessness and displacement that come with old age.

Light of the Thorn Bush concludes with a section called "Yerusholaim" ("Jerusalem"), comprised of poems written in the 1950s. This ending parallels that of her autobiography, which also concludes in the midst of Molodowsky's narration of her three-year sojourn in the newly formed State of Israel. Both endings express Molodowsky's love for the State of Israel and her sense of the hope it embodied for the Jewish people. By juxtaposing, at the end of her last book, poems that either idealize Jerusalem ("In yerusholaim kumen malokhim" ["In Jerusalem, Angels Come"], "In land yisroel" ["In the Land of Israel"]) or show the ragtaggle survival of refugees from Eastern Europe ("Unzer shif" ["Our Ship"] and "A polet" ["A Refugee"]), Molodowsky offers an answer to her own displacements, exiles, and losses. She seems to have chosen to conclude the coherent story of her own life and work with a political statement that espoused the Jewish nation.

Some contemporary readers have commented on the absence of an explicitly feminist voice in the poems Molodowsky wrote after her emigration to America. In fact, it is true that, after settling in America, she did retreat from her 1930s, preimmigration, prewar feminism. Perhaps this retreat is partly a response to what Irena Klepfisz calls "a stronger sexism" in the United States.[93] It may also be a reaction to the shock of her cultural transplantation at the very moment that her old, native world in Poland was destroyed. Another writer at another time or place with such experiences might have spoken out with a stronger sense of feminism. Molodowsky did not react this way, nor did other women writers of her generation, who typically responded to the historical trauma of the Holocaust by focusing on a unified Jewish peoplehood, on the strongest manifestations of *yidishkayt*, and by identifying with the "universal," the "mainstream," which had a male-identified voice. This was, at any rate, the outward appearance of things. In fact, though, many poems in *Light of the Thorn Bush* are subtly engendered. In many poems, the speaker takes the voice of an old woman whose age, although diminishing her physically, empowers her in wisdom. In "Gots kinder" ("God's Children"), the "old woman, no longer lovely," makes the wise king weep at her truth. In "Shulames" and "Tsum melekh shloyme kumt di herlekhe shulames" ("Glorious Shulames Comes to Solomon the King"), the speakers, while expressing comic envy of Shulames' eternal beauty, make it a point to comment both on the transience of actual beauty and on the dangerous ideal of beauty that entraps women within the cultural constructs that praise them.

The full answers to the questions of Molodowsky's feminism are difficult to assess, in part because we lack Molodowsky's account of this last period of her life. During the 1960s and 1970s, she and her husband lived in New York City, although she maintained her ties to Israel. After 1965, Molodowsky continued to publish: in addition to her novel *Baym toyer: roman fun dem lebn in yisroel* in 1967 and her serialized autobiography in *Svive*, another edition of her children's poems *Martsepanes* (Marzipans) (New York, 1970). A small selection of her poems was translated into English and included in the anthology, *A Treasury of Yiddish Poetry*, edited by Irving Howe and Eliezer Greenberg (New York, 1969), and she participated in the poetry reading celebrating that anthology at the 92nd Street YMHA in the Fall of 1969. A book of her Jerusalem poems was published in Hebrew translation in 1971, the same year that, in Tel Aviv, Molodowsky was awarded the Itzik Manger Prize for Yiddish Literature, the most prestigious award in the Yiddish literary world, and her acceptance speech, which argues for the commonality between modern Yiddish and Hebrew authors, appeared in the literary journal, *Di goldene keyt* (The Golden Chain).[94]

A photograph of Kadya Molodowsky from this period is telling. An old woman sits in a winged armchair next to a light-flooded window. Wearing a flower-print blouse, a skirt and sweater of a nubby fabric, she rests one hand in her lap. The other holds a cigarette, burned down to a stub with a crown of ashes, as though she had forgotten to attend to her smoking for several minutes. Her hair, pulled back into a knot, is hardly visible, but for the halo of runaway strands. Drawing her brows together with concentration, she directs her eyes, their long lids etched in light, at something beyond the frame. Her mouth opens partially to let out a ghost of smoke. This photograph was taken by a young man in the winter of 1970, an amateur photographer who had set himself the task of photographing the aging writers and performers of Yiddish culture in New York City. The poet had invited the photographer to lunch in her apartment on Grand Street, and he asked her, seated there by the window, to recite one of her poems. His camera immortalized the word she uttered in the wisp of smoke rising pale against the dark wing of the chair.[95]

Not long after this photograph was taken, Molodowsky's husband Simche Lev died in New York City in 1974. As Molodowsky's health declined, and she became incapacitated, Molodowsky's sister Dora, her niece Edith Schwarz, and her nephew Ben Litman moved her to a nursing home near their homes in Philadelphia. There, on March 23, 1975, Kadya Molodowsky died.[96]

Conclusion

The shape of Molodowsky's life and career as a poet is important on account of both its typicality and its uniqueness. What her story shares with those of other women of her generation who wrote poetry in Yiddish are the instabilities and uncertainties of life during the first decades of this century: the poverty, displacement, and political furor caused by the First World War, the pogroms, and the Russian Revolution. Her movement from a shtetl to the large cities of Eastern Europe was an experience shared by many young Jewish women who aspired to publish their writing in both verse and prose. Her immigration to the United States was also a shared experience, although Molodowsky came at a later age (forty-one) and during a later decade than many other women writers, such as Malka Heifetz Tussman, Anna Margolin, and Celia Dropkin, all of whom arrived as girls or young women, before the 1924 reduction of mass immigration. As a witness to the Holocaust from the safety of the United States, Molodowsky was more fortunate than poets such as Roza Yakubovitsh and Miriam Ulinover, both of whom perished under the Nazi regime. Unlike Rokhl Korn and Chava Rosenfarb, who survived the war years in Eastern Europe and later came to Canada, where they continued to write, Molodowsky's expression of loss and grief came from a more indirect but no less felt experience. Her support for the State of Israel, which had its roots in her Hebrew language group and teaching in Europe, developed now in part as a reaction against that grief.

On the other hand, what was unusual in Molodowsky's life were the facts that she married relatively late (at age twenty-seven), that she had no children, that she kept her own name, and that she continued to publish her books from the age of thirty-three until the last years of her life. The variety, quantity, and quality of her writing reveal Molodowsky to be a poet of the first rank in the history of Yiddish poetry.

The "Synagogue of the Wealthy" on Shosayne Street near the Post Office in Bereza Kartuska. (Caption in Pinkes fun finf fartilikte kehiles: Pruzshere, Bereze, Maltsh, Shershev, Selts, *ed. Mordechai V. Bernshteyn and David Fover. Buenos Aires: 1958, p. 336.) Molodowsky sent this postcard, two others of Bereza—the marketplace and street scene below—and a photograph of herself and her husband Simche Lev from Warsaw on July 23, 1925, to her sisters Lena (Libe) and Dora (Dobe) and their families in Philadelphia, with a note of greeting on the back (in Yiddish).*

The marketplace in Bereza Kartuska.

A street in Bereza Kartuska.

Kadya's father, Isaac Molodowsky, brother, Leybl Molodowsky, and mother, Itke Molodowsky, in Bereza, in the 1910s. Courtesy of Edith Schwarz.

Molodowsky, age 18 (center, in glasses), Dora Molodowsky, age 16 (on the right) and an unidentified friend, Bereza, 1912. Courtesy of Edith Schwarz.

Molodowsky (lower left) with two women friends, around 1912–13, probably in Bialystok.

Lena Molodowsky Pritsker and Dora Molodowsky (later Litman) in Philadelphia, around 1915. Courtesy of Edith Schwarz.

Molodowsky, February 12, 1926. Molodowsky inscribed this message on the back of the photograph to Simche Lev, "I look like a calf here because the photographer is a shlimazl."

Molodowsky, her brother Leybl (Louis) Molodowsky (bottom right) and Simche Lev (standing). Warsaw, 1920s.

Left to right: Isaac Bashevis Singer, Itsik Manger, Molodowsky, and Joseph Kerman. Warsaw, late 1920s.

Left to right: Molodowsky, Joseph Kerman, Joseph Opatoshu (front, center), Isaac Bashevis Singer (back, center), Aaron Zeitlin, and Melech Ravich. Warsaw, late 1920s.

Left to right: Mendel Elkin, Joseph Kerman, unidentified woman, Molodowsky, Aaron Zeitlin, and Itsik Manger. Warsaw, late 1920s.

Left to right: Melech Ravich, Joseph Kerman, Molodowsky, Samuel Jacob Imber, and Isaac Bashevis Singer. Warsaw, late 1920s. Inscribed on the back in Yiddish, "To my dear friend Leybl Molodowsky, I. Bashevis."

Left to right, seated: unidentified woman, Molodowsky, unidentified woman, and Samuel Jacob Imber. Standing: Leybl Molodowsky, unidentified woman, Joseph Kerman, Uri Zvi Greenberg.

Molodowsky, in Warsaw, early 1930s. On the back is written, "L. Blet," signifying the Warsaw literary journal Literarishe bleter.

Molodowsky (standing, second row, left) with other teachers and students at the TSHIO school in Warsaw, around 1930.

Molodowsky and Simche Lev. Warsaw, 1925. (Sent by Molodowsky from Warsaw with the three postcards of Bereza Kartuska to her sisters in Philadelphia on July 23, 1925.)

Molodowsky and Simche Lev in Paris, around 1931–32. Courtesy of Edith Schwarz.

Portrait of Molodowsky, around 1938, in the United States.

On the deck of a ship, in port. Probably New York, 1935 or 1936. Joseph Opatoshu (second from left), Molodowsky (third from left), H. Leyvik (fifth from left).

Passport photograph, Molodowsky, United States of America. Around 1950.

Molodowsky (second from left) in Tel Aviv with Simche Lev, the Yiddish poet Abraham Sutzkever, and Yiddish playwright David Pinski, 1951 or 1952.

Molodowsky, with Yiddish poets Rokhl Korn and Ida Maze, in Montreal, late 1950s.

Molodowsky, 1955–59.

Simche Lev and Molodowsky (at left) with her sister, Dora, and brother-in-law, Isadore Litman, at the Statue of Liberty, 1959.

Molodowsky at the podium, May 1964.

Molodowsky seated on stage between the poet-translators Adrienne Rich and John Hollander, at the 92nd Street YMHA on November 2, 1969. They were participants in the reading to celebrate the publication of A Treasury of Yiddish Poetry, *edited by Irving Howe and Eliezer Greenberg. Photo © Arnold Chekow (used with permission).*

Molodowsky reciting a poem in her apartment on Grand Street, January or February 1970. Photo © Arnold Chekow (used with permission).

Molodowsky, seated before her portrait, in her apartment, October 1973.

Illustration by Mane Katz for Molodowsky's children's poem, "A Tale of the Washtub," in Marzipanes *(New York: Education Committee of the Workmen's Circle and CYCO Press, 1970, p. 6). Original illustration courtesy of Ben Litman and Edith Schwarz.*

Notes

All translations of sources cited are by Kathryn Hellerstein unless otherwise indicated.

1. The date, May 10, 1894, is given in Marion Handgratinger, "Mein Leben—einem Gebetbuch entrissen: Zum literarischen Raum jiddischer Schriftstellerinnen zu Beginn des 20. Jahrhunderts am Beispiel von Kadya Molodowskys *Froyen-Lidern* (Wilna 1927)." (master's thesis, Ruprecht-Karls-Universitat, Heidelberg, 1992), 14. I have not been able to verify this date in another source.

2. "Bereza Kartsuka," *Encyclopaedia Judaica*, vol. 4. (New York: Macmillan, Jerusalem: Keter, 1971), 606. *Pinkes fun finf fartilikte kehiles: Pruzshene, Bereze, Maltsh, Shershev, Selts*, ed. Mordehai V. Bernshteyn with David Forer. (Buenos Aires: Landslayt Farayn fun Pruzshene, Bereze, Maltsh, Shershev, un umgegnt in Argentine, 1958), 328–466. Details provided by Gaston L. Schmir, Bob Rothstein, Michael Shimshoni, Michael Steinlauf, Jacob Buck, and Paul Pascal on the electronic mail newsletter Mendele 4.237 and in private e-mail correspondence. Also, Sallyann Sack and Gary Mokotoff, *Where Once We Walked: A Guide to the Jewish Communities Destroyed by the Holocaust* (Teaneck, NJ: Avotaynu, 1991), 22.

3. Kadya Molodowsky, "Mayn elterzeydns yerushe" ("My Great-Grandfather's Legacy"), *Svive* 17 (October 1965): 41; also *Svive* 24 (February 1968): 33–34. Molodowsky stemmed from a family of teachers: her father, his two brothers, and both of their parents were teachers.

4. Kadya Molodowsky, *Svive* 20 (September 1966): 63.

5. Ibid., 61; also, Kadya Molodowsky, *Svive* 21 (December 1966): 25.

6. Molodowsky's mother Itke grew up with seven stepsisters and two

stepbrothers from her father Kadish Katz/Kaplan's three wives in Frampolye, a village near Slonim. Kadya Molodowsky, *Svive* 15 (March 1965): 34–35.

7. Molodowsky, *Svive* 20 (September 1966): 62.

8. Kadya Molodowsky, *Svive* 16 (July 1965): 42. As Molodowsky uses the word *rebetsn* here, she seems to mean "female *rebe*" (rabbi or teacher), although the term usually refers to the wife of a rabbi.

9. Ibid., 42–43; also Molodowsky, *Svive* 24 (February 1968): 34.

10. Molodowsky, *Svive* 16 (July 1965): 44.

11. Ibid.; also Molodowsky, *Svive* 17 (October 1965): 40–41.

12. Molodowsky, *Svive* 21 (December 1966): 27.

13. Edith Schwarz and Ben Litman, niece and nephew of Kadya Molodowsky and children of her sister Dora Molodowsky Litman, interview with the author, Philadelphia, Penn., March 30, 1993.

14. Kadya Molodowsky, *Svive* 23 (October 1967): 25–28.

15. Kadya Molodowsky, *Svive* 25 (May 1968): 46, 49–50.

16. Kadya Molodowsky, *Svive* 28 (May 1969): 63.

17. Kadya Molodowsky, *Svive* 31 (May 1970): 60–61.

18. Kadya Molodowsky, *Svive* 32 (September 1970): 57.

19. Kadya Molodowsky, *Svive* 33 (January 1971): 54.

20. Kadya Molodowsky, "Dorsht" ("Thirst") and "Shtot" ("City"), in *Eygns*, book 2 (Kiev: Kiever Farlag, 1920), 73–77.

21. Molodowsky, *Svive* 33 (January 1971): 54–57. The rigor with which Molodowsky revised her poems is borne out in her manuscripts, found in the Kadya Molodowsky Archives at the YIVO Institute for Jewish Research.

22. In later years, Simche Lev wrote historical essays and earned his living as a Yiddish typesetter.

23. Molodowsky, *Svive* 33 (January 1971): 59–62. Molodowsky's niece and nephew reported in an interview that for a brief period during the 1920s, Molodowsky lived in Paris with Simche while he studied at the Sorbonne. Her niece and nephew believed that Kadya, too, studied there. Ben Litman and Edith Schwarz, interview with the author, Philadelphia, PA, March 30, 1993.

24. Melekh Ravitsh presents a different picture of Molodowsky's years in Warsaw. He writes that she lived with her brother Leybl, an electrical technician, on Dzshike Street, while her husband, Simche Lev, studied in Paris, and the couple endured years of separation. He implies that she also lived in Paris for a time. Melekh Ravitsh, "Kadya Molodowsky," *Mayn leksikon: Yidishe dikhter, dertseyler, dramaturgn in poyln tsvishn di tsvey groyse veltmilkhomes* (Montreal: A Committee in Montreal, 1945), 122–24.

25. Kadya Molodowsky, *Svive* 34 (August 1971): 39.

26. Ibid., 40–41.

27. Kadya Molodowsky, "Haynt iz a shtiler tog" ("Today Is a Quiet Day II"), in *Kheshvndike nekht* (Vilna: B. Kletskin, 1927), 90.

28. Molodowsky, "Oreme vayber" ("Poor Women"), *Kheshvndike nekht*, 90.

29. Kadya Molodowsky, *Svive* 35 (December 1971): 59; also, Molodowsky, "A matseyve" ("A Tomb"), *Kheshvndike nekht*, 76–81.

30. Molodowsky, *Svive* 35 (December 1971): 60–61.

31. Molodowsky, *Svive* 28 (May 1969): 61. Dora (Dobe), the younger sister, emigrated to America in the winter of 1913–14, joining Lena, the eldest sister, who had come earlier.

32. Molodowsky, "A matseyve IV" ("A Tomb IV"), *Kheshvndike nekht,* 79.

33. Molodowsky, "A matseyve V" ("A Tomb V"), *Kheshvndike nekht,* 80.

34. Molodowsky, "Oreme vayber II" ("Poor Women II"), *Kheshvndike nekht,* 91.

35. The exact title and date of this collection are not clearly established. In her autobiography, in *Svive* 36 (April 1972): 56, Molodowsky refers to her first book of children's poems as *Geyen shikhelekh avek vu der velt hot nor an ek* (Little Shoes Go Away to the Ends of the Earth) and says that it was published in Warsaw by the TSISHO Press (Farlag Tsentrale Shul Organizatsye). She gives no date. The earliest version of these poems I have located (at the YIVO library) is *Mayselekh* (Tales) (Warsaw: Yidishe Shul Organizatsye fun Poyln, 1931). The colophon of Molodowsky's 1942 novel, *Fun lublin biz nyu-york,* lists 1930 as the date for *Geyen shikhelekh avek.* However, this list errs in the dates for other works.

36. Molodowsky, *Svive* 25 (May 1968): 48–50.

37. Molodowsky, *Svive* 28 (May 1969): 59–60.

38. See Kadya Molodowsky, *Pitḥu et hasha'ar: shirei yeladim* (Open the Gate: Children's Poems), trans. Fanye Bergshteyn, Natan Alterman, Lea Goldberg, Avraham Levinson, Yankev Fikhman. With a story about the poet by Yankev Fikhman. Illustrated by Tirtsa. (Israel: Hakibbutz Hameuchad Publishing House, 1945; 2d. ed., 1979). Also see the article by an 11th grade student named "Ruthy" that celebrates the Hebrew translations of Molodowsky's children's poem, in the Hebrew paper, *Hevriah,* November 9, 1945. (Mirik Snir, unpublished summary of Molodowsky's time in Israel, 3).

39. Molodowsky, *Svive* 34 (August 1971): 44.

40. Michael Silver, interview with the author, Jerusalem, May 21, 1995.

41. Kadya Molodowsky, "Olke," in *Mayselekh* (Warsaw: Yidishe Shul Organizatsye in Poyln, 1931), 71–78.

42. Molodowsky, *Svive* 36 (April 1972): 57–58.

43. Rokhl H. Korn, "Dzshike gas un ir dikhterin" ("Dzshike Street and Its Poetess"), *Literarishe bleter,* 11th year of publication, 10, no. 506 (3), Warsaw (January 19, 1934): 36–37.

44. Nakhman Mayzel, "Dzshike-gas," in undesignated newspaper; judging from the page format, it is probably not *Literarishe bleter,* no date. Folder 156, Kadya Molodowsky Archives, YIVO.

45. Sh. Niger, "Shver tsu zayn a poet" ("It's Hard to be a Poet"), *Der tog,* February 10, [1933]. Folder 156, Kadya Molodowsky Archives, YIVO.

46. Kh. Sh. Kazdan, "Di dikhterin af der dzshike gas" ("The Poetess on Dzshike Street"), *Vokhnshrift far literatur, kunst, un kultur* (Weekly for Literature, Art, and Culture) 22, no. 122 (June 9, 1933): 2. Jewish National Library at Hebrew University, Jerusalem.

47. Ibid., 2.

48. Nakhman Mayzl writes in his memoirs that the censor forced Molodowsky to change "Nakht" ("Night"), a poem in *Dzshike Street*, about a nighttime police raid so that it referred to the troubles of the Jews in Nazi Berlin, rather than in Warsaw. Molodowsky added "Berlin, April, 1933" to the bottom of the page. Nakhman Mayzl, *Geven amol a lebn: dos yidishe kultur-lebn in polyn tsuishn beyde velt-milkhomes* (Once There Was a Life: Jewish Cultural Life in Poland between the World Wars). (Buenos Aires: Tsentral farband fun poylishe yidn in Argentine, 1951), 291–98. Thanks to Dovid Fishman for this reference.

Further evidence for Molodowsky's complex political alliances is detailed by Anna Gonshur, Department of Jewish Studies at McGill University, Montreal, Canada, in her master's thesis-in-progress, "Kadya Molodowsky: The Warsaw Years."

49. Molodowsky, *Svive* 36 (April 1972): 57.

50. Molodowsky, *Svive* 35 (December 1971): 63. "We lived then on Dzshike Street in a building of several stories, a huge building that stretched over two courtyards."

51. Source for information on Dzshike Street and Pawiak, David Rosenthal (native of Warsaw and student of Kadya Molodowsky), conversations with author, Philadelphia, Penn., 1990–91.

52. Molodowsky, *Svive* 35 (December 1971): 56.

53. Molodowsky, *Svive* 33 (January 1971): 56–57.

54. Kadya Molodowsky, "Bagegenishn" ("Encounters"), *Literarishe bleter* 5, no. 300 (January 31, 1930): 95. Thanks to Anna Gonshur of McGill University for the reference.

55. The following poems from *Kheshvndike nekht* appeared in variant form in Ezra Korman, *Yidishe dikhterins: antologye* (Chicago: L. M. Stein, 1928): "Froyen-lider I, II, VI, VII, VIII"; "Opgeshite bleter II"; "Otwock I"; "Nit loz mikh untergeyn" ("Tfiles I"); "S'iz gut dem kop bahaltn" ("Opgeshite bleter IX"); and "A matseyve" ("A matseyve I").

56. Molodowsky, "Meydlekh, froyen, vayber, un . . . nevue." *Literarishe bleter*, 4th year of publication, 3, no. 22 (June 3, 1927): 416; Melekh Ravitsh, "Meydlekh, froyen, vayber—yidishe dikhterins," *Literarishe bleter*, 4th year of publication, 3, no. 21 (May 27, 1927): 395–96.

57. Hannah Levin (1900–24), a Yiddish poet from Ekaterinoslav in Ukraine. A selection of her poems in translation is in *The Golden Peacock: An Anthology of Yiddish Poetry*, ed. and trans. Joseph Leftwich (London: Robert Anscombe, 1939), 741–43.

58. Molodowsky, "Bagegenishn," 95. Moyshe Khashtshevatsski (1897–1943) and Itsik Fefer (1900–1952) were both Ukranian-born Soviet Yiddish writers.

59. Kazdan, "Di dikhterin af der dzshike gas," 2.

60. Paula Hyman, *From Dreyfus to Vichy: The Remaking of French Jewry, 1906–1939*. (New York: Columbia University Press, 1979), 98, 106: "Restrictive legislation was imposed upon immigrant workers, artisans, and merchants, beginning with the law of August 10, 1932, which limited the ratio of

foreign workers to be employed in any industry or trade to 10 percent of the total. . . . the impact of this decree upon the Jewish trades was particularly severe, and the number of immigrant *faconniers* ["home workers, who were provided with raw material by an entrepreneur and who often subcontracted their work to other laborers" (98)] increase substantially as workers attempted to evade the provisions of the decree and its successors in 1934 and 1935."

61. Lafcadio Hearn, *Khinezishe legendn*, trans. Bernard Witt. (New York: Trio Press, 1930).

62. Molodowsky, *Svive* 36 (April 1972): 61.

63. Ibid. The reasons for and circumstances of Molodowsky's departure from Poland are ambiguous. According to her autobiography, in *Svive* 36 (April 1972): 60–64, Molodowsky decided rather casually to leave Poland for the United States, where her two sisters and father had settled, by accepting a 1935 invitation from the Sholem Aleichem Folk Institute as a visiting writer. That this "visit" enforced a three-year separation from her husband renders the casualness of this retrospective account suspect. The gaps in Molodowsky's narration of her departure from her husband and brother, the focus upon marginal details, and the oddly cheery tone all suggest an intentional obfuscation of the actual reasons for her emigration. My sense of this ambiguity was confirmed in a conversation on March 19, 1993, with Anna Gonshor, a master's candidate in Jewish Studies at McGill University, whose thesis-in-progress, "Kadya Molodowsky: The Warsaw Years," reveals that Molodowsky was very likely motivated to leave Poland because of conflicts in her political activities on the Jewish Left.

64. Ibid., 63; also, Kadya Molodowsky, *Svive* 38 (January 1973): 58: "In the year 1938, Simche came to America." Molodowsky's letter to Yosel Drost in Cleveland, dated March 26, 1938, mentions that she had trouble arranging the papers for her husband to come to the United States. According to the dates and addresses on the Drost letters, by November 21, 1938, Simche Lev had arrived in New York City, and he and Molodowsky had moved to 297 East 10th Street. Previously, Molodowsky's return address had been c/o Buff, 144 East 22nd Street. In contradiction, Molodowsky's niece and nephew, Edith Schwarz and Ben Litman, recalled their impressions that Simche Lev had come to America at the same time as Kadya. Edith said, in an interview with the author, "I was 14 in 1937, that summer we went to Rockaway, and Simche was there with Kadya."

65. H. Leyvik, "Kadya Molodowsky—Dikhterin fun *unzer* dzshike gas" ("Kadya Molodowsky—Poetess of *Our* Dzshike Street"), *Fraye arbeter shtime*, New York, October 11, 1935, 5. Folder 156, Kadya Molodowsky Archives, YIVO.

66. Molodowsky, *Svive* 37 (September 1972): 61.

67. Ibid., 57.

68. Ibid., 58.

69. Ibid., 59. Leyvik recorded his version of this incident atop the Empire State Building in his greeting to Molodowsky. Leyvik, "Kadya Molodowsky," 5. Leyvik quotes Molodowsky as she exclaimed at the view, "Vos hekher un grandiezer di moyern raysn zikh in di himlen arayn, alts sharfer,

dukht zikh, hert men vi es shpart der troyer fun di gor untershte kelern fun nyu york" ("The higher and more grandiosely the walls invade the sky, all the more sharply can one hear how the sorrow of New York's lowest cellars presses down").

70. Molodowsky, *Svive* 37 (September 1972): 61–62.

71. According to Molodowsky's letter to Yosel Drost, dated November 11, 1941, her novel, probably *Fun lublin biz nyu-york*, was "reprinted" in the "Presse" in Argentine, in 1941. It seems, then, that the novel was published in Argentina before it appeared in New York.

72. Melekh Ravitsh, "Kadya Molodowsky," *Mayn leksikon*, 124.

73. The typescripts of Molodowsky's columns on women, published under the pseudonym of Rivke Zilberg, are found in the Kadya Molodowsky Archives at YIVO. Molodowsky wrote about women, including the Biblical prophet Miriam; the nineteenth-century poets Elizabeth Barrett Browning and Emily Dickinson; Gela, the young girl whose 1710 Yiddish poem is included in Korman's anthology; Miriam Ulinover, a Yiddish poet of the 1920s; and Zionist women. These columns were published on page three of the second section of the Sunday edition of *Forverts* during the mid-1950s. For example, in January and February 1955, seven of these columns appeared: *Forverts* 58, no. 20971 (January 9, 1955); no. 20978 (January 16, 1955); no. 20985 (January 23, 1955); no. 20992 (January 30, 1955); no. 21006 (February 13, 1955); no. 21013 (February 20, 1955); and no. 21020 (February 27, 1955).

74. Molodowsky's brother Leybl was taken by the communists and died trying to escape from the communist concentration camp, probably in 1942 or 1943. His wife and baby daughter Edith were captured by the Nazis and did not survive. Edith Schwarz and Ben Litman, interview with the author.

75. Molodowsky, *Svive* 38 (January 1973): 59.

76. Ibid., 60.

77. Ibid.

78. Molodowsky edited *Svive* from 1943–44. She revived the journal in 1960, and it appeared until 1974. Melekh Ravitsh calls her almost mockingly, "Eyne fun di ershte un efsher di same ershte in der yidisher literatur tsu trogn redaktorske hoyzn" ("One of the first and perhaps the very first female in Yiddish literature to wear editorial trousers"). Ravitsh, "Kadya Molodowsky," *Mayn leksikon*, 124.

79. Molodowsky mentions here that this volume received the Louis Lammed Prize after its publication, but that she was not in the mood to rejoice over the award. Molodowsky, *Svive* 38 (January 1973): 60.

80. The colophon for *Only King David Remained* acknowledges Simche Lev, Molodowsky's husband, as the typesetter and arranger of print columns.

81. Molodowsky, *Svive* 38 (January 1973): 60.

82. Yankev Glatshteyn, in a contemporary review of *Der melekh dovid aleyn iz geblibn*, compares the 1946 book with the 1935 *Dzshike gas* and emphasizes Molodowsky's transformation from a Polish to an American Yiddish poet, focusing less on the *khurbm-lider* than on her *poeme* (narrative poem se-

quence) "Bronzvil" ("Brownsville"). Yankev Glatshteyn, "In tokh genumen: Kadya Molodowsky's nay bukh lider" ("The Essence of Things: Kadya Molodowsky's New Book of Poems"), *Yidisher kemfer* (New York) 28, no. 678 (November 29, 1946): 14–15. Folder 156, Kadya Molodowsky Archives, YIVO.

83. Alan Mintz, *Ḥurban* (New York: Columbia University Press, 1984), 21.

84. David Roskies, *Against the Apocalypse* (Cambridge, Mass.: Harvard University Press, 1984), 30.

85. Handgrattinger, "Mein Leben," 23.

86. Molodowsky, *Svive* 38 (January 1973): 59–60.

87. Molodowsky, *Svive* 39 (May 1973): 57; also interview with Edith Schwarz and Ben Litman: "Kadya and Simche bought an apartment and lived in Tel Aviv for up to three years, maybe more, in two installments during the early 1950s."

In her unpublished synopsis of Molodowsky's connections to Israel, the Israeli writer Mirik Snir states that Molodowsky and Lev "made aliyah" in 1949, but returned to the United States in 1952. Mirik Snir, "Manuscript summary of Kadya Molodowsky's time in Israel," (Hebrew), fax to the author, Netanya, March 10, 1997. Includes a bibliography of seventeen articles about Molodowsky, which appeared in the Hebrew press between August 30, 1938 and February 1976.

According to the return address on the letter to the Drosts dated January 2, 1952, Molodowsky and Lev's apartment was located at Rehov Yehuda Hamakabi 5, Shkhunat Riskin B'Tsfon, Tel Aviv.

88. Twelve numbers of *Heym* were published from June 1950 through October 1952. The complete collection can be found in the Jewish National and University Library in Jerusalem.

89. Kadya Molodowsky to Yosel and Bessie Drost, January 2, 1952. Drost family letters, private collection of Elaine Drost Friedman. The return address on this letter is Rehov Yehuda Hamakabi 5, Shkhunat Riskin B'Tsfon, Tel Aviv.

90. Telephone interview with Mordechai Tsanin, conducted by David Stern, in Hebrew, Tel Aviv, July 1996.

91. Snir, "Manuscript summary of Kadya Molodowsky's time in Israel."

92. Telephone interview with Mordechai Tsanin.

93. Irena Klepfisz, "Di mames, dos loshn/The Mothers, The Language: Feminism, Yidishkayt, and the Politics of Memory," *Bridges* (spring 1994): 12–47. "These are indications that Jewish sexism intensified on this side of the Atlantic and is far worse than it was in Eastern Europe. Perhaps this explains in part Kadya's shift from writing feminist poetry like 'Froyen-lider' in the 1920s in Poland to ignoring women altogether 40 years later in the States. Consciously or not, she was responding to a stronger sexism" (38).

94. Kadya Molodowsky, "Di eygnartikayt fun literatur bay yidn: rede baym bakumen dem manger-prayz" ("The Peculiarity of Literature by Jews: Speech upon Receiving the Manger Prize"), *Di goldene keyt* 73 (1971): 68–70.

95. The photographer was Arnold Chekow. See Kathryn Hellerstein, "Famous Long Ago: Yiddish in New York, 1967–1972," photographs by Arnold Chekow, *The Book Peddler* 18 (spring 1993): 44–57.

96. The date of her death was established in an interview with Edith Schwarz and Benjamin Litman. A different date, March 21, 1975, is asserted by Handgratinger, "Mein Leben," 25.

A Note on the Translation

The translator of Kadya Molodowsky's poetry into English, and perhaps of all Yiddish poetry, faces more challenges than I can enumerate here, but I will discuss two. The first of these evolves from the cultural assumptions surrounding particularities of diction. The second is prosody. Yiddish is syntactically a Germanic language with a rich dictionary of Hebraic and Slavic words (as well as of medieval French, American English, and other sources), upon which Molodowsky often capitalized. Although English has a Germanic base, Anglo-Saxon, the modern language is strongly influenced by the Romance languages, both in syntax and in diction. Because the cultural matrix of Yiddish is Jewish and that of English is Christian, a translator will never find exact equivalents, especially for the Hebraic words that refer to religious objects, practices, or concepts. For example, in the first poem in this book, "Women-Poems I," the second line presents the Hebraic adverbial phrase *in tsnies* to describe the virtuous, modest, even chaste way that "the women of our family" carried a lineage of purity from one generation to the next through the strict observance of Jewish law and custom in their sexual conduct and their dress. The options offered by English for this Hebraic word are all Latinate—"in virtue," "in modesty", "in chastity"—and, in reference to women, denote an obedience to a religious or moral code of conduct that is essentially Christian. It is tempting but unwise to draw an equation between the Latinate aspects of English and the

Hebraic aspects of Yiddish. The best one can try for are correspondences. I chose the adverb "modestly," perhaps the least religiously connotative of the words—hoping that a few lines later, both the word "kosher," which has been absorbed by the English dictionary, and the peculiarly Jewish conundrum of the abandoned wife (*agune*) will direct the reader toward the Jewish notions of sexual purity.

In other cases, I chose not even to attempt to translate the Hebraism and left it intact in the translation. In both "My Father's Fur Coat" and "Khad Gadya," Molodowsky uses the Aramaic phrase "khad gadya"—the title of a well-known Passover song that literally means "one kid"—in a colloquial Yiddish manner to denote a tedious tale that has no end. Because, in both poems, Molodowsky has rhymed "khad gadya" with her own name, "Kadya," it seemed important to keep the phrase, the name, and the rhyme in the English version, and to let a note explain the idiom's meaning.

One other example will introduce yet another kind of problem I encountered trying to convey the cultural ramifications of particular words, in the phrases "mamzer gonoruk" and "katshke-dreydl," both found in "In My Hand Two Feathers from a Pheasant." The first phrase consists of a common Hebraic word, *mamzer* (bastard), and *gonoruk*, which is not to be found in any dictionary. Not one of the several informants I consulted (all native Yiddish speakers from various regions) understood or recognized the word *gonoruk* in this phrase. The linguist Dr. Mordekhe Schaechter hypothesized that it means "gonorrheal" for *-uk* is a pejorative suffix. He said that this phrase may have been an urban, Warsaw insult. On the other hand, the late Yiddish translator of the French Symbolist poets, M. Litwin, told me that he thought the phrase somewhat stilted for a curse. To his Lithuanian ear, *gonor* was medical terminology, while the crass, common term for gonorrhea, *triper*, came from the Russian and was more likely to have been used in a curse. He speculated that Molodowsky chose *gonor* because it sounds like *goner* (gander, male goose). This wordplay would connote the same family of associations as *katshke* (duck) in the next line. Although both components of the second phrase were found in Weinreich's dictionary (*dreydl* here means chicanery or, humorously, scheme), the literal translation of *katshke-dreydl* as "duck-chicanery" made no sense. Two informants from Rumanian Yiddish backgrounds, Dr. Schaechter and Dr. Itzik Gottesman, identified *katshke-dreydl* as a nonsense rhyme in a children's counting or game song, like "eenie meenie minie mo." Another informant, Gella Schweid-Fishman, reports that the phrase appears in a rhyme that pokes fun at someone's self-importance. In the poem these two phrases seem to signify to the poet two extremes of diction—the insulting sexual curse of the city street and the intimate rhyme of a childhood in a specific locality. In contrast, the word *fazan* (pheasant), which the poet associates with the newly founded utopian Jewish State of Birobidzhan, sounds "too foreign, too delicate," and, like the other two terms, alludes to a bird. Because both of the impenetrable, connotative phrases serve as word-objects in this poem, I have kept them intact in the translation, following each with an interpretive phrase in English.

Just as I did not translate certain Hebraisms, I also left some Americanisms intact. In "In My Hand Two Feathers from a Pheasant," the English word "store" occurs in the Yiddish line: "s'iz nisht keyn krom, es iz a stor" ("It is not a *krom* [shop], it is a 'store'"). And in "Alphabet Letters," the English words "city," "business," and "Boy Scouts" occur ironically within the Yiddish sentences. However, in order to convey in the translations something of the ironic, comic effect of foreignness that Molodowsky intended with these American imports, I have selectively offset the Americanisms, which become invisible in English, with a few Yiddish words or phrases.

The complex, irregular prosody of Molodowsky's poems presents a particular challenge to the translator. Some poems adhere to strict, conventional forms, while others change their line lengths and rhyming patterns from strophe to strophe, or even line to line, as in "My Ultimate Biography." However, because most of Molodowsky's poems conform to some sort of metrical line based on a pattern of alternating stressed and unstressed syllables, they are not free verse in the strict sense. In translating Molodowsky's prosody, I have thus tried either to follow the Yiddish meter and rhyme or to find or invent corresponding forms, hoping to make each poem read well in English.

Rhyme is a very important tool in Molodowsky's poems. Where the end rhymes of the couplets seem essential to the Yiddish poem, that is, where the poet uses them for emphasis, a turn of wit, or to build to a climax, I have rhymed the English, too, as in "Blue Dawn, I, II, and IX," in "Shloyminke the Blacksmith," and in the first section of "In the Green Tree Lies Gray Ash":

> forst avek—derken ikh nisht keyn gas,
> un oyb kh'derken zey yo—zenen zey mir fremd.
> di ershte shure kon men gramen mit monparnas,
> di tsveyte—mit a hemd[.]
> . . .
> You leave. I can't recall the streets, alas,
> And those I recognize are strange, inert.
> The first line can be rhymed with Montparnasse,
> The second, with a shirt.

In another example, the refrain of "A Poem to My Clothes Closet," Molodowsky rhymes the two key words, the Hebraic *dveykes* (religious ecstasy, excessive devoutness), and the Slavic *katsaveyke* (a quilted peasant jacket), comically harnessing together their sacred Hebrew and the earthy Slavic connotations, as the speaker bemoans the poverty that forces her to remake her old-fashioned jacket into a modern dress. It was essential to produce a corresponding rhyme in the translation:

> Lig ikh azoy in dveykes,
> un trakht vegn mayn broyner katsaveyke.
> . . .
> Then I lie in devout, ecstatic guilt
> And think about my jacket of brown quilt.

If following a strict English rhyme scheme forced me to change the poem radically or to distort normal syntax, I substituted half-rhyme, assonance, consonance, or alliteration to give the effect of rhyme. In a poem filled with strong images and language, where the Yiddish poet used end rhyme in such an awkward or obligatory way that translating the rhyme strained the English poem, I often did not attempt to rhyme at all, but instead gave the translation texture with meter, rhythm, and internal sound patterns.

On the Yiddish Texts

These translations are based on the Yiddish texts of eight books of poetry by Kadya Molodowsky: *Kheshvndike nekht* (1927), *Mayselekh* (1931), *Afn barg* (1938), *Dszhike gas* (1933, 1936), *Freydke* (1935, 1936), *In land fun mayn gebeyn* (1937), *Der melekh dovid aleyn iz geblibn* (1946), and *Likht fun dornboym* (1965). Both *Dszhike gas* and *Freydke* were issued twice, and I have compared the two editions. In the few cases of their minor discrepancies, I have relied upon the earlier edition, the publication of which Molodowsky oversaw in Warsaw.

Because the spelling in Molodowsky's poems varies from book to book, I have standardized it, in collaboration with Gitl Schaechter-Viswanath, according to the Standardized Yiddish Orthography ("YIVO spelling"). This task raised some complex and unanswerable questions about the poet's intentions, her control over the final production of her books, and her own Yiddish dialect. We had to make a distinction between questions of spelling and those of dialectal usage. We standardized the spelling, despite the fact that such alterations sometimes also slightly changed the sound of the poem. With one exception, we retained Molodowsky's dialectal choices, including her inconsistencies, for instance the use of both *nit* and *nisht.* The only dialectal change we made was to the plural forms of the verb *zayn* (to be). In the books published in Warsaw, before 1935, and in Buenos Aires, in 1965, Molodowsky used the forms *zenen* and *zent*, while in the books published in the United States after 1937, she used *zaynen* and *zayt*. Reluctant to tamper with the poet's idiom, I sought advice from several colleagues in the field, sage advice, generously given, and ultimately contradictory. In the end, I turned to the manuscripts of Molodowsky's letters, where *zaynen* and *zayt* abounded, spontaneous and unedited proof of the poet's usage.

I

חשוונדיקע נעכט

ווילנע, 1927

I

Kheshvndike nekht

(NIGHTS OF HESHVAN)

VILNA, 1927

פּרויען-לידער

I

עס וועלן די פּרויען פֿון אונדזער משפּחה בײַ נאַכט אין חלומות
מיר קומען און זאָגן:
מיר האָבן אין צניעות אַ לויטערע בלוט איבער דורות געטראָגן,
צו דיר עס געבראַכט ווי אַ ווײַן אַ געהיטן אין כּשרע קעלערס
פֿון אונדזערע הערצער.
און איינע וועט זאָגן:
איך בין אַן עגונה געבליבן ווען ס'זײַנען די באַקן
צוויי רויטלעכע עפּל אויף בוים נאָך געשטאַנען,
און כ'האָב מײַנע ציינער די ווײַסע צעקריצט אין די איינזאַמע נעכט פֿון
דערוואַרטונג.
און איך וועל די באָבעס אַנקעגן גיין זאָגן:
ווי האַרבסטיקע ווינטן יאָגן נאָך מיר זיך
ניגונים פֿאַרוועלקטע פֿון אײַערע לעבנס.
און איר קומט מיר אַנקעגן,
ווו די גאַס איז נאָר טונקל,
און ווו ס'ליגט נאָר אַ שאָטן:
און צו וואָס אָט דאָס בלוט אָן אַ טומאה
ס'זאָל זײַן מײַן געוויסן, ווי אַ זײַדענער פֿאָדעם
אויף מײַן מוח פֿאַרבונדן,
און מײַן לעבן אַן אויסגעפּליקט בלאַט פֿון אַ ספֿר,
און די שורה די ערשטע פֿאַרריסן?

Women-Poems[1]

I

The women of our family will come to me in dreams at night
and say:
Modestly we carried a pure blood across generations,
Bringing it to you like well-guarded wine from the kosher
Cellars of our hearts.
And one woman will say:
I am an abandoned wife,[2] left when my cheeks
Were two ruddy apples still fixed on the tree,
And I clenched my white teeth throughout lonely nights of
waiting.
And I will go meet these grandmothers, saying:
Like winds of the autumn, your lives'
Withered melodies chase after me.
And you come to meet me
Only where streets are in darkness,
And where only shadows lie:
And why should this blood without blemish[3]
Be my conscience, like a silken thread
Bound upon my brain,
And my life, a page plucked from a holy book,
The first line torn?[4]

II

צו דעם וועל איך קומען,
ווער ס'האָט דער ערשטער מיר מײַן פֿרויענפֿרייד געבראַכט
און זאָגן: מאַן,
כ'האָב נאָך איינעם מײַן שטילן בליק פֿאַרטרויט
און אין אַ נאַכט לעם אים מײַן קאָפּ געלייגט,
ערשט האָב איך מײַן צער,
ווי בינען אָנגעשטאָכענע אַרום מײַן האַרץ געבראַכט
און האָב קיין האָניק ניט אויף לינדערן מײַן ווונד.
און ס'וועט דער מאַן מיר נעמען פֿאַרן צאָפּ,
וועל איך אַנידערברעכן זיך אויף ביידע פֿיס
און בלײַבן אויפֿן שוועל ווי די פֿאַרשטיינערונג פֿון סדום,
איך וועל די הענט אַרויפֿהייבן צום קאָפּ,
ווי ס'פֿלעגט מײַן מאַמע בײַם בענטשן ליכט,
נאָר ס'וועלן מײַנע פֿינגער שטיין ווי צען געציילטע זינד.

II

I will come to the one
Who first brought me woman's delight,
And say: Husband,
I trusted someone else with my quiet gaze,
And one night laid my head down near him.
Now I bring my sorrow
Like bees stinging around my heart,
And have no honey to soothe the hurt.
And when my husband takes me by the braid,
I will drop to my knees
And remain on the doorsill like the petrifaction of Sodom.
I will raise my hands to my head
As my mother used to, blessing the candles,
But my fingers will stand up like ten numbered sins.

III

אַ מאָל איז אַ שטיינערנער טרעפּ אַזוי זיס ווי אַ קישן,
אַז כ'לייג זיך אַנידער לענגאויס אויף זײַן קאַלטקייט,
ווען כ'קאָן נישט דערטראָגן צום שטאָק צו דעם דריטן,
מײַן קאָפּ מיט די דינע פֿאַרטריקנטע ליפּן.
כ'בין דעמאָלט אַ שטילע פֿאַרחלשטע מיידל,
וואָס שאַרט זיך אָן דר'ערד מיט פֿאַרגליווערטע גלידער,
און בלײַבט ערגעץ ליגן
אַליין בײַ דער נאַכט אויף די שטיינערנע שטיגן.

1924

III

A stone step is sometimes as sweet as a pillow,
If I stretch my whole body the length of its coldness,
When all the way up to the third floor, I cannot
Carry my head with its lips thin and arid.
I am, then, a swooning girl, fainting and silent,
Who, shuffling across ground on limbs numb and stiffened,
Stops somewhere and lies down
In the night on these stone stairs, alone.

1924

IV

דעם שפּיגל מוז איך אָפּקערן,
עס זאָל מײַן פּנים איצט אין שטילער נאַכט
אויף מיר ניט קוקן מיט שטײַפע ליפּן:
איך וועל שוין ניט באַרעכענען וואָס כ׳האָב ביז איצטער ניט באַרעכנט.
שאָקל איך דעם קאָפּ אַנטקעגן וואַנט,
ווי צו אַ לעבעדיקן מענטשן וואָס באַדויערט,
ווי צו אַן אַלטן גוטן-פרײַנד.
אין שטילקייט פֿון דער נאַכט איז גאַנץ עגאַל
צי כ׳בין גערעכט צו אומגערעכט,
עס זײַנען מײַנע ברעמען שווער און נאָך נישט אויסגעלאָדן,
און ס׳ציִען זיך די גלידער מײַנע צו דער ערד,
אויף שטומער אָנפּאַרטרויִונג צו איר אוראַלטן געוויסן.

IV

I must turn the mirror aside,
So that now, in the still night, my face
Does not look at me with prim lips:
I'm not going to solve what I haven't yet solved.
I nod my head to the wall,
As if to a living person who feels sorry,
As if to an old, good friend.
In the still of the night, it is all the same
Whether I am right or wrong.
My brows are heavy and still not unburdened,
And my limbs gravitate to the earth
In mute trust of her primordial conscience.

V

לאַנג און מילד זײַנען די תּמוז־אָבֿיקע באַגינענס,
ווען כ׳האַלט מײַן קאָפּ דעם וואַכן
אויף אַ ברוינער אָפּגעברענטער האַנט:
מאַן,
איך האָב לעם זיך פֿאַר דיר אַן אָרט אַן אָפּגעהיטן,
פֿאַר מיר האָב איך ניט אָפּגעהיט קיין רו און אָרט.
דורך צוגעמאַכטע אויגן פֿאַלן לאַנגזאַמער און וואַרעמער די טרערן,
און שטילקייט לייגט זיך אויס,
ווי העזלעך דרימלענדיקע אַרום בעט,
אָט וועט דער טאָג אַן ערשטן רוף טאָן
און אַלע וועלן זיך צעלויפֿן
און איך וועל אויפֿשטיין צו אַ שווערן לאַנגן וועג.

1926

V

Long and mild are the dawns of Tammuz and Av,[5]
When I hold my wakeful head
On a brown, sunburned hand:
Husband,
I have a place for you near me, a cherished place,
But I have not kept any peace or place for myself.
Through closed eyes, my tears fall slow and warm,
And stillness spreads,
Like drowsy hares around my bed.
Soon the first cry of day will sound,
And they will scatter,
And I will rise to a long, hard way.

1926

VI

פֿאַר כּלות אָרעמע וואָס זײַנען דינסטמיידלעך געווען,
צאַפּט די מוטער שׂרה פֿון פֿעסער טונקעלע
און קרוגן פֿונקלדיקן ווײַן.
ווען ס'איז אַ פֿולער קרוג באַשערט,
טראָגט די מוטער שׂרה אים מיט ביידע הענט,
און ווען ס'איז באַשערט אַ בעכערל אַ קליינס
פֿאַלט דער מוטער שׂרהס טרער אין אים אַרײַן.
און פֿאַר גאַסן-מיידלעך
ווען ווײַסע חופּה-שיכלעך חלומען זיך זיי,
טראָגט די מוטער שׂרה האָניק לויטערן,
אויף קליינע טעצעלעך,
צו זייער מידן מויל.
פֿאַר כּלות אָרעמע, פֿון אַ מיוחסדיקן שטאַם
וואָס שעמען זיך דאָס אויסגעלאַטעטע וועש
ברענגען צו דער שוויגער פֿאַרן אויג,
פֿירט די מוטער רבֿקה קעמלען אָנגעלאָדענע
מיט ווײַסן לײַוונט-לײַן.
און ווען די פֿינצטערניש שפּרייט אויס זיך פֿאַר די פֿיס,
און ס'קניִען אַלע קעמלען צו דער ערד צו רו
מעסט די מוטער רבֿקה לײַוונט אייל נאָך אייל
פֿון די פֿינגערלעך פֿון האַנט ביזן גאָלדענעם בראַסלעט.
פֿאַר די וואָס האָבן מידע אויגן
פֿון נאָכקוקן נאָך יעדן שכנותדיקן קינד,
און דאַרע הענט פֿון גאַרן
נאָך אַ קליינעם קערפּערל אַ ווייכס
און נאָך אַ וויגן פֿון אַ וויג,
ברענגט די מוטער רחל היילונגס-בלעטער
אויסגעפֿונענע אויף ווײַטע בערג,
און טרייסט זיי מיט אַ שטילן וואָרט,
ס'קאָן יעדע שעה גאָט עפֿענען דאָס צוגעמאַכטע טראַכט.
צו די וואָס וויינען אין די נעכט אויף איינזאַמע געלעגערס,
און האָבן ניט פֿאַר וועמען ברענגען זייער צער,

VI

For poor brides who were servant girls,
Mother Sarah draws forth from dim barrels
Pitchers of sparkling wine.
To those so destined, Mother Sarah
Carries a full pitcher with both hands.
And for those so destined, Mother Sarah's
Tear falls into the tiny goblet.
And for streetwalkers
Dreaming of white wedding shoes,
Mother Sarah bears pure honey
In small saucers
To their tired mouths.
For high-born brides now poor,
Who blush to bring patched underclothes
Before their mothers-in-law,
Mother Rebecca leads camels
Laden with white linen.
And when darkness spreads before their feet,
And all the camels kneel on the ground to rest,
Mother Rebecca measures linen ell by ell
From her rings to her golden bracelet.
For those whose eyes are tired
From watching the neighborhood children,
And whose hands are thin from yearning
For a small, soft body
And for the rocking of a cradle,
Mother Rachel brings healing leaves
Discovered on distant mountains,
And comforts them with a quiet word:
At any hour, God may open the sealed womb.
To those who cry at night in solitary beds,
And have no one to share their sorrow,

רעדן זיי מיט אויסגעברענטע ליפּן צו זיך אַליין,
צו זיי קומט שטיל די מוטער לאה
האַלט בײדע אויגן מיט די בלייכע הענט פֿאַרשטעלט.

Who talk to themselves with parched lips,
To them comes Mother Leah, quietly,
Shielding both eyes with her pale hands.

VII

אין נעכט אַזױנע פֿרילינגדיקע דאָ,
װען ס'װאַקסט אונטער אַ שטײן אַ גראָז
פֿון דר'ערד
און ס'בעט דער פֿרישער מאָך אַ גרינע קישן אױס
אונטער אַ שאַרבן פֿון אַ טױטן פֿערד
און אַלע גלידער פֿון אַ פֿרױ בעטן זיך צו װײַטיק פֿון געבורט.
און פֿרױען קומען און לײגן זיך װי קראַנקע שאָף
בײַ קרענעצעס אױף הײלן װײער לײַב,
און האָבן שװאַרצע פּנימער
פֿון לאַנג־יעריקן דאָרשט צום קינדס געשרײ.
אין נעכט אַזױנע פֿרילינגדיקע דאָ,
װען בליצן שנײַדן אױף מיט זילבערנע חלפֿים
די שװאַרצע ערד,
און פֿרױען שװאַנגערע צו װײַסע טישן פֿון שפּיטאָל
קומען צו מיט שטילע טריט
און שמײכלען צום נאָך נישט געבאָרענעם קינד
און אפֿשר נאָך צום טױט.
אין נעכט אַזױנע פֿרילינגדיקע דאָ,
װען ס'װאַקסט אונטער אַ שטײן אַ גראָז פֿון דר'ערד אַרױס.

VII

These are the spring nights
When up from under a stone, a grass blade pushes forth from
 the earth,
And fresh moss makes a green cushion
Under the skull of a dead horse,
And all of a woman's limbs beg for the hurt of childbirth.
And women come and lie down like sick sheep
By wells to heal their bodies,
And their faces are dark
From long years of thirsting for the cry of a child.
These are the spring nights
When lightning splits the black earth
With silver slaughtering knives,
And pregnant women approach
White tables in the hospital with quiet steps
And smile at the yet-unborn child
And perhaps even at death.
These are the spring nights
When up from under a stone, a grass blade pushes forth from
 the earth.

VIII

אין נעכט ווען איך בין וואַך,
און ס׳קומען צו מיר טעג מײַנע פֿאַרגאַנגענע
זיך פֿאַר די אויגן שטעלן,
קומט פֿאַר מיר מײַן מאַמעס לעבן.
און אירע אויסגעדאַרטע הענט
אין צניעותדיקע אַרבל פֿון נאַכטהעמד אײַנגעהילט
ווי אַ גאָטספֿאָרכטיקע שריפֿט אין ווײַסע גווילים
און ס׳בייזערן זיך ווערטער פֿון המפּיל,
ווי פֿײַערדיקע קוילן געלאָשן פֿון איר שטיל געבעט
און אויסגעטריקנט איר דאָס מויל
ווי אַ פֿאַרדאַרטע פֿלוים.
און ס׳קומען אירע טרערן ווי אַ קאַרגער-איינציק-טראָפּנדיקער רעגן,

און ערשט, אַז כ׳בין אַליין אַ פֿרוי
און גיי אין ברוינעם זײַד געקליידט
מיט בלויזן קאָפּ
און נאַקעט האַלדז,
און ס׳האָט דער אומגליק פֿון מײַן אייגן לעבן מיך דעריאָגט
און ווי אַ קראָ, אויף אַ קליין הינדעלע אַרויפֿגעפֿאַלן,
איז אָפֿט באַלויכטן העל מײַן צימער אין די נעכט,
און כ׳האַלט די הענט איבער מײַן קאָפּ פֿאַרוואָרפֿן
און ס׳זאָגן מײַנע ליפּן אַ שטילן איינפֿאַכן
געבעט צו גאָט
און ס׳קומען טרערן, ווי אַ קאַרגער-איינציק-טראָפּנדיקער רעגן.

1925

VIII

Nights when I'm awake
And one by one my past days come
To place themselves before my eyes,
My mother's life comes to me.
And her emaciated hands
Wrapped in modest nightgown sleeves
Are like a God-fearing script on white parchment
And the words of *Hamapil* are angry[6]
Like fiery coals quenched by her quiet plea,
And they shrivel her mouth
Like a withered plum.[7]
And her tears come drop by drop like a stingy drizzle.

And now that I myself am a woman,[8]
And walk, clad in brown silk
With my head bare
And my throat naked,
And now that my own life's misfortune has hunted me down
Like a crow falling upon a chick,
Often my room is lit up all night,
And I hold my hands, reproaches, over my head,[9]
And my lips recite a quiet, simple
Plea to God.
And tears come drop by drop like a stingy drizzle.

1925

אָפּגעשיטע בלעטער

I

ווערטער אָפּגעזאָגטע — אָפּגעשיטע בלעטער,
זאָל דער ווינט צעטראָגן אײַך,
און זאָל איך אײַך פֿאַרגעסן.
וועל איך בלײַבן ווי אַ בוים אַ ווינטערדיקער,
אונטער צוגעמאַכטע אויגן, שטיל
און שווײַגן.
אי וועט אײַנוויגן די נאַכט מיר אײַ-לו,
אי וועט אײַנוויגן די פֿינצטערניש מיר אײַ-לו,
נאָר די הענט מײַנע די ווײַסע
וועלן אויפֿכאַפּן זיך, וועקן,
זיי ווילן נאָך אַרומנעמען אַ לײַב אַ וואַרעמע
און אַ געטרײַע.
אָט די הענט מײַנע די ווײַסע.

Fallen Leaves[10]

I

Words forsaken—fallen leaves,
Let the wind scatter you,
And let me forget you.
I will remain like a wintry tree
Behind closed eyes, still
And silent.
Both the night will cradle me, *ay-lu*,
And the dark will cradle me, *ay-lu*.
But these arms of mine, these white arms
Will awaken, aroused,
Still wanting to hug a warm body,
A faithful body.
These arms of mine, these white arms.

II

אַן אַלטער סידור ליגט פֿאַר מיר,
מיט בלעטער געלע אײַנגעבויגענע אין ראָגן.
בײַ תּחינות וועגן טל און מטר
בײַ דער עקדה יצחקס
און בײַ דעם ברענענדיקן קאַלעך-אויוון פֿון נמרוד.
עס זײַנען טרערן דאָרט געפֿאַלן שטילע,
און ווייך געמאַכט דאָס בלאַט,
ווי ווייך אַ האַרץ ווערט בײַ אַ תּחינה,
און יהי רצונס אַלע זײַנען אויסגעטייטלט מיטן פֿינגער.
און שוואַרץ פֿאַרלאָפֿן פֿון דעם זיבנמאָליקן זאָגן.
און ווער וועט איצטער דעם סידור גאָטספֿאָרכטיק
אונטערן אָרעם טראָגן?
און ווער וועט איבערמישן געלע בלעטער?
אפֿשר גאָר זאָל איך אים נעמען אויף מײַן גרין געדעקטן טיש
אַוועקלייגן אין מיטן,
און ווען אַ טריקעניש וועט פֿאַלן אויף מײַן האַרץ
דעם סידור נעמען צו די ברענענדיקע ליפּן.

II[11]

Before me—an old prayerbook
With yellowed leaves bent at the corners,
Marking women's prayers about dew and rain,
Marking the Binding of Isaac
And Nimrod's fiery lime-kiln.[12]
Tears fell quietly there
And made each leaf soft,
As soft as a heart grows with prayer.
Fingers that followed the prayers beginning
"May it be Thy will,"
Darkened those lines recited seven times.
And who will now, God-fearing,
Carry the prayerbook under her arm?
Who will turn the yellowed leaves?
Perhaps I shall carry it to my green-covered table,
Place it in the middle,
And when a drought falls upon my heart,
Take the prayerbook to my burning lips.

VIII

בײַ דר'ערד אַ נידעריקער פּלויט,
און פֿעלדער אונטער בלויער ווײַכקייט גרינען,
קומט מײַן בליק דער אָפֿענער צו רו,
און די פֿיס אָן אָפּהאַלט גייען.
ציט דער וועג זיך סתּם אַזוי,
פֿירט אין ערגעץ ניט, נאָר צו מײַן האַרץ,
און די ליפּן הייבן אָן צו בליִען,
רעדן אויס דאָס ניט־דערדעדטע וואָרט.
הערן פֿעלדער אויפֿמערקזאַם זיך צו צו מײַנע רייד
און ענטפֿערן מיט שטילקייט און מיט דורכזיכטיקן רוים,
קומען מײַנע ווערטער צוריק צו מיר צו פֿליִען
און פֿאַלן צו, ווי זומער־פֿייגעלעך צום קלייד.
בײַ פּראָסטע מענטשן עס איך ברויט מיט האָניק
און ס'קומט דער ריח אין מײַן מויל פֿון פֿעלד און בינען,
און ווערטער לויטערע ווי שטערן,
און וואַרעמע ווי זון אין מיטן דרינען.

VIII

A low fence hugging the earth,
And fields under blue softness turning green,
Then my open gaze comes to rest,
And my feet walk unhindered.
The path extends as it will,
Leading nowhere but to my heart,
And my lips begin to bloom,
Uttering the unfinished word.
Fields listen, attentive to my speech,
And answer with stillness and transparent space.
My words come flying back to me
And land on my dress like butterflies.
I eat bread and honey with humble people,
And into my mouth comes the scent of fields and bees,
And words clear as stars,
Warm as the sun, all of a sudden.

IX

ס׳איז גוט דעם קאָפּ באַהאַלטן אין אַ סקירדע היי,
און אײַנשלאָפֿן פֿון שמעקעדיקן גראָז.
און ס׳חלומט זיך אַ פֿעלד, און האָז
און אַלץ וואָס ליב איז הערן און געדענקען.
נאָר ס׳שטעלט אַ קראָ זיך אויפֿן סקירדע אויפֿן שפּיץ,
און עפֿנט אויף אַ הייזעריק מויל אַ ברייטן.
און קראַקעט אויס, אַז ס׳איז שוין שפּעטער האַרבסט,
אַז ס׳זײַנען פֿעלדער וויסט
און פּוסט זײַנען די בייטן.
און ווען דער ערשטער שניי וועט פֿאַלן
וועט גרוי ווערן דער קאָפּ,
און ס׳וועט די ליפּ די אייבערשטע זיך אָנהייבן צו קנייטשן.

IX

How good to hide my head in a haystack
And grow drowsy from fragrant grasses.
I dream of a meadow and a hare
And hear and remember all I hold dear.
But a crow perches on the tip of the haystack
And opens its wide, hoarse throat,
Cawing that it is already late fall,
That the fields are bleak
And the gardens bare.
And, when the first snow falls,
My head will turn gray
And my upper lip will begin to wither.

X

עס האָט זיך איצטער ווינטערצײַט פֿאַרשמעקט מיר
די ערבֿ-פּסחדיקע לויטערקייט פֿון נעכט
און מילדע וואַרעמקייט פֿון דינעם זײַדענעם רעגן,
און ס׳גלאַנצעדיקע שטראַלונג פֿון מײַן קינדערישן קלייד.
גייט אום דאָ אפֿשר נאָענט אליהו,
און גייענדיק לאָזט פֿאַלן ווו אַ זיסן וואָרט,
איך האָב געוואַרט אויף אים אין קינדערנעכט אין העלע
יאָר-אײַן יאָר-אויס נעבן זײַן כּוס,
און טרעפֿן אים איז נאָך בײַ מיר אַ האָפֿענונג געבליבן.
אויב ס׳וועלן שויבן טונקעלע זיך אָנצינדן און ווערן העל
און שטומע הערצער וועלן זיך צעוויגן ווי אַ זינגעדיקער וואַלד
וועל איך דעם פּנים צולייגן צו דר׳ערד,
ווײַל נאָענט וועט אומגיין אפֿשר אליהו.

X

Now, in the winter, I have a hankering for
The clearness of nights just before Pesach[13]
And the mild warmth of thin, silken rain,
And for the shiny radiance of my girlhood dress.
Perhaps Elijah is walking near here
And, in passing, lets a sweet word fall somewhere.
I waited for him in the bright nights of my childhood,
Year in, year out, by his cup,
And I am still hoping to meet him.
If dark windowpanes kindle and brighten,
And mute hearts rock themselves like a singing forest,
I will put my face to the earth,
Because near here, perhaps, Elijah will walk.[14]

XI

פֿאָר איך מיט דער באַן אויף מערבֿ,
בלאָזן אויף זיך אַרבל פֿון מײַן לײַכטן קלייד, ווי זעגלען
יאָגן זיך אַנקעגן פֿעלדער,
שוואַרצע,
פֿעטע,
אויפֿגעשניטענע פֿון אַקער.
פֿעלדער, װעמען טראָגט איר גוטס און זאַטקייט?
און פֿאַר מײַן פֿאַרבליבענער משפּחה וועט אַ ברויט אַ שוואַרצער אָ סטײַען?
פֿאָר איך מיט דער באַן אויף מערבֿ.
לויפֿן ווינטן פֿאַר מײַן פּנים.
הייבן אויף די האָר זיך אויף מײַן קאָפּ,
ווי רופֿנדיקע האָרנס:
ווינטן, װעמען זוכט איר!
אפֿשר טראָגט איר מיר אַ בשׂורה?
פֿון אַן אָרט, וואָס וועט אַ היים מיר ווערן,
פֿון אַן ערד אַ מילדע און געטרײַע.
פֿאָר איך מיט דער באַן אויף מערבֿ.
קומען מיר אַנטקעגן הײַזלעך רויִקע
מיט פֿעלד און וואַלד באַזאָרגטע,
האָט איר ווו פֿאַר מיר ערגעץ געלאָזט אַ טיר און פֿענצטער
צי אַזוינע נישט געפֿונען?
פֿאָר איך מיט דער באַן אויף מערבֿ
בלאָזן אויף זיך אַרבל פֿון מײַן לײַכטן קלייד,
ווי זעגלען.

XI

I travel westward on the train.
Sleeves of my light dress inflate like sails
Racing against fields—
Black,
Fertile,
Split by the plow.
Fields, for whom do you bear goodness and fullness?
Will black bread suffice for my family, left behind?
I travel westward on the train.
Winds rush before my face.
The hair on my head rises
Like horns calling:
Winds, whom do you seek!
Do you bring me news?
News of a place that will become home to me,
Of a mild and faithful earth?
I travel westward on the train.
Calm cottages come to meet me
With anxious fields and forests.
Have you left a door and window open for me somewhere
Or aren't they to be found?
As I travel westward on the train,
Sleeves of my light dress inflate
Like sails.

אָטוואָצק

I

ווילעס עגונות פֿאַרלאָזטע פֿון מענטש און פֿון ווינען.
נידעריק פּלויטן ס'דאָ קיינער ניט קומען,
אויף גנבֿענען עפּעס בײַ נאַכט.
ווענעלעך שמאָלע — פֿאַרגליווערטע פֿינגער אין פּאַרק
און ביימער מצבֿות פֿון עמעצנס אויסגעשפּעט האַרץ.
ניט קיין טראָט. ניט קיין קול.
כאָ-כאָ-כאָ — הילכט אַ הוסט פֿון אַן אָפֿענעם פֿענצטער אַרויף.
ס'גייט דאָרט עמעצער אויס.
איז מײַן האַרץ דאָ אַ גאַסט.
אַ צעשראָקענע האַסטיק צעיאָגט עס מײַן בלוט.
איך בין דאָ?
דאָ, דאָ, דאָ קלאַפּט מײַן האַרץ,
איז די ערד דאָ פֿאַרקאַמט מיטן שניי און פֿאַרגלעט,
און ס'האָט קיינער מיט טריט ניט צעפּודלט דעם וועג
נאָר אַ הענדלער גיט הילכיק אַ מאָל אַ געשריי:
„פּאָמעראַנצן ווער קויפֿט?"
שטעקט אַרויס זיך אַ האַנט — שוין
אַן אָפּגעוועלקט בלאַט:
Proszę mnie.

Otwock[15]

I

Villas are abandoned wives,[16] neglected by people and
unoccupied.
Fences are low, because there is no one to come
Steal things at night.
Narrow pathways—stiffened fingers in the park,
And the trees, gravestones of someone's spent heart.
No footsteps. No voices.
Kho-kho-kho—a cough drifts down from an open window.
Someone is dying there.
Here my heart is a guest.
My frightened blood races quickly.
Am I here?
Here, here, here, beats my heart.
The earth here is combed back with snow and smoothed
down,
And no one has ruffled the path with footsteps.
Only a vendor's shout echoes sometimes:
Oranges! Who will buy them?"
A hand juts out—
Already a withered leaf:[17]
Proszę mnie.[18]

II

מיר זײַנען קראַנקע דאָ — אַ מחנה
הײשעריקן צוגעפֿאַלענע צו װײַסקײט פֿון דעם
װינטערדיקן װאַלד.
מיט מײַלער אָפֿענע אין פֿוילן אָטעם,
װי הײזעריקע פֿידלען צ׳ען מיר אַ װאָרט,
אין טיכער אײַנגעהילט, מיט פֿיבערדיקע אויגן,
װער דאַרף אונדז נאָך?
און װאָס קענען מיר טויגן?
ס׳פֿאַרהײבן סאָסנעס הויך אַרויף די צװײַגן,
כּדי אונדז ניט באַרירן,
כּדי אונדז מײַדן, מײַדן.
מיר גװאַלטעװען דעם װאַלד,
און שפּײַען בלוט אַרײַן צו זײַנע שמעקעדיקע װאָרצלען,
דערפֿאַר באַװעגן זיך בײַ נאַכט די בײמער און דערצײלן,
װי גרויס עס איז דאָ דער בית-עולם,
און שפּאָטן נאָך בײַ גוססע
דעם לעצטן שאָטן פֿון געדאַנק,
מיט גרויס געװיקס, מיט פֿעטן שטאַם
אין טויזנט-יאָרעדיקן לעבן.
בין איך דאָ אויך... אַן אײנע.
אַ קראַנקע אײַנגעהילט אין טוך,
און טרעט פֿאַמעלעך אינעם שניי צװישן בײמער
און ס׳װײסט ניט קײנער
אַז איך בין עס דאָך, איך.

II

We are sick here—a multitude of locusts
Fallen suddenly upon the whiteness
Of the wintry wood.
With mouths open in putrid breathing,
We draw out a word like hoarse fiddles.
Who still needs us,[19]
Wrapped up in shawls, with feverish eyes?
And what use are we?
Pines raise their branches high
In order not to touch us,
In order to shun us, shun us.
We scream to the woods
And spit blood into their fragrant roots.
That's why the trees stir at night and tell
How big is the cemetery here,
And mock the dying
To the last shadow of memory
With their tall growth, with their fat trunks
And millennial lives.
I am here, too, solitary,
Sick, wrapped in a shawl,
And I step slowly in the snow among the trees,
And no one knows
That I am still myself.

IV

מ'קומט אַהער נאָך שמייכלענדיק,
ווי גוטע־פֿרײַנד געאָרעמט מיטן טויט,
פֿון שטורמישן וואָקזאַל אַרויס,
אין קליידער מאָדישע
און אין פֿאַריזשער היט.
ס'איז אַ קוראָרט.
יונגע קומען, שפּאַנען הפֿקרדיק אַרײַן,
אין באָרדיקער אין גרינער שטאָט,
און ווערן דאָרט פֿאַרשוווּנדן, און פֿאַרפֿאַלן.
און ס'בלייכט פֿאַמעלעך אויס
אַ בליִענדיק געזיכט,
און שפּיציק ווערט אַ מיידלש קײַלעכדיקע קני.
ווי יורדים נאָך אַ גרויסן רעשיקן יריד,
שלעפּט מען זיך אַרום דאָ הין און צוריק.
און הייסע פֿינגערלעך פֿאַלן צו אַ מאָל
צום ברוינעם שטאַם פֿון בוים,
ווי ס'וואָלט געבעטן זיך אַ יונגע האַרץ
בײַ ביימער פֿון דעם וואַלד:
רעטונג, רעטונג!
און ס'ליגט אַ גאַנצע שטאָט
אַן אויסגעהייליקטע פֿאַר טויט,
מיט וועגן אָפֿענע,
און באַנען — פֿיאַוּוקעס צוגעזויגענע בײַם זײַט,
און ס'קאָן פֿון דאָרטן קיינער נישט אַנטלויפֿן.
און איך בין אויך אַן אויסגעבאָדענע אַהער געקומען,
אין ווײַסן וועש,
אַ זבֿח פֿאַרן וואַלד,
פֿון שטעט און וואַנדער.
נאָר ס'זײַנען עלאַסטיש פֿריש
בײַ מיר די אָדערן און בלוט.
און אפֿשר, כ'וועל די איינציקע אַנטלויפֿן
פֿון שטאָט געהייליקטער פֿאַר טויט.

IV

They arrive here still smiling,
Like good friends arm in arm with death,
From the tempestuous depot,
In fashionable clothes
And in Parisian hats.
This is a spa.
The young come, striding
Carefree into the green, bearded city,
Disappear there, and are lost.
And a blossoming face
Pales slowly, too,
And a girl's round knee grows sharp.
Like poor folk after a great, noisy fair,
People drag themselves around here, back and forth,
And hot fingers sometimes
Grasp a brown tree trunk,
As if a young heart were pleading
With a tree in the woods:
Save me!
And an entire city lies
Unhallowed before death,
With open paths
And trains—leeches sucking at its side,
And no one can escape from there.
And I, too, came here, bathed,
In my white underclothes,
A sacrifice to the forests,
From cities and wandering.
But my veins are limber
And my blood is fresh.
And maybe I am the only one who will
Escape from this city unhallowed before death.

VI

איך בין אַ וואַנדערמיידל
אין בענקעניש איז אויסגעאיבט מײַן האַרץ.
און ווען ס'עסט אויף דער טאָג די טויען פֿון בײַנאַכט,
פֿאַרשאַר איך דאָס ווײַסע פֿאָרהאַנגל בײַ מיר אין שויב,
כ'קוק אָן אַ נײַע גאַס.
און ס'ליגט פֿאַרקנוילט
אין ווינקעלע בײַ מיר פֿון האַרץ
אַזאַ מין ציטעריק געדאַנק:
און טאָמער וועט מיך קײנער דאָ ניט וועלן ליבן
און טאָמער וועט מיר קײנער דאָ ניט וועלן זײַן באַקאַנט!
נאָר גאָט באַהיט!
ווי רעגנס אָנגעלאָדן הענגען שטענדיק אין דער לופֿט
און פֿאַלן אומגעריכט אַ שפֿע אויף דער ערד,
אַזוי איז פֿאַר מיר יעדע נײַע שטאָט,
אַזוי איז פֿאַר מיר יעדער נײַער אָרט.
און כ'ווייס שוין נישט, פֿילפֿאַכיק איז מײַן לײַב.
ס'וואַקסט יעדעס יאָר אין מיר אַ נײַער רונג ווי אין אַ בוים,
איך בין מאַזאַ־ש אויסגעוועבט פֿון אויפֿגיין און פֿאַרגיין.
איך בין אַ וואַנדערמיידל,
אין בענקעניש איז אויסגעאיבט מײַן האַרץ.

VI

I am a wandering girl.
My heart is practiced in longing.
And when the day eats up the dew of the night,
I tuck up the small white curtain from my window pane,
And look upon a new street.
There lies coiled up
In a little corner of my heart
Such a singular, trembling idea:
Maybe no one here will love me.
Maybe no one here will want to know me!
But God forbid!
Like the threat of rain always hanging in the air
And falling in unexpected abundance on the earth,
That's how each new city is for me,
Each new place.
And I don't know how manifold my flesh is.
Every year a new ring
Grows in me, as on a tree,
I am mazily woven of rising and setting.
I am a wandering girl,
My heart is practiced in longing.

VII

געזונטערהייט, עס האָבן מײַנע חבֿרטעס
שוין קינדער פּיצעלעך אין ווײַסע וויגן
און בייגן צערטלעך זיך צו זיי
מיט שטילע מאַמישע געזיכטער,
מיט ברוסטן נאַקעטע און פֿולע —
אויסגעגאַנגען דאָס מיידלש לעבן.
און קוקן שטיל צו מיר אַריבער,
מיט פֿײַכטן גלאַנץ און טונקלדיקע בליקן,
ווי שוואַרצער קוק פֿון וואַסער האַרבסט
ערבֿ פֿאַרפֿרירן.
עס ענדיקן די טעג זיך ניט בײַ זיי
מיט גליקלעכע פֿאַרנאַכטן,
אָדער מיטן לאַנגן שלעפּעניש אויף גאַסן,
אין וויסטן שמייכל אויף די ליפּן,
ווי ס'טרעפֿט בײַ מיר.
און שלאָפֿן שטיל מיט רונדע פּנימער,
אויף בײַכיקע אויף ווײַסע קישנס,
און שטרעקן אויס אַ שלעפֿערדיקע האַנט צום וויג.
און האָבן ניט אין בין-השמשות פֿון פֿאַרטאָגן
קיין אויסגעבלייכטן בליק
צו גרויער שויב,
פֿאַר עמעצנס אַ ניט-דערזאָגטן וואָרט,
אָדער אַ שמייכל ווּעמעס
וואָס חזרט זיך מיר איבער אויף די ליפּן.
עס האָבן מײַנע חבֿרטעס שוין קינדער פּיצעלעך
אין ווײַסע וויגן.
געזונטערהייט!

VII

Good health to you! My women friends
Already have babies in white cradles
And bend tenderly over them
With quiet, motherly faces,
With full, naked breasts—
The girl's life is gone.
And they look quietly over to me,
With damp luster and dark gazes,
Like the black look of water in autumn
On the eve of freezing over.
For them, the days don't end
With exuberant evenings
Or with long strolls in the streets,
Their lips wearing a desolate smile,
As it happens to me.
Sleeping quietly, their round faces
On full-bellied, white pillows,
They stretch out a sleepy hand to the cradle.
And they don't, in the twilight of dawn
Send pale glances
To the gray windowpane
For someone's unfinished word
Or for someone's smile
Repeating itself on my lips.
My women friends already have babies
In white cradles.
Good health to you!

אין בלויען באַגינען

I

אַ בלויער באַגינען קומט אָן.
עס בלויט שוין אַ הימל, עס קרייט שוין אַ האָן,
מיַין בעט איז אַ בלימל אַ וויַיסע און בלוי,
און איך בין אויף אים אַ געפֿאַלענער טוי.
ס'איז הייס נאָך דער אָטעם
דאָס לייַב איז נאָך מיד
עס שוועבט נאָך פֿון חלום פֿון לעצטן אַ געליד,
כ'שאַר אָפּ פֿון די ליפּן דעם הייס פֿון דער נאַכט
אַ תּפֿילה אַ ריינע ט'דער טאָג מיר געבראַכט.

At Blue Dawn

I

A blue dawn enters slowly.
Sky grows blue. Roosters crow.
My bed is a blossom, white and blue,
And I am a fallen drop of dew.
My breath is still warm,
My body still tired.
Part of my last dream won't disappear.
I scrape the night's heat from my lips.
The day brings me a pure prayer.

II

מײַן פֿאַרמעגן נישט צו מעסטן נישט צו װעגן,
ליגט צעװאָרפֿן װוּ אױף װעגן,
ליגט באַהאַלטן אױף דער װעלט אין אַלע שפּאַלטן.
טױזנט גלעטן אױפֿן נאַקן,
הײסע קושן אױף די באַקן, װי די זון.
אױף װעגן ראָגן
ליגט פֿאַרבונדן און פֿאַרבאָרגן
קלאַפּן פֿון מײַן יונגן האַרץ,
און חלומות אױף די בעטלעך
אין די שטעט און אין די שטעטלעך
שלאָגן זיך מיט װײַסע פֿליגל
אױף די האַרטע מױער-ציגל.
מײַן פֿאַרמעגן נישט צו מעסטן,
נישט צו װעגן.

II

For what I own there is no weight or measure.
Strewn on streets, unburied treasure,
It hides in all the crevices, in every crack.
Caresses by the thousands on my neck,
Kisses as hot as sunlight on my cheeks.
Bound up with fraying strings
And concealed at the corners of streets
Lie my tender heartbeats.
And dreams floating up from all
The beds at night in cities and towns
Beat their white and fragile wings
Against the hard brick wall.
For what I own there's no weight
Or measure.

III

בערגלעך, בערגלעך שטילע צוגעטופּעטע,
כ'שטעל מײַן טראָט אויף אײַך ניט-ווילנדיק,
טרעט אײַך צו נאָך מער;
שלאָפֿט איר דאָרטן באָבעס אײַנגעהויקערטע?
טראַכט איר עפּעס זיידעס גרויע?
און פֿאַר וואָס איז אַזאַ שטילקייט?
ווער האָט אײַך געהייסן טויטע זיך ניט רירן?
איך וועל קומען! אָט וועט הוליען דער בית-עולם
כ'וועל אַ לויף טאָן
און דעם קבֿר איבערקערן,
אויסלאַכן די בני-לוויה
און מיט מײַנע פֿיס דעם גרוב פֿאַרשיטן, און פֿאַרטאַנצן,
מיט די הענט אַ פּאַטש טאָן
און אַרויסרופֿן די יונגע און די שטאַרקע,
איך וועל קומען אָט וועט הוליען דער בית-עולם!

III[20]

Little mounds, quiet mounds, patted down,
I set my foot on you unwillingly,
Stepping near you once again;
Are you sleeping there, hunchbacked grandmothers?
Are you pondering something, gray grandfathers?
And why is there such quietness?
Who told you, the dead, not to stir?
I will come! Then, won't the graveyard have fun!
I'll start to run
And overturn the tombstone,
Mock the mourners,
Kick dirt into the grave and dance on it,
Clap my hands
And call up the young and the strong,
I will come and, then, won't the graveyard have fun!

IV

פֿליִען פֿייגלען מחנות, מחנות,
שרײַען עפּעס איבער מיר,
ווײַסע פֿליגל אין דער לופֿטן,
ווײַסע אַלע איין קאָליר.
שרײַט בײַ מיר עפּעס אין האַרצן,
זײַ אַ ווידערקול צוריק
ווערט געבאָרן ווײַסע לידער,
ווײַסע לידער פֿון מײַן גליק.

IV

Hordes and hordes of birds are flying,
Shouting high above me,
White wings beating in the air,
All white, all one color.
Something in my own heart shouts.
They echo with a countervoice
And white poems spring forth from that call,
White poems of my joy.

V

ווײַסע קוימענס, רויטע דעכער,
גרויע ווענט און פֿענצטערלעכער.
אַלע טאָג איז אַלץ דאָס זעלבע,
גרויע, ווײַסע, רויטע, געלבע!
אוי אַ פֿײַער זאָל זיי נעמען,
כ׳שטיי אויף בײַ דער נאַכט באַגינען,
גלאַט אַזוי אין מיטן דערינען
כ׳גיב אַ קוק אויף די דעכער:
ווײַסע קוימענס, רויטע דעכער
גרויע ווענט און פֿענצטער-לעכער.

V

White chimneys and red rooftops,
Gray walls, broken window panes,
It's all the same, day after day,
Red and yellow, white and gray.
Let it all go up in flames!
I wake up in the darkest dawn
For no reason, all at once,
And peer out at the rooftops:
White chimneys and red rooftops,
Gray walls, broken window panes.

VI

ס׳פֿאַלן טראָפּנס פֿון מײַן דאַך,
װעקן מיך און מאַכן װאַך,
און זײ רעדן, און זײ בעטן:
מיר זײַנען דעם רעגנס אױגן,
קום אונדז גלעטן, קום אונדז גלעטן.
ס׳פֿאַלן טרערן אין מײַן בעט
פֿאַלן זײ פֿון מײַנע אױגן,
און איך װײס ניט װאָס איך בעט,
און איך װײס ניט װאָס איך בעט.

VI

From my rooftop drops are falling
Waking me and making wakeful,
And they're talking, and they're asking,
We are the eyes of the rain,
Come and stroke us. Come and stroke us.
In my bed the tears are falling,
Falling rainy from my eyes,
And I don't know what I am asking,
And I don't know why.[21]

VII

נעם אַ שטיין און גיב אַ וואָרף
צי אין שטאָט,
צי אין דאָרף,
ווו ער זאָל ניט בלײַבן ליגן
ט'עמעצער געזאָגט אַ ליגן.
און דעריבער קומען וואָלקנס איבער שטעטלעך און וועלדער,
און דעריבער ווילדע חיות רײַסן שעפּעלעך אין פעלד,
און דעריבער קליינע קינדער וויינען שרײַען אין די נעכט,
און דעריבער ווינט און שטורעם דעכער אָרעמינקע ברעכט.

VII

Pick up a stone and throw it
In the city
Or the countryside.
Wherever it may land,
Someone has told a lie.
And that's why clouds come over towns and forests,
And that's why wild beasts devour sheep in the fields,
And that's why small children cry out in the nights,
And that's why the wind breaks down the roofs of the poor.[22]

VIII

האַרבסט.
פֿעלדער אָפּגעשאָרענע פֿאַרוועלקטע
מיט קעפּלעך געגאַרטלטע גאַרבן.
וואָס דולט אײַך דער ווינט
מיט אַ פֿײַף און געפּילדער
דערשפּירט שוין אַ האַרבסטיקן שטאַרבן?
לאַכט אויס אים זײַן שרעקן,
נאָך ברייטער,
נאָך נענטער צום הימל ליגן פֿעלדער אום ווינטער,
און איך וועל אַנטלויפֿן צו אײַך צו די פֿעלדער
דעם ריח פֿון ווינטער דערשמעקן.
דערטרונקען געוואָרן די לידער פֿון שניטער
אין ערגעץ צוזאַמען מיט לאַנגע פֿאַרנאַכטן,
ניט בענקט נאָך זיי פֿעלדער,
ווען ווינטער וועט ליגן ווי סאַמעט ווי ווײַסער צעוואָרפֿן
פֿון שטוב מײַן וועל איך צו אײַך פֿעלדער אַנטלויפֿן.

VIII

Autumn.
Withered, raked-over fields
With heads of belted sheafs,
Why does the wind annoy you
With a whistle and a bluster
Intimating an autumnal death?
Scoff at its whistling,
Scoff at its terrors.
In autumn, the fields are
Wider and even closer to the sky.
And I will run away to you, to the fields,
Sniffing out the scent of winter.
The harvesters' songs have drowned
Somewhere together with long twilights.
Fields, don't long for them.
When winter lies like white velvet thrown down
   every which way
I will run from my house to you, fields.

IX

זיצן זיי און שפּינען
זיבן ווײַבער בײַ דעם ברונעם.
צען פֿעדעם ווײַסע ווײַסע,
שעפּטשען אָן אַ סוף אַ מעשׂה.
זאָגט די ערשטע:
כ'פֿיטער ציגן, ווײַסע ציגן,
פֿאַר די קינדער אויף פֿאַרוויגן.
זאָגט די צווייטע:
איך פֿלאַנץ ביימער, איך זיי בלומען
פֿאַר די קינדער וואָס'ן קומען.
זאָגט די דריטע:
איך בייג בויגן, איך שלײַף פֿײַלן
אויף זיך שפּילן און פֿאַרווײַלן.
זאָגט די פֿערטע:
איך מאַך קייטן, קייטן רונגען
אויף פֿאַרבינדן הערצער יונגע.
פֿינפֿטע שווײַגט;
ציט זיך פֿעדעם רויט ווי פֿונקען
און זי גייט אין ברונעם טונקען.
זאָגט די זעקסטע:
איך מאַך מאָס,
איך מאַך וואָג
מעסט איך וועג איך מײַן פֿאַרמאָג.
זאָגט די לעצטע:
פֿעדעם קורצע,
פֿעדעם ווײַסע,
ענדיק איך אַזוי די מעשׂה.

IX[23]

By the well they're sitting, spinning,
Seven women, seven women,
Ten threads, white on white, they're spinning,
Whispering the story, never-ending.
Says the first:
White goats are what I raise and keep
For rocking children fast asleep.[24]
Says the second:
I plant the trees and sow the flowers
For children in the coming hours.
Says the third:
I sharpen arrows and bend bows
For amusement and repose.
Says the fourth:
I make chains, link part to part
For the binding of young hearts.[25]
The fifth says nothing:
Red as sparks, the thread she pulls
And dips into the well and cools.
Says the sixth:
I determine weight
And measure
To measure fortune and weigh treasure.
Says the last:
This thread of mine
Is white, short-spun—
And with this thread, the story's done!

X

אַן אָפֿענער פֿענצטער, אַ בלימל, אַ נאַכט,
עס פּלאַפּלען די בלעטער.
ס׳איז האַרבסטצײַט, ס׳איז געל און עס איז נאַס.
פֿון עפּעס וואָס לעבט ניט
און שטאַרבט ניט
וואָס אײביקײט איז
האָב איך דורך די האַרבסטיקע בלעטער
געהאַט אַ גריס.

X

An open window, a blossom, a night,
Leaves jabber.
It is fall, yellow and damp.
Something that is neither living
Nor dead,
That is forever
Has sent me a greeting
Through the fall leaves.

XI

פֿון פֿינצטער פֿון באַהעלטעניש בין איך אַרויס
אוּן ברייט דער טראָט
פֿון קליינעם פֿוס,
אוּן שטאַרק דער קלאַפּ
פֿון שמאָלן פֿויסט,
פֿון פֿינצטער פֿון באַהעלטעניש בין איך אַרויס.
אוּן כ'וואַש די הענט,
אוּן הייב צום ערשטן מאָל די אויגן צו דער זון,
אוּן כ'צינד די ליכט צום וועלט-יום-טובֿ
די ליכט וואָס דורות לאַנג
האָט מען געצונדן פֿרום.
כ'שפּאַן טריט פֿון שײַן,
אוּן פֿאַרב אין יום-טובֿדיקע פֿאַרבן,
די פֿעדעם וואָס איך וועב אויס און וועב אַרײַן.

1920

XI

I have come out of darkness and hiding,
And my small feet
Take large strides,
And my thin fists
Knock, loud and strong.
I have come out of darkness and hiding.
I wash my hands,
Raising my eyes to the sun for the first time,
And light the candles for the festival of the world,
Candles that were piously lit
For generations.
I take steps of light
And, with festive colors, dye
The threads that I'm weaving in and out.[26]

1920

ס'איז היינט אַ שטילער טאָג

I

ס'איז היינט אַ שטילער טאָג.
עס האָבן איינגעשלאָפֿן מײַנע דאגות,
ווי קינדער נאָך אַ לאַנגן וויינען,
און וועלן אויפֿכאַפּן זיך ווידער
הונגעריקע צופֿאַלן צום מוח.
וועל איך אַנטלויפֿן אין אַן אַנדער שטאָט,
און אומבייטן די קליידער
נאָר אומעטום —
גיט אַ מאָל דער טויט אַ בליץ פֿון ווײַטן
מ'הערט נאָך ניט דעם דונער
מאַכן מיר אַ טריט אויף צוריק,
פֿאַר שרעק אַ טריט אויף צוריק,
לייקענען די פֿרויען יאָרן צוויי צי דרײַ
און באַקומען קרומע ליפּן פֿון ליגן זאָגן,
און מענער בלײַבן שטיין די קעפּ צום האַרץ פֿאַרבראָכן,
ווי איינגעשפּאַרטע אָקסן.

Today Is a Quiet Day

I

Today is a quiet day.
My worries have worn themselves out
Like children after a long cry,
And will awaken again
To hurl themselves hungrily at my mind.
I will run away to another city,
And change my clothes,
But everywhere—
When death flashes in the distance
You still can't hear the thunder,
So we take a step backward,
A step backward in fear,
The women deny two or three years
And get crooked lips from telling lies,
And men stand still, their heads bent to their hearts
Like stubborn oxen.

II

כ׳טראָג העלע זאָקן און מיידלשע לאַקירע שיך,
נאָר ס׳יאָגן מיך שוין אָן
די פֿרײַע מיטל-יאָרן פֿון אַ פֿרוי,
און איך האָב מורא אָפּקערן אויף הינטן מײַן געזיכט.
עס האָבן מענער שטאַרקע פֿיס,
און שטייען אײַנגעאַנקערט פֿעסט אַקעגן צײַט,
און דאָך גייען מיר ערגעץ אַלע גלײַך,
ווער אַ טריט פֿון הינטן
און ווער אַ טריט פֿאָרויס.
נאָר פֿעסטונגען איז דאָ, ווו מענטשן לעבן לאַנג,
דאָס זײַנען הויכע תּפֿיסות פֿון די שטעט,
וווּהין מ׳פֿירט די אויפֿגעבונטעוועטע קעגן אונדז און קעגן גאָט.
עס האָבן יענע ווײַסע ווענט
נאָר בלינדע פֿענצטערלעך מיט בלעך פֿאַרשלאָגענע פֿון זון,
נאָר ס׳זעט די תּפֿיסה מיט איר גלאָצעדיקער ווײַטקייט
גוט און ווײַט.
נעבן אירע שטילע אײַנגעשמידטע ווענט
גיי איך דורך אַ מאָל פֿאַר טאָג
ווי אין די קינדער-יאָרן לעם דער שטעטלדיקער שול
ניט זיכער, צי איז טאַקע דאָרט פּוסט און שטיל
און אפֿשר שטייט דאָרט עמעצער בײַם עמוד
מיט פֿײַערדיקע אויגן דורך די ווענט
געווענדט צו מיר.
כ׳טראָג העלע זאָקן
און מיידלשע לאַקירטע שיך,
נאָר ס׳יאָגן מיך שוין אָן
די פֿרײַע מיטל-יאָרן פֿון אַ פֿרוי
און איך האָב מורא אָפּקערן אויף הינטן מײַן געזיכט.

II

I wear bright socks and girlish, lacquered shoes.
But still I am pursued
By the early middle age of a woman,
And I am afraid to turn my face back.
Men have strong legs
And stand anchored, fixed against time,
And yet we're going somewhere, all the same,
Some a step backward
And some a step forward.
But there are fortresses where people live a long time,
These are the tall prisons in the cities
Where those who rebelled against us and against God are
taken.
With such white walls
But with blind windows of tin beaten by sun,
The prison sees with its staring distance
Good and far.
Sometime, near the silent forged-in walls,
I take a walk at dawn
As in my childhood, near the shtetl[27] synagogue
Not sure whether it is really empty and silent there—
Perhaps someone is standing by the pulpit
With fiery eyes following[28] me
Through the walls.
I wear bright socks
And girlish, lacquered shoes,
But I am still pursued
By the early middle age of a woman,
And I am afraid to turn my face back.

דאָרשט

I

אײן טרעפּ, צװײ... נאָך... נאָך...
שױן איבער קעפּ,
שױן איבער דעכער
נאָר ס'איז ניט העכער.
װײַט דער הימל
װײַט,
אונטערן װאָלקן,
אונטער אײביקײט.
און שװאַך די הענט
און קורץ די גלידער
און כ'פֿאַל אַרונטער
און כ'פֿאַל אַנידער
פֿאַרן הימל
און פֿאַרן װײַט.
כ'פֿאַרשטעל דאָס פּנים
פֿול מיט שאַנד
פֿאַר עפּעס פֿאַר אַ האַנט,
אַ שװערער האַנט.

Thirst

I

One step, two steps, . . . more and more
Out the door
And over heads
Above the rooftops
But—it stops.
The sky stays distant,
Constant,
Beneath the clouds,
Beneath eternity.
My hands weakening
And my limbs shrinking,
I fall down,
Fall down
Before the sky,
The infinite.
I cover my face
Filled with shame
Before some kind of a hand,
A heavy hand.

II

דורכגעפּיבערט איבער לופֿט,
צערונצלט זיך אויף ווענט,
אַרײַנגעקוקט אין פֿענצטער
אַ בינטל נעכטנס ט'אָנגעבראַכט
די נאַכט.
האַלב נאַקעטע,
האַלב טויטע,
אין שטעט פֿאַרשלאָסענע,
פֿאַרבויטע,
יאָרן שוין ווי שנײַ צעגאַנגענע,
און פֿנימער מיט צײַט פֿאַרהאָנגענע.
דורכגעפּיבערט איבער לופֿט,
צערונצלט זיך אויף ווענט,
פֿאַרשוווּנדן אינעם פֿענצטער
פֿון וואַנען און וווּהין?
איר קינדער פֿון דער פֿינצטער.

II

Fevering through the air,
Wrinkling on the walls,
Peering into windows
A bundle of yesterdays brought on
The night.
Half naked,
Half dead,
Locked up in cities,
Crowded,
Years already like melted snow,
And faces curtained with time.
Fevering through the air,
Wrinkling on walls,
Disappearing in the window
Where from and where to?
You, children of the darkness.

III

אויף מײַן יום-טובֿ קומען טויבע
פּאַטשן מיט די הענט.
ברענגען שטײנער האַרטע, גרויע,
ווי די אויגן ווי די שטומע,
ווי די האַרטע ווענט.
שרײַ איך זײ אַ וואָרט אין אויער
און די צײנער האַלט פֿאַרפּרעסט,
קוקן זײ ווי טויבע שטײנער, מײַנע געסט.

III

The deaf come on my holiday,
Clapping their hands.
They bring stones, hard, gray,
Like mute eyes,
Like hard walls.
When I shriek a word in their ears
And hold my teeth tightly pressed,
They stare like deaf stones, my guests.

IV

אַ טרוקענער אַ דאָרשטיקער ליגט מײַן קרוג,
און איך גיי אום איבער די גאַסן
און איך זוך אַ טראָפּן וואַסער
און איך גיי אויס
און איך גיי אויס
נעבן מײַן קרוג.
לייג איך מײַנע ליפּן
צו די וואָרצלען פֿון די ביימער,
צי איך זוך מיט אויגן און מיט מויל
צו רעגנס פֿון דעם הימל,
און ביטער איז מײַן צונג פֿון וואָרצלען פֿון די ביימער
און דאָרשטיק איז מײַן מויל,
און מיד זײַנען די אויגן צום הימל קוקן,
און כ'זוך מײַן קרוג,
און ער איז טרוקן.

IV

My pitcher lies, dry and thirsty,
And I walk through all the streets
Seeking out a drop of water,
And I am spent
Near my pitcher.
I lay my lips
To the roots of the trees,
I stretch with eyes and mouth
To the sky's rains.
And my tongue is bitter from roots of the trees,
My mouth is thirsty,
And my eyes are tired from looking at the sky.
I seek my pitcher,
And it is dry.

V

שווימענדיקע קעפּ
און שפּאַנענדיקע פּיס,
און אײַליקע באַוועגונגען פֿון הענט.
איך זע ניט קיין געזיכטער.
מ׳קוקט אַראָפּ,
מ׳זוכט אַן אָרט
אויף שטעלן דאָרט
אַ טראָט.
נאָר איינִיקע געציילטע,
לאַנג געוואַרטע,
שיקן מיר אַ פֿרעגנדיקן בליק
פֿון אונטן אויף אַרויף
און שפּאַנען הפֿקרדיק אָן שרעק
צום גאַס, צום עק.
און ס׳רעדט די גאַס מיט צענדליקער מיט פֿאַרבן,
וואָכעדיקע, יום-טובֿדיקע,
כ׳קאָן זיי קוים באַנעמען
מיט פֿאַרבן-קולות
און מיט קולות-טריט,
וואָס האָבן ניט קיין נעמען.
ווהין? נאָך וואָס? פֿאַר וועמען?
מיט אַן אייביק רעדעוודיקן מויל,
און מיט אַן אייביק וואָכנדיקן לעבן,
ווײַל די גאַס קיין ענטפֿער מיר נישט געבן.

1920

V

Swimming heads
And striding feet,
And quick-gesturing hands.
I don't see any faces.
They're looking down
At the ground for where
To take a step.
Only a very few,
Long awaited,
Send a quizzical gaze
To look me up and down
And stride recklessly, fearlessly
To the end of the street.
And the street speaks with scores of colors,
Ordinary, festive,
I can hardly grasp them
With color-voices
And with voice-steps
That have no names.
Where are they going? After what? For whom?
With a mouth forever talking
And with a life forever wakeful,
The street does not want to give me an answer.

1920

תּפֿילות

I

ניט לאָז מיך אונטערגיין,
ווי ס׳פֿאַלט אַראָפּ אַ שטיין אויף האַרטן גרונט.
און מײַנע הענט זאָלן ניט דאַר ווערן,
ווי צווײַגלעך פֿון אַ בוים,
ווען ס׳שלאָגט אַראָפּ דער ווינט די לעצטע בלעטער.
און ווען דער שטורעם רײַסט פֿון דר׳ערד דעם שטויב
מיט כּעס און ווייען,
זאָל איך נישט זײַן די לעצטע פֿליג,
וואָס צאַפּלט זיך צעשראָקן אויף אַ שויב.
נישט לאָז מיך אונטערגיין.
כ׳האָב אַזוי פֿיל געבעט,
נאָר ווי אַ גראָז דײַנס אין ווײַטן ווילדן פֿעלד
פֿאַרלירט אַ קערנדל אין שויס פֿון דר׳ערד
און שטאַרבט אַוועק,
פֿאַרזיי אין מיר דײַן לעבעדיקן אָטעם,
ווי דו פֿאַרזייסט אַ קערנדל אין דר׳ערד.

Prayers

I

Don't let me fall
Like a stone that drops on the hard ground.
And don't let my hands become dry
As the twigs of a tree
When the wind beats down the last leaves.
And when the storm rips dust from the earth
Angry and howling,
Don't let me become the last fly
Trembling terrified on a windowpane.
Don't let me fall.
I have so much prayer,
But, as a blade of Your grass in a distant, wild field
Loses a seed in the lap of the earth
And dies away,
Sow in me Your living breath,
As You sow a seed in the earth.

II

איך ווייס נאָך ניט צו ווּעמען,
איך ווייס נאָך ניט פֿאַר וואָס איך בעט,
אַ תּפֿילה ליגט בײַ מיר געבונדן,
און בעט זיך צו אַ גאָט
און בעט זיך צו אַ נאָמען.
איך בעט
אין פֿעלד,
אין רעש פֿון גאַס,
מיט ווינט צוזאַמען, ווען ער לויפֿט מיר פֿאַר די ליפּן,
אַ תּפֿילה ליגט בײַ מיר געבונדן,
און בעט זיך צו אַ גאָט
און בעט זיך צו אַ נאָמען.

II

I still don't know whom,
I still don't know why I ask.
A prayer lies bound in me
And implores a god,[29]
And implores a name.
I pray
In the field
In the noise of the street,
Together with the wind, when it runs before my lips,
A prayer lies bound in me,
And implores a god
And implores a name.

III

איך ליג בײַ דר׳ערד,
איך שטיי געקניט
אין רונג פֿון מײַנע האָריזאָנטן,
און שטרעק די הענט
מיט אַ געבעט
צו מערבֿ, ווען די זון פֿאַרגייט,
צו מזרח, ווען זי גייט דאָרט אויף,
צו יעדער פֿונק
באַווײַזן מיר דאָס ליכט
און העל מאַכן די אויגן,
צו יעדעם ווערעמל וואָס גליט אין פֿינצטערקייט בײַ נאַכט,
ער זאָל זײַן ווונדער ברענגען פֿאַר מײַן האַרץ
און אויסלייזן די פֿינצטערקייט, וואָס איז אין מיר פֿאַרמאַכט.

1922

III

I lie on the earth,
I kneel
In the ring of my horizons,
And stretch my hands
With a prayer
To the west, when the sun sets,
To the east, when it rises there,
To each spark
That it show me the light
And make my eyes bright,
To each worm that glows in the darkness at night,
That it shall bring its wonder before my heart
And redeem the darkness that is enclosed in me.

1922

ליימגרונט

I

פֿאָרן פֿורן גײַשע צום נאָענטן ייִשובֿ
צלמען די יונגע שיקסעס די פֿולע ברוסטן
בײַ גריבער פֿון צעגעלניע:
היט אויס אונדז, גאָט, פֿון שלעכטע רוחות.
און ס'ציטערן דערנאָך זייערע ברייטע אַקסלען
אין רויטע קאָפּטעלעך
אויף שאָקלענדיקע פֿורן
און זיי ווישן זיך מיט האַרטע דלאָניעס
דאָס מויל און שטערן.

Clay-Ground

I

As peasant[30] wagons drive to the nearby settlement
The young girls[31] cross their full breasts
Passing the pits of the brickyard:
Protect us, God, from evil spirits.
And then their broad shoulders tremble
In red jackets
On shaking wagons,
And they wipe their mouths and foreheads
With the hard palms of their hands.

II

האַרט איז זײַן קנאָכעדיקער שטעקן
און האַרט איז די ליימיקע ערד
בער צעגעלניקס.
קלאַפּט ער מיטן שטעקן ווי מיט אַ לאַנגן שנאָבל
און ס'ענטפֿערט אים די ערד מיט אַ לויטערן קול.
און ער ציילט ווי אַן אַלטער זייגער זײַנע טריט
אויף די שטחים פּאָרצעלאַן-ליים.
ביז ס'ווערן זײַנע אויגן ווי צוויי פֿאַרשימלטע וואַסערגריבער
— איין גראָז ניטאָ — שמייכלט בער
אויף דער עקרהדיקער ערד.
קלאַפּט מיטן שטעקן ווי מיט אַ לאַנגן שנאָבל
און ס'ענטפֿערט אים די ערד מיט אַ לויטערן קול.

II

Hard is his boney staff
And hard is the clayey earth
Of Bear of the Brickyards.
He knocks with the stick as if with a long bill
And the earth answers him with a clear voice.
He counts his steps like an old clock
On the areas of porcelain clay,
Until his eyes become like two moldy waterholes
—No grass at all—smiles Bear
At the barren[32] earth.
He knocks with the stick as if with a long bill
And the earth answers him with a clear voice.

III

פֿיר פֿאַרעלטערטע טעכטער
ווי ווײַסע לאַנגווײַליקע גענדז
האָט בער צעגעלניק.
באָדן זיי זיך פֿאַר טאָג אין די ליימגריבער,
און טוקן זיך שווער, ווי ווייך געפֿלאָכטן טייג.
ווי לאַנג וועט מען אַזוי די גריבער מעסטן?
פֿרעגט די עלטסטע:
ווי לאַנג וועט מען אַזוי מעסטן?
ענטפֿערט דער ליימגרוב פֿון דער צווייטער זײַט
ליגן זיי אויפֿן ברעג מיט פֿולע, צײַטיקע לײַבער
מיט שטערנס ווי פֿאַרלעגענער אַלטער זײַד.

III

Bear of the Brickyard has
Four aging daughters
Like weary white geese.
They bathe before daybreak in the clay—
And plunge heavily like soft braided dough.
How long will the pits be measured this way?
Asks the eldest.
How long will they be measured this way?
The clay pit answers from the other side.
They lie on the shore with full, ripe bodies,
With foreheads like desiccated silk.

IV

בּרענגען אָן די נעכט אויף דער צעגעלניע לאַנגע שעהען
און די קוימענס וויען אָפּ פֿאַרצוקטע יאָרן,
און די טעכטער קאָרטשען זיך ווי קראַנקע קי
און קערן ביז פֿאַר טאָג די קישעלעך פֿון איין זײַט אויפֿן צווייטן
אויף קילן זיך דאָס פּנים.
און פּלוצלינג לאַכן אַלע,
און האַלטן אָרעמס נאַקעטע אויף ווײַסע העלדזער
— בער צעגעלניק ציילט שוין זײַנע טריט,
די אוצרות פּאָרצעלאַן-ערד.

IV

The nights bring long hours to the brickyard,
And the chimneys breathe out[33] devoured years,
And the daughters writhe like sick cows
And turn their pillows from side to side until daybreak
To cool their faces. And suddenly they all laugh,
Holding their naked arms on their white necks:
—Bear of the Brickyard is still counting his steps,
The treasures of the porcelain earth.

V

גייט זי אויף אַ דאַרן שטעקן אָנגעלענט
די אַלטע מאַמע.
און ס'קלעפּט דער ווינט איר אויס די ביינערדיקע קנ׳ען,
שווער צו אויסהערן דעם ווינט
פֿאַר איר שוואַכן קאָפּ,
און זײַן אויסגעלאַסן שטורעמען דאָס איינזאַם הויז
אויף די אויסגעגאָלטע שטחים פֿאָרצעלאַן-ליים.
קומט זי ווי אַ גרויע בעטלערין צום יישובֿ,
בײַ די קרובֿים אָפּדאַגהן אַ נאַכט.
שאָקלען קרובֿים מיט די קעפּ,
וויגן אויפֿן וואַנט זיך לאַנגע שאָטנס
קענען נישט פֿאַרוויגן דער שלאָפֿעדיקער מאַמעס צער
פֿרי נאָך לאָזט זי אויפֿן טיש אַ קופּערנע מטבע
(קליינוואַרג איז בײַ לײַטן דאָ)
און טראָגט צוריק איר אויסגעדאגהטן קאָפּ,
ווי אַן אויפֿגעפּלאָנטערטן קנויל,
צו דעם הויכן צוים פֿון דער צעגעלניע.

V

The old mother
Walks leaning on a thin stick.
And the wind strikes her on her boney knees,
It's hard for her weak head
To listen to the wind
And its wanton storms buffet the lonely house
On the gilded areas of porcelain clay.
Like a gray beggar woman, she comes to the settlement
And worries away a night with her relatives.
As the relatives shake their heads,
Rocking long shadows rock on the wall,
They can't lull the sleeping mother's sorrow.
When it is still early she leaves a copper coin on the table
(These people have young children)
And she bears her worried[34] head
Like an untangled ball of thread
Back to the high fence of the brickyard.

VI

ציִען זיך אַ שורה פֿורן ציגל
שווער און לאַנגזאַם.
און די טעכטער בײַ די פֿענצטער
שפּאַרן אונטער שווער די געמבעס אויף די עלנבויגן
און קוקן נאָך די רויטע פֿורמאַנישע נאַקנס
ביזן לעצטן.
און ס'ציִען זיך די בליקן זייערע ווײַט אויפֿן וועג אַראָפּ
און בלײַבן הענגען אויף דער גרויער ליידיקייט.
דערנאָך צעגייען זיך די טעכטער איבער צימערן
און בלאָנדזשען לאַנגזאַם איבער די שוועלן,
ווי קראַנקע שאָף
מיט האַלב פֿאַרמאַכטע אויגן.

VI

Wagons of bricks stretch out in a line[35]
Heavy and slow.
And the daughters at the windows
Lean their chins heavily on their elbows
And stare after the red napes of the foremen
Until the very last one.
And their gazes stretch far down the road
And remain hanging on the gray vacancy,
After that the daughters scatter throughout the rooms
And stray slowly through the doorways
Like sick sheep
With half-closed eyes.

VII

יענע נאַכט קרעכצן שלעפֿעריק די טעכטער פֿון צעגעלניע
פֿאַר שטילן ווייטיק
און שלאָגן מיט די קעפּ זיך אָן די ווײַסע קישנס
און שרײַען:
מאַמע, ס'זויגט אונדז אײַן דאָס ליים דאָס נאַסע,
און צאַפּלען זיך אין בעט, ווי גרויסע פֿיש געכאַפּטע.
לויפֿט די אַלטע מאַמע אַ נאַקעטע פֿון איין בעט צו דעם צווייטן
און שאַרט מיט אָדערדיקער האַנט איבער
אַ רונדיק ווייכן אַקסל,
און רעדט מיט ליפּן בלוילעכע, אַראָפּגעפֿאַלענע פֿאַרצערטע,
— אויף ווייסטע דערפֿער, קינד, דײַן שרעק און אומעט.

VII

That night the daughters of the brickyard groan sleepily
In quiet pain
And beat their heads on the white cushions
And scream:
Mama, the damp clay sucks us in,
And toss about in bed like huge, hooked fish.
The old mother runs naked from bed to bed
And, with her veined hands, brushes over
A soft, rounded shoulder,
And speaks with bluish lips, sunken and consumed,
—On deserted villages, child, your misery and fear.[36]

VIII

נאַכט איז טונקל.
אויסגעלאָשענע און לאַנגע
קאַזאַרמעס איינציקע צעוואָרפֿן דרימלען,
און אויף דער ערד ווייך האָבן זיך אויסגעשפרייט די שאָטנס.
פֿון צעגעלניע מיטן פֿעלד צו זיי אַ פֿרוי גייט
טראָט בײַ טראָט, ווי נאָך אַ בײַנאַכטיקער לוויה.
און פֿאַר איר ווי אַ טונקל אָרון שווימט איר שאָטן.
און פֿאַר טאָג בלײַבן אויפֿן פֿײַכטן זאַמד די קליינע טריט
איינס נעבן אַנדערן
אויף הין און צוריק.

VIII

Night is dim.
Extinguished and elongated
Barracks, strewn every which way, doze,
And the shadows spread out softly across the earth.
Toward them, from the brickyard, through a field, a woman
  walks.
Step by step, as if following a nighttime funeral.
And before her, like a dark coffin, her shadow swims.
And at daybreak the small footprints remain on the damp
  sand
One after the other,
There and back.

IX

עס זײַנען װײַסע פֿאָרהאַנגען פֿאַר טאָג אױפֿן שױבן,
װי צוגעמאַכטע אױגן.
און די טעכטער הײבן שװער די קעפּ,
און שטעכן אױף מיט שפּילקעס בײנערנע
דאָס ביסל אױפֿגעפּלאָנטערט האָר.
און גוט איז װאָס איז קאַלט דער אײַזן פֿון דעם בעט.
דעם שטערן צולענען,
און הערן, װי עס זױגט אין ערגעץ אין א גרוב,
דאָס װאַסער מיט אַ רירעװודיקער צונג די װײכע ערד.
און האַרט צ׳ען זיך אָן פֿון דער פֿאַרטאָגעדיקער קעלט
צװײ אַפּלען ברױנלעכע
גרײטע פֿאַר אַ קינדס אַן אױסגעשטרעקטן מױל,
און װײך דער בליק װערט
װי דאָס מוטערלעכע צערטלענדיקע אױג.
און ס׳קען באַגעגענען אַ בליק אַזאַ,
אַ נישט קײן אױסגעבעטע בעט
מיט קישנס שטײַפֿע שטאַרק געפּרױרענע פֿון נאַכט
פֿון אַ שװעסטער װאָס ט׳אַװעקגעבלאָנדזשעט ביז פֿאַר טאָג,
אױף זוכן װוּ אַ װאַרעם לײַב,
פֿאַלט דאָס פּנים צו דעם װײַס געװעב פֿון ציך,
און דאָס מױל און ברעמען,
און קנײטשן צװײ און דרײַ,
װי אותיות פֿאַרבליבענע פֿון אױסגעבליאַקעװעטן כּתבֿ.

IX

At daybreak there are white curtains on windowpanes
Like closed eyes.
And the daughters raise their heads heavily
And with bone pins stick up
Strands of untangled hair.
And it's good that the iron of the bed is cold,
For leaning the forehead
And hearing how somewhere in a pit
Water sucks at the soft earth with a lively tongue.
And two brownish apples
Stiffen with the daybreak chill
Ready for a child's reaching mouth,
And the gaze grows soft
Like a fond motherly eye.
And such a gaze can meet
An unmade bed
With rigid cushions frozen solid from the night
Belonging to a sister who wandered off until daybreak,
Seeking a warm body.
Then the face falls onto the white weave of the pillowcase,
The mouth and the brow
And two or three wrinkles
Are like traces of letters in a blanched script.[37]

X

ציילט די ייִנגסטע טאָכטער אירע וועש
און ס׳גליטשן זיך פֿון אירע קני̇ען
געפּרעסטע לײַלעכער אויף דר׳ערד.
און זי האַלט לאַנג צו זיי דעם קאָפּ אַראָפּגעבויגן
ווי צו קינות.
צו וואָס דאָס שמעקעדיקע וועש,
אַז ט׳געלאָזט איר ווײַס געלעגער קאַלט אויף ביז פּאַר טאָג
און איצט האָט זי פֿון נאַכט געבראַכט אַראָפּגעלאָזטע אַקסלען
און אַ מידקייט אונטער די ברעמען
ערגעץ טיף אין קאָפּ.
ציילט די ייִנגסטע אירע וועש
און ס׳גליטשן זיך פֿון אירע קני̇ען
געפּרעסטע לײַלעכער אויף דר׳ערד.

X

The youngest daughter counts her linens,[38]
And pressed bedsheets
Slip from her knees onto the earth.
And for a long while she holds her head bent down to them
As if lamenting.
What are the fragrant linens for,
If her white bed was left cold until daybreak?
And now from the night she has brought lowered shoulders
And an exhaustion beneath her brows
Somewhere deep in her head.
The youngest counts her linens,
And pressed bedsheets
Slip from her knees onto the earth.

אָרעמע ווײַבער

I

אַרום די נעגל האָבן שוואַרצע רעמלעך אײַנגעגעסן זיך אין לײַב
ווי בײַ אַלטע ווײַבער די פֿאַראָרעמטע, וואָס שײַערן פֿאַרברענטע טעפּ.
כ'האָב אויך שוין פֿינגער געלבלעכע
וואָס טראָגן ביינערדיק אַ קויש.
און אויגן ליידיקע ווי אַן אויסגעטרייסלטער זאַק.
באַגינען טרעף איך טרעגערינס פֿון מילך,
מיט קאַנען זילבערנע
וואָס ציִען זיי די אַקסלען נידעריק אַראָפּ,
און איינס לעם צווייטן טראָגן מיר אַדורך די שווערע לאַסט
ווי שטומע אייזלען אײַנגעשפּאַנטע,
וואָס האַלטן שווער די קעפּ צו דר'ערד.
כ'האָב אויך שוין פֿינגער געלבלעכע
וואָס טראָגן ביינערדיק אַ קויש.

Poor Women

I

Around the nails, black rims have eaten into flesh
As with all impoverished women who scour burnt pots.
I too have yellowish, boney
Fingers carrying a basket,
And eyes empty as a sack shaken out.
At dawn I meet the women carriers of milk,
With silver cans
That drag their shoulders down,
And one by one we bear the heavy load
Like donkeys, dumb, in harness,
Holding their heads heavily to the ground.
I too have yellowish, boney
Fingers carrying a basket.

II

אין תמוז נאָך פֿאַלט אַ מאָל אַ בלאַט אַראָפּ פֿון בוים,
און אַן אומגליק קומט צו פֿריִער צײַט
און ברענגט אַ מאָגערקייט צום לײַב.
מיט מיר האָט אויך דער אומגליק פֿרי גענומען זיך בײַם האַנט
ווי אַרעסטאַנטן צוזאַמען אויפֿגעשמידטע אויף אַ לאַנגן וועג.
גייען מײַנע פֿיס פּאַמעלעך,
ווי נישט-געצאָלטע בעל-מלאָכות
אומעטיק און מיד.
אין מײַנע חלומדיקע נעכט
בין איך אין אַ טונקעלער שטוב,
צווישן ווײַבער אויסגעמאַטערטע און צוגעפֿאַלענע צו דר'ערד.
און זייערע הענט זײַנען מיר גוט באַקאַנטע הענט,
מיט נעגל אויסגעשטשורבעטע פֿאַר אויסגעהאָרעוועטע יאָרן.
כאַפּ איך אויף זיך מיט אַן אָפּגעליימטע האַרץ,
און ס'גייען מײַנע פֿיס פּאַמעלעך,
ווי נישט-געצאָלטע בעל-מלאָכות אומעטיק און מיד.

II

Even in Tammuz, sometimes a leaf drops from a tree,
And misfortune arrives prematurely
And brings a leanness to the flesh.
Early on, unhappiness took me by the hand,
Like prisoners handcuffed to each other on a long road.
My feet walk slowly,
Like unpaid artisans
Careworn and tired.
In my dream-filled nights
I am in a dim house
Among women, exhausted and collapsed on the ground,
And their hands are hands well known to me,
With nails notched from years of drudgery.[39]
I arise with a clay-weighted heart
And my feet walk slowly,
Like unpaid artisans, careworn and tired.

VI

צום קליינעם שטעטעלע צו מײַנעם,
וואָס איז געבליבן שוין כּמעט אין גאַנצן וויסט,
קער איך זיך אַ מאָל, ווי צו אַ מיזרח-וואַנט
און בעט פֿאַר זיי פֿאַר אַלעמען,
וואָס זײַנען דאָרט פֿאַרבליבן.
עס זײַנען הײַזלעך דאָרט פֿאַראַן
ווו מ'האָט שוין לאַנג קיין לאָמפּ נישט אָנגעצונדן,
און אין די ווינקלען זיצן די פֿאַרבליבענע
און זאָגן מיטן אַלטן נוסח
און בעטן פֿאַר דער אָרעמער חיונה.
נאָר ס'זײַנען אַלע וועגן מיט הויכן שניי פֿאַרוואָרפֿן
און אַלע ברונעמער מיט אײַז אַרומגעפֿראָרן.
טראָגן יונגע זיך מיט האַרטע זוכעדיקע שנאָבלען אין דער וועלט אַוועק,
און אַלטע בלײַבן אין ווינקלען נישט-באַלויכטענע אין ערגעץ ליגן.

VI

Sometimes I turn my face, as to an Eastern wall,
Toward my tiny shtetl,
Almost entirely devastated,
And pray for every single person
Left behind.
There, in cramped houses,
No one has lit a lamp for a long time.
Those left behind sit in the corners,
Reciting in the old tradition
And praying for their poor livelihood.
But all roads are blocked with high snow
And all wells are choked with ice.
Young people with hard, seeking beaks pack off into the
world,
And the old stay behind to lie somewhere in unlit corners.[40]

VII

עס הענגט נאָך אַלץ דאָס בילד פֿון משה מאָנטעפֿיאָר,
אַ לאַנג פֿאַרגעלטעס שוין אונטערן גלאָז
אין טאַטנס שטוב אויף מיזרחדיקער וואַנט.
אַהער האָב איך געבראַכט
פֿון בלויער וואַרעמער אוקראַיִנע
בלייכע און באַרויבטע הענט
און אויגן טונקעלע ווי אויסגעבערענטע היילן,
און חלומות לאַנגע פֿון וויעדיקע קינדער און פֿון הינט,
און מײַן קאָפּ צום לעבן אַ באַשערטן.
נאָר ס'הענגט דער טויט אַ נאָענטער,
ווי אַ בגד איבער מײַן בעט
אָט נעבן בילד פֿון משה מאָנטעפֿיאָר
דעם לאַנג פֿאַרגעלטן שוין אונטערן גלאָז
אין טאַטנס שטוב אויף מיזרחדיקער וואַנט.

1925

VII

The picture of Moses Montefiore[41] still hangs,
Long-yellowed under the glass,
On the Eastern wall in my father's house.
I brought here
From the blue, warm Ukraine
Pale and deprived hands[42]
And eyes as dim as burned-out caves,
And prolonged dreams of howling children and of dogs,
And my own head destined for life.
But nearby, death hangs
Like a garment above my bed,
Near the picture of Moses Montefiore,
The one long-yellowed under the glass
On the Eastern wall in my father's house.

1925

II

מעשׂהלעך

וואַרשע, 1931

II

Mayselekh
(Tales)
Warsaw, 1931

אָלקע

הינטער וואַרשע, עק אָכאָטע,
אַ הויף מיט בלאָטע.

וווינט דאָרט אָלקע
מיט דער בלויער פּאַראַסאָלקע.

דער טאַטע אַ שמיד
די מאַמע אַרבעס בריט,

דער דאַך איז איַינגעבויגן האַלב,
אונטערן דאַך ווינט אַ שוואַלב.

אין שטוב — אַ טיש מיט אַ בעט
און אַ בוידעם מיט גרעט.

און לעפּל, און טעלער, און טעפּ, און קריג,
און אַ קינד אין וויג.

און דאָס מיידעלע אָלקע
מיט אַ בלויער פּאַראַסאָלקע.

אַ מויד פֿון זעקס יאָר,
מיט גאָלדענע האָר.

איז אין דרויסן העל,
און דער זאַמד איז געל,

נעמט אָלקע זאַמד קנעטן,
אַלע חבֿרטעס פֿאַרבעטן.

רופֿט די מאַמע די מויד,
אַז עס ציטערט אַ שויב,

Olke

In the back streets of Warsaw, at the end of desire,
A yard filled with mire,

There lives Olke
With her blue parasol-ke.[43]

Her father's a blacksmith,
Her mother boils peas.

The roof tilts aslant; in a hollow
Beneath the roof lives a swallow.

In the house, a table and a bed,
And a garret hung with laundry, a washshed.

And spoons and plates, pitchers, pans, and a pot,
And a baby on its cot.

And this girl Olke
With her blue parasol-ke.

A maid, six years old,[44]
With hair like spun-gold.

Outside it's bright and mellow,
And the sand is yellow,

Olke picks up some sand to knead—
She wants to invite her friends in for bread.

But her mother yells to the maid
So that the window panes quake,

און דער טאַטע, דער שמיד,
העלפֿט מיט:

— גיי אין שטוב!
מען דאַרף דאָס ברודערל וויגן,
וואַשן טעפּ און קריגן.

מען דאַרף וואַסער ברענגען,
מען דאַרף העמדעלעך שווענקען,

מען דאַרף קאַרטאָפֿעלעך שיילן,
מען דאַרף מעשׂהלעך דערציילן.

אַ ביסעלע לייענען,
אַ ביסעלע שרײַבן,
געדענק, כ'וועל דיך פֿון שטוב פֿאַרטרײַבן!

גייט אָלקע וואַסער ברענגען,
העמדעלעך שווענקען.

זעט זי:
גענדז גייען.
גייט די גאַנדז גורע,
די קליינע גענדזעלעך אין שורה,
פֿעדערן ווײַסע, פֿיס רויטע,
און דער גאָנער, דער שוטה.

עפּנט אָלקע
די בלויע פֿאַראַסאָלקע,
האָט זי אַ שטוב, און אַ דאַך,
און גענדזעלעך אַ סך.

וויל אָלקע מיט גענדזעלעך גיין
ביז די זון וועט פֿאַרגיין.

And her father, the blacksmith, then
Joins in:

"Get into the house!
Little brother needs rocking,
Pots and pitchers need washing.

Water needs bringing,
Shirts need rinsing,

Potatoes need peeling,
Stories need telling.

A little to read,
A little to write—
Remember, I'll drive you out of the house tonight."

When Olke goes to bring
Water for shirt-rinsing,

She sees:
Geese walking:
The goose walks proud and fine,[45]
And the goslings in a line,
Feathers of white,
Feet of red,
Then comes the gander, that noodlehead.[46]

Right then and there, Olke
Opens up her blue parasol-ke,

And she has a roof and a house
And geese numerous.

Olke wants to walk with the geese all the way
Until the sun sets at the end of the day.

רופֿט די מאַמע די מויד,
אַז עס ציטערט אַ שויב,

און דער טאַטע, דער שמיד,
העלפֿט מיט:

גיי אין שטוב!
עס איז אין דער וואָכן,
מען דאַרף קאַשע קאָכן,

מען דאַרף האָלץ שפּאַלטן,
מען דאַרף דאָס קינד האַלטן,

מען דאַרף שוועבעלעך צינדן,
מען דאַרף וויקעלעך בינדן,

אַ ביסעלע לייענען,
אַ ביסעלע שרײַבן, —
געדענק, כ׳וועל דיך פֿון שטוב פֿאַרטרײַבן!

גייט אָלקע האָלץ שפּאַלטן,
דאָס קינד האַלטן.

זעט זי:
פֿייגעלעך פֿליִען,
אַ שורה לאַנג ווי אַ באַן
און איבער זיי אַן עראָפּלאַן.

פֿליגעלעך ווײַס,
פֿייגעלעך הויך.
און איבער זיי אַ וואָלקן,
ווי בלויער רויך.

עפֿנט אָלקע
די בלויע פֿאַראַסאָלקע

But her mother yells to the maid
So that the window panes quake,

And her father, the blacksmith, then
Joins in:

"Get into the house!
It's the workaday week,
There's kasha to cook,

Wood to split,
Matches to be lit,

A baby to hold,
Diapers to fold,

A little to read,
A little to write—
Remember, I'll drive you out of the house tonight."

When Olke goes out to split the wood,
To hold the child,

She sees:
Birds flying
In a line as long as a train
And, above them, an airplane.

Wings of white,
Birds up high,
And above them clouds,
Like blue smoke in the sky.

Right then and there, Olke
Opens up her blue parasol-ke,

האָט זי אַ שטוב און אַ דאַך
און פֿייגעלעך אַ סך.

ווײַל אָלקע דאָ שטיין,
ביז די זון וועט פֿאַרגיין.

רופֿט די מאַמע די מויד,
אַז עס ציטערט אַ שויב,

און דער טאַטע, דער שמיד
העלפֿט מיט:

— גיי אין שטוב!
מען דאַרף זאָקן צירעווען,
מען דאַרף פֿעדעם קירעווען,

מען דאַרף קניפּלעך דרייען,
קנעפּלעך פֿאַרנייען,

אַ ביסעלע לייענען,
אַ ביסעלע שרײַבן, —
געדענק, כ'וועל דיך פֿון שטוב פֿאַרטרײַבן!

גייט אָלקע פֿאָדעם דרייען,
קנעפּלעך פֿאַרנייען.

גיבן קנעפּלעך זיך אַ שאָט
און צעלויפֿן זיך איבערן שטאָט.

ווערט יעדעס קנעפּל אַ ראָד,
יאָגן זיך די רעדער קאַראַהאָד.

איינס יאָגט זיך איבער דער גאַס,
קײַקלט זיך און פֿירט אַ פּאַס.

And she has a roof and a house
And birds numerous.

Olke wants to stand there stock-still
Until the sun sets over the hill.

But her mother yells to the maid
So that the window panes quake,

And her father, the blacksmith, then
Joins in:

"Get into the house!
Socks need darning,
Thread needs turning,[47]

Knots need tying,[48]
Buttons need sewing,

A little to read,
A little to write—
Remember, I'll drive you out of the house tonight."

When Olke unwinds some thread
To sew on buttons,

Suddenly the buttons spill down
And strew themselves all across the town.

Each button turns into a wheel,
And the wheels begin to dance a reel.[49]

One of them races across the cobbles,
Rolling as fast as a runaway barrel.

צוויי דרייען אַ וועלאָסיפּעד,
דריַי רעדער פֿירן אַ ברעט.

פֿיר רעדער אין אַ וואָגן,
איַינגעשפּאַנט זיך אין אַ וואָגן.

עפּנט אָלקע
די בלויע פּאַראַסאָלקע,

האָט זי אַ שטוב און אַ דאַך,
און רעדער אַ סך.

וויל אָלקע דאָ שטיין,
ביז די זון וועט פֿאַרגיין.

רופֿט די מאַמע די מויד,
אַז עס ציטערט אַ שויב,

און דער טאַטע, דער שמיד,
העלפֿט מיט.

נאָר אָלקע וויל ניט הערן, וויל ניט וויסן,
די רעדער רודערן, און בייגן זיך צו איר, און גריסן.

נעמט אָלקע אַלע רעדער אין אַ שפּאַן
און מאַכט אַ לאַנגע באַן.

און ס'פֿיַיפֿט די באַן, און אָלקע פֿאָרט אַוועק,
העט וויַיט, העט וויַיט, איבער אַ וויַיסן וועג.

Two spin a bicycle, straight and narrow,
Three wheels on a plank make a wheelbarrow,

Four wheels get themselves into a brawl
And harness themselves as a wagon to haul.

Right then and there, Olke
Opens up her blue parasol-ke,

And she has a roof and a house
And wheels numerous.

Olke wants to stand there stock-still
Until the sun sets over the hill.

But her mother yells to the maid
So that the window panes quake,

And her father, the blacksmith, then
Joins in:

But Olke does not want to hear or to know,
The wheels stir and bow to her and greet her, "Hello."

Then Olke hitches all the wheels in a harness
And makes a long train to go farther than farness.

Then the train whistles, and Olke travels away,
Far, far away on a glowing, white way.

דער טײַך

האָט מען אַ גולם געהייסן וואַסער טראָגן,
האָט ער צוויי עמער גענומען
און איז אַוועק צום ברונעם.

טראָגט ער וואַסער און טראָגט
וויפֿל כּוח ער פֿאַרמאָגט.

עמער נאָך עמער, אַ פּאָר נאָך אַ פּאָר,
אַזש עס שטייען אים קאַפּויער די האָר.

איז דאָס פֿאַס געוואָרן פֿול,
די באַלעבאָסטע איז געוואָרן דול:
— ס'גייט דאָס וואַסער אַריבער די ברעגן,
ס'איז די שטוב געוואָרן אַ טײַך,
צו טײַכן גלײַך.

האָט די גאַנצע שטוב גענומען שווימען:
פֿר:ער די פֿענצטער מיט די בלומען.
ווידער די טישן מיט די בעטן,
העמדער, זאָקן און קאַשקעטן.

אַ כוואַליע אויף אַ כוואַליע —
און די קינדער שווימען אין באַליע.

און דער גולם טראָגט וואַסער און טראָגט
וויפֿל כּוח ער פֿאַרמאָגט.

איז דאָס וואַסער פֿון שטוב אַרויס אין הויף,
האָבן העגער גענומען קרייען,
האָבן אינדיקעס גענומען גרעגן —
ס'לויפֿט דאָס וואַסער אַריבער די ברעגן.

The River

A golem got orders to go fetch some water,[50]
So in each hand he took up a pail,
And headed off to the well.

Water, more water, he carried and carried,
With all of his strength, the water he ferried.

He carried the buckets, pair by pair,
Until the hair on his head stood up straight, all his hair.

After the barrel was all filled up,
The housewife became completely mixed-up:
"The water is rising and running over!"
And the house turned into a river,
As great as any river.

Then the whole house began to float:
First the windows and the flowers,
Next, the tables and the beds,
Then shirts and socks, caps, a coat.

Wave upon wave, another, another,
And there goes the washtub with sister and brother.

Water, more water, he carried and carried,
With all of his strength, the water he ferried.

When the water ran out of the house to the yard,
Roosters began to cock-a-doodle and crow,
Turkeys began to gobble and go:
"The water is rising and racing over!"

האָט דער הויף געגומען שווימען:
שווימט אַ בעזעם און אַ ברעט,
און אַ שטריקל מיט גרעט,
און פֿון דאַך אַ שינדל,
און אַ ראַבע הינדל.
איז געוואָרן פֿון הויף אַ טײַך
צו טײַכן גלײַך.

און דער גולם טראָגט וואַסער און טראָגט
וויפֿל כוח ער פֿאַרמאָגט.

איז דאָס וואַסער פֿון הויף אַרויס אין גאַס.
האָבן די גלעקער גענומען קלינגען,
האָבן קינדער זיך גענומען שרעקן,
ס'לויפֿט דאָס וואַסער אַריבער די ברעגן.

האָט די גאַס גענומען שווימען:
שווימט אַ לייטער, שווימט אַ שטרוי,
שווימט אַ וואָגן מיט אַ גוי.
שווימען וועגענער מיט היי,
מאַמעס, קינדער מיט געשריי.
איז די גאַס געוואָרן אַ טײַך
צו טײַכן גלײַך.

איז דאָס וואַסער פֿון גאַס אַרויס אין פֿעלד.
און אין פֿעלד האָט געפּאַשעט זיך אַן אָקס.
האָט ער דאָס וואַסער גענומען טרינקען,
האָט ער דאָס וואַסער גענומען שלינגען,
מיט אַזוינע גרויסע שלוקן
אַז אין איין ויהי איז אַלץ געוואָרן טרוקן.
און אַזוי גיך איז דאָס געשען,
פּונקט ווי ס'וואָלט אַ מעשׂהלע געווען.

Then the yard began to float:
A broom swam by, and then a board,
And laundry hanging on a rope,
A shingle from the roof's tiptop
And a fawn speckled with white spots.
And the yard turned into a river,
As great as any river.

Water, more water, the golem still carried,
With all of his strength, the water he ferried.

When the water ran out of the yard to the street,
Bells began ringing, over and over,
The children were whimpering, trembling with fear:
"The water is rising and racing over."

Then the street began to float:
A ladder swept past, a piece of straw,
A wagon, its driver, his mouth ajar,
Carts loaded with hay,
Mothers and children, *oy vey*!
And the street turned into a river,
As great as any river.

Then the water ran down from the street to the meadow.
And there was an ox grazing, down in the meadow,
With a lick of its tongue, it drank up the water,
With a flick of its tongue, it swallowed the water
With such a huge slurp, in such a great gulp
Before you could say "Once . . . ," the whole world was dry,
And indeed, this took place in the wink of an eye,
Just like a story that's passing you by.[51]

אַ מעשׂה מיט אַ באַליע

אין אַ ליכטיקן טאָג, אין אַ גליקלעכער שעה,
די זון איז געשלאָפֿן אויף טישן און בעטן,
האָט כאַנטשע געקויפֿט אַ דייזשע, ברויט קנעטן.

קנעטן הײַנט און קנעט מאָרגן —
ווי לאַנג עס זאָל נישט דויערן
וויל דער טייג אַלץ נישט זויערן.

האָט כאַנטשע געזאָגט אָט אַזוי:
אַז די דייזשע איז קאַליע,
וועט זי זײַן פֿאַר אַ באַליע.

איצט גייט ווונדער אויף ווונדער,
אַז קינדערשע קליידער און העמדער מיט שמוץ און מיט פֿלעקן
וואַשט די באַליע אַליין, אָן אַ פּיצעלע זייף, אָן אַ האַנט צו פֿאַרשטעקן.

ווי אַזוי?
ס׳גיט אַ העמדל זיך דרײַ מאָל אַ דריי ווי אַ רייף
ווערט אַ באַליע מיט זייף.
לינקס אַ ראָד,
רעכטס אַ ראָד —
שוין פֿון באָד.

קומען שכנות פֿון קעלערס, פֿון בוידעמס, פֿון מיטלסטע שטאָקן:
כאַנטשע-לעב, כ׳האָב קינדערלעך זיבן, רק וואַש און צוואָג,
אַנטלײַ מיר די באַליע אויף הײַנטיקן טאָג.

איז די באַליע געגאַנגען אַזוי ווי אַ בשׂורה:
פֿון קעלער אַרויף, אויף אַן אייבערשטן שטאָק,
פֿון דאָרטן אין הויף, אין אַ פֿינצטערן ראָג.

The Tale of a Washtub

One bright day, at a lucky hour,
When the sun was dozing on table and bed,
Khantshe bought a wooden trough for kneading bread.

But knead as she might, today and tomorrow—
As long as the sun stayed up in the skies,
The dough simply refused to rise.

So this is what Khantshe said:
If the kneading-trough is spoiled
I'll make it a washtub where laundry is boiled.

Now came the wonder of wonders:
The tub scrubbed every spot, speck, and stain
From the children's clothes! With no soap, with no drain!

How did that happen?
A shirt rolled three times around, like a hoop,
The tub became soap.
Turn to the left,
Turn to the right—
Out of the washtub, clean and bright.

Neighbors popped up from cellars, from attics:
Khantshe dear, with seven children, it's always wash and scrub!
Please, just for today, lend me your new washtub.

So the washtub travelled like gossip
From the cellar up to a floor on top,
Down to the yard's darkest nook, didn't stop.

דערנאָך:
אויף אַ בוידעם, אין אַ שטוב אָן אַ טיר,
און אַרויף ווי אַ וויאַטראַק אויף טרעפּלעך פּיר.

דערנאָך:
אין אַ שטוב מיט אַ הרובע אַ בלויער,
פֿון דאָרט צו אַ שכנישער גויע.

האָט די מעשׂה געדויערט
אַזוי ברייט, אַזוי לאַנג,
ביז די באַליע אַליין האָט געוווּסט שוין דעם גאַנג.

האָט די באַליע געוואַגט
און גענומען אַליין
פֿון דירה צו דירה זיך קײַקלען און גיין.

טראַכט די באַליע און זאָרגט:
פֿייגע-ביילע אין די מאַנצבילשע קאָמאַשן
מוז מען צו איר זונטיק קומען וואַשן,

ווײַל זי האָט קליינע קינדערלעך,
מוז אָפּטער וואַשן ווינדעלעך.

און מאָנטיק וואַשט מען העמדעלעך אין אייבערשטיבל.
און דינסטיק, האָט נישט קיין פּאַראיבל,
וואַשט מען מײַטקעלעך.

און וואַשן לײַבעלעך און זאָקן
קײַקלט זיך די באַליע מיטוואָך מיט גערויש און מיט געהילך
צו שׂרה-זלאַטען וואָס האַנדלט מיט ציגנמילך.

דאָנערשטיק איז אַ געשפּאַר,
קײַקלט זיך די באַליע, ווערט צוויי מאָל אַזוי ברייט.
וואַשט העמדעלעך פֿאַר קינד-און-קייט.

After that:
Up to an attic in a house with no door,
Like a windmill, whirled up the steps, one-two-three-four.

After that:
Into a room with an oven that's blue,
From there, to a Gentile neighbor's, too.

And the story went on
So long and so slow
That the washtub itself knew which way to go.

And it dared to set out
All alone, just like that,
Rolling and bumping from flat to flat.

Worriedly, the washtub thought:
There's Feyge-Beyle in her men's mackintosh—
On Sunday I have to go do *her* wash.[52]

Because she has small children,
She must wash diapers much more often.

And Monday, I'll launder blouses in garrets.
And Tuesday, no offense intended,
I'm due to wash breeches stained with carrots.[53]

And on Wednesday, the tub noisily rolled
To wash jackets, socks, and a coat
For Sore-Zlate, who sells milk from her goat.

Thursday was all push and shove
As the washtub rolled, expanded its girth,
And washed shirts for everyone on earth.

פֿרײַטיק גייען קינדער אין קלאָרן וועש,
פֿרײַטיק ווערט די באַליע זייער פֿרום —
און וואַשט זיך גאָר אַליין אַרום.

Friday, the children wore clean underwear,
Friday, the washtub became quite devout,
And did nothing else but wash itself out.

שיכעלעך

אָט-אָ, אָט-אָ איז אַ באַרג,
אָט-אָ, אָט-אָ איז אַ טאָל,
זיצט אַ שוסטער אויפֿן באַרג
מיט אַ האַמער, מיט אַן אָל.

שטעכט דער שוסטער מיטן אָל,
מיטן האַמער שלאָגט ער גיך,
איינס און צוויי,
איינס און צוויי,
וואַקסן אויס צוויי קליינע שיך.

זאָגט דער שוסטער:
— שיכלעך, גייט!
גייען שיכעלעך אַוועק,
וווּ די וועלט האָט נאָר אַן עק.
גייען שיכעלעך אַרום,
וווּ דער שוסטער שיקט זיי אום.

גייען שיכעלעך נאָך ברויט,
גייען שיכעלעך נאָך זאַלץ,
גייען שיכעלעך אַרום
פֿאַרן שוסטער ברענגען אַלץ.

איין מאָל נעמען שיכלעך גיין,
בײַ אַ טויער בלײַבן שטיין.

קלאַפּט דאָס רעכטע שיכל: איינס,
קלאַפּט דאָס לינקע שיכל: צוויי,
עפֿנט זיך אַ טיר פֿאַר זיי.

זיצט אַ קינד דאָרטן אַליין,
באָרוועס, נאַקעט, ווינד און ווײ.

Little Shoes

Come and look at this high hill,
Come and look at this deep vale,
A cobbler's sitting on the hill
With his hammer and his awl.

The cobbler punches with the awl,
He pounds the hammer quickly,
A-one and a-two,
And a-one and a-two,
Small shoes appear there magically.

The cobbler says:
—Go, little shoes!
The shoes go off wherever he sends,
To the place where the world ends,
The little shoes go everywhere
The cobbler orders, anywhere.

The little shoes go seeking bread,
The little shoes go seeking salt,
The little shoes go everywhere
To bring the cobbler whatever he wants.

Once, as the shoes pass by a gate,
They stop and wait.

The right shoe knocks for the first time.
The left shoe knocks a second time,
A small door opens up for them.

There a child sits, all alone,
Barefoot, naked, on a stone.[54]

דאָרטן בלײַבן שיכלעך שטיין,
ווילן ערגעץ מער נישט גיין.

און דער שוסטער אויפֿן באַרג
וואַרט, און וואַרט,
און וואַרט, און וואַרט.

The little shoes stand stock-still there,
No more will they go anywhere.

The cobbler, high upon the hill
Waits and waits,
He's waiting, still.

די גריל

גרילט אַ גאַנצע נאַכט אַ גריל,
ווייס ניט קיינער וואָס זי וויל.
צירי-רי, צירי-רי
גרילט אַ גריל ביז אין דער פֿרי.

ווייס ניט קיינער וואָס זי עסט,
זאָגט די באָבע, אַז זי פֿאַסט,
זאָגט דער זיידע, אַז זי נאַשט,
און די גריל זאָגט:
צירי-רי,
צירי-רי,
צירי-רי ביז אין דער פֿרי.

ווייס ניט קיינער ווו זי וווינט.
זאָגט די באָבע: אין אַ שפּאַלט,
זאָגט דער זיידע: אין אַ וואַנט.
און די גריל זאָגט:
צירי-רי,
צירי-רי,
צירי-רי ביז אין דער פֿרי.

גייט אַרויס די העלע זון,
זוכט דאָס גרילכל אומעטום.
גייט די זון אונטערן טיש,
שאַרט די זון איבערן דיל,
און דאָס גרילכל ליגט פֿאַרשטעקט,
ליגט פֿאַרשטעקט און שאַ, און שטיל.

ווי די זון גייט נאָר אַוועק
הייבט די גריל אָן:
צירי-רי,
צירי-רי,
צירי-רי ביז אין דער פֿרי.

The Cricket

Under the table, a cricket trills,
Not knowing herself what she wants or wills.
Chirrup, chirrup,
The cricket cricks till the sun comes up.

Nobody knows what she eats,
Grandma tells us that she fasts,
Grandpa tells us that she snacks,
And the cricket says:
Chirrup,
Chirrup,
Chirrup until the sun comes up.

Nobody knows where she lives—
Grandma tells us: in a hole,
Grandpa tells us: in a wall,
And the cricket says:
Chirrup,
Chirrup,
Chirrup until the sun comes up.

The bright sun rises, goes here and there,
Looks for the cricket everywhere,
The sun goes under the table,
The sun scrapes across the floor,
And the little cricket lies, silenced, stilled,
And doesn't crick anymore.

But when the sun has finally gone,
The cricket begins again:
Chirrup,
Chirrup,
Chirrup until the sun comes up.

עפּנט דעם טויער

עפּנט דעם טויער, עפּנט אים ברייט,
ס'וועט דאָ דורכגיין אַ גאָלדענע קייט:
דער טאַטע,
די מאַמע,
דער ברודער,
די שוועסטער,
חתן-כּלה אין מיטן
אויף אַ גאָלדענעם שליטן.

עפּנט דעם טויער, עפּנט אים ברייט,
ס'וועט דאָ דורכגיין אַ גאָלדענע קייט:
דער זיידע,
די באָבע,
דער פֿעטער,
די מומע,
די אייניקלעך אין מיטן
אויף אַ גאָלדענעם שליטן.

עפּנט דעם טויער, עפּנט אים ברייט,
ס'וועט דאָ דורכגיין אַ גאָלדענע קייט:
אַ באַר
און אַן עפּל,
און האָניק אַ טעפּל,
און אַ לעקעך אַ געלער
אויף אַ גאָלדענעם טעלער.

Open the Gate

Open the gate, throw it wide open,
Through it must pass a chain that is golden:[55]
Papa
And Mama,
Brother
And Sister,
And among them, a bride and groom, happy and gay,
Riding upon a golden sleigh.

Open the gate, throw it wide open,
Through it must pass a chain that is golden:
Grandpa
And Grandma,
Uncle
And Aunt,
And among them, the grandchildren, happy and gay,
Riding upon a golden sleigh.

Open the gate, throw it wide open,
Through it must pass a chain that is golden:
A pear
And an apple,
A cup filled with honey,
And a yellow ginger cake
Set upon a golden plate.

III

אויפֿן באַרג

ניו-יאָרק, 1938

III

Afn barg
(On the Mountain)
New York, 1938

מאַרצעפּאַנעס

גערוען אַ טאַטע מיט אַ מאַמע.
דער טאַטע איז דין,
די מאַמע איז גראָב,
און קינדער ווי באָב.

וויל איינס עסן היידעלעך,
דאָס צווייטע קניידעלעך,
און די אויסטראַכטערקע חנה
וויל אַ מאַרצעפּאַנע.

ווייס ניט קיינער ווו די מאַרצעפּאַנעס קריגן.
ווייס ניט קיינער ווו האָט עס צו ליגן.

זאָגט דער טאַטע:
מאַרצעפּאַנעס וואַקסן אויף אַ בוים,
גלײַך אַן עפּל, גלײַך אַ באַר און גלײַך אַ פֿלוים.

זאָגט די מאַמע:
מאַרצעפּאַנעס קויפֿט מען אין די קראָמען.

זאָגט די שוועסטער:
מאַרצעפּאַנעס וואַקסן ווי די שוואָמען.

און די באָבע אַלט און אײַנגעבויגן:
— נישט געהערט פֿון מאַרצעפּאַנעס קיין מאָל.
נישט-געשטויגן,
נישט-געפֿלויגן.

קומט אַ בריווטרעגער מיט אַ בריוו:
— מאַרצעפּאַנעס? — זאָגט ער —
ברענגט מען מיט אַ שיף.
פֿון אַ שטאָט אַזאַ וואָס הייסט האַוואַנע.
ס'וואַקסן דאָרטן אויף יעדער בוים אַ מאַרצעפּאַנע.

Marzipans

Once there were a mother and a father.
The mother was fat,
The father was thin,
And each of their children was shaped like a bean.

One child wanted to eat noodles,
A second—strudels,
And the fastidious girl Ann,[56]
Wanted nothing but marzipan.

No one knew what marzipans are
Or how to find marzipan, find near or far.

The father said: Marzipans grow on a tree,
Just like apples, pears, and plums, you see.

The mother said: Marzipans are bought in the store.
A sister said: They grow like mushrooms on the forest floor.

The old grandmother, bent in two,
Said: Marzipans? Fiddlesticks! Untrue!

A postman came with a letter to deliver:
Ships bring marzipans across the sea, up the river,

From a city called Havannah,
Where on every tree there grows *marzipannah.*

But no one believed the postman,
So he swore with such venom
That nobody wanted to see him or hear him.

האָט דעם בריווטרעגער קיינער ניט געגלייבט,
און ער האָט געמעגט מיט שבֿועות שווערן —
האָט מען סײַ ווי ניט געוואָלט ניט זען, ניט הערן.

קומט אַ שוסטער מיט אַ זויל:
— מאַרצעפּאַנעס? — לאַכט ער מיט אַ פֿולן מויל.
מאַרצעפּאַנעס עסן גרויסע, גרויסע פּריצים.
אונדזער איינער קען צווישן זיי ניט זיצן.
און אַפֿילו ראָטשילד, וואָס האָט אַ רײַכן טאַטן
און אַ רײַכע מאַמע —
עסט איין מאָל אין אַ יאָר אַ מאַרצעפּאַנע.

האָט דעם שוסטער קיינער ניט געגלייבט,
און ער האָט געמעגט מיט שבֿועות שווערן,
האָט מען סײַ ווי ניט געוואָלט ניט זען, ניט הערן.

האָט מען אַלץ געשר״ען:
מאַרצעפּאַנעס הין, און מאַרצעפּאַנעס הער,
ערשט ס'עפֿנט זיך די טיר,
און ס'קומט אָן יאָסל בער.

יאָסל בער? איז פּונקט מן-השמים.
ער ווייסט ווו ס'ווינט אַ האָז אין וואַלד,
פֿון קאָרן ווייסט ער און פֿון קלײַען.
ער ווייסט ווו אַ קאַנאַריק שלאָפֿט,
און וואָס עס עסן בערן,
און ווו עס שווימען אַלע טײַכן
און וואָס די פֿייגל קלערן.
ער ווייס אַפֿילו אין אַמעריקע די שטעט און לענדער.
ער ווייס, בקיצור, אַלץ — און ענדע.

זײַנען אַלע אים באַפֿאַלן ווי די פֿליגן —
זאָל ער זאָגן ווו די מאַרצעפּאַנעס ליגן.

A shoemaker then arrived with nails and a sole:
—Marzipans!—he laughed with his mouth full—

The landlords who eat marzipan are so enormously fat
That not one of us could squeeze between them like that![57]

And even Rothschild, with his rich mom and dad,
Eats marzipan just once a year, it is said.

But no one believed the shoemaker,
So he swore with such venom
That nobody wanted to see him or hear him.

An uproar began—Marzipan here,
Marzipan there,

Then a door opened
And in came Yosl-Bear.

Yosl-Bear must have been heaven-sent, what a man!
He knew where rye grows, and which grain is bran,
And where hares rest their feet,
And what the bears eat.

And what the birds think,
And where rivers run.
He knew all the cities and states in America
In short, he knew everything under the sun.

Everyone fell upon him like flies,
Asking him to tell where marzipan lies.

And Yosl-Bear, being such a clown,
Winked at Ann, one eye up, one eye down:

Just look here, you see! Such a fine girl, this Ann!
Wants nothing other than a marzipan!

און יאָסל בער איז נאָך געווען דערצו אַ לץ,
פינטלט ער צו חנהן מיט די אויגן: זעטס נאָר, זעטס!
אַ מויד אַזאַ, אַ חנה — וויל דווקא גאָר אַ מאַרצעפּאַנע?

הער-זשע: ס'איז דאָ אַ שטאָט —
ליגן מאַרצעפּאַנעס דאָרט אויף גאָלדענע געפּעסן,
נאָר ווי עס הייסט די שטאָט האָב איך פֿאַרגעסן.

לאַכן אַלע פֿון דער אויסטראַכטערקע חנה:
— נאַ דיר גאָר, פֿאַרגלוסט אַ מאַרצעפּאַנע!

און קומען אין דער שטאָט קען קומען יעדער,
אויף אַ פֿור אָן פֿערד און רעדער.

לאַכן אַלע פֿון דער אויסטראַכטערקע חנה:
— נאַ דיר גאָר, פֿאַרגלוסט אַ מאַרצעפּאַנע!

און ס'ווינען דאָרטן לײדיק-גײער, שפּאַסער,
וואָס טוען ניט אַרײַן אַ האַנט אין קאַלטן וואַסער.

לאַכן אַלע פֿון דער אויסטראַכטערקע חנה:
— נאַ דיר גאָר, פֿאַרגלוסט אַ מאַרצעפּאַנע!

און פּלוצלינג צעלאַכט זיך יאָסל בער אַליין.
און כאַ-כאַ-כאַ.
— אַ מאַרצעפּאַנע איז אַ בייגעלע אַזאַ,
און מען באַקט אים אין אַן אויוון,
און מען מעג שוין יאָסל בערן זיכער גלייבן.
און אַ מויד אַזאַ, אַ חנה,
מעג פֿאַרקאַשערן די אַרבל ביז די עלנבויגן,
און זיך צושטעלן צום מולטער קנעטן,
עס וועט שוין עפּעס טויגן.

און כּך-הווה, אַזוי איז שוין געווען די מעשׂה.
ס'האָט די אויסטראַכטערקע חנה אויסגעבאַקט אַ מאַרצעפּאַנע,
איז איר די גאַנצע שטאָט געווען מקנא.

So listen, there is a city—
Where marzipans lie on golden plates, very pretty,
But I've forgotten what they call this city.

Then everyone laughed at the fastidious Ann:
—Here, dear, you're craving a marzipan.

And its inhabitants are lazy jokers
Who sit all day and poke with pokers.[58]

Then everyone laughed at the fastidious Ann:
—Here, dear, you're craving a marzipan.

And the people there ride in vehicles
That move without horses and without any wheels.

Then everyone laughed at the fastidious Ann:
—Here, dear, you're craving a marzipan.

And suddenly Yosl-Bear himself burst out laughing,
Ha-ha-ha, and ha-ha-ha . . .

A marzipan is just a little cookie,
And it's baked in an oven,
Believe Yosl-Bear, and you'll be lucky.
And such a little girl as Ann
Who rolls up her sleeves to her elbows can
Knead the dough, pat it, and put it in a pan,
And soon there will be some marzipan.

And indeed, this is the actual story.
The fastidious girl baked marzipan to perfection,
And everyone's mouth watered for the confection.

אַ בריוועלע

די מאַמע האָט געהייסן שרײַבן קיין אַמעריקע אַ בריוועלע
צו דער מומע חנה-שיינע-שׂרה-ציוועלע.

שרײַבן אַ בריוו? פֿאַר וואָס ניט?
איז נישטאָ קיין פּאַפּיר, איז נישט גוט.

זאָגט שיינדל: פּאַפּיר? איך ווייס ווו און וואָס און ווי
און ס'וועט זײַן פּאַפּיר אין איין ויהי.

איז שיינדל אַוועק מיט פּאַראַד און געשריי
און מען האָט זי אָנגעזען ווי דעם פֿאַראַיאָריקן שניי.

האָט די מאַמע געהייסן אַז בערל און מאָטל און פּרץ
זאָלן ברענגען פּאַפּיר און אָן אַ תּירוץ.

האָבן בערל און מאָטל און פּרץ אַזוי לאַנג געהאַקט מיט די שטיוול
ביז מען האָט געבראַכט פּאַפּיר אויף אַ בריוול.

דעם טינט האָט פֿרומע געזוכט צוויי שעה נאָך אַנאַנד
און געפֿונען אונטערן בעט, אין אַ ווינקל, בײַ דער וואַנט.

און די פּענע האָט שׂרהקע געזוכט מיט היץ און קוראַזש —
זי שטייט גאָר פֿאַרשטעקט מיטן שפּיץ אין אַ פֿלאַש.

אַלץ געבראַכט —
ט'מען געשריבן אַ בריוול, אַ בריוול אַ פּראַכט.

האָט בערל פֿאַרקאַשערט די אַרבל ביז די עלנבויגן
און האָט גענומען שרײַבן פֿײַל אויסן בויגן.

געשריבן און געשריבן זייער שיין און זייער דין
ביז ער איז געקומען צו אַ שין.

A Letter

Mother ordered us to write a letter to America,
To Auntie Khane-Sheyne-Sore-Tsivele, now known there as
Erica.[59]

Sure, write a letter, of course we should!
But if there's no paper, that's no good.

So Sheyndl said, "Paper? I know all about it
And there'll be paper, don't you doubt it."

Then Sheyndl set out with parades and brass bands,
But soon returned, shamefaced, with empty hands.

Then Mother ordered Peretz, Motl, and Berl
To go find some paper without a quarrel.

So Peretz, Motl, and Berl, those go-getters,
Wore out their boots and got paper for letters.

Frume, looking for ink two hours, all-in-all,
Found it under the bed, near a crack in the wall.

And Sorke searched for the pen with such mettle
That she found it with its point stuck in a bottle.

All gathered together, all for the better—
So a letter was written, a magnificent letter.

Berl rolled up his sleeves just to the elbow
And began to write fast as a bow and arrow.

He wrote and he wrote, each stroke nice and thin,
Until he came to a *shin*.[60]

און דער שין איז אים פֿון קאָפּ אַרויסגעפֿלויגן,
גלײַך קיין מאָל נישט געזען אים פֿאַר די אויגן.

זאָגט שיינדל: אַ שין? מיט דער פּענע נאָר אַ דריי, אַ פֿלי
וועט זײַן אַ שין אין איין ויהי.

און אַז שיינדל האָט אַזוי אַ שרײַב געטאָן —
איז אַרויסגעקומען אַ ווינטמיל מיט אַ האָן.

האָט שוין מאָטל פֿאַררוקט דאָס היטל ביז די אויערן
און גענומען פּערלדיקע אותיות מויערן.

געשריבן און געשריבן מיט חשק און מיט ברען
ביז ער איז געקומען צו אַ מעם.

און דעם מעם האָט ער געשטעלט קרום און לאָם, קאַפּויער אין צווייען —
זאָגן אַלע: ס'טויג נישט, אַ מעם דאַרף שטיין ווי אַלע מעמען שטייען.

זאָגט שיינדל: אַ מעם? אַ פּאַסיקל אַהין, אַ פּאַסיקל אַהער, אַ פּאַסיקל
אין מיטן —
וועט זײַן אַ מעם ווי אויסגעשניטן.

און אַז שיינדל האָט אָנגעהויבן שרײַבן און מעקן
איז אויסגעקומען אַ שטעקן אויף אַ שטעקן.

דעמאָלט האָט שוין פּרץ אַראָפּגעוואָרפֿן שיך און זאָקן
און האָט גענומען וואָרט נאָך וואָרט ווי טשוועקעס שלאָגן.

און ס'איז אַרויסגעקומען אַ גאָלדן בריוועלע
צו דער מומע חנה-שיינע-שרה-ציוועלע.

האָט מען אין גאַנץ אַמעריקע דעם בריוו געלייענט, געלויבט אין הימל:
— זעט אַן אַלף, זעט אַ בית, און זעט א גימל,

And the *shin*—whoosh!—flew right out of his brain,
Just as if such a letter had never been.

Then Sheyndl said, "A *shin*?
Just swoop up and touch the pen down once again,
And you'll have such a *shin* as has never been."

And Sheyndl wrote with such a gesture
That what emerged was a windmill and rooster.

Then Mottl shoved his hat down over his ears and curls,
And built up a wall of letters like pearls.

He wrote and wrote with great vigor and vim
Until he came to a *mem*.

And he set down the *mem* like a crooked, lame "m,"
So everyone said, "No way! A *mem* must be a *mem*!"

Then Sheyndl said, "*Mem*? Stroke here, there, the middle,
And you'll carve out a *mem* that's fit as a fiddle."

When Sheyndl began to write and blot,
What emerged was a stick on a log with a knot.

At that point, Peretz kicked off his shoes and socks,
And hammered out word after word like tacks.

And what emerged was a golden letter to America
For Auntie Khane-Sheyne-Sore-Tsivele, now known there as
Erica.

So all of America read the letter and praised it to heaven,
"See, an *alef*! Look, a *beys* and a *giml*, even!

הײַנט דער שין, דער מעם, דער לאַמעד און דער כאָף, —
גאָלד מיט זילבער פֿון דעם אָנהייב ביזן סוף.

האָט מען אין גאַנץ אַמעריקע דערציילט, אַז פֿרומע און שיינדל און שׂרהקע
און בערל און מאָטל און פּרץ (קיין איינס נישט פֿאַרפֿעלט)
האָבן אָנגעשריבן אַ בריוועלע איינס אין דער וועלט.

See the *shin*, the *mem*, the *lamed*, and the *khaf*, how they
bend?
Silver and gold from beginning to end."

All of America knew how Frume, Sheyndl, Sorke, Berl, Mottl,
and Peretz (no one left out)
Wrote a letter worth writing home about.

IV

דזשיקע גאַס

וואַרשע, 1933, 1936

IV

Dzshike gas
(Dzshike Street)
Warsaw, 1933, 1936

דזשיקע גאַס

י. אָפּאַטאָשון

ס'איז פּופּצנטער אין חודש אייר,
עס זײַנען טעג, ווי גאָלדענער זאַפּרען,
עס שמעקט מיט פֿייגלמילך. שיעור, שיעור
דאַכט זיך — עס איז גאָט פֿאַראַן.
עס קלינגט די לופֿט. זומער בליט אין מײַנע האָר.
נאָר איבער מיר שטייט שאַרף די טאָגעדיקע וואָר:
דאָ וווינען אַרבעטסלאָזע,
קאָמוניסטן,
און נאָך — דער דלות.
טאָג-טעגלעכקייט איז אַ בלוטיקער פֿאַל,
קלינגען אַלע דעכער מיט אומגליק,
טישן מיט — הונגער,
און דער באָרוועס — מיט אינטערנאַציאָנאַל.
ייִדן וווינען דאָ, —
אַ פֿאָלק צום אויסגיין פֿאַר געלעכטער —
עס ליפֿערט פֿאַר דער וועלט בראַקירטע סחורות
און בלוט פֿון זין און טעכטער.
און איך — מען טײַט אויף מיר דאָ מיט די פֿינגער:
„אָט זי, די זינגערין,
אַ רוח אין איר מאַמען,
זי שלעפּט זיך דאָ אַרום,
און פֿלעכט פֿון אונדזער אומגליק גראַמען.
וואָלט זי נעכטן גיין מיט אונדז אין גאַס אַרויס און זען —
מען האָט פֿאַרקאַטעוועט דעם צוואַנציק-יעריקן
אויף דזשיקע נומער צען”.
און איך — איך האָב נישט וואָס צו ענטפֿערן אַ וואָרט,
איך ווייס —
איך בין נישט פֿון די מענטשן „פּערווי סאָרט”.
און כאָטש עס שטייט אַ קוואַל פֿון טרערן הינטער מײַן אויג,
בין איך פֿאַרליבט אין לעבן, ווי אַ צויג.

Dzshike Street[61]

To J. Opatoshu

It's the fifteenth of the month of Iyar,[62]
Days are like golden saffron,
Fragrant with starflowers.[63] Almost, it almost
Seems that God is there.
The air rings. Summer blossoms in my hair,
But the everyday facts stand starkly over me:
Here live the unemployed,
Communists,
And even more—poverty.
Day-in, day-out, it's a bloody affair:
All the roofs ring with despair,
Tables with hunger,
And the barefoot with the "Internationale."
Jews live here,
What a people—you could die from laughter—
Delivering rejected wares to the world
And the blood of sons and daughters.
And I—they point at me with their fingers:
"There she is—the lady singer,
The devil take her mother,—
She hangs around here all the time
And braids our misery into rhymes.
Yesterday, she should have gone into the street with us and
seen
The twenty-year-old man flogged to death
In Dzshike Number Ten."
And I—I don't have a single word with which
To answer. I know—
I'm not one of those "first-rate" folks.[64]
And although tears well up behind my eyes,
I am in love with life like a bitch.

מאַרש

איך שרײַב נישט קיין ליד, איך פּרוּוו
געפֿינען אַ וואָרט פֿאַר מײַן בלוט,
וואָס ווײנט אין מײַן גוף.
פֿאַר טשאָבאָטעס צוויי — מײַנע שיך —
וואָס שטייען בײַ מיר נעבן בעט,
גרייט אָן אַ קלער,
אין גאַס אַרויס,
ברענגען דעם הונגער אַהער
און נאָך:
ברענגען מיט זיך,
אַ מאַרש פֿון צעריסענע שיך.

כ׳ווייס דעם אומעט פֿון באָרוועסן גיין,
פֿון מײַן גאַס
און מײַן אייגענער היים.
און כ׳דערקאָן יעדן טראָט:
ס׳זײַנען לאַפּטשעס פֿון ליטע, מײַן היים,
וואָס שמעקן מיט וואַסער-טשעראָט,
ס׳זײַנען שטיוול, וואָס כ׳קען זיי געוויס און געוויס,
נישט איין מאָל צוזאַמען געשפּאַנט איבער גאַסן,
און צוריקגעבראַכט:
ביינער,
און הונגער,
און שטרויכלונג פֿון פֿיס.

גייט דער מאַרש איבער מיר,
און אויף זײַטן פֿון ווײַסן פּאַפּיר
שרײַבט מיט פֿינצטערן שטריך.
הער איך מיט אויגן פֿאַרמאַכטע
דעם מאַרש פֿון צעריסענע שיך.

Marching

I don't write a poem, I try
To find a word for my blood
That cries in my body,
For two clodhoppers—my shoes[65]
That stand near my bed,
Ready—nothing to lose—
To walk out in the street
To bring hunger back here
And more:
To bring back
A marching of worn-out shoes.

I know the sadness of walking barefoot
From my street
And my own home,
Recognize every footfall:
Lithuanian bast shoes,[66] from my home,
With their water weed smell,
Leather boots that, I know very well,
More than once strode together from street to street
And brought back
Denials
And hunger
And the stumbling of feet.

Then it's me that the marching walks over,
And upon white pieces of paper[67]
Writes its dark stroke.
Eyes closed, I hear: it ensues,
The marching of worn-out shoes.

אַ מאַמע

די מאַמע אין גרינעם סוועטער גייט איבערן גאַס און גייט.
אלול הוידעט זיך דער ווינט,
טבֿת שנייט,
זון איבער די שויבן פּסח רינט.
דער גרינער סוועטער גייט איבערן גאַס און גייט
שוין זומערן,
שוין ווינטערן,
שוין וויפֿל ציַיט —
די גאַסן שווימען אין דער לענג און אין דער קרים,
דער הימל הוידעט זיך אַזוי ווי אַ האַמאַק,
און אַלע גאַסן,
אַלע פֿירן צום פּאַוויאַק.
דאָרט ווי אַ ווונד אַ קאַמער בריט,
אַ קאַמער וויגט זיך טאָג און נאַכט;
אונטער די גרויע וועגט אַ טאָכטער זיצט פֿאַרמאַכט,
פֿאַרשלאָסן,
שטיל,
מיט אויפֿגעלייגטע הענט,
מיט שאַרפֿן הערן,
און זעגט די קראַטן מיטן בליק
און ציילט די שטערן.
אַרום די שטילקייט קלינגט,
עס בלענדט די ליידיקייט מיט וויַיסע שפּיזן.
— — —
— — —
— — —

דער גרינער סוועטער גייט איבערן גאַס און גייט.
אלול איז נישט נאַס,
און טבֿת איז נישט קאַלט,
און פּסח איז קיין יום-טובֿ נישט.

A Mother

The mother in the green sweater walks and walks along the
street.
In Elul, the wind swings,
Tebeth snows,
Pesach leaks sun over windowpanes.[68]
The green sweater walks and walks along the street,
Through summers,
Through winters,
Through so much time.
The streets swim lengthwise and aslant,
The sky swings like a hammock,
And all the streets,
All lead to Pawiak.[69]
There, like a wound, a prison cell burns,
A cell sways day and night;
Beneath the gray walls a daughter sits closed,
Locked,
Silent,
With folded hands,
With keen hearing,
And saws the bars with her gaze
And counts the stars.
Around her, the silence resounds,
The vacancy dazzles with white spears.
—[70]
—
—
The green sweater walks and walks along the street.
Elul is not damp,
And Tebeth is not cold,
And Pesach is not a holiday.

דער הימל הוידעט זיך אַזוי ווי אַ האַמאַק,
און אַלע גאַסן,
אַלע פֿירן צום פּאַוויאַק.

The sky swings like a hammock,
And all the streets,
All lead to Pawiak.

אַ גאַס אין יאָר 1930

ווי־טרינעס. דענקמעלער.
ווי אַ דזשענטלמען געקרויזט רוסאָ.
יאָגט און שווימט דער שטאָטישער פּאַרקער,
דער גאָלדענער פון אויבן,
און דער טונקעלער פון דנאָ.

כוואַליעט זיך די גאַס אין רעש.
אַ רויטע דאַמענהוט,
און אַ צילינדער, ווי אַ שוואַרצע פלאַש.
אַ הויקער, ווי אַ פּראַגע-צייכן אויפן טראָטואַר.
און אַ רעקלאַמע-טרעגער מיט לאַנגע אויערן — גרימירט צום נאַר.

און בײַ אַ וואַנט שטייט איינער אָפּהענטיק און מאַט,
מיט הוט און שטעקל,
ווי טשאַרלי טשאַפּלין זעט ער אויס כמעט,
געקליידט אין ביליקן טאַנדעט,
אָן אַ וווּהין.

הונגעריק און שאַרף זײַנען זײַנע אויגנשפּאַלטן
(אַרום איז העל).
ער האָט פון טויט אַ שטרענגן בריוו דערהאַלטן,
מיט בלוט געשריבן אויפן ברוק פון גאַס,
און אַ פּאָסטסקריפּטום:
וועגן הונגערטויט אין קעלער, ווו ס'איז נאַס.

לייענט ער דעם בריוו פאַר אַלע מיט הונגעריקן קוק.
הערן אַלע:
עס איז מיט בלוט געשריבן אויפן ברוק,
און אַ פּאָסטסקריפּטום:
וועגן הונגערטויט.

פּאַריז, 1931

A Street in the Year 1930

Shop windows. Monuments.
(Like a gentleman, a crimped Rousseau.)
The metropolitan traffic chases and swims,
The golden traffic from above,
And the dark traffic from below.

The street pounds with noise like waves.
A red ladies' hat
And a top hat like a bottle, black.
Like a question mark on the sidewalk, a hunchback.
And a sandwich-board man with long ears—made up as the
fool.

And by a wall stands a man, limp and dull,
With hat and stick,
He almost looks like Charlie Chaplin,
Dressed in cheap old clothes,
Without a destination.

The slits of his eyes are hungry and keen.
(It's bright all around.)
He's received a harsh letter from death,
Written in blood on the cobblestone street,
With a postscript
About dying of hunger in the damp cellar.

He reads the letter for all with a hungry gaze.
They all hear:
It is written in blood on the cobblestones,
With a postscript
About dying of hunger.

Paris, 1931

כראָניק

איך בין די נידערטרעכטיקסטע פֿון די לבֿנה-זינגער,
דער אומגייטיקסטער מענטש פֿון אונדזער צײַט,
און אַנדערש ס׳קאָן נישט זײַן,
כאָטש כ׳ווייס, ווי ס׳איז געמיין, און כ׳ווייס ווי ווײַט...

בײַ נאַכט — אַפֿילו אונטער אַ דרימלענדיקן מוח,
געדענק איך:
זעלבסטמאָרדן אין לאָדזש אויס נויט,
און ברויט,
געהיט פֿון באַיאָנעטן,
און אַלע וועגן פֿאַרשטעלט
מיט הונגער,
מיט פּאָליציי,
און מיט פּאָעטן.

און ווײַט אין ערגעץ שלאָגט מען די הינדוסן,
שנײַדט מען ייִדן אין סאַלאָניק,
אַזוי איז דאָס אין טאַנצנדיקן חלום
פֿון דער כראָניק.
און אין אַ נישע פֿון אַ וואַנט וווּנדערט זיך אַ בעטלער,
ס׳זעט קיינער נישט זײַן אויסגעשטרעקטע האַנט די שמאָלע,
פֿאַרבײַ אים שפּרינגען די צײַטונגס-קינדער, ליאַרעמען:
— קראַך פֿון פֿונט,
און בעסע פֿון דאָלאַר!
בײַם בעטלער לעם די פּיס איז שוואַרץ דער שניי,
בײַ די צײַטונגס-פֿאַרקויפֿער זײַנען בלוי די פֿינגער,
און אין הימל שטייט די גאָלדענע בעריכע
אויף שטראַלנדיקע שטערן צוויי.
כ׳געדענק דאָס אַלץ,
כ׳געדענק דאָס אַלץ,
די נידערטרעכטיקסטע פֿון די לבֿנה-זינגער.

1932

Chronicle[71]

I am the most contemptible of the moon-singers,
The most unnecessary person of our time,
And I can't be otherwise,
Although I know how it's base, and I know how far-gone . . .

At night, even beneath a dozing mind,
I remember:
In Lodz, suicides of want,
And bread guarded by bayonets,
And all roads blocked
With hunger,
With police,
And with poets.

And somewhere faraway they're beating Hindus,
Stabbing Jews in Salonika,
That's how it is in the dancing dream
Of the chronicle.
And in a niche of the wall a beggar marvels.
No one sees his scrawny, outstretched hand.
Newsboys leap past him, ranting:
—The pound's crashed,
The dollar rises!
Near the beggar's feet, the snow is black,
The fingers of the newspaper-vendors are blue,
And in the sky stands the Golden Bear
On two radiant stars.
I remember all this,
I remember all this,
The most contemptible of the moon-singers.

1932

מײַן פֿאַפּירענע בריק

דוד בערגעלסאָנען

הײַנט איז איבערגעגאַנגען מײַן פּאַפּירענע בריק
(אָט די, וואָס איך גיי איבער איר צו מײַן גליק)
אַ זעכציק-יעריקע פֿרוי (שוין זעכציק געוויס),
מיט דערפֿראָרענע, באָרוועסע פֿיס.

מיר האָבן געטראָפֿן זיך, אַ ווײַלע געבליבן דאָרט שטיין.
איך גלאַט אַזוי, ווײַל איך האָב נישט געהאַט וווּ צו גיין,
און זי האָט גערעדט, ווי צו מיר און צו זיך,
וועגן ברויט, וועגן האָלץ, וועגן שיך.

מײַן פּאַפּירענע בריק, איך האָב זי געבויט,
ווען נישט נאָר דער הימל — מײַן אויג האָט געבלויט,
און די זון איז געווען אַ גאָלדענע ראָד
און איר אײנציקער וועג צו די פֿיס מײַנע גראָד.

האָב איך פֿאַרטראַכט זיך אַ שטוב און אַ בעט
און גאָלדענע טעג, און צעשטערנטע נעכט,
האָב איך פֿאַרטראַכט זיך אַ מאַן און אַ קרוין,
און פֿרילינגען גרין, און זומערן ברוין.

האָב איך פֿאַרטראַכט זיך אַ וועג און אַ בריוו,
און אַ כוואַליקן ים, און אַ ליכטיקע שיף.
האָב איך פֿאַרטראַכט דאָס געזאַנג פֿון די באַנען,
און בלויע מאַטראָסן, ווער ווייסט זיי פֿון וואַנען.

נאָר כ׳האָב נישט פֿאַרטראַכט די שיך פֿאַר דער זעכציק-יעריקער פֿרוי, —
זײַנען מיר הײַנט דאָ געשטאַנען, געשמועסט אַזוי,
זי וועגן שיך, אַז עס פֿרירט איר די ביין,
און איך גלאַט אַזוי, ווײַל איך האָב נישט געהאַט וווּ צו גיין.

1930

My Paper Bridge[72]

For David Bergelson

Today she walked across my paper bridge
(The very one I cross to happiness)
A sixty-year-old woman, surely sixty,
With freezing-cold, bare feet.

We met each other, stayed there for a while.
I, simply because I had nowhere to go.
And she spoke, as if to me and to herself,
About bread, about wood, about shoes.

That paper bridge of mine, I built it when
Not only the sky but also my eyes turned blue,
And the sun was a golden wheel on its own path
That led to my feet straight and true.

I contemplated a household and a bed,
And golden days and nights bursting with stars,
I contemplated a husband and a child,
And green springs and brown summers.

I contemplated a letter and a road,
A wave-filled sea and a ship of radiant light.
I contemplated the singsong of a train
And sailors from wherever, blue as night.

But I didn't conceive of shoes for this sixty-year-old woman.[73]
And today we stood here, chatting away, just so,
She about shoes, while her bones were freezing,
And I, simply because I had nowhere to go.

1930

אויטאָפּאָרטרעט

איך בין אַ פֿרוי
און שמייכל אָפּט, ווי די לבֿנה,
סתּם אַזוי.
גייט אַלץ מיט אַלעמען פֿאַר מײַן באַטראַכט,
ווען אויגן מײַנע זײַנען אָפֿן,
נאָך מער,
ווען ז'זײַנען צוגעמאַכט.
און מײַנע הענט זײַנען שוין געווינט
בלייך געקרייצט צו זײַן איבער מײַן קאָפּ.
עס איז אין מײַנע הענט דער ווייטיק שטענדיק דאָ,
כאָטש אָן דעם טשוואָק.
און מײַנע ליפּן זײַנען נישט געפֿאַרבט,
נאָר רויט,
ווײַל ס'איז מײַן פּנים הייס,
און אָפּט און אָפֿטער אויסגעקרימט,
מסתּם פֿאַר זינד.
פֿאַרגלוסט זיך מיר אַ מאָל בײַ נאַכט
אַ ווונק טון צו מײַן גורל אויף אַ שפּאַס,
קומט אַ פֿינצטערקייט,
פֿאַרנייגט זיך ביזן פּאַס,
שמייכל איך צו פֿינצטערקייט
ביז שפּעטער נאַכט.

1928

Self-Portrait

I am a woman
And smile often, like the moon,
For no reason.
The whole world parades before me
When my eyes are open,
Even more
When they are shut.
And my hands, ever pale,
Are accustomed to being crossed above my head.
Pain is always in my hands,
Although without the nail.
And my lips are not painted,
But red
Because my face is hot,
And more and more often twisted,
As likely in sin as not.
Sometimes I get a hankering at night
To wink just for fun at my fate.
Then comes a darkness
Bowing deeply at the waist,
And I smile at the darkness
Late into the night.

1928

אַ בריוו

שרײַב בריוו צו מיר אַזוינע לאַנגע, לאַנגע,
ביז דער שטח צווישן אונדז וועט ווערן אַזוי ווײַט,
אַז דיר וועט מער נישט קאָנען באַנג טון,
ווי איך זע אויס פֿאַר גאָט און קעגן לײַט.

און זאָג, צי איז דאָס נישט אַ שטילער פֿרידלעכער שגעון
מיט זיך אַליין צו שמועסן אַ שעה און צוויי און דרײַ,
און אויפֿן קול, דער גרויער ווײַטקייט צו פֿאַרטרויען,
אַז מיר איז דאָס אַלץ איינס: געטרײַ, צי אומגעטרײַ.

אַז איך פֿאַרגעס אַ מאָל מײַן שטאָט און נאָמען,
און ווי אַ בוים אַ נאַקעטער בלײַב שטיין פֿאַר גאָט,
און ווי אַ בלאַט אַ דאָרשטיקן הייב אויף מײַן פּנים,
צו זון, צו ווינט און צו גענאָד.

און זאָג, צי איז דאָס נישט אַ שטילער, פֿרידלעכער שגעון:
אין טאָג אין זוניקסטן געדענק איך פֿון דעם תּהום,
וואָס וואַרט געדולדיק אויף מײַן קומען,
אַפֿילו אין דער זוניקסטער, אין צוועלפֿאַזייגערדיקער שעה.

1928

A Letter

Write such long, long letters to me,
Make the distance between us so great
That the way I appear, for, God, against people,
Will not cause you more regret.

And say if it's no harmless quirk, quiet whim
To chat with myself for two hours, or three,
And right out loud, to trust the gray distance,
Since faithful or false, it's all one to me.

I sometimes forget my city, my name.
I stand before God, a stripped tree, my face
Uplifted like a thirsty leaf
To sun, to wind, and to grace.

And say if it's no harmless quirk, quiet whim:
On the sunniest day, I recall the abyss
Patiently waiting for me to come,
Even at the sunniest noontime, like this.

1928

בײַם שפּיגל

I

אָט שטיי איך בײַם שפּיגל און האַלט אַלץ אין בעטן,
די האָר מײַנע לאָז נאָך מיר איבער,
און זאָל נאָך זײַ עמעצער גלעטן.
און ס׳געשעט בײַ מײַן שפּיגל אַ נס,
אָט שטיי איך, ווי אַ ווײַסינקע צווײַגעלע בעז,
כ׳דערקען מײַנע קינדערשע שיך
און די ווײַסקייט פֿון קלייד,
נאָר כ׳דערקען נישט מײַן קינדערשע פֿרייד.

At the Mirror

I

I stand at the mirror in constant prayer,
Dear God, let my hair remain
And let someone stroke it again.
At my mirror, a miracle occurs.
I stand here like a white lilac twig,
And I recognize my childhood shoes
And the whiteness of my dress,
But I don't recognize my childhood bliss.

II

גאָט,
כ׳האָב קאַרשן אין קינדערשער לוסט געגנבֿעט פֿון שכנישן סאָד,
און געוויינט מיטן פּנים אין היי,
דערנאָך אַ טאָג דרײַ אָדער צוויי.
ווי קאָן דאָס געשען, אַז בײַ דיר, אין דײַן זוניקן רײַף,
זאָל מען ווערן אַזוי-אָ ווי איצט, אַזוי העפּלעך און טרייף.

און מיט באָרוועסע פֿיס
איז געווען אַזוי גוט, אַזוי זיס,
שוואָמען צו קלײַבן אין וואַלד, אָדער נאָדלען פֿון כוואָיע,
ווי אַ קליינינקע גויע,
און הערן, ווי ס׳רעדט אין טשעראָט
אַ זשאַבע מיט גאָט.
זיך לײַגן און שווײַגן
און ציילן אויף קינדערשע פֿינגער די צווײַגן.

איך קאָן דיך גאָר איצט נישט דערקענען
אין שפּיגל מײַן אייגענעם פּנים,
ס׳זײַנען נישט מײַנע אויגן,
וואָס האָבן די גרינקייט פֿון זומער געזויגן,
ווען איך בין דורך גערטנער צום טײַכל געלאָפֿן זיך באָדן,
און געקריגן מיט ריטער פֿאַר טרעטן די בייטן און שאָדן.
ווי קאָן דאָס געשען, אַז בײַ דיר אין דײַן זוניקן רײַף,
זאָל מען ווערן אַזוי-אָ ווי איצט, אַזוי העפּלעך און טרייף!

II

God,
I stole cherries from the neighbors' orchard with girlish glee,
And wept with my face in the hay
Afterwards for two or three days.
How can it be, that with you, sun-ripe and mature,
One becomes now so overly civil, impure?[74]

And it was so good, so sweet
With bare feet
To gather forest mushrooms or needles of evergreen,
Like a tiny colleen,[75]
And to hear in the reeds
How a frog talks with God.
To keep still and to sprawl,
And to count branches on fingers so small.

Even now I cannot recognize
My very own face in the mirror,
Those eyes in there are not my eyes
That sucked the green from the summer
When I ran through the gardens down to the brook for a
swim,
And got a lashing with rods for trampling beds, doing harm.
How can it be, that with you, sun-ripe and mature,
One becomes now so overly civil, impure?

איז מײַן שטוב דען אַ שיף

איז מײַן שטוב דען אַ שיף,
וואָס עס וויגט מיך אַזוי אין מײַן בעט,
פּונקט ווי ס׳גאַנצענע הויז
וואָלט אויף כוואַליעס געשטאַנען געבעט.

און כאָטש קיינער אין שטוב איז נישטאָ,
איז מײַן שטוב אַזוי פֿול מיט גערויש,
און כאָטש טירן און פֿענצטער פֿאַרמאַכט,
איז עס אָפֿן דורכויס און דורכויס.

און איך כאָטש אין העמד און אין קלייד,
בין איך נאַקעט אין גאַנצן און גאָר,
און מײַן האַרץ איז בײַ גאָט
נאָר אַן אימה צעוויגט מײַנע האָר.

1929

My Room, Then, Is a Ship

My room, then, is a ship, because
It rocks me in my bed,
Exactly as if the whole house
Stood praying on the waves.

And though no one is in the room,
My room is full of noise.
And though the windows and doors are closed,
It's open through and through.

And I, though wearing skirt and blouse,
Am nude from head to toe,
And though my heart is with my God,
A terror sways my hair.

1929

איך האָב קיין אײנציקע נאָך נישט קיין גרויע האָר

איך האָב קיין אײנציקע נאָך נישט קיין גרויע האָר,
נאָר שוין בין איך ווי יעדערער געגוג געמיין,
וויגן זיך די אַקסלען מײַנע, ווי פֿון ווינט געשלאָגן,
ווען כ'זיך סתּם אַזוי בײַ נאַכט און וויין.

עס זײַנען נאָך די פֿיס מײַנע, ווי פֿעסטע שטאַמען,
און די הענט, ווי בייגעוודיקע צווײַגן,
טאָ פֿאַר וואָס ווילן אָפּט אַזוי אַראָפּזינקען די ברעמען,
און די ליפּן ווילן מער און מער אַלץ שווײַגן?

און שווער איז גלייבן, אַז איך בין שוין נאָך די דרײַסיק, —
פֿון אונדזער דור דער סאַמע, סאַמע מיטן,
אַז ס'וועלן ייִנגערע, ווי מחנות שוועלבעלעך, אַ הייב טאָן זיך, מיך מײַדן
ווי איך די זיידעס האָב געמיטן.

1928

I Still Don't Have a Gray Hair, Not a One

I still don't have a gray hair, not a one,
But I'm commonplace enough, like everyone,
My shoulders sway and rock as if wind-beaten
At night when I sit crying for no reason.

My legs still are like the firm trunks of trees,
And my arms, like branches bending in the breeze,
Then why do my brows frequently sink down,
And my lips purse in silence with a frown?

I'm over thirty—a thought of consternation,—
The very middle of our generation,
Like flocks of swallows they'll rise up—the young—
To shun me like the grandfathers I've shunned.

1928

יאַנואַר

ס'איז יאַנואַר.
(העט ווײַט הינטער די שנייען חלומט זיך מיר פֿייגלמילך און רויטער מאָן)
און כ'גיי אין פּאָר
מיט דער לבֿנה,
מיט דער נאַכט,
און מיטן שניי,
וואָס מאַכט מיר ווײַס מײַן טראַכטן.
אויף דינעם שטענגל
גייט אויף דער רויך פֿון מײַן ציגאַר,
בלײַבט הענגען פֿאַר מײַן אויג,
ווי אַ פֿאַרזאַמטער פֿויגל.
ס'איז יאַנואַר.
מײַן גרינער בערעט העלט, ווי פֿרישע בלעטער.
כ'געדענק:
ס'איז שפּעט אין ווינטער,
און ס'איז שפּעט אין נאַכט,
און פֿון די פֿיס מײַנע די שאָטנס אויפֿן שניי,
ווי שווערע ווײַזערס שלעפּן זיך,
און צייכענען: ס'איז שפּעטער נאָך,
נאָך שפּעטער.
ס'איז יאַנואַר.
(העט ווײַט הינטער די שנייען חלומט זיך מיר פֿייגלמילך און רויטער מאָן).
1932

January

It's January.
(I dream of starflowers and red poppies far beneath the snow.)
And I walk arm-in-arm
With the moon,
With the night,
And with the snow
That turns my thoughts white.[76]
On thin stems
The smoke of my cigar rises
And hangs before my eyes
Like a lingering bird.
It's January.
My green beret brightens like fresh leaves.
I remember:
It's late in winter,
And it's late at night,
And the shadows of my legs on the snow
Drag like heavy clock hands
And indicate: it's even later,
Even later.
It's January.
(I dream of starflowers and red poppies far beneath the snow.)

1932

האַלאָ, מײַן האַרץ!

האַלאָ, מײַן האַרץ!
גענוג געדרייט די קאַטערינקע!
עס פֿאַלן מײַנע לידער טויב און שווער,
ווי זילבערשטיק פֿון איינעם פֿון יענע לײַט,
וואָס ווײַנענדיק אין הויפֿן רויטן גאָלד,
האָט מען פֿאַרקויפֿט דעם גאָט,
אָדער אַ פֿרײַנד.
האַלאָ, מײַן האַרץ!
פֿאַר וועלכן טײַוול האָסטו מיך פֿאַרקויפֿט,
וואָס פֿון שטוב מײַנער איז אַנטלאָפֿן שוין די לעצטע מויז?
אַזוי איז אימהדיק בײַ מיר:
אָן גאָט,
אָן ברויט.
נאָר ס'לעשט זיך נאָך אין מיר אַ לעצטע בענקעניש,
ווי אין אַ יולי-נאַכט אַ לעצטער שטערן,
וואָס וויל פֿון הימל נישט אַראָפּ,
ביז גרויסן טאָגן.
כאָטש ס'זײַנען מײַנע אויגן זאַט פֿון ביטערניש,
און יעדער טראָט,
געשריי,
און בליק,
אַפֿילו דער צאַרטער בינענווינט, וואָס פֿאַר מײַן פֿענצטער פֿליט,
וואַרפֿט אין מײַן שויב
די מעשׂה פֿון דעם וואָלף און ציג,
אָט יענע מעשׂה פֿון דעם וואָלף און ציג.
האַלאָ, מײַן האַרץ,
עס כריפּעט די קאַטערינקע!

1932

Hello, My Heart!

Hello, my heart!
Enough barrel-organ grinding!
My poems fall deaf and heavy
Like silver-coins from one of those folks
Crying in a heap of red gold, who
Sold their god
Or a friend.[77]
Hello, my heart!
Which devil did you sell me to,
To make the mice run out of my house?
I dwell in such dread:
Without God,
Without bread.
But one last longing still flickers out,
Like the last star in a July night
That does not want to fall from the sky
Until the great dawning.
Although my eyes are sated with bitterness,
And every step,
Every shout,
Every gaze,
Even the gentle bee-wind flying before my window
Throws into my pane
The tale about the wolf and the kid,
That same tale about the wolf and the kid.
Hello, my heart,
The barrel organ rasps!

1932

אין גרינעם בוים ליגט גרויער אַש

פֿאָרסט אַוועק — דערקען איך נישט קיין גאַס,
און אויב כ'דערקען זיי יאָ — זײַנען זיי מיר פֿרעמד.
די ערשטע שורה קאָן מען גראַמען מיט מאָנפּאַרנאַס,
די צווייטע — מיט אַ העמד,
נאָר כ'וויל קיין גראַמען ניט,
עס איז מיר אומעטיק, וואָס דו האָסט מיך נישט ליב.
פּונקט ווי די ליכטיקייט וואָלט הײַנט אויף לאַנג, אויף לאַנג פֿאַרגאַנגען.
פּונקט ווי אַ פֿעלד וואָלט אויפֿגעהערט צו רוישן מיט די זאַנגען.
נאָר כ'וויל קיין פֿאַרגלײַכן ניט,
עס איז מיר אומעטיק, וואָס דו האָסט מיך נישט ליב.

In the Green Tree Lies Gray Ash (Selections)

You leave. I can't recall the streets, alas,
And those I recognize are strange, inert.
The first line can be rhymed with Montparnasse,
The second, with a shirt.
But I don't want to rhyme—
For you don't love me. I'm sad all the time,
As if the sun had set for years and years today,
As if a field ceased rustling its cornstalks and hay.
But I don't want a simile,
I'm sad because you don't love me.[78]

איך שרײַב דיר נישט קיין ליבעבריוו,
נאָר אין דער טיף
ווײַנט מײַן האַרץ צו דיר.
ווײַנט מײַן האַרץ צו דיר אַצינד,
ווי ס'פּלעגט זיך בעטן צו דער מאַמען,
ווען כ'בין געווען אַ קינד.
אונטער דער מאַמעס אויג
בין איך געוואָקסן הייס, און ברוין, און שטאַרק
איצט זײַנען קרעלן דײַנע,
ווי אַ שניט אַ רויטער אויף מײַן קאַרק.
אונטער דער מאַמעס זון
בין איך אַ ביימל מאַלינעס געווען,
רויט אָנגעגאָסן מיט שטראַלנדיקער פֿרייד,
איצט בין איך אַ ווינטערדיקער בוים,
צו בייזע ווינטן גרייט.
איך שרײַב דיר נישט קיין ליבעבריוו,
נאָר אין דער טיף
ווײַנט מײַן האַרץ צו דיר.

I'm writing you no love letters,
But deep inside
My heart cries out to you.
My heart cries to you now,
As it used to plead with my mother
When I was a girl.
Beneath my mother's eye
I grew strong and brown and hot.
Now your beads are
Like a scarlet slash on my throat.
Beneath my mother's sun
I was a raspberry sapling,
Streaming red with lustrous joy,
Now I am a wintry tree,
Ready for vicious winds.
I'm writing you no love letters,
But deep inside
My heart cries out to you.

בײַ אַ הינקלדיקן טישל אונדזער ראַנדעװו,
איך די ערשטע בין געקומען,
און נישט דו,
(יאָ צי ניט,
אַזוי קומט אין אַ ליד).
האָט דאָס טישל זיך אַ װיג געטון,
דיך באַגעגענען, אַװעק אין ליכטיקן גאַלאָפּ,
און איבער מיר האָבן זיך בײַטשלעך גאָלדענע צעפּאָכט,
ביז אין בלױען רױך ביסט שטײן געבליבן נעבן מיר.
האָט דער גאַלאָפּ אַ זעץ געטון זיך אױף אַלע פּיר,
און מיט טלאָען זילבערנע אָפּגעטופּעט אין מײַן בלוט:
טופּ-טופּ,
טופּ-טופּ.
גוט, װאָס ביסט געקומען,
גוט.
(יאָ צי ניט,
אַזוי קומט אין אַ ליד).

At a limping table, our rendez-vous—
I was the first to come,
Not you
(Yes or no,
That's how poems go).
The table gave a wobble
And took off to meet you at a gallop.
Above me, golden whiplets fanned the air,
Until, wrapped in blue smoke, you stood near.
At once the gallop set down on all fours
And with silver hooves tapped out in my blood:
Tup-tup,
Tup-tup.
Good, that you came,
Good.
(Yes or no,
That's how poems go.)

צווישן מיר מיט דיר איז מער נישטאָ קיין רייד,
און שטילקייט האָט זיך אויסגעשפּרייט
און פֿאַרטײַעט זיך אונטער די טריט פֿון פֿיס.
כ'וואָלט עפּעס זאָגן נאָך געוואָלט פֿאַר איידלקייט.
און האָב נישט וואָס.
הייב איך אויף מײַן פּנים,
עס איז מײַן שמייכל, ווי אַ דינע אָנגעצונדענע ליכט,
און כ'ווייס נישט, ווען וויל איך צולויכטן
אין פֿינצטערער פֿאַרשוויגנקייט,
זיך אַליין,
צי דיר.
אויף אונדזער טיש איז עפּל דאָ און ברויט,
און אַלץ וואָס זומערדיקע שפּע ט'פֿאַר אונדז צוגעגרייט.
גאָר ווי די בלעטער, וואָס האָבן אָנגעדאַרט,
זײַנען אונדזערע רייד.

Between you and me there is no more to say,
And silence spreads across our way
And entangles itself in our footsteps.
Out of courtesy, I would like to say something,
And I have nothing.
So I raise my face.
My smile is like a candle gleaming thinly,
And I don't know whom I'll light up
In the dark taciturnity,
Myself
Or you.
On our table there are apples and bread
And everything prepared for us by summer's prosperity.
But like the withering leaves
Are our words.

ירמיהו

א

וועו דאָס האַרץ מיט אַ שווערקייט ווערט פֿול,
אַז ס׳קאָנען די פֿיס מער דעם גוף נישט פֿאַרטראָגן,
און ס׳ווילט זיך מיר פֿאַלן אויף פֿיר
און זיך הינטיש צעוויען,
ווי אַ חיה נישט וויסן פֿאַר וואָס
און פֿאַר וועמען —
איז דעמאָלט, ווי מילך אויף די ליפּן,
קומען עטלעכע נעמען:
דער ערשטער איז זיס — ירמיהו.
זײַן גוף ווי אַ בוים אַ פֿאַרברענטער פֿון דונער
איז שוואַרץ און פֿאַרוואָגלט,
מיט ליפּן, וואָס האָבן קיין זון נישט געטרונקען,
נאָר ביטערן וואַסער.
זײַנע הענט — לענג-אויס מיטן ווינט זיך צעעפֿנט,
אויף אייביקן פֿרעגן,
ווי צווײַגן, וואָס דאַרפֿן צעבלײַען
און וואַרטן אויף רעגן.

Jeremiah

I

When my heart grows so full of heaviness
That my legs can't hold my body any more,
I want to fall onto my hands and knees,
Howling windily, down on all fours
Like an animal that knows not why
Or for whom—
It's then, like milk upon the lips,
That several names come:
The first one is sweet—Jeremiah.
His body, like a tree burned through by thunder,
Is blackened and wasted,
With lips that have not drunk any sun
But bitter water.
His arms—opened their full length with the wind
In eternal asking, a refrain,
Like branches needing to blossom
That wait for rain.[79]

ב

עס שרעקט, ירמיהו, דײַן קאָפּ ווי אַ וואָלקן,
דײַנע הענט איבער אים,
ווי צוויי ווײַסע לבֿנות.
אויפֿן נאַקן דער יאָך האָט געגראָבן אַ ליג-אָרט,
אַזוי טיף ווי אַ מולטער,
און דער ווײ ביזן האַרצן.
דײַנע פֿיס, ווי די פֿיס פֿון אַ קעמל,
וואָס האָפּט נישט צו וואַרפֿן די משׂא
און גרויס איז דער מידבר,
און ווײַט איז דאָס וואַסער —
אַזוי דײַנע פֿיס, ירמיהו.
און געגרייטע פֿאַר דיר
דאָס אַש
מיטן זאַק,
און דער גוף, ווי אַ בוים
וואָס וואַרט אויפֿן האַק.

II

Jeremiah, your head frightens like a cloud,
Your hands over it
Like two white moons,
On your neck the yoke has dug a lying-place
As deep as a trough,[80]
And pain all the way into your heart.
Your legs, like the legs of a camel
With no hope of throwing its burden
And the desert is huge,
And water is far—
These are your legs, Jeremiah.
And the ashes
Are ready for you
And the sacks,
And the body like a tree
Awaiting the ax.

ג

בײַ נאַכט פֿאַרמאַכט זײַנען די טירן,
נאָר די הערצער אָפֿענע זײַנען פֿאַר בשׂורות גרייט.
טראָגט אויף ליפּן ביטערע דער נבֿיא
דעם טאָג פֿון טויט.
שלאָפֿט דער קייסער אויף אַ ווײַסער העלפֿאַנט־ביינערנער בעט,
איז די לבֿנה, ווי אַ זילבערנער פּעכער איבער דער שטאָט,
שטעלט זיך ירמיהו בײַ דעם קייסערס טיר
ווערט זי, ווי אַ ווײַסער, טויטער קאָפּ.
וועקט דער קייסער זיך און ס׳ווערן בײַ אים שאַרף און בלאַנק די ציין.
שטייט ירמיהו אײַנגעוואָקסן בײַ זײַן בעט.
וויל דער קייסער נעמען אין האַנט די שפּיז,
זעט ער — זײַן האַנט איז טויט.

III

At night, the doors are closed,
But hearts are open, ready for news.
On bitter lips the prophet brings
The day of doom.
The moon above the city is like a silver fan.
The emperor sleeps on a white, ivory bed.
When Jeremiah stands at the emperor's door,
The moon becomes a white death's-head.
The emperor awakens. His teeth are sharp. They gleam.
Jeremiah stands transfixed, next to his bed.
When the emperor wants to take his lance in hand,
He sees—his hand is dead.

ד

איבער מערק ירמיהו רעדט מיט זײַן מרה-שחורה.
טאַנצט דער מאַרק אין זײַן רונדקייט,
אין אַ פֿריילעכער מהומה.
זײַנען הײַזער צעשראָקן, ווי רינדער פֿאַר שחיטה,
און מײַלער ווי היילן,
און צינגער, ווי גלעקער פֿון טומאה.
צימבלען פֿריילעך מטבעות
אויף סוחרישע הענט,
נאָר עס ליגט מרה-שחורה,
ווי בלויע סיניאַקעס,
אונטער בעטלערשער העמד.
קאָכן ווײַבער דאָס פֿעטס פֿון די רינדער
אין טעפּ אויפֿן פֿריילעכן פֿײַער,
נאָר אַ פֿינצטערקייט הענגט איבער טירן
און אין שפּאַלטן פֿון הײַזער.
איבער מערק ירמיהו רעדט מיט זײַן מרה-שחורה,
שטיקן זיך ווערטער אין שטומקייט,
ווי מען שרײַט אין אַ חלום.
ווי שיכּורע מײַלער צעקרימט זײַנען טירן פֿון הויפּט-שטאָט —
בן-עזור זאָגט נבֿואה:
אָ פֿרידן אײַך, פֿרידן,
די זון קומט און גאולה.

IV

Above the markets Jeremiah speaks with melancholy.[81]
The market dances in its roundness,
In a joyous riot.[82]
Panicking, the houses seem like cows before the slaughter,
And mouths like caves,
And tongues like sullied bells.[83]
Joyous coins are jingling
In the hands of merchants,[84]
But melancholy is lingering,
Livid as blue bruises[85]
Underneath the paltry shirt of a beggar.
Women cook the rendered fat of cattle
In pots upon the joyous fire,
But a darkness hangs above the doorways,
And in the cracks and crevices of houses.
Above the markets Jeremiah speaks with melancholy.
Words suffocate in muteness,
Like shouting in a dream.
Like drunken mouths, the doors of the capital are smirking—
Ben Azzur recites prophecy:[86]
O, peace unto you, peace,
The sun is coming and redemption.[87]

ה

שעלט ירמיהו זײַן טאָג אָט אַזוי:
חנינה בן-עזור אין קלייד פֿון ווײַסן זײַד.
אַז ווײַסקייט איז אַלץ איינס, ווער ס'טוט עס אָן,
און זײַד איז גלאַטער אויף אַ פֿעטן לײַב.
און טרייסט איז זיסער,
און ביטער איז געשריי פֿון פּײַן,
נאָר ס'ענטפֿערט דער ווידערקול אויף אַלע ווערטער גלײַך.
חנינה בן-עזור אין קלייד פֿון ווײַסן זײַד.
און ס'וואַרטן גריבער אויף העלקייט פֿון מײַן לײַב,
און ס'וואַרט געפּענגעניש אויף אומרו פֿון מײַן האַרץ,
און ס'האָט אַ שטאָט אַ לייב פֿאַרטריבן
און געבליבן איז בײַ הינט.
ענתות — איז מײַן שטאָט.
און אַלע טירן זײַנען ענג פֿאַר מיר פֿאַרקריצט,
און אַלע גרענעצן ווי זעגן זיך פֿאַרשאַרפֿט,
מיט צייַנער אָנגעשפּיצט זיך צו מײַן קאָפּ.
חנינה בן-עזור אין קלייד פֿון ווײַסן זײַד.

V

This is how Jeremiah curses his day:
Hananiah ben Azzur in clothes of white silk,
Since white is the same, no matter who wears it,
And silk is much smoother upon a fat body.
Though comfort is sweeter,
And the shout of pain, bitter,
An echo answers all words alike.
Hananiah ben Azzur in clothes of white silk.
Graves are awaiting my own body's brightness,
And capture awaits my own heart's disquiet,
A city has exiled a lion
And is left with dogs.
Anathoth—is my city.[88]
And all doors are gritted narrow before me,
And all borders sharpened like saws,
With teeth pointed toward my head.
Hananiah ben Azzur in clothes of white silk.

אַ ליד צו מײַן קליידערשאַנק

עס הוידען זיך די שאָטנס אויף די ווענט,
און דורכן פֿענצטער קומט אַ גרויע שײַן.
ס'איז נאַכט. איך ליג און טראַכט אַרײַן
וועגן מײַן ברוינער קאַצאַווייקע.

זאָל איך מאַכן דערפֿון אַ קלייד,
וועט זי שמאָל זײַן און וועט זײַן קורץ,
פֿונדעסטוועגן — — —
אַ קלייד איז פֿאָרט אַ שטיקל גוטס.

ליג איך אַזוי אין דבֿקות,
און טראַכט וועגן מײַן ברוינער קאַצאַווייקע.

גיט דערווײַל די בעט אַ רוק זיך און אַ פֿאָר.
און ס'קריפּעט ווי אַן אַלטער שׂונא: נאַר,
אַ קליידל מער, אַ קליידל ווייניקער,
דער עיקר זײַנען גאָר די האָר.

און די אַלטע קאַץ מיאַוקעט מיט אַ ברייטער קעל:
— איך בײַט אויך אַ מאָל די לאַטעס אויף דער פֿעל,
זײַ שוין נישט אַזאַ-אָ קאַרגער דרייקאָפּ
און זאָג אַ גוטן טאָג דער ברוינער קאַצאַווייקע.

ליג איך אַזוי אין דבֿקות
און טראַכט אַרײַן וועגן מײַן ברוינער קאַצאַווייקע.

A Poem to My Clothes Closet

The shadows see-saw on the walls,
And through the window comes gray light.
I lie and cogitate all night
About my brown quilt-peasant-jacket.[89]

If I should make a dress from it,
It will be short, with a tight fit,
Nevertheless—
It's still worth something, such a dress.

Then I lie in devout, ecstatic guilt
And think about my jacket of brown quilt.[90]

Meanwhile the bed gives a push and a pull,
And creaks like an old enemy: Fool,
A dress more, a dress less,
The main thing is, your hair's a mess.

And the old cat meows with a wide-opened throat:
—Sometimes I, too, change the patches on my coat,
So don't be such a stingy flibbertigibbet,
And bid farewell to your brown peasant jacket.

Then I lie in devout, ecstatic guilt
And think about my jacket of brown quilt.

שלמינקע דער שמיד

כ'האָב די ווערטער דײַנע, שלמינקע שמיד,
אַזוי געהיט, אַזוי געהיט,
פּונקט ווי מײַנע הילצערנע ליאַלקעס.

און אַזוי טײַער איז געווען מיר יעדעס וואָרט
ווי איצט דער אָנדענק פֿון דײַן וויסטער באָרד,
און ווי דעמאָלט מײַנע הילצערנע ליאַלקעס.

אַ שוימיקער איז דײַן פּעגאַז געווען, שלמינקע שמיד,
דו פֿלעגסט אַ פֿלי טאָן אַזש ביז וולאָדעווער יאַריד,
און צוריק נישט מיטן גלײַכן וועג.

נאָר אין אַ גרוב פֿלעגט זיך אַרײַנדרייען אַ ראָד,
און לעבן וואָגן, לעבעדיקער גאָט,
שטייט אַ ציג.

און דער וואָגן איז פּלוצלינג אַזוי שווער
און דער וועג צעלויפֿט זיך, ווי אַן אָפֿענע שער
און מען ווייס נישט ווו דער טראַקט.

בײַ דײַן שוימיקן פּעגאַז, שלמינקע שמיד,
האָט די ציג געדאַוונט, ווי אַ גוטער ייִד,
(נישט דאָ געדאַכט).

און פּלוצלינג ליגן רודעס געלט,
און ליכטיק ווערט אין פֿעלד,
נאָר נישט ווי פֿון גאָטס זון.

זעט מען שוין: מען איז פֿאַרקראָכן אויף אַן אָרט,
זוכט מען גאָטס וואָרט,
איז דער זכּרון, ווי אַ שטיין.

Shloyminke the Blacksmith[91]

Shloyminke Blacksmith, how I've hoarded
And kept all your words well-guarded,
Just like my wooden dolls.

So dear to me, your every word
As now the memory of your white beard,
As then, my wooden dolls.

Shloyminke Blacksmith, how your Pegasus frothed there,
When you'd fly off for the distant Vlodev Fair,
Returning not by the direct road.

In a hole, one wheel would spin,
And, Living God!, right by the wagon
There would stand a goat.

And suddenly the wagon's heavy and, like shears
Opening, the road disappears
And the highway cannot be found.

Next to your frothing Pegasus, Shloyminke, there,
Like a good Jew, the goat sways in prayer,
(Heaven preserve us all around!)

And suddenly, right there, mounds of money lie,
And the field grows bright as the sky
But not as from God's sun.

See how it is: when stuck somewhere odd
And groping for the word of God,
Your memory is like a stone.

גיט מען פֿון די נײַנציקער אַ היפּשן זופּ אַזאַ,
ווערט ליכטיק דער זכּרון, מען דערמאָנט זיך: שמע,
איז די ציג געלם ווי אין דר'ערד.

דײַן שוימיקער פּעגאַז, שלמינקע שמיד,
אין מײַנע טרוקענע פֿערזן שטייט געשמידט
אויפֿן צוימל פֿון דײַן וואָרט.

און כ'האָב צו זיך אַליין פּרעטענזיע —
וואָס דאַרף איך הערן M — — — סקעס בעקעמעקענע רעצענזיע,
אַז כ'האָב דײַן גאָלדענעם אוצר פֿאַר אַ שפּיגל זיך געמאַכט.

So, you take a gulp of ninety-proof and sigh, Ah!
Then memory brightens. You remember: *Shema,*
And the goat vanishes into the earth.

Shloyminke Blacksmith, how your frothing Pegasus
Stands forged in my withered verses
On the bridle of your word.

And I've been fooling myself, it's true—[92]
Why do I need to hear M—ske's bleating review,
When I've made a mirror of your golden treasure?

V

פּריידקע

וואַרשע, 1935, 1936

V

Freydke

(Freydke)

Warsaw, 1935, 1936

פֿון פֿריידקע: אַ פּאָעמע

I

פֿריידקע

פֿריידקע מײַן העלדין,
מיט געשוירענעם קאָפּ און מיט אײַליקע טריט.
זיי שיטן זיך אויס אויף דער גאַס
נישט געציילט,
נישט געהיט.
הונדערטער, טויזנט און טויזנטער טריט.

פֿריידקע מײַן העלדין,
זי וואָלט געקאָנט זײַן אַ געוואַגטער מאַטראָס,
און פֿירן אַ שיף,
און זײַן באַלעבאָס,
אַזאַ הילכיקע שטים האָט זי.

זי וואָלט געקאָנט האַלטן אין האַנט אַ לונעט
און זוכן אין הימל
אַ נײַעם פּלאַנעט.
אַזעלכע ליכטיקע אויגן האָט זי.

זי וואָלט געקאָנט זײַן אַ בויער אין לאַנד
און אויסמעסטן פֿעלדער
און שיטן אַ פּלאַנט.
אַזעלכע שטאַרקע הענט האָט זי.

זי האַנדלט מיט אייער,
פֿרידקע מײַן העלדין,
איך זע אירע טעג, אירע שעהען,
איך קען אירע פּעקלעך,
פֿאַרקניפּטע מיט שטריק

From Freydke: A Long Poem

I

Freydke[93]

Freydke, my heroine,
With her shorn head and her hurrying gait.
Hundreds of thousands and thousands of steps,
Uncounted,
Uncautious,
Spilling onto the street.

Freydke, my heroine,
She could have been a daring sailor,
And steered a ship,
And been master,
She had such a resounding voice.

She could have held a telescope in her hands[94]
And in the heavens sought out
A new planet.
She had such luminous eyes.

She could have been a builder on the land
Surveying the fields
And laying down a railroad.
She had such powerful hands.

She dealt in eggs,
Freydke, my heroine.
I see her days, her hours,
I know her bundles,
Knotted with string

און פֿאַרטיק צום וואַנדער,
אין לײַוונט אין געלן, אין גרינעם און בלויען.

ווען איר האָט נישט איין מאָל
פֿאַר טאָג בײַ מײַן פֿענצטער
אַ וואָלקן געהאָנגען,
אַ טונקעלע כמאַרע.
און לערמאָנטאָוו האָט מיר געשושקעט אין אויער:
אויפֿן מאַרק צווישן קיישלעך
זיצט דײַן טאַמאַרע.

ווען איר האָט מײַן זייגער געקלונגען:
ס'איז זעקס.
די גאַס גיט אַ רוף.
פֿריידקע, איר קויש אויף דער האַנט,
איר אַרבעט, איר ברויט, איר באַרוף.
די קופּערנע גראָשנס,
דאָס קופּערנע אומגליק,
איז ערגעץ באַהאַלטן.
זי יאָגט זיך נאָך זיי

איבער שטיין,
איבער שטאָק
ווי צעריסענע זעגלען,
פֿלאַטערן מידע
פֿון קליידל די פֿאַלדן.

ווען איר האָט נישט איין מאָל
פֿאַר טאָג בײַ מײַן פֿענצטער
דער רעגן געאומערט (אויף דעם איז ער אַ מײַסטער).
עס קענען נישט דעקן דעם דאַך און די קוילן
די קופּערנע גראָשנס בײַ פֿריידקען אין טײַסטער.

דער טײַסטער אָוואַ!
אָט דער ברודיקער טײַסטער,
וואָס גייט בירושה פֿון טאַטן צו קינדער,

And ready for her wandering,
In canvas, yellow and blue and green.

Regarding her, more than once
By my window at dawn,
There hung a cloud,
A dark thunderhead.
And Lermontov whispered in my ear:
Your Tamara sits in the market,
Among baskets.[95]

Regarding her, my clock chimed:
It's six.
The street calls out.
Freydke, basket on her arm,
Her work, her bread, her calling.
Copper pennies,
That copper misery,
Are hidden somewhere.
She chases after them

Over stones,
Up flights of stairs.
Like torn sails,
The folds of her skirt
Flutter wearily.

Regarding her, more times than one,
By my window at dawn,
The rain cast a gloom (it's champion of that).
The copper pennies in Freydke's purse
Cannot cover the roof and the coals.

The purse, oh, my!
That filthy purse,
A legacy passing from father to children,

וואָס קען נישט פֿאַרדעקן די לעכער אין דאַך
מיט הילצערנע שינדלען.

דער טײַסטער אָוואַ!
וואָס יאָמערט אין ערגעץ אַזוי ווי אַ האַרץ.
אין קעשענעס, ווײַבערשע, מאַנצבילשע, קאַלטע,
וואָס שענדט און ליגט, ווי אַ לאַסט,
ווי די לאַטע די געלע אין מיטל-אַלטער.

דער טײַסטער אָוואַ!
אָט די אָרעמע טאָרבע פֿון ייִדישן מאַרק,
אין ציטעריקע, געלע שווינדזיכטיקע פֿינגער,
ס'זײַנען טאַטשקעס מיט ליים, ס'זײַנען הילצערנע קלעצער,
ס'זײַנען אײַזערנע שטאַבעס שוין טויזנט מאָל גרינגער,
שוין טויזנט מאָל גרינגער.

דער טײַסטער, אָוואַ!
די טאָרבע פֿון אומגליק,
די טאָרבע פֿון סם,
עס שטייען די בעבעכעס שטענדיק פֿאַרקניפּטע,
פֿאַרפֿאַקטע אויף לויפֿן לעבֿר-הים.

Can't cover over the holes in the roof
With wooden shingles.

The purse, oh, my!
Laments like a broken heart, somewhere or other.
In the pockets of women, of men, such cold pockets,
It disgraces and burdens
Like the medieval patches of yellow.

The purse, oh, my!
That self-same, poor sack of the Jewish market
In tremulous, yellow, tubercular fingers.
Wheelbarrows filled with clay, thick wooden logs,
Iron staffs are a thousand, a thousand times lighter.

The purse, oh, my!
Old sacks of misery,
Old sacks of poison,
So the raggedy bedding is always knotted,
Packed up for escaping across the ocean.[96]

II

די סטעליע נידעריק

די סטעליע נידעריק איבערן קאָפּ,
דאָס פֿענצטער קרום (ווי אין אַ טעאַטער-דעקאָראַציע),
רעמבראַנטס אַ בילד, (האָ-האָ).
געקויפֿט מסתּמא אויף אַ ליציטאַציע,
אַ קינדערבעטל מיט אַ הויבן שעניק,
אַ ביכער-פּאָליצע „טבֿיה דער מילכיקער" און „פּענעק",
אַ וואַסערקראַן.
אַ שענקל פֿאַרן ברויט און פֿאַר געפֿעס,
און פֿריידקע, די באַלעבאָסטע, געשוירן ווי אַ ייִנגל,
מיט ייִנגלערישן זשעסט.
— די הענט, דאָס זײַנען וועסלעס — זאָגט זי —
און דער קאָפּ דער רודער,
אַ שאָד, עס איז קיין שיף נישטאָ,
דער ים איז אָט די בודע.
און ייִנגלעריש שאַרט זי אַרויף די האָר מיט ביידע הענט,
איר דינער שאָטן
טוט אַ טאַנץ, אַ הוידע זיך, אַ פֿאַל
אויף בלויע נידעריקע ווענט,
צעברעכט זיך אויף דרײַ שטיגן,
עס וואַרט די סקריפּענדיקע טיר —
(די טיר זינגט אויס אַן אָפּגעהאַקטן ניגון,
אַ קורצן מאַרש, אַ זיפֿץ אַ שוואַכן,
בײַם עפֿענען און בײַם פֿאַרמאַכן.)
דערנאָך דער הויף מיט שפּיציקע און גרויע שטיינער,
דערנאָך דער טויער און די גאַס — — —
די גאַס — דער באָרוועסער דער ייִדישער יאַריד,
אָ, פֿינצטערניש —
איך קאָן פֿאַר איר קיין ווערטער נישט געפֿינען,
דער קויש — מיט אייער,
קנאָבל,
און ציטרינען,

II

The Low Ceiling

Overhead, the low ceiling,
The crooked window (as on a theater set),
One of Rembrant's pictures (ho-ho).
Probably bought at an auction,
A child's bed with a high hay mattress,
A bookshelf holding *Tevye the Dairyman* and *Penek*,[97]
A water faucet.
A closet for bread and dishes,
And Freydke, the housewife, shorn like a boy,
With her boyish gesture.
—My hands, these are oars—she says—
And my head the helm,
It's a shame there's no ship here,
This dog house is the sea.
And boyishly she rakes her hair with both hands,
Her thin shadow
Dances, swings, falls,
Breaks upon three flights of stairs,
The creaking door waits—
(The door sings out a chopped-up melody,
A short march, a weak sigh,
Opening, closing.)
Then the yard with pointy, gray stones,
Then the gate and the street—
The street—that barefoot, Jewish fair,
O, darkness—
I cannot find any words for her,
That basket—of eggs,
Garlic,
And lemons,

אָ, פֿינצטערניש, איך קען פֿאַר זיי קיין ווערטער נישט געפֿינען,
אין אַ פֿענצטער מאַטערט זיך אַ נײַמאַשין,
דאָס רעדל כריפּעט, שנאָלט.
אָ, פֿינצטערניש —
אַ נס... די זון אַ נס — — —
האָט אויסגעשאָטן דאָ אַ קויש מיט גאָלד.

O, darkness, I cannot find any words for them,
In a window a sewing machine labors,
The wheel rattles, fillips.
O, darkness—
A miracle . . . right here,—a miracle,
The sun has spilled a basket of gold.

IV

בײַ פשעניצאַן אין וואַרשטאַט

פֿאָרויס, פֿאָרויס — די יאָרן יאָגן זיך נאָך קײַלעכדיקער זון,
נאָך רויש פֿון רעגן, נאָך גערוך פֿון בלום.

פֿאָרויס — עס טרײַבט דאָס גרינע ראָד,
דער ווינט, וואָס גלעט, דער הונגער, וואָס באַדראָט.

דער טאָג, וואָס קומט מיט קאַלטער, דראָענדיקער קעל
אויף דאַך און וואַרעמקייט, אויף בעט און שוועל.

פֿאָרויס,פֿאָרויס מיט יונגע פֿיס,
מיט אַלטע, מיט רעוומאַטישע און מידע,
אין מאַרש נאָך זון, אין גאַנג נאָך ברויט, נאָך רעגן און נאָך ליבע.

פֿאָרויס.
ס'איז צוויי אַ האַלבע יאָר כמעט,
זינט פֿריידקע האָט געאַרבעט בײַ פשעניצאַן אין וואַרשטאַט.
און דער באַלעבאָס, פשעניצאַ, אַ ציוניסט און אַ בעל-מוח,
אַ לייענער אַ שטענדיקער פֿון „השלח",
אַ דעמאָקראַט —
האָט ליב געהאַט אַ פּסוק זאָגן און אַ פּשט.
— אַז די מאַשינערקע — זאָגט ער — פֿאַרשטייט נישט שיר-השירים.
אַ נעטעלע מוז האָבן חן,
מוז שעמערירן.
ווער רעדט אַ קעשענע — — — און בײַ שיינדל קאַנאַריי אין שירץ
איז גראָד דאָס קעשענקע אויף צוויי אַ האַלבן סאַנטימעטער קורץ.
געהערט?
און בײַ פשעניצאַן ווערט
איין אויג אַ ביסל שיקלדיק און קלענער,
און ביידע אויגן פּיקן זיך, ווי הענער.

IV

In Pshenytsa's Workshop

Onward, onward—the years chase after the circular sun,
The scent of flowers, the sound of rain.

Onward—the green wheel drives
The wind that strokes, the hunger that rives.[98]

The day that comes with a cold, menacing chill
Upon roof and warmth, upon bed and doorsill.

Onward, onward, young feet,
Old feet, rheumatic and tired feet,
On the march toward sun, toward bread, toward rain, toward love.

Onward.
It is almost two and a half years
Since Freydke has worked at Pshenytsa's workshop.
And the owner, Pshenytsa, a Zionist and a brainy man at that,
A steady reader of the Hebrew "Messenger,"[99]
A democrat—
Loved to quote chapter and verse and interpret.[100]
—Since a machine-operator, a woman, he says, can't understand The Song of Songs.
A hem must have charm,
Must shimmer.
Even more so, the pockets in Sheyndl Kanarey's aprons!
That pocket is too short—two and a half centimeters.[101]
You hear?
One of Pshenytsa's eyes
Squints a little and grows smaller,
And both eyes peck like hens.

נאָר מאָנטיק איז געווען אַ גוטער טאָג,
(ס'האָט יעדערער דערקענט)
ס'פֿלעגט אָנקומען אַ טשעק פֿון מײַזנערן, דעם קאַטאָוויצער פּראָקורענט.
פּשעניצאַ פֿלעגט דעמאָלט אַרײַנכאַפּן אַ קערטל, אַ ביסל שלאָפֿן,
און דער עיקר אַ קריג טאָן זיך מיט פֿילאָסאָפֿן.
אַחד-העם איז מיט זײַן רוחניות אין גאַנצן נישט גערעכט.
געהערט?
ייִדן זײַנען טאַקע אַן עם-הבחירה,
פֿונדעסטוועגן איז קודם-כּל דאָס שטיקל לאַנד, די דירה.
דער חומר איז אויך אַן עיקר — מוז מען זאָגן,
און אויב אין קעלער רודערט זיך,
וועט ליכטיק זײַן ממילא אין די הויכע שטאָקן.

דער קעלער הודעט.
מען הערט ווי נאָדלען ציקן, צאַקן, פּוצן,
און די מאַשינען שטעפּן, שיפּן, יאָגן אין געלאַף.
און שײנדל קאַנאַריי צעזינגט זיך פּלוצעם,
„גענוג צו זײַן אַ שקלאַף".
די לערנמיידלעך שלייפֿן לעכלעך, בײַסן שנעל די פֿאָדעם,
די בלאָנדע ברומט אַ לידל „פֿון חווה און פֿון אָדם".
אַ פּרעסאײַזן האָט זיך צעשיפּעט ווי אַ שלאַנג,
געטאָן אַ הייסן כלופּ און זיך צעפֿאָכעט מיט אַ פּאַרע,
און זיבן פּרעסלעך יאָגן נאָך און זינגען אונטער:
מאַך אַ וואַרע.
מאַך אַ וואַרע.

פֿריידקע, די ווילנערקע, ציק-צאַקעט מיט דער שער,
די אַלטע פּעסל הוסט אַ ביסל אונטער — קכע און קכע,
שוין אַ יאָר צוואַנציק, ווי זי טרײַבט אַלץ די מאַשין.
בײַ הענדלערן געווען, בײַ פֿעכטן און איצטער בײַ פּשעניצאַן,
(עס מעג אין זיי — זאָגט זי — אין אַלעמען אַרײַן אַ בראָך).
איצט האָט זי נישט אַפֿילו מיט וואָס באַצאָלן פֿאַרן לאָך,
פֿאַרן אייבערשטיבל מיט די צעוויגטע שטיגן,
און ס'זשומעט די מאַשין, ווי בייזע האַרבסטיק-הונגעריקע פֿליגן.
עס מאַטערט זי, וואָס שׂהלע די בלאָנדע יאָגט אַזוי מיטן פּעדאַל,

But Monday was a good day
(Of this everyone was cognizant)
A check would arrive from Mayzner, his Katovitz agent.[102]
Then Pshenytsa used to sneak in a game of cards, take a nap,
And, most important, quarrel with philosophers' claptrap.
Ahad Ha'am with his spiritual Zionism is totally wrong.[103]
You hear?
Indeed, the Jews are a people of free will,[104]
Nonetheless, first and foremost is the land, the place to dwell.
Matter is also a principle—one must say,
And if there's stirring down in the cellar,
Then automatically on the top floors, it'll be bright as day.

The cellar hums.
One hears how needles click, clack, thump,
And the machines stitch, advance, pursue in a stampede.
And Sheyndl Kanarey suddenly bursts into song,
"Enough of being a slave!"
The apprentice girls thread needles, swiftly bite the thread,
The blonde one hums a ditty, "All about Adam and Eve."
All at once a pressing-iron advances like a snake,
Gives a hot sob and blows a sudden breath of steam,
And seven irons pursue and softly sing:
Make way.
Make way.

Freydke, the Vilna girl, click-clacks with the shears,
Old Pesl sputters a little—cough and cough,
She's been running the machine, without a break for twenty
years,
She was with Hendler, with Fekhtn and now with Pshenytsa
(May they—she says—have a disaster, each and all).
Now she doesn't even have enough to pay for that hole,
That garret with its swaying flights of stairs,
And the machine buzzes, like ugly autumn-hungry flies.
She's tormented by the way blonde Sorele races with the
pedal,

און פּעסל גיט זי מיט אַלע פֿינגער איבער דער נאָז אַ שאַר,
שנעלער, שׂרהלע, דו'סט קריגן אַ מעדאַל:
„פּשעניצאַס גרעסטער נאַר".

דער קעלער הודעט.
מען הערט ווי נאָדלען ציקן, צאַקן, פּוצן,
און די מאַשינען שטעפּן, שיפּן, יאָגן אין געפּעכט.
און ער, פּשעניצאַ, צעקרעכצט זיך פּלוצעם:
— איַי, שלעכט, איַי שלעכט, איַי שלעכט...
פֿריידקע די דעלעגאַטקע וועט דאָס געשעפֿט אים רוי:נירן,
ס'האָט אָפּגעשיקט אַ האַלבן טראַנספּאָרט שירצן דער פּויזנער פּראָקורענט, פּאָפּערנע,
די קעשענעס — שרייַבט ער — זייַנען גרויסע, ווי פּאַר זעלנער,
נו, און שיינדל אויך האָט קרום געשטעלט די קעלנער.
פּשעניצאַ זיפּצט. די ליפּן אָנגעבלאָזן ווי צוויי אונגערישע פֿלוימען,
— אַזעלכע ביטערע פֿאַרדינסטן, אַזעלכע הויכע לוינען — — —
ער זייט אַזוי די ווערטער און ער זיפּט,
גלייַך אויף דער גאַס אַן אָסיענדיקער רעגן טריפּט.
— אַז דעלעגאַטקעס דאַרף מען נאַר, וואָס טויגן די פּאַראַדעס?
און שטאַרק אין כּעס נעמט ער זיך לייענען קלויזנערס „אנושיות ויהדות".
נאָר פֿרייַטיק, פֿאַרן אויסצאָלן איז דאָס געווען אַ וואָלקן, נישט קיין באַלעבאָס.

דער קאָפּ אַראָפּגעזונקען,
די ברילן אויף דער נאָז.
אָן „השלח", אָן אַ פּסוק, אָן אַ פּשט.
פֿאַרוויקלט אין גרויען אָפּגעריבענעם כאַלאַט.
פֿרייַטיק צום אויסצאָלן הייבט אָן די קאַסע קרעכצן און דער שופֿלאָד שפּילן,
און ס'הייבן אָן צו סקריפּען און ווי פֿאַרקילטע הוסטן אַלע שטולן.
פּשעניצאַ זיצט. דער שופֿלאָד איז האַלב אָפֿן,
און ס'דאַכט, דער שופֿלאָד ט'באַלד צערעדן זיך:

And Pesl scrapes at her nose with her finger:
Faster, Sorele, you'll get a medal—
"Pshenytsa's greatest, stupidest humdinger."

The cellar hums.
One hears how needles click, clack, thump,
And the machines stitch, advance, pursue in combat.
And he, Pshenytsa, suddenly bursts out with a groan:
—Ay, terrible, terrible, terrible . . .
Freydke the delegate, will send his business to ruin.
The procurer from Poyzn, Paperne, returned half a shipment
of aprons,
The pockets—he writes—are huge, like for soldiers,
Well, and also Sheyndl set the collars crooked.
Pshenytsa sighs, each lip inflated like a Hungarian plum,
—How bitter the gains, how high the stakes have become—
He sows the words like this and faintly breathes,
Just like an autumn rain dripping on the street.
—Since you've got to hire delegates, aren't parades just
vanity?
And, deeply angry, he starts reading Klausner's "Judaism and
Humanity."[105]

But Friday, before paytime, he's become a cloud and not a
boss.
His head sunken down,
His glasses on his nose.
Without "The Messenger," without a verse, without a quote.
Wrapped up in a worn-out, loose, gray coat.
Friday at paytime the moneybox begins to groan and the
drawer to scold,
And all the chairs to creak and cough as if they'd caught a
cold.
Pshenytsa sits. The drawer stands half-ajar.
And it seems that all of a sudden words will come from the
drawer:

ניטאָ אויף וואָס צו האָפֿן, ניטאָ אויף וואָס צו האָפֿן.
פּשעניצאַ זעגנט זיך מיט יעדן פֿינפֿער, און מיט יעדן צווייער.
פֿאַמעלעך נעמט ער מיט די פֿינגער יעדע אייציקע מטבע,
פֿאַמעלעך גיט ער זי אַ שאַר פֿון זיך אַוועק,
און ציט צוריק אַ ווײַלע צום באַטראַכטן,
רוקט אָפּ די צענערגילדן, די יחסנים, צו דער וואַנט,
און גיט אַוועק דערנאָך פֿון האַנט צו האַנט.
אַוועקגעגעבן — זאָגן זײַנע פֿינגער, איז פֿאַרפֿאַלן,
אַוועקגעגעבן אַ צענערל, וועט עס צוריק נישט קומען,
און ס'סקריפּעט און ס'הוסט זײַן בענקל: צוגענומען, צוגענומען.
און שיינדל קאַנאַריי האָט פּריַיטיק ליב אַ שפּאַס טאָן מיטן באַלעבאָס.
זי גיט אַ פֿינטל מיט די אויגן, אַ שאַר די נאָז —
— שוין צײַט צו ציילן שנעלער, פּאַן פּשעניצאַ,
די גילדנס זײַנען סײַ ווי סײַ, ווי קײַלעכדיקע רעדער — — —
— געלט האָט ליב אַ חשבון — ברומט פּשעניצאַ,
און טונקט פֿאַמעלעך אײַן די פֿעדער.

אַ זומערדיקער טאָג. די היץ, אין סאַמע פֿלאַטער.
די נייטערקעס זײַנען געזעסן אויסגעבלייכט, פֿאַרמאַטערט.
בײַ פּעסלען האָט זיך גראָד צעשפּילט דער לונגען-פֿעלער.
קומט איין מאָל די פּשעניציכע אַראָפּ אין קעלער.
דאָס בלויע קלייד מיט זילבערנעם גאַלון,
האָט שטראַלן מיטגעבראַכט פֿון דרויסנדיקער זון.
אַרײַנגעשוווּמען, פֿאָכעט זי זיך אָפּ, און ס'טופּען אירע קנאַפּל,
איינס און צוויי, און איינס און צוויי.
זי קוקט זיך אום, גייט צו צו שיינדל קאַנאַריי:
— קאָכאַניע, זאָגט זי, כ'בעט אינען, מײַן דינסטמיידל צו אַל די שלעק,
איז ערגעץ ווו אַוועק,
און איך מוז אָפּנעמען אַ וואָלסקע פּאַלמע,
נישט ווײַט פֿון דאַנען, אויף קראָכמאַלנע.
איך בעט אינען — — —

בײַ שיינדלען די מאַשין האָט זיך געטאָן אַ וואַרג,
זי האָט צו דער פּשעניציכע אַ דריי געטון דעם קאָפּ צוזאַמען מיטן
גאַנצן קאַרק:
— וואָס איז, איר ווייסט נישט ווי מ'טראָגט אַ וואָלסקע פּאַלמע
אויף די הענט?

Nothing to hope for, nothing to hope for.
Pshenytsa bids farewell to every coin worth five, worth two.
Slowly he takes every single coin between his fingers,
Slowly he pushes it away,
And draws it back a while for consideration,
Shoves the ten-gildn pieces,[106] those aristocrats, to the wall,
And subsequently from hand to hand, gives them away.
Given away, his fingers say, means lost,
A tenner given away—will not come back,
And his stool creaks and coughs: taken away, taken away.
And on Fridays, Sheyndl Kanarey likes to joke with the boss.
She gives a blink of her eyes, a poke with her nose—
—It's time to count faster, Mr. Pshenytsa,
Afterall, gildns are round like wheels—
—Money loves an accounting—Pshenytsa growls,
And slowly dips his pen.

A summer's day. The heat, aflutter.
Pale, exhausted, the seamstresses were sitting.
Pesl's consumption was acting up.
Once, down into the cellar, Pshenytsa's wife comes.[107]
Her blue dress with its silver trim
Brings in with it the outdoors and a sunbeam.
Floating in, she fans herself, and her heels stamp,[108]
One and two, one and two.
She looks around, approaches Sheyndl Kanarey:
—Dearie, she says, I beg you, unfortunately, my servant girl
Is off today,
And I must take an Italian palm tree away
From a store not far from here, on Krokhmolne Street.
I beg you—[109]

Sheyndl's machine halts with a choke,
Toward Pshenytsa's wife she turns her head, her whole neck:
—What's the matter? You don't know how to carry an Italian
palm tree in your arms?

אַזוי-אָ-אָ, מען נעמט —
און שיינדל האָט אַ בלאַנק געטאָן מיט ווײַסע ציין,
מען נעמט זי אָט אַזוי-אָ און מען טראָגט אַהיים.
בײַ דער פּשעניציכע זײַנען די גוידערס אויפֿן האַלדז געוואָרן אָנגעדראָלן.
— מײַן מאַן — — — האָט זי געשטיקט זיך, סטײַטש...

דערנאָך האָבן אַ יאָג געטאָן אין אַ געוויטער די פּעדאַלן,
דער לינקער פֿוס שלאָגט אויס דעם טאַקט,
דער רעכטער כאַפּט אים אונטער אויף פֿאַרפֿאַלן.
די נאָדלען ציקן, יאָגן נאָך אַ ווײַסן קאַנט.
זיי ווילן אויפֿפּרעסן די ראָגן,
און אַקסלען בייגן זיך אויף רעכטס, אויף לינקס,
זיי לויפֿן, לויפֿן, ווילן עמעצן דעריאָגן.

פּשעניצאַ האָט לאַנג געטראַכט,
אַז פּעסל, וואָס האָט דעם לונגען-פֿעלער,
איז דאָ בײַ אים אַן איבעריקער מענטש אין קעלער.
די פּעדאַלן האָבן ליב אַ יונגן פֿוס,
בײַ יונגע פֿיס זינגען די רעדלעך גאָר אַן אַנדער ניגון,
און זי האָט כּסדר אָט דעם הוסט.

און איין מאָל גראָד אַ מאָנטיק,
ס'האָט פֿאַרשפּעטיקט די אָנווײַזונג פֿון קאַטאָוויצער פּראָקורענט.
פּשעניצאַ האָט זיך אַרומגעדרייט, געזאָטן און געברענט.
פֿאַר נאַכט האָט ער אַ זאָג געטאָן,
(געערדט אַ ביסל שנעלער)
— הערט נאָר, פּאַני דעלעגאַטקע,
צו פֿיל מאַשינערקעס בײַ מיר אין קעלער — —
און איך אין חובֿות בין פֿאַרקראָכן,
וועל פּעסלען אָפּשיקן,
זי האָט נאָך די צוויי וואָכן.

און איבער די פּעדאַלן זײַנען די ווערטער דורכגעפֿלויגן.
די פֿיס געטאָן אַ ברען.
און ס'האָבן די רעדלעך אָפּגעזשומעט:
- מען וועט נאָך זען, מען וועט נאָך זען — — —

One picks it up, like this, . . . from beneath—
And Sheyndl flashes her white teeth,
Just like this, it's picked up and carried home.
Pshenytsa's wife's goiters swell up on her throat.
—My husband—she sputters, After all, how could you . . .

Afterwards, in a whirlwind, the pedals start to race.
The left foot beats out the time,
The right foot accompanies it at a hopeless pace.
The needles click, chase after a white border, a hem.
They want to devour the corners,
And shoulders bend to the left, to the right,
They run, run, run, trying to overtake someone.

For a long time, Pshenytsa has thought
That Pesl, who has consumption,
Is superfluous in the cellar.
The pedals love a young foot,
With young feet, the wheels sing an entirely different tune,
And she always has that cough.

And once, it happened to be a Monday,
The draft of the Katovitz agent was delayed.
Pshenytsa went back and forth, boiled and burned.
At dusk he made an announcement
(Spoke a little faster)
—Just listen, Madam Delegates,
Too many machine operators in my cellar—
And I am deep in debt,
So I will get rid of Pesl,
She has only two weeks left.

And these words flew over the pedals.
The feet worked up a sweat.
And the wheels buzzed away:
—It's not finished yet, it's not finished yet—

V

שטרײַק

ווי פֿערד נאָך הייסע שלאַכטן, שווײַגנדיקע אין אַ ריי
שטייען די מאַשינעס,
פֿאַרקלעמט דעם לעצטן לויף פֿון נאָדלען דינע.
עס וואַרטן אויף אָנריר פֿון אַ פֿוס פּעדאַלן.
די נייטערקעס מיט פֿיבערדיקע אויגן
די אַקסלען אין די שאַלן.
עס איז די טיר — דערוואַרטונג.
דאָס פֿענצטער — לויער.
דער טאָג אַן אומהיימלעכער,
פֿאַרדראָסיקער
און גרויער.
שיינדל קאַנאַריי האָט הויך גערעדט:
(ס'איז שאַרף די בלאַסקייט פֿון איר פּנים.
די שוואַרצקייט פֿון בערעט).
— מען דאַרף דאָ לאָזן אויף בײַ נאַכט אַ וואָך,
אַט דער פּשעניצאַ מיט די קאָסע אויגן
קען צוטראַכטן אַ זאַך.

פּשעניצאַ איז אין קעלער נישט אַרײַנגעקומען.
געדרייט זיך אויפֿן הויף,
(ס'האָט זײַן כאַלאַטל געפֿאָכעט ווי אַ פֿאָן),
גלײַך ער זאָל זיך אויף אויסנווייניק חשבונען,
און גלײַך ער האָט דאָ עפּעס וואָס צו טאָן.

ס'האָט שיינדל קאַנאַריי צו מאָרגן אין דער פֿרי
געטראָפֿן: דער קעלער צוגעשלאָסן.
אַ ווײַסער צעטל האָט געטאָן אַ ברי:
„דאָ ווינײַענטשאַ".
ס'האָט פּשעניצאַ זײַן פֿאַבריק אַוועקגעפֿירט קיין לאָדזש,
(און די פּשעניציכע אַוועקגעפֿאָרן איז דערווײַלע קיין נאַלענטשאָוו.)

V

Strike

Like horses after heated battle, the machines
Stand silently in a row,
Caught in the last run of thin needles.
A pedal waits for the touch of a foot.
The seamstresses with feverish eyes,
Their shoulders in shawls.
The door is—expecting.
The window—lurking.
The day is weird,
Irksome
And gray.
Sheyndl Kanarey speaks loudly:
(Her beret's blackness
Sharpens the paleness of her face.)
—Someone needs to stand guard here at night,
That cross-eyed Pshenytsa
Might devise some plan.

Pshenytsa does not enter the cellar.
He comes and goes through the yard
(His loose cloak flapping like a flag),
As if he had figured it all out by heart,
And as if he had something to do here.

Bright and early in the morning, Sheyndl Kanarey
Confronts the cellar all locked up.
A white note scalds:
"For Rent."[111]
Pshenytsa has moved his factory to Lodz,
(And Pshenytsa's wife meanwhile has travelled off to
Nalentshov.)[112]

אַ וואָגן איז געקומען נאָך פֿינצטערלעך באַגינען,
און צוגענומען די קעפּ פֿון די מאַשינען.
דורך די שויבן,
ווו ס'האָבן פֿליגן געזשומעט און געדרימלט,
האָט שיינדל קאַנאַריי געזען:
די פֿיס פֿון די מאַשינעס, שטויב און שימל.

ס'האָט שיינדל קאַנאַריי געקוקט אַ ווײַלע.
איבער די ליפּן איז אויפֿגעגאַנגען אַ האַלבער שמייכל, אַ האַלבער גרימאַס.
— זע נאָר, פּשעניצעלע ט'אַרויסגעגנבֿעט אונדזערע מאַשינעס.
זי האָט אַ שאַר געטאָן דעם בערעט העכער אויפֿן קאָפּ,
און האָט גענומען אַ שמאָלן שלאָסערישן לאָס,
(און כאָטש מען טוט אַזוי נישט אין קיין לײַטישע פּאָעמעס —
האָט שיינדל קאַנאַריי אַזוי געטאָן)
דאָס שלעסל אַ זעץ געטאָן פֿון אויבן אויף אַראָפּ.
עס האָבן די נייטערקעס צו איר געטאָן אַ שאָס,
דערזען — שיינדל קאַנאַריי
האָט מיטן פֿוס די טיר געטאָן אַ דריי.
און איז אַרײַן אין קעלער מיט טריט געלאַסענע און פּראָסטע,
גלײַך זי זאָל דאָרטן זײַן די באַלעבאָסטע.

זי האָט זיך צוגעזעצט צו איר מאַשין.
עס האָבן אירע פֿינגער שנעל און דין
געמײַסטרעוועט בײַ די פּעדאַלן.
זי האָט זיך אויסגעשרויפֿט. אַ ווײַלינקע באַטראַכט.
גלײַך זי וואָלט עפּעס גערעדט צו זיי,
מיט זיי אַ חשבון אויסגעגלײַכט,
אַ רעכענונג געמאַכט.

דערנאָך האָט זי פּאַמעלעך, אָן געאײַל,
בײַ פּעסלען אין מאַשין אויסגעשלאָסן דעם פּעדאַל.
דערנאָך בײַ שׂרהלע דער בלאָנדער — — —
פֿריידקע האָט איר מאַשין אַליין פֿאַרפֿאַרטיקט
אויפֿגערעגטער,
שנעלער —
אוןביידע זײַנען זיי אַרויס פֿון קעלער.

A wagon arrived in the dark just before dawn,
And took away the heads of the machines.
Through the window panes,
Where flies buzz and doze,
Sheyndl Kanarey sees
The feet of the machines, dust and mould.

For a while, Sheyndl Kanarey looks.
Across her lips passes a half-smile, half-grimace.
—Well, look at that! Our Pshenytsele's stolen our machines.
She shoves the beret higher on her head,
And takes a slender locksmith's crowbar
(And although this is not done in refined poems—
Sheyndl Kanarey does this)
She pries off the lock from top to bottom.
The seamstresses pour toward her,
To watch. Sheyndl Kanarey
Gives the door a kick with her foot
And enters the cellar with calm, ordinary steps,
Exactly as if she were the proprietress.

She sits down at her machine.
Her fingers, swift and thin,
Work at the pedals.
She unscrews them, meditates a while
As if she were saying something to them,
Settling an account with them,
Balancing the books.

After that she slowly, without haste,
Disconnects the pedal of Pesl's machine.
And then, of Sarah the blonde's machine—
Freydke prepares her own machine
More excitedly,
Faster—
And both come out of the cellar.

ס'האָט שיינדל קאַנאַריי די צוועלף פּעדאַלן
געטראָגן לײַכט מיט גלײַכע, יונגע טריט.
דאָס פּנים ווײַס.
די אויגן האָבן בלוי געגליט.
זי איז אַרויס פֿון הויף.
עס האָבן די מאַשינערקעס נאָך איר אַ שאַר געטאָן זיך.
מיט פֿיבערדיקע בליקן דורכגענומען.

פּשעניצאַ איז דערנאָך אַרומגעלאָפֿן מיט שיקלדיקע אויגן,
איבערן הויף.
זײַן גרוי כאַלאַטל האָט געפֿאָכעט,
ווי אַ פֿליגל,
ווי אַ שלייף.
— ער וועט זי שמירן,
אַזוינס געשעט נישט אין פֿאַבריקן.
ער וועט זי — — — ער וועט פֿאַרשיקן — — —

אין אַ טאָג דרײַ אַרום איז שיינדל קאַנאַריי
מיט זיבן גילדן,
און שוואַרצן ברויט אַ פּענעך —
צו פֿוס אַדורך די קאַטאָוויצער גרענעץ.

Sheyndl Kanarey carries the twelve pedals
Lightly with straight, young steps.
Her face is white.
Her eyes glow blue.
She leaves the yard.
The women who ran the machines poke after her.
Penetrating with feverish gazes.

Then cross-eyed Pshenytsa races
Across the yard.
His gray cloak fans out
Like a wing,
Like a noose.
—He will smash her!
Such things don't happen in factories.
He will—he will have her deported—

Three days later Sheyndl Kanarey
With seven gildens,
And a slice of black bread—
Crosses the Katovitz border on foot.

מײַן שלעפּשיף

מײַן שלעפּשיף,
מיט צעאָדערטער פֿאָן,
מיט צעשלאָגענע שויבן.
און איך, דער טרויעריקער קאַפּיטאַן,
האָב צעטריבן די ווערטער די שטילע —
די טויבן,
זיי זאָלן נישט ברומען אין אויערן,
זיי זאָלן נישט וואָרקען,
נישט לויבן.
איך האָב זיי גענוג מײַנע ווערטער —
די ערלעכע טויבן.

עס וויאַנעט און וויאַנעט דאָס לעצט ביסל בלוי פֿונעם הימל,
וואָס כ'האָב ערגעץ פֿאַרמשכּונט,
בײַ קינדערשער חבֿרה,
ווען כ'האָב זיי געלערנט צו זאָגן אַן אַלף,
צו שרײַבן אַ בית
און צו לייענען אַ גימל.

עס וויאַנעט און וויאַנעט דאָס לעצט ביסל בלוי פֿונעם הימל,
וואָס כ'האָב ערגעץ באַהאַלטן
פֿון שטיינער פֿון שׂונאים,
פֿון קאַלטקייט אין צימער,
פֿון פֿינצטערע נעכט פֿון פּאָגראָמען.

איך פֿיל אַזוי דײַטלעך אויף זיך איצט מײַן בעטלעריש העמד,
און אַזוי איבעריק זײַנען פֿון ווערטער די זײַדענע לאַטעס.
עס איז מיר דערווידער און פֿרעמד
דאָס געדריי אַרום מיר, און דער טומל:
פֿון ווערטער דער טריפֿענער שעטנז.

אין פֿאַרפֿײַניקטן מוח לויפֿט דורך דער געדאַנק, ווי אַ נאָדל, —
כ'קריג בריוו אַנאָנימע פֿאַרבונדן מיט בלוטיקן פֿאָדעם,

My Tow-Boat

My tow-boat,
With a tattered flag,[113]
With beaten panes.
And I, the sorrowful captain,
Have driven away the silent words—
The doves,
So they shall not hum in ears,
So they shall not coo,
Not praise.
I have enough of them, my words—
The virtuous doves.

The last bit of blue in the sky fades and fades—
I pawned it somewhere
With a group of children,
When I taught them to say an *alef*,
To write a *beys*
And to read a *giml*.[114]

The last bit of blue in the sky fades and fades—
I hid it somewhere
From the stones of enemies,
From the cold in the room,
From the dark nights of pogroms.

I feel so clearly myself, now in my beggar's shirt,
And the silken patches of words are superfluous.
How repugnant and foreign to me are
The shouting around me and the din:
The impure weave of words.[115]

Thoughts race through my tormented brain like a needle,—
I receive anonymous letters bound with bloody thread,

כ׳קריג בריוו אַנאָנימע פֿאַרפֿלעקטע מיט ווײַבערשע טרערן.
זיי בעטן:
מיר קענען דעם פֿלאַטער פֿון זײַדענע ווערטער נישט הערן,
מיר קענען נישט לייענען —
מיט ביטערע אויגן...

טססס...
אַ ווײַלע פֿון רו.
מײַן טויבנשלאַק שטייט אַ פֿאַרוויסטער,
אַזוי ווי מײַן שלעפּשיף פֿאַראומערט,
און וואַרט אויפֿן חלף פֿון בליץ,
אויף צעטרייסלונג
פֿון דונער...

טססס...
אַ ווײַלע פֿון רו.
עס בלויט נאָך אין ערגעץ אַ שטיקל פֿון הימל,
וואָס כ׳האָב פֿאַרבאַהאַלטן בײַ גאָט...

טססס...
אַ ווײַלע פֿון רו.

I receive anonymous letters spotted with womanly tears.
They plead:
We cannot hear the flutter of silken words,
We cannot read—
With bitter eyes . . .

Hush . . .
A moment of calm.
My dove-cote stands desolate,
Just as my tow-boat saddens,
And waits for the slaughtering knife of lightning,
For the paroxysm of thunder.

Hush . . .
A moment of calm.
Somewhere that bit of sky that I hid with God
Still turns blue . . .

Hush . . .
A moment of calm.

מײַן טאָג

מײַן טאָג —
איז אויסגעשטאָכן, ווי אַ זיפּ,
און אויסגעלאַכט, ווי אַ שגעון.
זאָל די ווײַסקייט ווינטער בליִען,
זאָלן האַרבסטן גראָען,
זאָלן זומערס פּײַפּן —
סאָלאָווייען.
ס'האָט אַ קאָרנווינט
געוואָלט מײַן האַרץ פֿאַרדרייען,
פֿאַרשיכּורן,
פֿאַרזומערן, —
האָבן דאָ, עק גאַס
דרײַ פּרויען פֿון דרײַ חרובֿדיקע צימערן,
ווי פֿון זינקענדיקע שיפֿן,
אויסגעשטרעקט צו מיר די פֿויסטן:
בלייכע,
ביינערדיקע,
געשלעכטלאָזע —
פֿויסטן פֿונעם דלות,
און האָבן מיר באַשוואָרן:
עס זאָל מיר ענג זײַן
אין מײַן זומער, אין מײַן ווינטער, — —
אין צפֿון און אין דרום.
און כ'קען אין ערגעץ נישט אַנטלויפֿן.
עס זײַנען די וועגן פֿאַרנומען, פֿאַרנומען.
אָט שטייען די קולבאַקישע בראָנדזענע יונגען,
מיט פֿאַפּירענע בלומען,
מיט ליאַלקעס פֿון גומע.
די יונגען, וואָס קענען צעטראָגן אַ שטאָט,
און אויסבויען באַנען
און אײַנזייען גערטנער און פלאַנטן.
זיי האַנדלען, ווייסט דער טײַוול מיט וואָס —
מיט מײַן האַרץ און מיט פֿאַפּירענע פֿאַנטן.

My Day

My day—
Is punctured like a sieve,
And ridiculed like a whim.
May winter whiteness blossom,
May autumns turn gray,
May summers whistle—
Become nightingales.[116]
When a rye-wind
Would have twisted my heart,
Intoxicated it,
Transformed it into summer—[117]
Here, at the end of the street,
Three women stretched out their fists to me
From three wasted rooms,
As from sinking ships,
Pale,
Boney,
Sexless
Fists of poverty,
And swore at me:
May my life be miserable
In my summers, in my winters,
In the north and the south.
And I can escape nowhere.
The roads are busy, busy.
Here stand the Kulbak-like bronze youths,[118]
With paper flowers,
With rubber dolls.
The youths, who can turn a city upside down,
Build railroads
And sow gardens and train tracks.
They deal with the-devil-knows-what—
With my heart and with paper pledges.

זייער קול:
ס'איז חוזק,
ס'איז שפּאָט,
און ס'איז בלוטיקער דראָען.
און אַזאַ איז מײַן טאָג:
אויסגעלעכערט, ווי אַ זיפּ.
און אויסגעלאַכט, ווי אַ שגעון.

Their voice
Is derision,
Mockery,
And bloody menace.
And such is my day:
Punctured like a sieve.
And ridiculed like a whim.

דעם טאַטנס פּעלץ

גערעדנקסט דײַן פּעלץ דעם היימישן און שווערן,
אַ ירושה פֿון פֿעטער שײַע,
מיט אַרבל שווערע, ווי די בערן
און ווי אַ קישן, גינציקע, געטרײַע.

אין טיפֿער קעשענע געפֿין איך אָפֿטער דײַנע אַלטע ברילן.
באַטראַכטן זיי מיך זייער פֿילאָסאָפֿיש
און מורמלען צו פֿאַרדראָסיק: קאַדיע, קאַדיע,
ווי ווערט נישט נימאס דיר צו וואַלגערן אונטערן פּעלץ
און שרײַבן אַ חד-גדיא, און אַ חד-גדיא.

און גלייב מיר, אַלע לידער וועלן נישט געפֿינען,
וואָס עס שמועסט אַ ווײַסער שטיין פֿון אַ מצבֿה מיטן בלויען הימל,
און וואָס עס רעדט דאָס גרינע פֿרילינגדיקע גראָז
צו דעם אַלטן גערטנער, דעם גרויעם באַלעבאָס.
און אַפֿילו, ווי עס קריגן זיך געזאַנג פֿון לויפֿנדיקן באַן
מיט די טריט פֿון פֿוסגייער, דעם אָרעמאַן.

דערזען — די ברילן זײַנען אַוועק אין הויכע דרכים,
בין איך מיט ביידע אויערן אונטערן פּעלץ פֿאַרקראָכן.
נאָר אויך דאָרט, אין דעם באַהעלטעניש דעם שטילן,
הער איך אַלץ, ווי ס'זשומען נאָך דעם טאַטנס אַלטע ברילן.

My Father's Fur Coat

Remember your heavy, familiar fur,
A legacy from Uncle Shaye,
With heavy sleeves, like bears,
Sincere and faithful as a pillow.

In its deep pocket, I find your old glasses.
They watch me philosophically
                    and mutter irksomely: Oh, Kadya, Kadya,
How tedious for you to loll beneath the fur
And write those endless tales, each one a *khad-gadya.*[119]

And believe me, all those poems will not supply
What the white gravestone says to the blue sky,
And about what green spring grasses chatter
With the old gardener, the gray householder.
And not even how the song of the racing train
Quarrels with the footsteps of the poor man.

I saw—the glasses have vanished on paths high and far,[120]
So I crept up to my ears beneath the fur.
But even there, in the hidden quietness,
I hear the constant buzz of father's old glasses.

VI

אין לאַנד פֿון מײַן געביין

שיקאַגע, 1937

VI

In land fun mayn gebeyn
(In the Country of My Bones)
Chicago, 1937

מײַן אַרציביאָגראַפֿיע

מײַן טײַערינקע אַרציביאָגראַפֿיע,
טאַטעלעך, מאַמעלעך, האַרצעלע, קרוין —
אַך, ווי נישט פֿײַן, און אַך, ווי נישט שיין,
אַזוי באַהאַנדלען אַ פּאַרשוין.

נאָך דאָס האָט מיר צום רומל געפֿעלט —
מיט לידער האַנדלען אויפֿן הילכיקן יריד.
עס זאָל מײַן קאָלירטער סטראַגאַן*
זיך וואַקלען, ווי אַ קרעמל מיט שניט.

און אַ שפּרונג זאָל מיך וואַלגערן איבער דער וועלט,
אַזוי אַז די האָר זאָלן שטעכן קאַפּויער.
אין מידבר פֿון פֿרעמדן און טונקעלן פֿעלד,
און אונטער די פֿיס גראָבט זיך אונטער אַ טכויער.

אין לאַנגאַניקן וואַנדער, אין טרוקענעם גאַנג,
ווי האַסטיק די באַן זאָל נישט געבן אַ ריס,
גיי איך סײַ ווי אַ וואַכע אין דרויסן פֿאַרבײַ
מיט באָרוועסע, שטענדיק פֿאַרטיליקטע פֿיס.

און דאַרע, געמאָסטענע בינטלעך „קולטור"
צעטראָג ווי אַ פּעדלער אויפֿן אַקסל די סקרינעס.
און אין מיטן אַ רוישיקן, אויגיקן זאַל
מיט טראַסק גיי איך פּלוצלינג אַראָפּ פֿון די שינעס.

און ווו אַראָפּ? און ווו?
אָט דאָרט טאַקע, ווי איינס און צוויי,
אָט דאָרט ווו ס'שײַנט די לאָך פֿון מײַנע שיך,
אָט דאָרט ווו ס'זינגט מײַן תּמעוואַטער סאָלאָוויי.

אָט פּונקט ווי בײַ דער קוואַסניצע דער מאַמען,
פּאָרויס, מײַן אַרציביאָגראַפֿיע, דרייסטער —
פּלעשער זײַנען הילכיקע גלאָקן,
און איך — אַ נאַסער קאַפּעל-מײַסטער.

My Ultimate Biography

My darling, ultimate biography,
Dear papas, dear mamas, dear hearts, I say—
Ah, it's not nice, and ah, it's not kind
To treat a person this way.

The last thing in the world that I need
Is to deal in poems at the boisterous fair.
So, may my crazy-quilt market-stall
Wobble like a shop full of ready-to-wear.[121]

And let a spell send me to wander the world,
A charm so terrific, my hair stands on end.
In some faraway desert of alien fields,
Under my feet, a skunk burrows in sand.

In endless wanderings, across arid ways,
No matter how fast trains approach and retreat,
I'm always outside, walking by watchfully
On permanently battered, bare feet.

I lug thin, measured bundles of "culture"
Like a peddler with crates on his shoulder,
And in the midst of a noisy, staring hall,
Suddenly plunging from the boards, down I fall.

And down? Where is down?
Out there, like a-one and a-two,
Out there, where the holes shine through my shoes,
Out there, where my dim-witted nightingale sings.

Just like my mother, the vendor of kvass,
Onward, biography, bold and bluster—
Bottles are ringing, ringing like bells,
And here I am—a drenched kapellmeister.

(קלינגט נאָך פּלעשער,
גרינע, יונגע, קלאָרע,
אין אַ קאָרעטע מיט וואַסער
קלינגענדיקע מעטעאָרן.

קלינגט נאָך פּלעשלעך,
אײַנגעבונדענע צוזאַמען,
קלינגט נאָך פּלעשלעך,
ס'האָט געשיקט ערגעץ די מאַמע).

נו, גיב דאָרט, יעזעפּקע, אַ מונטער דאָס וועגל,
און גרינגער זאָל זײַן — גיב אַ צמאָק מיט די ליפּן.
די פּאָדערשטע רעדלעך מיט הילצערנע סטרונעס —
די הינטערשטע — צוויי פּאַרחלומטע סקריפּען.

אַ גראָשן אַ וויאָרסט,
אַ דרײַער אַ טאָג,
דער פּרימאָרגן, ווי שטענדיק,
גייט אויף מיט פּאַרטאָג.

מיט בלויקייט, וואָס קעלטערט,
מיט זון, וואָס בריט,
זאָגט איין קינד צום צווייטן,
אַ קינד צו אַ קינד:

איצט לאָמיר זיך בײַטן
און דו שטופּ דעם וואָגן,
און שרײַ מיר העט-טאָ,
אַז אין פּיאַטע וועט שלאָגן.

נאָר רעדלעך, ווי רעדלעך,
זיי דרייען אַ מיזמור,
זיי זאָגן און זאָגן
אַ רונדיקן פּזמון:

(Keep ringing, ringing, bottles,
Green and fresh and clear,
In a trough of water—
Ringing meteors.

Keep ringing, ringing, bottles,
All bundled up together,
Keep ringing, ringing, bottles,
Mother's gone off somewhere.)

Look lively, Yezepke, and get the cart rolling,
Give a smack of your lips to make it move lightly.
The front wheels strum on wooden strings—
And the two back wheels squeak dreamily.

A penny a mile,
And three pennies a day,
As always, the morning
Comes up with the day.

In the chilly blue,
In the boiling sun,
Two children speak,
One to one:

Now, let's change places,
And you push the cart.
Shout "giddy-up," so
It strikes my heart.

But wheels, being wheels,
Spin out a song,
Repeat and repeat
A rolling refrain:

ה
ײַדאַ-רודאַ, שמעלקע-צאַלקע,
פּורים כ'וועל שפּילן אין אסתּר-המלכּה,

אין אסתּר-המלכּה מיט גאָלדענע שיך —
סקריפּען די רעדער טשי-ריך און טשי-ריך.

סקריפּען די רעדער טשי-ריך און טשי-ריך,
גייט אסתּר-המלכּה אין גאָלדענע שיך.

מיט קנעפּלעך פֿאַרשפּיליעט די בײַענע קלייד,
און פֿאָרויס, ווי געווײנלעך, טרומייטערט אַ פּלייט.

טרילער, און טרילער, און טרילער — לאַ-לאַ.
שרײַט דאָס פֿערדל פֿון פֿאָרנט:
— בלײַב שטיין און העט-טאַ!

דו זעסט נישט? ווו ביסטו?
מיר זינקען אין ליים.
פֿון פֿאָרנט — אַ גרוב,
און פֿון הינטן — אַ שטיין.

פֿאָרויס, מײַן אַרציביאָגראַפֿיע,
ווי קאָן זײַן דאָ אָן שלמינקע דעם שמיד?
אָט ציט ער מיך פֿעסט בײַ די צעפּלעך,
ער האָט אַ מעשׂה מיט אַ ציג.

ווער קאָן בײַשטיין דער ווונדערלעכער מעשׂה
(פֿון אַ ציג און אַ וואָלף און אַ קעפּל קרויט) —
עס מעג זיך ניו-יאָרק פֿאַרבאַהאַלטן
פֿאַר גאַלאָפּ פֿון אַ היימישער בויד.

און בלויז פֿאַרן סאָראָקער מלמד,
פֿאַר זײַן צעטומלטער, כוואַליקער באָרד,
ווען ער שפּאַנט אויפֿן מאַרק בין-הזמנים
מיט אַ נײַער אַ בלעכענער קוואָרט.

Shmelke-Tsalke, eenie meenie,
On Purim I'll be Esther Queenie,

Queen Esther with her golden shoes—
The wheels squeak sha-reek and sha-rooz.

As the wheels squeak sha-reek and sha-rooz,
Queen Esther walks in her golden shoes.

With her baize dress all fastened with buttons,
And before her, as always, a silver flute trumpets.

Trill, trill, and trill—high and low.
The horsey in front commands:
Stop! Stand still! Whoa!

Don't you see? Where are you?
We're sinking in loam.
Ahead lies a graveyard,
And behind lies a stone.

Onward, my ultimate biography,
But how can we ever move on without
The braid-tugging Blacksmith Shloyminke?
He has a tale to tell me about a goat.

Who can resist the wonderful tale
(Of a goat and a wolf and a head of kraut)?
I'd give the whole of New York City
For the familiar gallop of his cart.

And for the schoolteacher of Sorok,
For his beard, mixed-up, wavy,
When he strides across the market between terms
With a brand-new, tinny laver.

און נישט אַזוי ווײַט צוליב פֿאַרדינסטן
איז זײַן פּנים פֿאַרטראַכט און צעהעלט,
ער האָט געזען פֿאַר טאָג די זון און די לבֿנה
אין בערענע פּעלצן פֿאַרשטעלט.

און זיך געשלאָגן — ווי צוויי מלמדים פֿאַר אַ קנעלונג —
און אַ בערענע לאַפּע אַ פֿאַרהייב,
און עס יאָגן זיך פֿלאַמיקע כמאַרעס,
אַזש עס פֿאַלט אויפֿן שטעטל אַ שטויב.

מײַן טײַערינקע אַרציביאָגראַפֿיע
אין רויכיקן אומעט פֿאַרברענט.
לאַך איך אַזש ביז העט אין די ריפּן,
אַז מע פֿרעגט מײַן געבורטסטאָג איז ווען.

מײַן געבורטסטאָג — אויף אַ קאַרשנבוים-צווײַגל
אַ העמד אַ פֿאַרלאַטעטע שײַנט,
איך שיק אײַך מײַנע העפֿלעכסטע ווערטער
צו אײַער געבורטסטאָג, מײַנע פֿרײַנד.

(אין אונדזער משפּחה האָט געפֿלאַקערט
אַ פֿאַרעקשנטע שלאַכט װעגן מיר —
די באָבע האָט געציילט מיך פֿון אלול,
די מאַמע האָט געדענקט, אַז פֿון אייר.

נאָר ביידע האָבן געוווּסט, און אויף ריכטיק —
און דאָס האָט געשטילט זייער ברען —
אַז אין יענעם פֿרימאָרגן בלי-ספֿק
איז אַ רעגן געווען).

מײַן אַרציביאָגראַפֿיע, ס'איז באַשערט דיר
די הילצערנע סטרונעס אַ שפּאַן טאָן: פֿאַרפֿאַלן.
שטעפּ, מײַן זינגערווּקע, היפּער נישט —
עס מאַכט נישט אויס, אויב ס'זשאַווערן אַ ביסל די פּעדאַלן.

---

* מאַרק-געשטעל

And by no means on account of his wages
Does his face gleam, pensively glare;
At dawn he saw the sun and the moon
Masquerade in the pelt of a bear.

And wrestle—like schoolteachers over a post—
With a bearish paw raised high,
Till dust fell onto the shtetl
When flaming storm-clouds raced by.

My darling, ultimate biography,
Burned up in smoky gloom.
I laugh until my ribs crack
When they ask when my birthday will come.

My birthday—from a cherry-tree twig
A luminous, patched shirt depends,
I send you my most courteous words
For each of your birthdays, my friends.

(In our family, a battle raged
Stubbornly over me each year—
From Elul my grandmother counted my age,
My mother calculated it from Iyar.

But both knew for certain—
And this is what quieted their zeal—
That unquestionably on that morning
It was a heavy rain that fell.)

My ultimate biography, it is your fate
That the wooden strings stride forth: for naught.
Stitch, my sweet Singer, but don't skip—
It doesn't matter if the pedals rust a bit.

ווען קיינער רופֿט מיך נישט

מײַן מאַמע רופֿט מיך נישט בײַם נאָמען —
ווײַל מײַן מאַמע איז טויט.
מײַן טאַטע רופֿט מיך נישט בײַם נאָמען —
ווײַל מײַן טאַטע איז ווײַט.
און גאָט רופֿט מיך אויך נישט בײַם נאָמען —
ווײַל גאָט האָט געמאַכט אַ פּורים-שפּיל,
ער האָט פֿאַרשטעלט זיך פֿאַר אַ הונט,
און יאָמערט אין די נעכט אַזוי הויך,
אַז איך טרײַב אים מיט אַ שטעקן אַוועק
ער זאָל מיך לאָזן צו רו.

רו, מײַן האַרץ —
רו אַ ווײַלע ווען גאָט איז אַוועק.
רו אַ ווײַלע,
ווען מײַן גוף איז אויסגעצויגן מיט געדולד.
רו אַ ווײַלע,
ביז עס וועט רופֿן אַ גלאָק,
ביז עס וועט רופֿן דער יאָמער,
וואָס הענגט אויף מײַן רוקן — אַ זאַק.
רו אַ ווײַלע — — — —
איין ווײַלע אָן גאָט.

When Nobody Calls Me

My mother does not call me by name—
Because my mother is dead.
My father does not call me by name—
Because my father is gone.
And God does not call me by name—
Because God plays at a Purim masquerade,
He's disguised himself as a dog
And mourns loudly in the night.
I beat him off with a stick
To make him leave me alone.

Rest, my heart—
Rest a moment while God is away.
Rest a moment
While my body is drawn out with patience.
Rest a moment
Until a bell peals,
Until the mourning that hangs
Like a sack on my back calls.
Rest a moment—
One moment without God.

בײַם שוועל

דער ווינט האָט צוגענומען ס׳לעצטע וואָרט.
אַ ריר פֿון ליפּן,
אַ האַנט וואָס פּאָכט.
די ווײַטקייט האָט פֿאַרדעקט מײַן שטאָט —
מײַן פֿינצטערע נעסט.
מײַן גאַס — —
מײַן טרויער און מײַן פּאָן.

און ווערטער יאָגן, גרײַפֿן אָן:
פֿאַר וואָס האָסטו פֿאַרלאָזט?
אַוועק און צוגעמאַכט די טיר?
אָט איצט, ווען פֿינגער אונדזערע זײַנען אין קלעם,
ביסטו דער שוועסטער דעזערטיר.

די רעדער יאָגן זיך ווי בייזע הינט,
בילן, רײַסן שטיקער ערד.
און איך, ווי שטענדיק, זוך דאָס וואָרט
אויף ענטפֿערן —
ווײַל איך בין אויך גערעכט.

עס פֿאַלט ערגעץ אַראָפּ דער וועג.
מײַן גוף פֿאַלט אויך.
עס שרײַבט אַ שוואַרצן יעראָגליף
פֿון באַן דער יאָגנדיקער רויך
פֿון לאַנד צו לאַנד שיפֿרירטע בריוו.

— אָט נעמט אים דעם מענטש,
זײַן לעבן, זײַן געשריי,
און שטעלט אים הינטער דראָטן —
אין דער ריי.

אין נאָענטסטן קופּע פֿאָרט אַן אומשטערבלעכער פּאָעט.
(ס׳איז נישט מיצקעוויטש, ניין).

At the Threshold

The wind has taken away the last word.
A stir of lips,
A hand that waves.
Distance has covered my city—
My dark nest.
My street—
My sorrow and my flag.

And words chase, attack:
Why have you forsaken?
Left and slammed the door?
At this moment, when our hands are tied,[122]
You are the worst deserter.

The wheels chase like angry dogs,
Barking, tearing up chunks of earth.
And I, as always, seek the word
For answering—
Because I, too, am right.

Somewhere, the road falls away.
My body falls, too.
The smoke racing from the train
Writes a black hieroglyph—
From country to country, letters in code.

—Seize that person,
His life, his cry,
And set him behind wire
And bars, in prison!

An immortal poet travels on the closest heap.
(It is not Mickiewicz, no).[123]

ס'איז שטאָלץ זײַן לאַץ מיט פּרישן פּיאָלעט.
און ס'שמעקט זײַן אײראָפּעיִשקייט ווי פּאַסטע צו די ציין.

ער פֿאָרט איצט אין פֿאַרבלוטיקטן בערלין
אויף אַ באַבלומטן און אַ גלאַנציקן באַנקעט
אַ שמועס טאָן וועגן קולטור און פּאָעזיע,
דערמאָנען געטע און וואַן-גאָג.
(און אים, דעם פּערסישן, מיט טויזנט יאָר צוריק).
פֿון „שטערן גאָלדענע" די אײביקע מוזיק,
און פֿעלקער-ליבע הײַנט צו טאָג.

די גראַמען פּאָרן זיך ווי מײַז,
פֿלינקע. אונטערטעניק. פֿלײַסיק.
ס'איז יאָר — טויזנט נײַן הונדערט פֿינף און דרײַסיק.

His lapel is proud with fresh violets.
And his Europeanness smells like toothpaste.

He's travelling to bloodied Berlin now
For a flower-decked, gleaming banquet
To chat about culture and poetry,
Mentioning Goethe and Van Gogh.
(And that Persian, from a thousand years ago.)
The eternal music of "Golden Stars,"
And Brotherhood between Peoples nowadays.[124]

The swift rhymes mate like mice,
Submissively, diligently, they thrive.
It's the year nineteen hundred and thirty-five.

אין לאַנד פֿון מײַן געביין

דאָרט, ווו ס'ענדיקט זיך דער האָריזאָנט פֿון מײַנע אויגן,
הייבט זיך אָן דאָס לאַנד פֿון מײַן געביין.
מיט צען פֿינגער דורכגעקנאָטן,
דורכגעפֿלויגן אין אַ מעטראָ,
און פֿאַרהאַקט זיך לעם אַ ווײַסן קאַרשנבוים.

אַ גוט-מאָרגן! ס'איז אַ זוניקער מאָנטיק,
ס'איז אַ דינסטיק מיט אַ ווינטיקן רעגן,
(סאַראַ וווּנדער ס'איז, וואָס פֿיס פֿון מענטשן
קענען דורכגיין דורך אַזוי פֿיל טעג און וועגן).

עס ראַנגלט זיך אַ שטיבעלע מיט גרויער אָרעמקייט,
ווי מיט טריקעניש אַ שטאַרקער פֿלאַנץ.
שנײַדן אויף דעם טאָג די טירן מיט אַ כריפּע,
כאַפּט זיך אויף די קאַץ, די הינער און די גאַנדז.
כאַפּט זיך אויף אַ האָפֿענונג, אַז ס'וועלן אוגערקעס אין גאָרטן זיך צעגרינען,
און אַ הון וועט לייגן אַן איי.
ס'האָט די מאַמע — אַ קלוגער גענעראַל — געהייסן,
מען זאָל נישט וועלן קיין פֿלוימען-צימעס און קיין טיי.
ניין, איז ניין! ווער דאַרף זיך נאָך דעם פֿרעגן,
עס גרינען אַגרעסן, די וועלט איז העל.
עס ציטערן די פֿיס צו ווײַטע, זוניקע געיעגן,
נאָר דאָ קומט אָן אַ היימישער באַפֿעל:
— זע, די גאַנדז — וווּהין האָט זי אַוועקגעפּאַדעט?
שוין אַרײַן מסתּם צו חיים גדליהן אין סאַלאַטע.
גיט אַ ציטער דאָס בלויע בענדל אין מײַן צאָפּ
און ס'לעשט זיך אויס די זוניקייט און דער צעוויגטער פֿלאַטער.

עס זעגן איינס דאָס אַנדערע די כוואַליעס
פֿון אַלע ימען, וואָס איך בין דורכגעשווומען.
און ס'דאַכט זיך מיר: כ'האָב מענטשן און כ'האָב שטעט געזען
דורך אַ שפּיגל אַ פֿליסיקן און קרומען.
איך האָב מײַן זײַדן העמדל אויפֿגעפֿלאַטערט אויף אַ פּאָן,

In the Country of My Bones

There, where my eyes' horizon ends,
Rises the country of my bones.
Thoroughly kneaded with ten fingers,
Flown through in a metro,
And snagged near a white cherry tree.

Good morning! It's a sunny Monday,
It's a Tuesday with windy rain
(What a miracle, that people's feet
Can stroll through so many days and ways).

A cottage struggles against gray poverty
Like a hearty plant against drought.
The doors cut open the day with a rattle,
The cat awakens, and the hens, and the goose.
A hope awakens that cucumbers in the garden will turn green,
And a hen will lay an egg.
My mother—a clever general—ordered
That no one should want any plum-*tsimes*[125] and tea.
No, no! Who needs it?—
Cucumbers turn green, the world is bright.
My feet tremble toward distant, sunny races,
But now a familiar command arrives:
—Look, the goose! Where has she waddled?
Maybe into Khaim Gedalye's lettuce-patch.
The blue ribbon in my braid trembles
And the sunniness fades with the swaying flutter.

The waves saw away at one another, the waves
Of all the seas that I have floated through.
And it seems to me: I have seen people and cities
Through a crooked and fluid mirror.
I hoisted my silk shirt to flutter as a flag,[126]

און אין דער וועלט אַוועק אין העמד פֿון שווערער האָרעוואַניע,
בין איך גראָד געבליבן אַלעמען בעל־חובֿ,
און צו מיר שטעלט מען אַרויס די שווערסטע טענה.
אַזוי איז קלאָר.
דאָס קלאָרסטע שבקלאָרע.
דער יענקי וואָלט אויף דעם געזאָגט: אָקיי.
דער ליטוואַק זאָגט: עס טויג אויף אַ כּפּרה.

מאָדנע ווי די זון איז נאַקעט, און ס׳איז נאַקעט דאָס קלערן.
עס הענגט אַ כמאַרנעקייט אין מיר
און דעקט אַ זומערטאָג אַ ווייכן.
עס האָט זיך אַ קליין שטיבעלע באַגעגנט מיט עמפּײַער־סטייט
און איינס אַנטקעגן אַנדערן זיך אויסגעבויגן אין אַ פֿראַגע־צייכן:
דער עמפּײַער־סטייט האָט אָפֿן, פֿרעך
געטײַטלט מיטן העכסטן טורעם
און געשריבן בלאַנק און אומגעריכט,
ווי אַ בליץ אין פֿינצטערקייט פֿון שטורעם:
— זעסט, מיט מײַן העכסטן קופּערנעם שפּיץ
האָב איך פֿאַרשניטן אין הימל אַ בראָנע,
און אומזיסט האָט דײַן זיידע מיט ציטעריקע הענט
מחדש געווען די לבֿנה?

— זעסט, בײַ מײַן אײדלסטן געזימס,
מיט פֿינגער געפֿורעמט אין פֿיבער און פֿאָרכט,
זיצט פֿאַרלייגט אַ פֿוס אויף אַ פֿוס
דער גרעסטער פּאַסקודניאַק פֿון ניו־יאָרק?

און דאָס שטיבעלע, געוויינלעך, פֿרעגט זיך וואָס מען מאַכט,
און זאָגט מיר רויִק:
— אין האָניק איז נישטאָ פֿון בין די גיפֿטן — —
פֿאַרבעסער איך די טעותן אין לאַנד פֿון מײַן געביין
און פֿאַרצייכן זיי אין מײַנע שריפֿטן.

And went off into the world in a shirt of hard labor,
I seem always to be in debt to everyone,
And the worst complaints are always directed at me.
This is clear.
The clearest of all.
About this, the Yankee would say: Okay.[127]
The Litvak says: It's no damn good.[128]

Strange how the sun is naked, and thinking is naked.
A cloudiness hangs in me
And obscures a soft summer's day.
A cottage met up with the Empire State Building
And they bent together into a question-mark:
The Empire State Building openly, impudently
Pointed with its highest tower
And wrote as brilliantly and unexpectedly
As lightning in the darkness of a storm:
—See, with my highest copper tip
I've cut a harrow in the sky,
And your grandfather, for naught, with trembling hands
Blessed the new moon!

—See, at my most delicate cornice,
With fingers formed in fever and dread,
Sits, placing one leg upon the other
New York's greatest bastard?

And the cottage, as usual, asks how you are,
And calmly says to me:
—There's none of the bee's venom in honey—
I correct those mistakes in the country of my bones
And record them in my writings.

אַ ווײַסער פּאָעט

ה. לייוויקן

ניו-יאָרק.
אויף הונדערט פֿערטן שטאָק איז געשטאַנען אַ ווײַסער פּאָעט.
דער הימל און אַן אײַזערנע שטאָט
האָבן איינס מיט אַן אַנדער גערעדט.
עס האָט אַ דאָרשטיקער „אייביק" מאַרשירט
פֿאַרוואונדערט
און נישט אָרגאַניזירט.

ניו-יאָרק האָט געלויכטן מיט גרין,
מיט רויט,
מיט זוניקן בלענד.
ניו-יאָרק האָט פֿאַרטראַכט זיך
אויף ווײַטן און רוישיקן ענד.

אויף הונדערט פֿערטן שטאָק איז געשטאַנען אַ ווײַסער פּאָעט.
דער הימל און אַן אײַזערנע שטאָט
האָבן איינס מיט אַן אַנדער גערעדט.
דער באָרוועס האָט אויסגעבויט ניו-יאָרק,
שוואַרצע, איטאַליענער, אוקראַאינער, כינעזער, פּאָליאַקן און מיר.
— איך אַליין האָב דאָ געפֿאַרבט דעם העכסטן שטאָק,
איך אַליין האָב דאָ געקלעפּט פּאַפּיר.
ס'איז וואָרע וואָר,
אַ סימן: ס'איז דאָ אַראָפּגעפֿאַלן פֿון צענטן שטאָק
דער מוליער פֿון נאָווידוואָר.

אַלע פֿעלקער האָבן דאָ געזאָגט אַ וואָרט,
אַלע אויסגעזונגען זייער ליד.
אַ שוואַרצער איז געשטאָרבן פֿון אַ קלאַפּ אין קאָפּ.
אַן אוקראַאינער האָט זײַן סאָקאָל דערשטיקט.
אַ ייִד און אַ טשעך האָבן אָנגעפֿירט אַ שטרײַק.
אַ כינעזער האָט געדאַרט און געוויינט נאָך אַ בריוו.

A White Poet

For H. Leyvik[129]

New York.
A white poet stood on the hundred-and-fourth floor.
The sky and an iron city
Engaged in a conversation.
A thirsty "forever" marched on
In bewildered
Disorganization.

New York lit up green
And red,
With a dazzle of sun.
New York sank into thought
All the way to its far, noisy end.

A white poet stood on the hundred-and-fourth floor.
The sky and an iron city
Engaged in a conversation.
The barefoot built New York,
Blacks, Italians, Ukrainians, Chinese, Poles, and we Jews.
—I am the one who painted the highest floor here,
I am the one who pasted the wallpaper here,
It's absolutely true,
Here's proof: the bricklayer from Novidvor
Fell from the tenth floor here.

Here, all the peoples had their say,
All sang out their song.
A Black man died from a blow to the head.
A Ukrainian choked his falcon.[130]
A Jew and a Czech led a strike.
A Chinese man withered and wept for a letter.

איצט שטייען אַלע —
אין גרינער קורטקע פֿון רילעף
אויף פֿרעמדער גאַס.
מיסטער דזשאָ האָט אָפּגעריסן ווערטער פֿון פּאָעט:
— מעקס, דזשאַז!
און ס'האָבן אַ בלענד געטאָן צוויי הונדערט פּיס —
שוואַרצע, איטאַליענער, אוקראַינער, כינעזער, אַ ייִד און אַ גריך.
און האָבן אויסגעטאַנצט אַ זוניקן טאָג
און שטערנליכט
אַ לויכטנדיקן האַפֿן,
און דעם רקיע אין ערשטן ציטעריקן גליק
פֿון באַשאַפֿן.

אויף הונדערט פֿערטן שטאָק איז געשטאַנען אַ ווײַסער פּאָעט.
דער הימל און אַן אײַזערנע שטאָט
האָבן איינס מיט אַן אַנדער גערעדט.
אַ חלום איז —
עס איז נישט קיין וואָר,
אַז מײַן שטוב איז פֿאַרוואָקסן מיט דערנער און גראָז,
און ס'האָט אַ גאַנצע גאַס אין ניו-יאָרק
פֿאַרגעסן שוין דעם לעצטן אות.

ניו-יאָרק איז כלו ליכט.
ס'איז קיין שאָטן נישטאָ.
אַ חלום איז אַ קאָפּ אויפֿן שטיין,
וואָס דרימלט פֿאַרטוליעט אין בײַנאַכטיקער שעה.

אַ חלום איז — אַ ווײַסע טויב,
געזוכט אַ באַרגשפּיץ און אַ בלאַט,
און געקומען אויף צוריק
פֿון מאָרד, פֿון געוויין, פֿון פֿאַראַט.

דער פּאָעט האָט געשטיקט זיך מיט אייגענעם קול:
— אָט איז דער לאָם, די האַק,
דער עמפּײַער-סטייט זאָל ווערן צוריק צו ליים,
צוריק צו פֿעלזיקן שטיין.

Now all stand—
In gray jackets of Relief
On the foreign street.
Mister Joe interrupted words of a poet:
—Max, jazz![131]
And two hundred feet dazzled—
Blacks, Italians, Ukrainians, Chinese, a Jew and a Greek.
And danced out a sunny day
And starlight,
A luminous haven,
And the firmament in its first trembling happiness
Of creation.

A white poet stood on the hundred and fourth floor.
The sky and an iron city
Engaged in a conversation.
It's a dream—
It is not the truth
That my house is overgrown with grass and thorns,
And an entire New York City street
Has forgotten the last letter of the alphabet.

New York is all light.
There are no shadows.
A dream is a head on a stone, fast asleep,
Wrapped snugly in the hours of night.

It's a dream—a white dove
Seeking a mountaintop and a leaf,
That came back poisoned
From murder, betrayal, and grief.

The poet choked on his own words:
—Here is the crowbar, the ax,
The Empire State Building should return to clay,
Back to rocky stone.

איך גיי אַראָפּ...
איך גיי... איך גיי דאָס טאָן אַליין.

ניו-יאָרק איז כּלו ליכט
עס איז זוניקער ווײַס,
עס איז הימלשער גרין — —
מיסטער דזשאָ האָט אָפּגעריסן ווערטער פֿון פּאָעט:
— מעקס, מײַן מאַשין!

אויף הונדערט פֿערטן שטאָק איז געשטאַנען אַ ווײַסער פּאָעט.
דער הימל און אַן אײַזערנע שטאָט
האָבן איינס מיט אַן אַנדער גערעדט.

I'm going down . . .
I'm going . . . I'm going to do this alone.

New York is all light,
It is sunny white,
It is sky-green—
Mister Joe interrupted the words of the poet:
—Max, my machine!

A white poet stood on the hundred and fourth floor.
The sky and an iron city
Engaged in a conversation.

בײַ מיר אין האַנט צוויי פֿעדערן פֿון אַ פֿאַזאַן

בײַ מיר אין האַנט צוויי פֿעדערן פֿון אַ פֿאַזאַן.
פֿון יונגן לאַנד, פֿון בירעבידזשאַן.
בײַ מיר אין האַנט צוויי פֿעדערן פֿון אַ פֿאַזאַן —
שלאַנקע,
דינע.
אין זיי איז וווּנדער דאָ —
פֿון אַ פֿרימאָרגנדיקער, ליכטיקער מדינה.
פֿון שטעט און נעמען אומגעריכטע.
פֿון נײַעם ווענד אין דער געשיכטע.
נאָר מײַן זכּרון, די אַלטע קראָ,
וואָס טראָגט מיך נאָך דעם אַלטן פּויק פֿון דורות —
איז שוין דאָ.
מען רופֿט בײַם נאָמען מיך —
אַן אַלטער קול.
אַ הינקעדיקער טישל נידעריק, און שמאָל.
אַ פֿינפֿער-לעמפּל רייכערט צו און ברענט.
און אַלטע הענט פֿליקן פֿעדערן.
הײַפֿלעך ראַבע, גרויע.
ס'איז שפּעטער האַרבסט. ס'איז נאָגעניש. און קינדערישער טרויער.
און קרומע לאָדן
אויף זשאַווערדיקע לאָמען,
שרעקן מיט נאַכט, און מיט פֿאַרטײַעטע פּאָגראָמען.

און מײַן זכּרון, די אַלטע קראָ,
זי הויערט איבער מיר שוין דאָ,
אָט איצטער, אין ניו-יאָרק, אין בראָנקס.
ס'איז דאָ אַ לעבן, אַזוי צו זאָגן, אויך אַ קראַנקס.
די זעלבע וואָג. די זעלבע הענדלערישע לאַטע.
ס'איז נישט קיין קראָם, עס איז אַ סטאָר.
ס'איז נישט קיין בערדיקער, נאָר אַ געגאָלטער טאַטע.

בײַ מיר אין האַנט צוויי פֿעדערן פֿון אַ פֿאַזאַן.
כאָטש ס'קלינגט דאָס וואָרט פֿאַזאַן

In My Hand Two Feathers from a Pheasant

In my hand two feathers from a pheasant.
From the young land of Birobidzhan.[132]
In my hand two feathers from a pheasant—
Slender,
Thin.
There is in them the wonder
Of tomorrow's light-filled state.
Of unexpected cities and names.
Of a new turn in history.
But my memory, the old crow
That still carries the old drum of generations to me,
Is already here.
I am called by name—
An old voice.
A low and narrow, limping little table.
A five-penny lamp smokes and burns.[133]
And old hands pluck feathers.
Bunches of feathers, speckled, gray.
It's late autumn. It's anguishing, childhood sadness.
And crooked shutters
On rusty hinges
Terrify with night and with concealed pogroms.

And my memory, that old crow,
Hovers here, above me
Even now, in New York, in the Bronx.
There's a life here, that is to say, a sick life, too.
The same scales. The same mercenary patch.
No longer a "*krom*," it's a "store."[134]
No longer a bearded but a shaven father.

In my hand two feathers from a pheasant.
Although the word "pheasant" rings

צו פֿרעמד, צו איידל.
ס'איז נישט ווי ממזר-גאָנאָרוק,
און שוין אַוודאי נישט ווי קאַטשקע-דריידל.
עס קלינגט אָבער ווי טראַקטאָר, בירע, טײַגע —
ווערטער מונטערע, באַוואָפֿנטע,
און אויסגעטאָנענע פֿון אַלטער דאגה.
שטאַרק און אומגעריכט אַרויסגערעגנט —
ערשטע ייִדישע אויטאָנאָמע געגנט.

און כאָטש איך האָב די טײַגע קיין מאָל נישט געזען,
און נישט די בירע —
און ס'גאַנצע לאַנד האָב איך אויסגעחלומט
פֿון אַ טויזנט-מײַלעדיקער ווײַט —
הער איך: עס שרײַט
מיט וואַלד און וואַסערן,
מיט טאַנקס,
מיט געפּאַנצערטע, שטאָלענע מעווס —
דאָס ליד פֿון אַלע לידער:
וגר זאב עם כבש.

Too foreign, too refined.
It's not like "***momzer-gonoruk***,"
(the gander's gonorrheal bastard)
And certainly not like "***katshke-dreydl***"
(lucky-ducky, spin the top, you will win where it will stop).[135]
But it rings like tractor, Bire, Tiga—[136]
Hearty, armed words
That have shaken off those old worries.
Strong and unexpectedly raining down—
The first autonomous Jewish region.

And although I have never seen the Tiga area
Or the river Bire—
And I dreamed up this entire country
From a thousand-mile distance—
I listen: it shouts out
With woods and waters,
With tanks,
With armored, steel seagulls
The song of all songs:
And the wolf shall dwell with the lamb.[137]

אותיות

אין בראַנקס, אין ברוקלין און ניו-יאָרק-סיטי,
האָבן מײַנע שוועסטערקינדער קראָמען.
זיבן שוועסטערקינדער מיט זיבן קראָמען, ווי געבאָטן.
ביזנעסלײַט מיט לאַנגע צעטלען פֿון באַנקראָטן.
און מײַן פֿאַמיליע-נאָמען האָט אַ קוק געטאָן אויף מיר פֿון זייערע שילדן
מיט אַ בליק — אַ פֿרעמדן און אַ ווילדן.
עס האָט דער פֿלאַמעדיקער „מעם" (פֿון משה און פֿון מאַרקס)
געהיפּעט אויף אַ גרינעם פּיסל.
דער „אַלף" האָט בלאַנק געוווּנקען צו דער גאַס.
דער „למד" האָט אויסגעשלײַפֿט זיך ווי אַ תּליה.
און ס'האָט דער „אַלף-בית" געשריִען אין אײַזערנעם געבראַזג פֿון שטאָט:
— באַנקראָט, באַנקראָט און נאָך אַ מאָל באַנקראָט.
נאָר אונטערן שילד זײַנען דער פֿעטער מיכל און די מומע שׂרה
ברייט געוואָרן, קיין עין-הרע.
זי — אַ בלויע זײַדענע פּאַס,
און ער — אַ גרויע, שטאָלענע ספּרונזשינע.
און די קינדער: דזשולי, ביטריס, מעקס און קאַראָלינע,
האָבן שטאָלץ געטראָגן אויפֿן פּלייצע אותיות ווי שטערן,
צו וועלכן קאָרטנקלוב און בוי-סקאָוט זיי געהערן.

Alphabet Letters

In the Bronx, in Brooklyn and in New York City,
My cousins all have stores.
Seven cousins with seven stores, like commandments.
Business people with long lists of going bankrupt.
And my family-name stares at me from their signs
With a gaze that's wild and foreign.
The flaming *mem* (of Moses and of Marx)
Skips on one green foot.
The *alef* winks glossily at the street below.
The *lamed* loops a knot like a gallows.[138]
And the alphabet shrieks in the city's iron uproar:
—Bankrupt, bankrupt and bankrupt some more.
But beneath the sign, my Uncle Mikhl and Aunt Sore
Have gotten fat—evil eye, stay away—*keyn ayen hore.*[139]
She—a blue silk barrel,
And he—a gray steel spring.
And their children—Julie, Beatrice, Max and Carolyn—
Proudly wear letters like stars on short sleeves and long,
For the card clubs and Boy Scout troops to which they
belong.[140]

ירושה

אַ הימל איז דאָ — זײַנען שטערן פֿאַראַן.
און איך — האַלב אַ בדחן
און האַלב אָרעמאַן.

ווער ווייס צי אַ שווינדלער, ווער ווייס — אַ פּאָעט
אין אַנטליִענע שיך —
אין פֿאַרבלאָנדזשעטער בעט.

קיין זאַך נישט קיין סימן —
קיין זאַך נישט באַווײַזט.
ס'קען זײַן ס'איז דאָס לעבן אין גאַנצן פֿאַרגרײַזט.

נאָר די גראַמען שטאָלצירן מיט גאָלדענער סמיכה
פֿון שינדלנעם דאַך
מיט צעריסענער סטריכע.

אין פרײַסן געווען, און אַ ביסל פֿאַרטשאַדעט,
מיט אַ פּסוק פֿאַרשלייערט,
מיט אַ לאַטע פֿאַרלאַטעט.

נאָר די אותיות זײַנען געירשנט ווילגיביק,
פֿון דעם אַלטן מלמד
לייזער-בער מיטן ציבעק.

Legacy

Here is a sky—stars are there.
And I—half jester,
Half pauper.[141]

Who knows if a poet, who knows if a fraud
In borrowed shoes,
In a meandering bed.[142]

No thing is a symbol—
Nothing to reveal.
Maybe life is all wrong, a raw deal.

But in gold ordination, rhymes proudly sputter
From a shingled roof
With a torn gutter.

Was in Prussia, somewhat perplexed,
Veiled with a verse,
With a patch, patched.[143]

But the alphabet is bequeathed plentiful and ripe
By the old schoolteacher
Leyzer-ber with his pipe.

VII

דער מלך דוד אַליין איז געבליבן

ניו-יאָרק, 1946

VII

Der melekh dovid aleyn iz geblibn
(Only King David Remained)
New York, 1946

אל חנון

אל חנון,
קלײַב אויס אַן אַנדער פֿאָלק,
דערוויל.
מיר זײַנען מיד פֿון שטאַרבן און געשטאָרבן,
מיר האָבן ניט קיין תּפֿילות מער,
קלײַב אויס אַן אַנדער פֿאָלק,
דערוויל,
מיר האָבן ניט קיין בלוט מער
אויף צו זײַן אַ קרבן.
אַ מידבר איז געוואָרן אונדזער שטוב.
די ערד איז קאַרג פֿאַר אונדז אויף קבֿרים,
נישטאָ קיין קינות מער פֿאַר אונדז,
נישטאָ קיין קלאָגליד
אין די אַלטע ספֿרים.

אל חנון,
הייליק אַן אַנדער לאַנד,
אַן אַנדער באַרג.
מיר האָבן אַלע פֿעלדער שוין און יעדן שטיין
מיט אַש, מיט הייליקן באַשאָטן.
מיט זקנים,
און מיט יונגע,
און מיט עופֿעלעך באַצאָלט
פֿאַר יעדן אות פֿון דײַנע צען געבאָטן.

אל חנון,
הייב אויף דײַן פֿײַערדיקע ברעם,
און זע די פֿעלקער פֿון דער וועלט —
גיב זיי די נבֿואות און די יום-נוראָים.
אין יעדן לשון פּרעפּלט מען דײַן וואָרט —
לערן די מעשׂים זיי,
די וועגן פֿון נסיון.

Merciful God

Merciful God,
Choose another people,
Elect another.[144]
We are tired of death and dying,
We have no more prayers.
Choose another people,
Elect another.
We have no more blood
To be a sacrifice.
Our house has become a desert.
The earth is insufficient for our graves,
No more laments for us,
No more dirges
In the old, holy books.

Merciful God,
Sanctify another country,
Another mountain.
We have strewn all the fields and every stone
With ash, with holy ash.
With the aged,
With the youthful,
And with babies, we have paid
For every letter of your Ten Commandments.

Merciful God,
Raise your fiery brow,
And see the peoples of the world—
Give them the prophecies and the Days of Awe.
Your word is babbled in every language—
Teach them the deeds,
The ways of temptation.

אל חנון,
גיב פראָסטע בגדים אונדז,
פֿון פֿאַסטעכער פֿאַר שאָף,
פֿון שמידן בײַ דעם האַמער,
פֿון וועש־וואַשער, פֿון פֿעל־שינדער,
און נאָך מער געמיינעס.
און נאָך איין חסד טו צו אונדז:
אל חנון,
נעם צו פֿון אונדז די שכינה פֿון גאונות.

1945

Merciful God,
Give us simple garments
Of shepherds with their sheep,
Blacksmiths at their hammers,
Laundry-washers, skin-flayers,
And even the more base.
And do us one more favor:
Merciful God,
Deprive us of the Divine Presence of genius.[145]

1945

אַ בריוו צו אליהו הנבֿיא

אַלטער בשׂורה-טרעגער, אליהו,
איך האָב פֿאַרלאָרן אַלע אַדרעסן,
שרײַב איך איצט אַ בריוו צו דיר.
האָסט אַלטע פֿרײַנדשאַפֿט זיכער ניט פֿאַרגעסן,
ווען כ'פֿלעג דיר קינדווײַז עפֿענען די טיר.

ניט איין מאָל דיך געפֿירט מיט ציטער און מיט תּפֿילה
צום יום-טובֿדיקן טיש, צום כּוס מיט ווײַן.
עס קען ניט זײַן, זאָלסט איצט ניט וועלן אויסהערן
מײַן ביטערע מגילה,
עס קען ניט זײַן.

כ'האָב לײַכטזיניק פֿאַרשניטן אַלע דײַנע שפּורן
און אויך די ווײַטקייט פֿון מײַן הימל,
און אויך די וואָרעמקייט פֿון גלויבן.
עס שטייען מײַנע לידער איצטער נאַקעטע, ווי הורן,
נאָר דײַנע מעשׂהלעך פֿאַרדעקן זיי ווי טויבן.

צווישן אונדז אַזעלכע פֿרעמדע תּהומען זײַנען אויפֿגעקומען,
איך האָב, זעט אויס, געגראָבן זיי אומזיסט.
איך שווער, איך האָב געוואָלט פֿאַרזייען זיי מיט בלומען,
ס'איז ניט מײַן שולד, וואָס זיי זײַנען פֿאַרשאָטן איצט מיט מיסט.

איך האָב געוואָלט דערגראָבן זיך צו זיסע קוואַלן,
פֿאַר זיך קיין טראָפּן ניט גענומען,
ניט אײַנגעשלאָגן ערגעץ ניט פֿאַר זיך קיין סלופּ.
דו האָסט איידל אויסגעפֿורעמט מיר מײַן האַלדז און גומען,
ווי איידל דו פֿלעגסט טאָן פֿון כּוס אַ זופּ.

דו ביסט דער נבֿיא פֿון רחמים און נקמה,
דײַן פֿײַערדיקער רײַטוואָגן די וואָלקנס ברעכט,
דו ווייסט מײַן האַרץ, איך האָב געפֿירט די בראָנע
אויף רייניקן די בײַט פֿאַר גוטסקייט און פֿאַר רעכט.

A Letter to Elijah the Prophet

Old message-bearer, Elijah,
I have lost all the addresses,
So now I write a letter to you.
Surely you have not forgotten an old friendship,
When, as a child, I would open the door for you.

More than once, trembling and praying, I led you
To the holiday table, to the cup of wine.
It can't be that now you will not hear out
My long, bitter letter,
This bitter *megile* of mine.[146]

Reckless, I tore up all traces of you
And also the reach of my sky,
And also the warmth of belief.
Now my poems stand naked, like whores,
But your stories cover them like doves.

Abysses of strangeness have opened between us.
It seems that I dug them in vain.
I swear that I wanted to sow them with flowers,
It's not my fault they're now filled with dung.

I wanted to dig down deep to sweet springs,
For myself, not taking a drop,
Never pounding in a stake for myself anywhere.[147]
You delicately molded my palate, my throat,
As, nobly, you used to sip from the cup.

You are the prophet of mercy and vengeance,
Your fiery chariot shatters the clouds.
You know my heart. I have guided the harrow
To cleanse the garden for justice and good.

איך בין געפֿאַלן און צעטראָטן,
און יעדער הונט, וואָס לויפֿט פֿאַרבײַ, גיט מיך אַ ביס,
נאָר ס'קלאַפּט מײַן האַרץ, גאַרט ביזן לעצטן אָטעם
צום קוואַל צום אייביקן, וואָס איז נאָך אפֿשר זיס.

אַן עוולה, וואָס דו קומסט ניט און דו זעצסט זיך ניט אַנידער
בײַ סדרים אונדזערע מיט חמצדיקן ווײַן.
מיר זינגען דאָרט אַזעלכע לאַנגוויַיליקע לידער,
אַז דו אַליין וואָלטסט אפֿשר מציל זײַן.

אָפֿט ווילט זיך מיר, אַז דו זאָלסט ווידער קומען,
בקפֿיצת-דרך, אויף זילבערנעם לבֿנה-גראָז,
וואָלטסט ווי אַ מאָל מיך ווידער מיטגענומען
אין ליכטיקן מאַרשרוט פֿאַרזוכן יעדער כּוס.

צי ביסטו דאָרט געווען?
דאָרט... דאָרט... אונטערן בייזן מויער?
אין לאַנד פֿון פּײַן, אין היים פֿון בראָך?
צי איז אויף זייער יום-טובֿדיקן טרויער
די לאַטע גרעסער ווי אין מיטן וואָך?

צי האָסטו דאָרט געהערט אַ קינדס געלעכטער?
אַ קינד מיט בלאָנדע הערעלעך, געשאָרן.
צי האָסטו זייער כּוס פֿאַרזוכט?
צי זײַנען דײַנע ליפּן ניט פֿאַרברענט געוואָרן?

עס שטיקן זיך אין האַלדז בײַ מיר אַזוי פֿיל נעמען...
כ'האָב מורא פֿרעגן דיך, און זאָג מיר גאָרניט,
אויב ס'האָט עפּעס זיך געטראָפֿן...
גיב אַ ריר דײַנע רחמימדיקע ברעמען,
פֿאַרלעש מײַן לאָמפּ,
און אויב עס איז צו דיר קיין בשורה ניט דערפֿלויגן,
פֿאַרלעש מײַן לאָמפּ
און מאַך מיר צו די אויגן.

1942

I am fallen and trampled,[148]
Bitten by each dog running past on the street.
But my heart beats on, craving until my last breath
The eternal wellspring that may still be sweet.

What an injustice that you don't come take a seat
At our Seders with their everyday wine.[149]
The songs that we sing there are so tiresome,
Perhaps you'd want redemption in time.

Often I wish that you would come again
Over silver moon-grass, a magic shortcut,[150]
And take me with you again, as before,
On your bright route, tasting every cup.

Have you been there?
There . . . there . . . behind the evil wall?
In the land of pain, in the home of ruin?
Is the patch on their holiday despair
Larger than in the middle of the week?

Did you hear a child laughing there?
A child with shorn, blond hair?
Did you take a sip from their cups?
Did it scald your lips?

So many names stick in my throat . . .
I'm afraid to ask you, and don't tell me
If something has happened . . .
Bestir your compassionate brow,
Put out my lamp,
And if you have received no news,
Put out my lamp
And close my eyes.

1942

בריוו פֿון געטאָ

אײַערע קורצע בריוו —
דרײַ שורות אויף אַ קאַרטל, ניט מער.
ווי יעדע מײַל וואָלט צוגעלייגט אַ שטיין —
אַזוי זײַנען זיי שווער.

אַ שורה וועגן אַלעמענס געזונט,
בײַם נאָמען יעדערן דערמאָנט,
מען זאָל ניט דאַרפֿן איבערקלערן,
און רחמים בעט דער ווײַסער בלויז אויפֿן פּאַפּיר,
אַזוי מסתּמא איז דער כּתבֿ פֿון טרערן.

די קורצע בריוו —
זיי ליגן בײַ מיר אַלע אויפֿגעקליבן,
ביז סוף פֿון דורות וועלן זיי פֿאַרבלײַבן.
איך זע די ציטערדיקע האַנט, וואָס שרײַבט זיי איצט,
איך ווייס די פֿײַערדיקע האַנט,
וואָס וועט מיט רחמים דעם בלויז דערשרײַבן.

1941

Letters from the Ghetto

Your brief letters—
Three lines on a card, nothing more.
As if every mile added a stone—
That is how heavy they are.

A line about everybody's health,
Each one mentioned by name,
There is no need to worry,
And the white blankness pleads for mercy on the paper,
Thus, probably, is the script of tears.

These brief letters—
They all lie gathered to me,
They will remain until the end of generations.
I see the trembling hand that writes them now,
I know the fiery hand
That will inscribe the blankness with mercy.

1941

אַ ליד וועגן זיך

אַן אַלטע נאַרישע געוווינהייט — לידער,
די ערשטע שורה קומט אַליין פֿון זיך,
אַ ריר, אַ ברום, אַ קול, אַ ווידערקול און ווידער,
ווי אַלע אותיות וואָלטן געטראָגן שיך.

עס לויפֿט די ערשטע ריי,
די סטראָפֿע איז געשלאָסן מיט אַ ריג,
זי גיט אַ פֿלי, ווי ערשטער גרינגער שניי,
וווהין? וווהין? און פֿאַלט צוריק.

זי פֿאַלט צוריק איבער מײַן קאָפּ,
שוין נישט ווי גרינגער שניי, נאָר ווי אַ שטיין.
אָט גיב איך זיך אַ ריס... אין ערגעץ מוז מען גיין...
וווהין, וווהין זשע גיין?

איך האָב געוווּסט: אין מיזרח-זײַט גייט אויף די זון.
איך האָב געוווּסט, דער דרום איז די העלע שײַן.
איך האָב געוווּסט, דער מערבֿ איז די רײַפֿע בלום,
איך האָב געוווּסט, דער צפֿון איז דער ווײַסער לײַן.

די גאַנצע געאָגראַפֿיע ליגט קאַפּויער,
און אַלע מײַנע ליבשאַפֿטן — פֿאַרסמטע.
די קראָ — דער זינגער איז, דער טרייסטער — איז אַ טכויר,
און אַלע ליבסטע זעען אויס, ווי אומבאַקאַנטע.

ס'איז בלויז געבליבן נאָך אַ ווערוויק אויף אַ צווײַג,
דערשראָקן פּונקט ווי איך, און פּונקט ווי איך פֿאַרלאָרן,
ס'האָט זיך געחלומט אים אַ בלוט-געפֿאַרבטע שטײַג,
און זײַנע טענץ, ווי מײַנע לידער, זײַנען אײַנגעפֿראָרן.

איך האָב געהערט אַ מאָל דעם גאַנג פֿון הילכעדיקע מאַרשן,
איך האָב געזען אַ מאָל דעם פֿלאַם פֿון פֿײַערדיקע פֿאָנען,
איך האָב פֿאַרזוכט אַ מאָל דעם ווײַן פֿון רײַפֿע קאַרשן,
כ'האָב ליב געהאַט דאָס ליד פֿון רוישנדיקע שטראָמען.

A Poem about Itself

Old, idiotic habit—poems:
All by itself, the first line goes,
A stir, a voice, an echo hums,
As if all the letters were wearing shoes.

Running and hurrying comes the first row,
The strophe, closed with bolt and lock,
It flurries up, a first, light snow,
Where to go? Where? And then falls back.

Back it falls upon my head,
More like a stone, not like light snow,
Then I tug at myself . . . you must go somewhere . . .
Where, oh, where is there to go?

I once knew: the sun rose in the East.
I once knew: it shines brightly in the South.
I once knew: a ripe flower is the West.
I once knew: white flax is the North.

All geography lies topsy-turvy,
All my loves turned poison, lovesbane.
The crow—consoler, singer,—a coward;
All dearest are snuffed out, unknown.

All that's left is a squirrel, afraid
Like me, lost like me, on its branch,
Dreaming up a blood-colored cage,
And like my poems, frozen in its dance.

Once I heard the marches pass, resounding,
Once I saw the flame of fiery flags,
Once I sipped the wine of just-ripe cherries,
I loved the rushing river's song.

די וועלט איז יונג געווען,
געוואָלט משדך זײַן זיך מיטן הימל...
איצט האַלט איך אײַנגעטונקט אַ שווערע פּאַרקער-פּען
און שרײַב אַן אַלטן „בית", און וועק אַ דרימלענדיקן „גימל".

נאָר אויף קיין איינציקער פֿון מײַנע ליבעס האָב איך ניט חרטה.
פֿון יעדן פֿרילינג בלײַבט אין אויג אַ פֿלאַם
און וואַרעמט איצט אין נאַכט פֿון מיאוסער שלעכאָטע,
ווען יעדע מכשפֿה פּיקט אין באַראַבאַן.

ס'איז אפֿשר רעכט, וואָס כ'ליג איצט, ווי אַ מויז אין נאָרע,
אין איסט-ניו-יאָרק, אויף עשפֿאָרד סטריט.
און כ'הער בײַ נאַכט, ווי ס'כריפּעט און עס פּלאַצט די קאָרע
פֿון אַלע ליבשאַפֿטן, וואָס האָבן אָפּגעבליט.

און כ'הער די ווינטן שפּילן אויף, ווי הכנעהדיקע קלעזמער
די פֿייגל וואַקלען זיך ווי ווײַסע פֿלעקן,
איך גיב אַ ריס זיך — וויל אַ טרייסט פֿאַררופֿן,
אַ טרייסט פֿאַררופֿן, דעם חושך צו פֿאַרדעקן.

און שווערע רעדער זײַנען די מעת-לעתן,
ס'איז ניט קיין פֿיר און צוואַנציק שעה איצט אַ מעת-לעת.
אַ ים קען אויסרינען, אַ האַרץ קען זיך פֿאַרלעשן,
און אפֿשר, אפֿשר קען געשען אַ נס.

1941

Wanting to get married to the sky,[151]
The world was still young then . . .
I write an old *beys*, waken a dozing *giml*[152]
Now when I dip my heavy Parker Pen.

But I do not regret one single love.
From every springtime, my eyes keep a flame
That warms me on this ugly, slushy night
When every witch bangs on her drum.[153]

It may be fitting, that I lie at night,
A mouse curled in its lair, in East New York,
On Ashford Street, and hear the creak and burst
Of the bark on all my loves that bloom no more.

I hear winds playing, meek musicians.
Birds wobble like white blurs,
I tug at myself, I call forth consolation,
To cover up the dark and the obscure.

Nocturnal, diurnal, a night, a day,[154]
Not twenty-four hours, but heavy wheels.
A sea can drain out, a heart flickers away,[155]
I hope against hope for miracles.

1941

צו אַ קינדס פּאָרטרעט

דאָס קרײַזעלע אַרום דײַן קלייד,
איז קינדיש, איז מילד און זיס.
די זעקעלעך אויף דײַנע קליינע פּיס,
פֿון דײַנע שיכעלעך די זוילן אַרויסגעשטעלט
צו אונדזער גרויסער, נאַרישער און ווילדער וועלט.

עס שרעקט מיך די גרויסע פּילקע לעם דײַנע קליינע הענט,
אַ גלאָבוס דערמאָנט זי מיר, —
אַ וועלט וואָס יאָמערט און וואָס ברענט,
עס שרעקט מיך דער פֿײַער, וואָס איז אַזוי נאָענט —
צו דײַנע קליינע הענט.

עס שרעקט מיך די שטאָט אַוווּ דו וווינסט,
די געלע לאַטע אויף דײַן מאַמעס קלייד,
דאָס גרויסע שיסעלע מיט גריץ,
וואָס דו האַלטסט צו דעם די הענטלעך אויסגעשפּרייט.

עס שרײַבט דײַן מאַמע, אַז דו גייסט שוין און דו לאַכסט, —
גלייב איך ווידער, אַז וווּנדער האָבן נאָך ניט אויסגעפּעלט,
און אפֿשר וועסטו מיט דײַנע קליינע טריט
אונדז ברענגען ווידער צו אַ לאַכעדיקער וועלט.

1941

To a Child's Portrait

The little ruffle around your dress
Is girlish, mild, and sweet.
The little socks on your small feet,
The soles of your little shoes exposed
To our large, foolish, and wild world.

I'm frightened by the large ball near your hands,
It reminds me of a globe,—
A world that mourns, a world that burns,
I'm frightened by the fire that is so close
To your small hands.

I'm frightened by the city where you live,
The yellow patch on your mother's dress,
The gray dish of groats
To which your little hands reach out.

Your mother writes that you already walk and laugh,—
And I believe again that wonders never end,
And maybe with your little steps, you will
Bring us to a laughing world again.

1941

דער בעל־תּקיעה

דער בעל־תּקיעה יאָמערט אויס אַ ניגון,
אַן אַלטן ניגון צו גאָט.
איבער אים —
אַ הימל אָן שטערן,
חושך אין חושך פֿאַרלאָרן,
דער בעל־תּקיעה יאָמערט אויס אַ ניגון:
תּקיעה, תּרועה, שבֿרים.

די פֿינצטערקייט — אַ ווינט, אַ מויער,
עס איז קיין עדה,
קיין מנין נישטאָ.
דער בעל־תּקיעה יאָמערט אויס אַ ניגון:
הללויה.

לעבן אים אַ פֿאַרלאָשענער דאָרן,
אין חושך נאָך פֿינצטערער שטאַרט,
דער בעל־תּקיעה יאָמערט אויס אַ ניגון,
אַן אַלטן ניגון,
און וואַרט —
דער דאָרן זאָל אָנהייבן ברענען,
אויף אַ וואַנט זאָל אַ פֿלאַם טאָן אַ שריפֿט.
איבער אים אַ הימל אָן שטערן,
און חושך,
און טויטלעכער גיפֿט.
נאָר ס'איז נישט מפֿסיק,
עס שטילט נישט דער האָרן:
תּקיעה,
תּרועה,
שבֿרים.

1945

The Shofar Blower

The shofar blower keens a melody,
An old melody to God.
Above him—
A sky without stars,
Primordial darkness lost in darkness,[156]
The shofar blower keens a melody:
Teki'ah, *Teru'ah*, *Shebarim.*[157]

The blackness[158]—a wind, a wall,
There is no congregation,
No quorum at all.
The shofar blower keens a melody,
An old melody:
Hallelujah.

Near him, an extinguished thorn,
As he stares into even blacker darkness,
The shofar blower keens a melody,
An old melody,
And waits—
The thorn shall begin to burn,
A flame shall inscribe on a wall.
Above him, a sky without stars,
And primordial darkness,
And deadly venom.
But this does not interrupt,[159]
Does not silence the horn:
Teki'ah,
Teru'ah,
Shebarim.

1945

אָנבאָט

מײַן גאָט, ווי אַ גוטער עלטער-פֿעטער
ביסטו פֿול געווען אין שטוב בײַ אונדז אין אַלע ווינקלען.
פֿאַרבעט צו גאַסט מיך איצט און לייג ניט אָפּ אויף שפּעטער,
דײַן שור-הבר פֿאַרזוכן, דײַן אַלטן ווײַן כ׳וויל טרינקען.

און מאַך דאָס פּשוט, אין אַ מיטוואָך איין מאָל אין אַ העלן,
(נאָר גרייט דאָרט צו פֿאַר מיר אַ פּוסבענקל אַ שיינעם).
איינע פֿון די וועלטן דײַנע איז מיר ניט געפֿעלן,
כ׳האָב מורא פֿאַר די מושלים... טאָ זאָג דאָס ניט פֿאַר קיינעם.

דו מאַכסט אַזעלכע מאָדנע שפּאַסן
מיט דײַן שיינעם בלומען-גאָרטן,
און אין ניו-יאָרק אַפֿילו מיט דײַן פֿאָלק ישׂראל,
וואָס ווײנט אויף אונדזער חורבן, וויינט און שפּילט אין קאָרטן.

נאָר שיק נאָך מיר דײַן שענסטן מלאך,
עס זאָל מיר גרינג זײַן פֿליִען אין דײַן היכל,
טאָ שיק נאָך מיר דײַן סאַמע שענסטן מלאך,
עס זאָל מײַן לעצטער בליק פֿאַרלאָשן ווערן מיט אַ שמייכל.

1940

Proposition

My God, like a kindly great-uncle
You filled up all the corners of our home.
Invite me now to visit and don't postpone,
I'll sample your Wild Ox, I'll drink your ancient wine.[160]

And make it simple, one bright Wednesday
(But get a pretty footstool ready there for me).[161]
One of your worlds doesn't please me at all,
I'm afraid of the rulers . . . so be sure not to tell.

You play such odd jokes
On your beautiful flower garden,
And on your people Israel, even in New York,
Who weep over our destruction, and keep playing cards.[162]

Just be sure to send your most beautiful angel
To make it easy for me to fly to your Temple,[163]
Do send your most beautiful angel,
To snuff out my last glance with a smile.

1940

אין דער גרויסאַרטיקער ווינונג פֿון דער אייביקייט

ווען איר וועט קומען צו מיר, פֿרײַנד,
צו מײַן גרויסאַרטיקער ווינונג פֿון דער אייביקייט,
זאָגט גוט-מאָרגן מיט אַ שמייכל באַגלייט,
איך וועל אײַך הערן אין דער ווינונג פֿון דער אייביקייט.

ס'איז דאָרט ניט פֿינצטער און ניט פֿײַכט.
אַ פּאַלאַץ אייביק גרויס און גראָם,
כ'וועל האָבן דאָרט אַ טעלעפֿאָן
צו אים אַליין און צו זײַנע לײַט
אין מײַן גרויסאַרטיקער ווינונג פֿון דער אייביקייט.

די זון מיט וואַרעמקייט וועט קומען אויף באַזוך,
דער שניי וועט אויסשפּרייטן אַ ווײַסן פּוך,
און יעדער פֿויגל אין זײַן זומער
וועט אַ טרילער טאָן זײַן פֿרייד
און קומען צו מיר אין דער גרויסאַרטיקער ווינונג פֿון דער אייביקייט.

די שטערן וועלן קנעלן מיט איר פֿילאָזאָפֿי,
די לבֿנה וועט פּלאַפּלען פֿון הי און ניט-הי,
זיי וועלן אויך אַ מאָל אין רויטן פּלאַם פֿאַרדרייט
קומען צו מיר אין דער ווינונג פֿון דער אייביקייט.

ווען איר וועט קומען צו מיר, פֿרײַנד,
צו מײַן גרויסאַרטיקער ווינונג פֿון דער אייביקייט,
דערציילט אַ מעשׂה מיט אַ שמייכל אַ באַהעלטן,
ווײַל אונדזער וועלט איז סוף-כּל-סוף, ווי ס'זאָגט דער קלוגער פֿילאָסאָף,
נאָך אַלץ די בעסטע פֿון די וועלטן.

כאָטש קהלת האָט אַ סבֿרא,
אַז זי טויג אויף אַ כּפּרה.

1943

In the Magnificent Dwelling of Eternity

My friends, when you will come to visit me
In my magnificent dwelling of Eternity,
Say "Good morning" accompanied by a smile,
I will hear you in the dwelling of Eternity.

There, it is neither damp nor dark.
A palace, huge and roomy, eternally,
There I will have a telephone
To Him Himself and to His gentlefolk,
In my magnificent dwelling of Eternity.

With warmth, the sun will come to call,
The snow will spread out its white down,
And every bird in its own summer will
Warble its joy to one and all
And come to me in the magnificent dwelling of Eternity.

The stars will teach philosophy to me,
The moon will chatter about what's here and far away.
And sometimes, they, too, twisted in red flames,
Will come to me in the dwelling of Eternity.

My friends, when you will come to visit me
In my magnificent dwelling of Eternity,
Tell a story with a dazzling smile,
Because, in the long run, our world still
Is, as the clever philosopher says,
The best of all worlds, afterall.

Although Ecclesiastes has a hypothesis
That the world is worthless.[164]

1943

געזעגענונג

שוין לאַנג אַ שורה ניט געשריבן,
ס'ווערט אויסגעלאָשן מער און מער פֿון האַרץ דער פֿלאַם.
אַ דאַנק פֿאַר די געוועזענע חסדים,
פֿאַר מילדן אַלף-בית,
פֿאַר לידערטרייסט,
פֿאַר פֿידל פֿון דעם גראַם.

פֿון האַרץ די לעצטע פֿונקען אויפֿגעקליבן —
די קעלט דערוואַרעמען,
אין חושך ליכט דערזען —
כ'וואַרט יעדן טאָג אָן מינדסטן פֿאַראיבל
אַ ווינט זאָל קומען, אַרויסשאָקלען פֿון האַנט די פּען.

מסתּם, ווער ווייסט — מסתּם
האָב איך ניט שטענדיק אָפּגעהיט אין תּמימות
די לויטערקייט פֿון פֿלאַם.
מסתּם, ווער ווייסט — מסתּם
האָב איך געמאַכט פֿון ווײַן די ברכה
איבער אַ כּוס מיט סם.

כ'בין בלינד פֿון צער.
איך זע ניט מער קיין בערג.
איך גלייב ניט אין קיין לויכטנדיקע שפּיצן.
און גיין אויף פֿלאַכלאַנד איז דער וועג פֿון נאַר,
ער'ט קיין מאָל ניט דערגיין
צום הייל פֿון ליכט און בליצן.

ס'ווערט מער און מער אַלץ נאַכט.
די פֿינצטערקייט איז טיף,
ווי אין שייד פֿון אייביק שלאָפֿן.
אַ דאַנק פֿאַר די געוועזענע חסדים,
פֿאַר העלע אָנהייבן
און וואָלקנדיקע סופֿן.

Leavetaking

It's been so long since I've written a line,
My heart's flame is starting to die down.
Thanks for the past favors,
For the gentle alphabet,
For a poem's consolation,
For the fiddle of a rhyme.

The heart's last sparks are gathered
To warm up the chill,
Light glimpsed in utter dark.
Bearing no grudge, each day I wait for
The wind to shake the pen from my hand.

Who knows? Perhaps
I've not always cherished naively
That purity of flame.
Who knows? Perhaps,
I've recited the wine's blessing
Over a cup of poison.

I am blind with grief.
I can no longer see the mountains.
I don't believe in gleaming peaks.
And the road over the flatlands is for a fool
Who will never arrive
At light or lightning's cave.

Night takes over more and more.
The darkness is as deep
As the sheath of eternal sleep.
Thanks for the past favors,
For the bright beginnings
And cloudy endings.

ס'איז דורכגעברענט,
עס הוידעט זיך אַוועק דער לעצטער פֿאָדעם,
די אותיות קרישלען זיך,
די ווערטער בלייבן אויס,
אַ דאַנק, אַ דאַנק
פֿאַר די געוועזענע חסדים.

***

פֿאַר טרויער כ'האָב מײַן אַלף-בית פֿאַרגעסן.
פֿאַרקרימט די הייען, פֿאַרטעמפּט די חיתן,
דעם זין פֿון זיי כ'האָב נישט דערבליקט.
נו, מילא ווערלן ווערטער ניט פֿאַרענדיקט בלײַבן,
נאָך מיר וועט קומען עמעצער און וועט דערשרײַבן
דאָס וואָרט, ווו איך האָב זיך דערשטיקט.

דעם פּײַן פֿון שטום-לשון וועט עמעצער דערלייזן.
די פֿינצטערקייט פֿון תּהום מײַנעם דעם בייזן
וועט אויפֿלויכטן אַ יונגער מיט אַ גרינגער פּען.
די שטומע און פֿאַרבלאָנדזשעטע געשטאַלטן,
וואָס רינגלען מיך אַרום, מײַן אָטעם האַלטן,
וועט אים באַשערט זײַן אויפֿגעלעבטע זען.

איך הער זײַן גאַנג דעם גרינגן, ניט געצאַמטן,
ער ט'אויסלייזן מײַנע פֿאַרזעצטע פֿאַנטן.
און צושרײַבן די שורות מיט אַ פֿײַף.
כ'וועל דעמאָלט זיך דעם אַלף-בית צוריק דערמאָנען,
כ'וועל אין גן-עדן זײַן, נאָר כ'וועל סײַ ווי דערקאָנען
מײַן ניגון אין דעם לעצטן פֿולן רײַף.

1943

Burned through,
The last thread swings away,
Letters crumble,
And words pale.
Thanks, thanks
For the past favors.

* * *

I've forgotten my alphabet in sorrow.
The *heys* distorted, the *kheses* dulled,
I no longer discern their sense.[165]
Never mind, that words are not finished.
After me, someone will come and complete
The very word, where I choked.

Someone will redeem the anguish of sign-language.[166]
A youth with an easier pen will illuminate
The darkness of my angry chasm.
The mute and straying figures
That encircle me and hold my breath
Will be decreed to him and his revived vision.[167]

I hear his jaunty footsteps, unrestrained.
He will redeem the pledges that I pawned,
And add his verses, writing as he whistles.
Then I'll remember the alphabet again,
I'll be in Paradise, but I'll still recognize
My melody in its last, full ripeness.

1943

בײַנאַכטיקע געסט

בײַ נאַכט איז געקומען אַ פֿויגל צו מיר,
און געקלאַפּט מיט די פֿליגל,
אין מײַן פֿענצטער און טיר.
— קום אַרײַן, פֿויגל-פֿידל, גוטער קלעזמער פֿון מײַן יוגנטליד,
איך האָב ברויט נאָך און וואַסער פֿאַר דיר אָפּגעהיט,
קום אַרײַן, זײַ מײַן גאַסט, זײַ געערט.
ס'איז אונדז ביידן דאָס לעבן און דאָס שטאַרבן באַשערט.

און אַ קאַץ איז געקומען פֿאַרבלאָנדזשעט פֿון נאַכט,
געדראַפּעט מיט נעגל,
געדראַפּעט, געשאַרט.
— קום אַרײַן, קיצל-קעצל, פֿון מײַן קינדהייט סטראַשנער ווילדטיר,
איך האָב ניט איין מאָל דעם בעזעם פֿאַרזוכט צוליב דיר.
קום אַרײַן, זײַ מײַן גאַסט, זײַ געערט,
ס'איז אונדז ביידן צו בלאָנקען, נע-ונד זײַן באַשערט.

און אַ ציג איז געקומען, דאָס בערדל פֿאַרשפּיצט,
געקלאַפּט מיט די קלאָען,
מיט די הערנער געקריצט.
— קום אַרײַן, ציגל-מיגל, קורצע בערדל, מילך אין קריגל.
דײַן ליד נאָך ביז הײַנט מאַכט מײַן בעט פֿאַר אַ וויגל,
קום אַרײַן, זײַ מײַן גאַסט, זײַ געערט,
ס'איז אונדז ביידן אַ מלמדישע דאָליע באַשערט.

בײַ נאַכט, אַ מענטש איז געקומען, זיך געשטעלט בײַ מײַן טיר,
און אַן אַנגסטיקע שרעק
איז געפֿאַלן אויף מיר.
— ווער ביסטו? צי דו טראָגסט ניט אַ מעסער אין האַנט?
צי דו טײַעסט פֿאַרראַט? צי דו טל?עסט אַ בראַנד?
און די טיר כ'האָב פֿאַרשלאָסן, פֿאַרהאַקט און פֿאַרקלעמט,
און געפֿאַלן, דאָס פּנים פֿאַרדעקט מיט די הענט.

Night Visitors[168]

At night, a bird arrived at my door,
Knocked with its wings
On my window and door.
—Come right in, fiddle-bird, musician of my youth,[169]
I still put aside bread and water for you.
Come right in, and be my honored guest.
We've both been decreed this life and this death.

And then a cat strayed in from the night,
Scratched with its claws,
Scratched and scraped.
—Come right in, dread childhood beast, kitty-cat,[170]
I've never, not once, grabbed a broom and said, "Scat!"[171]
Come right in, and be my honored guest,
We've been given the fate to be homeless and lost.

A goat came next, with its pointy goatee,
Knocked with its hooves,
Ground with its horns.
—Come in, goaty-bloaty,[172] beard, milk from a ladle.
To this day, your song transforms bed into cradle.[173]
Come in, and be my honored guest,
We've both been decreed a schoolteacher's lot.

At night, a person came, stood by my door,
And I was befallen with
Such anxious fear.
—Who are you? Are you holding a knife in your hand?
Are you hiding betrayal? Do you hold smoldering brands?
And I slammed the door shut, turned the lock, threw the
bolt,
Fell to the floor, put my face in my hands.

איז די נאַכט געווען פֿינצטער, אַזוי פֿינצטער, אַז ש בלינד.
און מײַן דיל איז געווען אַזוי האַרט, ווי אַ שטיין,
און פֿון יענער זײַט טיר איז געשטאַנען דער מענטש,
און פֿון יענער זײַט טיר כ'האָב דערהערט אַ געוויין.

The night grew dark, then, as blindness is dark.
My floor became hard as stone,
And he stood on the other side of the door.
From the other side, I heard sobs and a moan.

חד גדיא

איך האָב אָנגעשריבן אַ ליד
און פֿאַרוואָרפֿן עס צוליב אַ גראַם.
אין ליד איז געווען אַ מעשׂה
פֿון אַ הויכן, גרויעם מאַן.

ער שטייט פֿאַר טאָג בײַ זײַן פֿענצטער
און רייכערט אַ ליולקע און ברומט,
ווי אַזוי עס גייט אַ לעבן —
און שלעפּט אַראָפּ צום גרונט.

ווי אַזוי עס שווימט דער הימל
און שווימט קיין מאָל ניט אַוועק,
ווי אַזוי דאָס אײַזערנע בעטל
איז מיט טונקעלע שאָטנס פֿאַרדעקט.

און ווי דער גרויער אומעט
האָט זיך אויף די ברעמען געזעצט,
און ווי דער טשײַניק דער קרומער
זומט אַ ניגון צו לעצט.

איז הײַנט מיט פֿאַרדראָס און צאָרן
געקומען דער הויכער מאַן,
און געפּאָכעט צו מיר מיט זײַן ליולקע:
— האָסט פֿאַרוואָרפֿן מיך צוליב אַ גראַם.

האָב איך געקוקט אויפֿן טרויעריקן מענטשן
און באַטראַכט אים פֿון דער נאָענט,
און איך האָב דעם רויך פֿון זײַן ליולקע
און זײַן גרויעם אומעט דערקאָנט.

דאָס איז ניט קיין רויך פֿון קיין ליולקע,
נאָר אַ פֿאַרוויקלטער אייביקער קנויל.
דאָס איז ניט קיין גרויער אומעט,
נאָר אַ וואָרט אויף פֿאַרשוויגענעם מויל.

Khad Gadya[174]

I once wrote down a poem
And discarded it because of a rhyme.
In the poem was a story
Of a tall, gray man.

At dawn he stands at his window
And smokes a pipe and hums,
This is how a life can go—
And drag one to the ground.

This is how the sky swims
And never swims away,
This is how the iron bunk
Is covered with dim shades.

And how that gray unhappiness
Has settled on the brow,
And how the dented teakettle
Finally buzzes a tune.

Today with resentment and fury
That same tall man has come,
And waved his pipe at me:
—You discard me because of a rhyme.

Then I looked at the sorrowing person
And considered him from up close,
And I recognized the smoke of his pipe
And his gray unhappiness.

That is not the smoke of a pipe,
But an entangled, eternal knot.
That is no gray unhappiness,
But a word on a taciturn lip.

און אָט־אָ האָסטו אַ חד גדיא —
איך לייען זי מיט זינגענדיקן טראָפּ,
איך אַליין, ווי מײַן נאָמען איז קאַדיע,
קוק פֿון שפּיגל, ווי ער, פּונקט אַראָפּ.

And right here you have a “Khad Gadya”—
I read it with the stress of the song,
I myself, as my name is Kadya,
Like him, from the mirror peer down.

די נישט-דערציילטע בלאַט

אין אַן אַלט פֿאַרהייליקטן און קלוגן ספֿר
פֿעלט די נישט-דערציילטע בלאַט.
ס'האָט מיר די בלאַט געבראַכט צו טראָגן
אַ ווינטערנאַכט, אין חודש שבֿט.

דערזען זי אויסגעשפּרייט אין וואָלקן,
געשריבן מיט גרויעם יעראָגליף,
פֿאַר יעדן האַרץ מיט אומעטן פֿאַרשאָלטן
איז אָפֿן דאָס פֿאַרהוילענע געשריפֿט:

ס'איז נאָך געווען אַ באַשאַף, נאָך אַ באַשאַף.
פֿון תּהום איז שרעק אַרויס, און צווייפֿל, און פֿאַראַט.
אויף דעם איז אויך כּי-טובֿ פֿאַרשריבן,
און צוגעדעקט מיט פֿײַגנבלאַט.

אַרום דעם וואָלקן נײַע וואָלקנס,
געטאָפּלט און געכּפּלט דאָס געשריפֿט.
איך האָב פֿאַרמאַכט די אויגן און פֿאַרשאָלטן
דעם אימהדיקן יעראָגליף.

די פֿרייד פֿון יעגער,
און דער צאַפּל פֿון געשאָסענעם פֿויגל,
און די רויטע שׂרפֿה פֿון בלוט.
אויף דעם איז אויך כּי-טובֿ פֿאַרשריבן,
און מיר טײַטשן עס — ס'איז גוט.

אויף מײַן טיש דער קלוגער ספֿר איז געלעגן,
אין שוואַרצע טאָוול, מיט חכמה זאַט.
נאָר איך מיט יאָמער האָב געלייענט
די אַלטע, נישט-דערציילטע בלאַט.

* * *

The Unrecounted Page

In an old, clever, and hallowed Book[175]
The unrecounted page is missing.
But I was brought this missing page
By a winter night in the month of Shebat.[176]

I glimpsed it, spread out across the clouds,
Written in gray hieroglyphs,
And the concealed script revealed itself
To every heart cursed with unhappiness:

There was once a Creation, another Creation.
Fear emerged with doubt and treachery from the abyss.
On that, *ki tov* was also written,
And covered up with a fig-leaf.[177]

Around that cloud, new clouds
Doubled and multiplied the script.
I closed my eyes and cursed
The terrifying hieroglyph.

The joy of the hunter,
And the jerk of the shot bird,
And the red blaze of blood.
On that *ki tov* is also written,
And we translate—"It is good."[178]

On my table, the clever Book lay,
In black boards, sated with wisdom.
But I, lamenting, have read
That old, unrecounted page.

* * *

ס'איז נאַכט אויף נאַכט געטאָפּלט, גאָט,
ווי קען מען דאָס פֿאַרטראָגן?
די זון, די שטערן — און דער קוואַל פֿון זייער ליכט —
אין זיי איז אויך אַ פֿינצטערקייט פֿאַרבאָרגן.

דו אייביק ביסט.
וועסט נאָך זען נײַע תּקופֿות, נײַע וועלטגעבורטן.
פֿאַר וואָס איז מיר באַשערט דער טאָג פֿון ווי און וויסט?
די בייזע נאַכט —
פֿון הרג און פֿון פֿלוכטן?

מײַן טאָג איז קורץ, איין אָטעם נאָר,
כ'בין ווי דאָס פֿלאַטערל, וואָס שטאַרבט אין איין מעת-לעת,
דאָס פֿלאַטערל אין לעצטער שעה
זעט כאָטש דעם פֿלאַם פֿון דײַנע פֿײַערדיקע האָר —
און איך?
אין פֿינצטערקייט דײַן לעצטער נס?

1942

Night is doubled upon night, God,
How can it be borne?
The sun, the stars—and the wellspring of their light—
In them, too, a darkness is hidden.

You are eternal.
You will witness new epochs, the births of new worlds.
Why am I decreed this day of desolate woe?
This evil night—
Of murder and of curses?

My day is brief, a single breath,
I am like the butterfly that dies in a single day.
In its last hour, the butterfly sees
The nimbus of your fiery hair—
And I?
Is darkness your last miracle?

1942

שיר-המעלות

מיט נאַכט, מיט ווינט, אָדער מיט שטורעם,
מיט וואָס איך זאָל נישט אָנהייבן מײַן ליד —
דער גרעסטער חוזק איז פֿורעמען אַ פֿורעם
פֿאַר אומגעלומפּערטן געמיט.

און וואָס איז נאַכט מיט פֿינצטערער פֿאַרצוקונג,
און וואָס איז ווינט מיט ביטערקייט פֿון בליט,
און וואָס איז שטורעם, וואָס פֿליקט דעם ים פֿון גרונטן,
אַנטקעגן הילוך פֿון אַ ייִד?

דאָס היטל דעם טרויער פֿון די אויגן צו פֿאַרדעקן
דאָס רעקל אויף ערגערן די ברוינע הינט.
די שיך אַ מידברדיקער פֿיבער זאָל זיי לעקן,
די שיך — די קלוגע, שלעפּערישע שיך.

אַ פֿאַלן האָט דערוואַכט אין מיר.
איך זע אַפֿילו נישט דעם גרונט פֿון תּהום,
אויף זײַנע הענט דער אייבערשטער ט׳מסתּם פֿאַרהאַלטן מיך,
ווײַל ער איז אייביק,
ווי דער געוויש פֿון אַ פּאָגראָם.

און אפֿשר וואַכט אין מיר די היץ,
וואָס שוידערט מיך אַ גאַנצע נאַכט,
און אפֿשר איז דאָס דער לעצטער בליץ,
וואָס האָט פֿאַרמאָסטן זיך איבער מײַן דאַך.

און אויב אַזוי, —
וועל איך נאָך אין די לעצטע ווײַלעס,
ביז וואַנען ס׳איז נאָך וואַך מײַן זינען,
וועל איך נאָך זאָגן שיר-המעלות
צום ערשטן שטערן
פֿון מאָרגנדיקן באַגינען.

Psalm of Ascents[179]

With night, with wind, or with storm,
With what else shall I begin my poem?
The worst mockery is to formulate form
For an unspeakable mood.

And what is night with its dark devouring,
And what is the wind with its bitter flowering,
And what is a storm that pulls the sea from its floor
When compared to the attire of a Jew?

The cap that covers the eyes' sadness.
The jacket that drives brown dogs to madness,
Those shoes lapped up by a desert fever,
Those clever, those destitute shoes.

Within me, a falling awakens.
I cannot even see the chasm's floor.
Maybe God Above held me back with His hands,
Because He is eternal,
Like a pogrom's roar.

And maybe a fever awakens in me,
Making me shiver the whole night through,
And maybe the lightning's final strokes
Spar above my roof.

And if that's so,
In my very last moments,
As long as my sense is awake,
I'll still recite the Psalm of Ascents
To the first star
At daybreak.

און אפֿשר איז דאָס שוין די שׂרפֿה,
וואָס שמעלצט אַראָפּ פֿון בוים די פֿרוכטן,
און ס'וועלן עפּל מער ניט וואַקסן
אויף דעם באָדן דעם פֿאַרפֿלוכטן.

און אויב אַזוי —
וועל איך נאָך אין די לעצטע ווײַלעס,
ביז וואַנען כּוח ס'וועט מײַן האַרץ געפֿינען,
וועל איך נאָך זאָגן שיר-המעלות
צום שטערן וואָס ברענט אין מיר אַליין,
צום שטערן וואָס ברענט נאָך אין מײַן זינען.

1938

And if this is the ultimate fire
That melts the fruit from its tree,
And apples will no longer grow
Upon this cursed terrain,

And if that's so,
In my very last moments,
As long as my heart finds the strength,
I'll still recite the Psalm of Ascents
To the star that burns in me,
To the star that still burns in my sense.

1938

באַדעקנס

הימל הויכער,
ס'מוז דאָך זײַן אַ טאָג פֿון פֿאַלן,
ס'מוז דאָך זײַן אַ טאָג אַזאַ בײַ דיר.
הימל הויכער,
אַלע זײַנען מיר שוין בלינד געוואָרן,
בלוטיק איז דער העלסטער שטראַל —
ס'מוז דאָך זײַן אַ טאָג פֿון פֿאַלן,
וואַרטן מיר איצט אויף דײַן פֿאַל.

נידעריקער קום,
און הייב אָן דעם באַדעקנס,
סײַ ווי האַלטן מיר די לעבנס אײַנגעקלעמט אין בלייכע הענט,
וואונדערלעך, עס היילט מײַן האַרץ די מעשׂה,
ווי עס שטאַרבט דער שטאַרקער שמשון,
און אויף די פּײַניקער צעשיטערט ער די ווענט.

הימל גרויער,
דײַנע בעטלערישע לאַטעס
קענען ווערן בלײַ —
הימל גרויער,
אויב עס פֿעלט דיר שווערקייט
נעם מײַן גוף —
אַנטלײַ.

Veiling[180]

High heavens,
Of course there must be a day of falling,
Of course there must be such a day for you.
High heavens,
We have all grown blind.
The brightest ray is bloody—
Of course there must be a day of falling:
Now we await your fall.

Come down lower
And begin the veiling,
As we still clutch our lives in pale hands,
How wonderfully it heals my heart, the tale
Of how strong Samson died,
As upon his tormentors he shattered the walls.

Gray heavens,
Your beggarly patches
Can become lead—
Gray heavens,
If you lack hardship,
Take my body—
On loan.

טויטער שבת

עס קומען שאָטנס בײַ נאַכט צו מיר טויט-שבת ביטן.
די הענט פֿאַרקלעמט,
אויף רוקנס אויפֿגעלייגט —
די טמא וועלט ניט אָנרירן,
דעם טויטן שבת היטן,
וואָס האָט די וואָך,
דאָס לעבן,
און אַלע יום-טובֿן פֿאַרברענט.

די טירן דרייען זיך אויף שטיל געוואָרענע זאַוויסעס.
דאָס אײַזן און דער זשאַווער זײַנען גרינג,
אַלץ האָט די וואָג פֿאַרלאָרן נאָך מיליאָנען מיתות,
אַ טויטער שבת רוט,
און ערשטע אייביקייט ביז לעצטער זינקט.

די שאָטנס שוועבן דורך,
נאָר איינער האָט אַ ווײַלע זיך לעם מיר פֿאַרהאַלטן.
כ׳בין קליין געוואָרן, נידעריק
און צוגעקלעמט צום שוועבנדיקן ווײ —
ביסטו, מײַן ברודער, דו?
געזען כ׳האָב רויטע זוימען
אַרום זײַנע איינגעשפּאַלטן.
ניטאָ קיין תּהום, וווּ איך זאָל פֿאַלן,
באַהאַלטן זיך פֿון טויטער רו.

ווי גליקלעך כ׳בין אַ מאָל געווען,
ווען ס׳איז מיט טרויער פֿול געווען מײַן ברונעם,
און כ׳האָב פֿון לעבעדיקער נויט
געהערט אַ לעבעדיק געוויין.
ער האָט געוווּנדיקט און געהיילט מײַן גומען,
מײַן חלום און מײַן וואַכן טאָג באַגלייט.
דאָס האַרץ האָט ווײ געטאָן אויף וואָכעדיקע לאַטעס,
און אויף יום-טובֿדיקע שקראַבעס.

Dead Sabbath

Shadows come at night to invite me to Dead Sabbath.
Their hands pressed,
Folded on spines—
In order not to touch the impure world,
In order to observe the dead Sabbath
That has burned up the week,
This life,
And all the holidays.[181]

Doors swing on silenced hinges.
Iron and rust are light.
All has lost its heft after millions of deaths.
A dead Sabbath rests,
And, first to last, eternity sinks.

As the shadows float by,
Only one pauses near me for a moment.
I grow small, stunted
And jammed up against the floating pain—
Are you, my brother, you?
Then I see red rims
Around his eye-slits.
There's no abyss where I can fall
To hide myself from the dead rest.

How happy I was, once,
When my well was full of sadness,
And from living need I
Heard a living cry.
It wounded and healed my palate,
Accompanied my dreams and my waking day.
My heart ached for weekday patches,
And worn-out shoes on holidays.

איצט האָב איך רו.
איצט רוט דער טויטער שבת.

דאָס ברויט אין אויוון איז געבליבן ניט-דערבאַקן,
די קינדער ניט דערוואָקסן ביזן אויפֿגאַנג פֿון דעם טאָג.
די אַלטע ניט דערזאָגט די וואָכעדיקע מנחה.
אַ טויטער שבת האָט דערשטיקט אַ שטאָט.
שיכעלעך אַ פּאָר האָבן ערגעץ זיך פֿאַרוואַלגערט,
בײַם קינד אין מיטן ווײַנען האָט מען אָפּגעשניטן דאָס געוויין,
און טירן זײַנען געבליבן צעפּראַלטע אָפֿן,
און שטילקייט האָט זיך אויסגעבעט
אויף ברוק און שטיין.

ווי גליקלעך כ׳בין אַ מאָל געווען,
ווען מײַנע פֿיס האָבן געשטרויכלט
אין ייִדנהאַס, אין דחקות און אין בלאָטע.
כ׳האָב דעמאָלט פֿון די שטערן מזלות ליכטיקע אַראָפּגעלייענט,
און אַלטער גלויבן —
לויטערער ווי וואַסערן פֿון ווײַסל —
דעם טרויער האָט צעוואָרפֿן און פֿאַרווייעט.

איצט איז רו,
און טרערן האָבן ניט אויף וואָס צו פֿאַלן,
פֿון שטילקייט כ׳ווער דערשטיקט,
אַפֿילו אין דעם רעש פֿון טאָג,
אַפֿילו ווען טרומפּייטן שאַלן,
איך הער קיין יובֿל ניט אין זיי,
אַפֿילו ניט קיין קלאָג.
איצט איז רו.
פֿון שטילקייט כ׳ווער דערשטיקט,
אַפֿילו ווען די פֿייגל זינגען,
ווען ווונדערלעכע תּפֿילות קוואַקען אויס בײַ נאַכט די זשאַבעס.
איצט איז רו,
די רו פֿון טויטן שבת.

Now I have rest.
Now the dead Sabbath rests.

The bread in the oven never finished baking,
The children never finished growing up as the day passed on.
The old never finished saying the weekday *Minkhe.*[182]
A dead Sabbath choked an entire town.
Little shoes, a pair of them, turned up somewhere,
The cry of the child was severed in the midst of crying,
And doors remained wide open,
And silence bedded down
On rock and cobblestone.

How happy I was, once,
When my feet stumbled
In Jew-hatred, in want, in mud.
Then, I read bright fortunes in the stars,
And old belief—
Purer than the Vistula's waters—
Scattered and snowed over the sorrow.[183]

Now there is rest,
And tears have nothing to fall on.
I choke on silence,
Even in the noise of day,
Even when trumpets sound,
I hear no gaiety,
Nor even a lament.
Now there is rest.
I choke on silence,
Even when the birds sing,
When, at night, the frogs croak wonderful prayers.
Now there is rest,
The rest of the dead Sabbath.

דער דודע-שפּילער פֿון סדום

אין סדום איז אַ דודע-שפּילער געווען.
פֿון אייביק אָן עד-היום
זײַן לײַב איז ברען אויף ברען,
אָ ווײ דעם דודע-שפּילער פֿון סדום.

זינגט דער דודע-שפּילער פֿון סדום:
ווען ס׳גייט דער שטערן-געשפּאַן
אויפֿן הימלשן ראָד —
ווער פֿאָרט אַזוי הויך?
מסתּמא גאָט.
פֿאַר וואָס בלײַבט ער ניט שטיין
איבער שטאָט פֿון געוויין?
איבער סדום,
ווו איך, דער דודע-שפּילער,
אויף באַרג מיט אַש האָב מײַן טראָן.
ער וואָלט דעמאָלט ווי איך,
זיך אַ דודע געמאַכט,
זיבן שפּאַלטן געשניצט —
פֿאַר ווינד און ווײ,
ווײ און ווונד,
ווונד און יאָמער.
עס קען ניט איין דודעקנעכט
אַליין —
אויסטראָגן אַ סדום מיט סדומער.

אַלמעכטיקער גאָט,
ס׳איז דם אויף דם
אין דײַן סדום.
פֿאַר וואָס האָסטו מיך אויסדערוויילט
זינגען פֿאַר דיר דאָס הללויה-ליד,
צו מעריבֿ, ווען די זון פֿאַרגייט,
צו שחרית, ווען דאָס ליכט קומט אָן?

The Fife-Player of Sodom[184]

In Sodom there was a fife-player.
Forever and a day.
His body is burn layered upon burn,
O, woe to the fife-player of Sodom.

The fife-player of Sodom sings:
When the stars, in harness, walk
On the heavenly wheel—
Who's travelling so high up there?
Probably God.
Why doesn't He stay standing here
Above the City of Tears?
Above Sodom,
Where I, the fife-player,
Have my throne on the mountain of ash.
Then, like me, He would
Make himself a fife,
Cut out seven slits
For wince and woe,
Woe and wound,
Wound and wail.
One fife-slave alone
Cannot
Redeem Sodom from the Sodomites.

Almighty God,
It's blood upon blood
In Your Sodom.
Why have you elected me
To sing this Hallelujah for You,
At evening prayer, when the sun sets,
At morning prayer, when the light arrives?[185]

סדום קען ניט,
און וויל ניט,
און דאַרף דײַן נאָמען ניט הערן.
מיט פֿײַער און רצח,
ווו איך שטיי און איך זעץ זיך —
קריצט מען מיתה בײַ מיר אויפֿן שטערן.
זאָג פֿאַר וואָס,
אָ, פֿאַר וואָס בליט דאָ גאָלדענער קאָרן?
זאָג פֿאַר וואָס,
אָ, פֿאַר וואָס איז מײַן דודע באַשערט
געשניצט זײַן פֿון פֿינצטערן דאָרן?
פֿון אייביק אָן עד-היום
אָ וויי דעם דודע-שפּילער פֿון סדום.

אַלמעכטיקער גאָט,
שווערד אויף שווערד — קלינגט אין סדום,
חטא אויף חטא רוט אין סדום,
מאַכט אויף מאַכט —
און איך מיט דער דודע
אין תּפֿילהדיקער האַנט
אין דעם פֿײַנבעטל ליג אַלע נאַכט.
פֿון אייביק אָן עד-היום
אָ וויי דעם דודע-שפּילער פֿון סדום.

אַלמעכטיקער גאָט,
זאָג אויף וועלכן יסוד
איז דײַן רו-פּלאַץ געבויט?
און וואָס איז רו-פּלאַץ פֿאַר גאָט,
ווען חידקל און פּרת און די ווײַסל —
איז רויט
פֿון מײַן אָפֿענער וווּנד,
פֿון מײַן פֿײַנלעכן טויט,
וואָס איז קיין מאָל נישט טויט?
פֿון אייביק אָן עד-היום
אָ וויי דעם דודע-שפּילער פֿון סדום.

Sodom cannot
And does not want
And does not need to hear Your name.
With fire and fury,
Wherever I stand and wherever I sit down—
Death is engraved upon my forehead.
Tell why,
O, why blooms the golden rye?
Tell why,
O, why is it decreed my fife to be
Carved from the dark thorn?
Forever and a day
O, woe to the fife-player from Sodom.

Almighty God,
Sword rings upon sword in Sodom,
Sin rests upon sin in Sodom,
Power upon power—
And I with the fife
In prayer-like hand
Lie all night on the pallet of agony.
Forever and a day,
O, woe to the fife-player of Sodom.

Almighty God,
Do tell, on which foundation
Is Your resting-place built?
And what is a resting-place for God,
When the Tigris and the Euphrates and the Vistula—[186]
Flow red
From my open wound,
From my anguishing death
That is never dead?
Forever and a day,
O, woe to the fife-player of Sodom.

דער מלך דוד אַליין איז געבליבן

דאָס פֿאָלק איז פֿאַרשניטן —
ווונד און טויט.
די וועגן פֿאַרשאָטן,
די הײַזער פֿאַרברענט.
דער מלך דוד אַליין איז געבליבן,
ער מיט דער קרוין אין די הענט.

געשטאָרבן דער שאַל פֿון דעם האָרן.
דער לעצטער שטאָפּעט איז געפֿאַלן —
ווונד און טויט.
עס רײַסן קריעה אין הימל
פֿאַרשרפֿעטע, חרובֿע ווענט.
דער מלך דוד אַליין איז געבליבן,
ער מיט דער קרוין אין די הענט.

עס הוילט דער ווינט אין צעשאָטענע נעסטן —
ווונד און טויט.
די לאָנקעס די גרינע פֿון קינדהייט,
די טשערעדע שאָף — איז פֿאַרלענדט.
דער מלך דוד אַליין איז געבליבן,
ער מיט דער קרוין אין די הענט.

דאָס לאַנד איז צעמאָסטן אויף קבֿרים —
ווונד און טויט.
אַ וועג אַן איינציקער גרינט און איז פֿריש.
דער וועג צו זײַן זון דעם משיח,
וואָס דאָס פֿאָלק האָט פֿאַרטרויט און צעשמט.
אַהין גייט דער אָבֿל, דער מלך,
ער מיט דער קרוין אין די הענט.

Only King David Remained

The nation was cut down—
Wound and death.
The roads bestrewn,
The houses burned.
Only King David remained,
He with his crown in his hands.

The horn's echo has died.
The last runner has fallen—
Wound and death.
Blazing, destroyed walls
Tear mourning-rents in the sky.[187]
Only King David remained,
He with his crown in his hands.

The wind whines in ruined nests—
Wound and death.
The green meadows of childhood,
The flocks of sheep—are wrecked.
Only King David remained,
He with his crown in his hands.

The land is measured in graves—
Wound and death.
One single path turns green and fresh.
The path to Messiah, His son,
Whom this people dreamed of and revered.
There walks the mourner, the king,
He with his crown in his hands.

ער טראָגט די פֿאַרהייליקטע ירושה —
וווּנד און טויט.
— אָט איז דײַן כּתר, משיח,
אַלע פּערל געשוינט, ניט פֿאַרשוועגדט.
אָט איז דײַן כּתר, משיח,
אויף די לעצטע צוויי ייִדישע הענט.

He carries the hallowed heritage—
Wound and death.
—Here, Messiah, your diadem,
All the pearls spared, not spent.[188]
Here, Messiah, your diadem
In the last two Jewish hands.

הבֿדלה

גאָט פֿון אַבֿרהם,
באַשאַף אונדז אַ צווייטן בראשית.
מעג קיין זון דאָרט ניט שײַנען —
דאָס ליכט האָט אונדז סײַ ווי פֿאַרראַטן.
מעג דער ווינט דאָרט ניט זינגען —
ער האָט מיט די דײַטשן צוזאַמען געטריבן
אונדזער פֿאָלק צו די שחיטה-וואַרשטאַטן.
מעג קיין ים דאָרט ניט רוישן קיין גרינער —
ער האָט געזונקען די שיפֿן — די שפּענדלעך
מיט אונדזערע לעצטע אַנטרינער.
מעגן בערג דאָרט ניט רײַסן צום הימל די שפּיצן —
זיי האָבן דעם וועג ניט פֿאַרצאַמט פֿאַר די רוצחים,
אַ פּיצעלע קינד צו באַשיצן.
מיר זאָגן זיך אָפּ פֿון דער שיינקייט.
מיר זאָגן זיך אָפּ פֿון דער גבֿורה.
מיר זאָגן זיך אָפּ פֿון דער שירה.
מעג אײַנשטיין קיין יורש ניט לאָזן.
מיר זײַנען אין חרם צוזאַמען
מיטן געטלעכן תּמים שפּינאָזע.

באַשאַף אונדז אַ וועלט מיט אַ פּאַסיקל הימל,
און איין מאָל אַ יאָר זאָל אַ שטערן דאָרט שײַנען,
און מאַכן הבֿדלה, און געטלעך פֿאַרטײַטשן:
ס'איז אַ צווייטער בראשית,
אויסער וועלט פֿון די דײַטשן,
אויסער חכמת-הדמים.
און עס וועלן די קינדער אונטער פּאַסיקל הימל
ענטפֿערן: אָמן ואָמן.

Havdalah[189]

God of Abraham,
Make us a second Beginning.[190]
May the sun never shine there—
Light betrayed us, anyway.
May the wind there not sing—
Joined with the Germans, it drove
Our people to the slaughter-shops.[191]
May a green sea not roar there—
It sank the ships—those splinters
With our last refugees.
May mountains there not tear at the sky with their peaks—
They did not block the road for the assassins
To protect a tiny child.
We renounce beauty.
We renounce valor.
We renounce the praise-song.
May Einstein not leave an heir.
We are excommunicated together
With the divine innocent, Spinoza.

Make us a world with a strip of sky,
Once a year, may a star shine there
And make Havdalah, and divinely interpret:
This is a second Beginning,
Without the world of the Germans,
Without the science of blood.[192]
And under this strip of sky, the children will
Reply: Amen and amen.

עס קומען ניט מער קיין בריוו

עס קומען ניט מער קיין בריוו,
קיין וואָרט,
קיין גערים —
ניטאָ בײַ וועמען צו פֿרעגן.
די שטילקייט ווערט הוילער,
און קלערער,
און וויסט —
פֿאַר דעם ווונדיקן פֿרעגער.

אין די אויגן ניטאָ קיין געוויין.
אַלע גלידער פֿאַרקלעמט.
עס ליגן שערבלעך פֿון אומגליק
בײַ מיר אין די הענט.

איך וויל דערפֿילן אַ כּוח פֿון לעבן,
אַ געשריי,
אַ געוויין איך וויל דערהערן.
אַ שטיקל פֿײַער אין הימל
— וויקלט אויס זיך אין גאָרניט
אין רויך.
אָט אַזוי-אָ מסתּמא
בײַ גאָט אין דער הייך —
וויקלט אויס זיך אַ ייִדישער שטערן.

1945

No Letters Arrive Anymore

No letters arrive anymore,
Not a word,
Not a greeting—
There's no one to ask.
The silence grows hollower,
Clearer,
And empty
Before the aching asker.

In my eyes, no weeping.
All my limbs are grieving.
Shards of calamity
Lie in my hands.

I want to sense a life-force,
A shout,
I want to hear a cry.
A bit of fire in the sky
Unravels into nothing—
Into smoke.
Probably, in just this way,
A Jewish star unravels
With God on High.

1945

אַ תּפֿילה

איך שטיי אויף אין פֿאַרטאָג און מײַן תּפֿילה —
איז סם.
איך בעט, אַז דער מבול זאָל נאָך אַ מאָל קומען.
ער זאָל אויפֿהייבן העכער פֿון טורעמס און דעכער
די פֿלייצונג פֿון ים.
עס זאָל די תּבֿה פֿון רעטונג ניט שווימען.

אוי ווײ, ווי ס'וועט גוט זײַן די קאַלטע באַרירונג
פֿון טויט.
זי וועט אויסלעשן אפֿשר דעם ווייטיק וואָס קרענקט
אין די גלידער,
די פֿאַרוויסטונג פֿון האַרץ און די חרפּה פֿון קײַען
דאָס ברויט
לעם דעם אַשבאַרג פֿון שוועסטער און ברידער.

אוי ווײ, ווי ס'וועט גוט זײַן באַרירן די וואָלקנס
אין פֿאַרלענדטן געשווים.
כ'וועל דאָרט אפֿשר די זיסקייט די לעצטע דערפֿילן —
פֿון צעפֿלויגענעם אַש פֿון די גופֿים דערהערן
אַ שטים,
און פֿאַרשליסן פֿון לעבן דעם קרײַז, און די ווונדיקע פּײַן
וועל איך שטילן.

1945

A Prayer

I arise at dawn and my prayer
Is poison.
I ask that the Deluge shall come again,
Raising the surge of the ocean
Higher than towers and rooftops.
The rescuing Ark shall not float.

Oh, how good it will be—death's
Cold touch.
Perhaps it will put out my limbs'
Sickening pain,
The heart's desolation, the disgrace of chewing
Bread
Near the ash-heap of brothers and sisters.

Oh, how good it will be to touch the clouds
In the annihilating flood.
Perhaps there I'll sense the ultimate sweetness—
Hear, in the ash flying forth from bodies,
A voice.
And, closing the circle of life, I will
Silence the pain.

1945

אַ ליד צו דער פּאַפּירענער בריק

פֿיר מיך, פּאַפּירענע בריק, אין דײַן לאַנד,
וואָס איז ווײַס, וואָס איז מילד און לאַנגאָניק.
איך בין מיד פֿון דעם מידבר, וווּ עס ליגט שוין דער מן
פֿון ברויט און פֿון מילך און פֿון האָניק.

ס'האָט דאָס פּשוטע פֿאָלק, מיט די ערדענע קריג,
מיט קינדער, מיט רינדער, מיט טרערן,
אַ שטאַרקע געבויט די פּאַפּירענע בריק,
מען זאָל זי ניט קענען צעשטערן.

געבויט און געצירט מיט פֿליגלען אַ סך,
צום הימל פֿאַרטשעפּעט אַ טרעפּל.
די בריק כ'האָב געזען דורך אַ פֿליגל פֿון דאַך,
דורך סכך און דורך האַרבסטיקע עפּל.

כ'האָב איר פֿלאַטער געהערט און איר רויש און איר שאָרך
אין דער ווייכקייט פֿון מענטעלעך סאַמעט,
און איר קול איך האָב דערקאָנט אין דעם טײַטש פֿון אַ וואָרט
פֿון אַ שטעטלשן אַלטן מלמד.

מײַן האַרץ האָט געקלעמט אויפֿן בראָך אין זײַן שטים,
אויפֿן ציטער פֿון פֿאַרטײַעטן חלום,
ער אַליין האָט געשפּאַנט אויף דער פּאַפּירענער בריק
און איז איבערגעגאַנגען בשלום.

ס'האָט נאָך קיין מאָל קיין אָפּרו מײַן האַרץ ניט געהאַט,
ווען אַפֿילו עס האָבן געטאַנצט מײַנע טריט.
עס קען זײַן, אַז דער סנה האָט געברענט — אפֿשר יע,
נאָר עס ווערט ניט געזאָגט, אַז דער סנה האָט געבליט.

כ'האָב שוין ווונדער געזען אַ סך אונטער זון:
ווי אַ בעכער פֿון בלום — ווערט אַ תּהום.
כ'האָב שוין ווונדער געזען אַ סך אומעטום:
ווי ליכטיקע שטעט ווערן — סדום.

A Poem to the Paper Bridge[193]

Oh, paper bridge, lead me into your land,
White and constant and mild.
I am tired of the desert where manna was strewn
Made of milk and honey and bread.

A simple people, with their earthen jugs,
With children, with cattle, with tears,
Constructed a paper bridge of such strength
It withstands the destruction of years.

Built and adorned with numerous wings,
A staircase hooked up to the sky.
I sighted the bridge through a wing of the roof,
Sukkah twigs, and fall apples hung high.[194]

I heard its flutter, its rustle and rush
In a velvet-soft Torah-scroll mantle,
And I recognized its voice in the gloss of a word
By an old schoolteacher from the shtetl.

My heart grieved at his cracking voice,
At the tremble of his hidden dream.
He himself trod over the paper bridge
And passed across it unharmed.

No rest, as yet, for my own heart,
Even when my footsteps danced.
Maybe the thorn bush actually burned—
But no one says that it bloomed.[195]

I've seen many miracles under the sun:
How a goblet of blossoms becomes a chasm.
I have seen many wonders everywhere:
How illustrious cities become Sodom.

פֿיר מיך, פֿאַפּירענע בריק, אין דײַן לאַנד,
וואָס מיר האָבן געבויט מיט ערלעכע הענט,
אין שײַן פֿון דער נויט און אין ריינקייט פֿון האַרץ,
קיין מענטש ניט געמאַטערט, קיין קינד ניט פֿאַרשעמט.

דאָרט בליט נאָך אַביימל,
דאָרט קרייט נאָך אַ האָן,
און דער ליכטיקער שחר
באַגינען זאָגט אָן.

1942

Lead me, paper bridge, into your land,
The one we have built with honest hands,
In the stark light of need and in pureness of heart,
No person was tormented and no child shamed.

There, a sapling still blooms,
There, a rooster crows on,
There, the brilliance of daybreak
Announces a new dawn.

1942

מײַנע קינדער

כ'האָב הײַנט געזען דורך נעפּל פֿון אַ פֿאַלנדיקן שניי
די קינדער מײַנע — צוויי און צוויי.

זיי האָבן מיך אַרומגערינגלט קינדער מײַנע
מיך פֿאַרן קלייד געצויגן מיט אַ טענה:
— שפּיל זיך מיט אונדז. מיר אין קאַראַהאָד
און דו אין מיטן,
און זאָג פֿאַר וואָס האָסטו פֿון אונדז די לעבעדיקע וועלט פֿאַרמיטן?

כ'האָב זיי געגעבן קיכעלעך און יעדערן געהייסן: עס.
און כ'האָב פֿאַרענטפֿערט זיך, אַז כ'האָב פֿאַרלאָרן זייער אַדרעס.
פֿיר זײַנען זיי געווען. דאָס ייִנגסטע מיידעלע — אַ פּיצל.
זי האָט די הערעלעך געקעמט, און אָנגעטאָן אַ פּורים-מיצל.
זיי האָבן מיט די הענט געפּאַטשט, געטאַנצט, אַרומגעלאָפֿן,
צעפֿרידענע, וואָס ס'האָט דער חלום אונדז צונויפֿגעטראָפֿן.

דער עלטסטער זון מײַנער האָט פּלוצלינג
אָנגעהויבן ריידן מיט אַ שטורעם.
— כ'בין גאָרניט איצט. כ'בין ניט געווען, און וועל ניט זײַן.
כ'ווייס ניט דעם טעם פֿון גליק און פֿון יסורים.
איך גיי אַ מאָל אַראָפּ אויף פֿרעמדע וועלטן,
איך הער דעם רויש פֿון זיי און הער אַ מאָל
דעם אָפּהילך פֿון דײַן שטימע.
פֿאַר וואָס האָסטו מײַן חלק דעם באַשערטן, דעם באַשטעלטן
נישט אָפּגעגעבן מיר —
אין אײַער וועלט פֿון טרערן און נגינה?
איך זע אַ מאָל ווי ס'פֿלאַטערט דורך פֿאַר מיר
מײַן רעיון וואָס איז נישט געבאָרן,
ער צאַפּלט זיך צווישן אַלע הימלען.
וואָס טויגן דײַנע לידער, די ניגונים און די כאָרן?
אַז הינטער זיי נשמות אונדזערע פֿאַרוועלקטעווימלען?
ביסט נישט דער לעצטער צוועק,
ביסט נישט קיין אָנהייב און ביסט נישט דער לעצטער מיין,
פֿאַר וואָס זאָל איך אָט דאָ אין גזר פֿון אָפּגעשטעלטע וועלטן זײַן?

My Children[196]

Today, through a haze of falling snow, I saw
My children—two by two.

They ringed around me, children dear,
Tugging at my skirt with complaints to air:
"Come play with us. We'll dance in a circle
And you'll stand in the middle
And tell us why you kept the living world from us."

I gave them cookies and bade them, "Eat."
And I made excuses that I'd forgotten their street.
There were four of them. The youngest girl, a tiny tot.
She combed her ringlets, and donned a Purim hat.
They clapped their hands, danced, ran about,
Delighted that the dream had let us meet.

Suddenly, my eldest son
Began to talk up a storm.
"I'm nothing now. I never was, will never be.
I don't know the taste of pleasure or of pain.
Sometimes I descend to foreign worlds,
I hear their noise and sometimes hear
The echo of your voice.
Why did you not deliver to me
My portion, the one reserved, the one decreed
In your world of music and tears?[197]
Sometimes I see how my vision that was never born
Flutters before me,
It quivers among all the heavens.
What do your songs matter, their melodies and choruses
While, behind them, our souls, all wilted, swarm?[198]
You are not the final cause,
You're not the beginning and you're not the last intent,
Why should I be condemned to unrealized worlds?

עס גליִען אין מיר פֿײַערן, נאָך נישט געצונדענע אַפֿילו,
עס וויינען אין מיר צערן אָן אַ תּפֿילה,
עס רופֿן מיך פֿון נישט-דערקענטע געגנט די שוועלן.
פֿאַר וואָס האָסטו פֿאַראורטיילט מיך אָט דאָ אין כּף-הקלע?

עס האָבן זײַנע רייד דעם שניי געצונדן און דערוואַרעמט
און מײַנע אויגן זײַנען פֿול געווען מיט טרערן.
עס האָט מײַן ייִנגסטע טאָכטער זיך אויף מיר דערבאַרעמט,
צו מײַנע קני זיך צוגעטוליעט מיטן שטערן.

— מיך אַרט ניט, — האָט זי געזאָגט,
און כ׳האָב דערקענט אויף איר מײַן שמייכל. —
— איך בענק ניט נאָך דער וועלט,
און כ׳בין דאָס גאַנצע גליק דיר מוחל.
כ׳וואָלט אויך מסתּמא אַזאַ שלאַק ווי דו געווען,
מיט אַלעמען געקריגט זיך און געברוגזט זיך אויף יאָרן.
און וואָס איז דאָ דער מאכל שטענדיק סקריפּען מיט דער פּען?
און ס׳אַרט מיך ניט וואָס איך בין ניט געבאָרן, —
כ׳האָב זי געוואָלט אָ קוש טאָן, נאָר אין מײַנע הענט
האָב איך געהאַלטן נאָר אַ קאַלטן שניי, וואָס איז צערונען.
כ׳האָב זי געוואָלט אַרומנעמען לעם מײַנע קני,
נאָר כ׳האָב איר קליינעם קעפּל נישט געפֿונען.

געדיכטער איז געוואָרן דער נעפּל פֿון דעם פֿאַלנדיקן שניי.
מײַנע קינדער זײַנען פֿאַרשוווּנדן אין דעם נעפּל דעם גרויעם.

כ׳האָב נאָר געהערט די טריטלעך זייערע,
ווי גלעקלעך אין אַ ווינטיקן געדריי,
און איך הער זיי איצט בײַ נאַכט אין שטילע שעהען.

Unlit fires glow in me,
Sorrows cry in me without a prayer,
The thresholds of unfulfilled journeys call me.
Why did you sentence me to limbo here?"[199]

His words caught fire, warming up the snow,
And my eyes filled with tears.
My youngest daughter took pity on me
And rested her forehead on my knee.

"It doesn't bother me," she said,
And I recognized my smile on her face.
"I don't long for this world,
And you may keep all that happiness![200]
I, too, would probably have been a wretch like you,
Quarrelling with everyone and holding grudges for years.
And what's so delightful about constantly creaking with that
pen?
It doesn't bother me that I was never born."
I wanted to give her a kiss, but in my hands
I held only cold snow that melted away.
I wanted to hug her at my knees,
But I could not find her little head.

The haze of falling snow grew thicker.
My children vanished in the gray haze.

All I could hear were their faint footsteps,
Like small bells in a windy whirl,
And I hear them now at night, in silent hours.

די קליינע פֿוקסעלעך — שועלים קטנים

עס האָבן זיך פֿאַרנאַדעט אין מײַן ווײַנגאָרטן, מײַן כּרם,
די קליינע פֿוקסעלעך, שועלים קטנים,
און פֿילן אָן בײַ נאַכט מײַן שטוב מיט רויטן שײַן.
זיי טראָגן אין די פּיסקלעך לויכטנדיקע גראַמען
די קליינע פֿוקסעלעך — שועלים קטנים,
און שטעלן זיי אין ליד צו מיר אַרײַן.

געוויס, זיי זײַנען קלייניקע מחבלים,
פֿאַר צײַטן אין די ווײַנגערטנער דעם צוויט געביסן,
מען האָט אין שיר-השירים זיי דערפֿאַר מיט רעכט געשמיסן,
מען וועט נאָך זיי מיט פּסוקים און מיט דרשות טאַדלען.

נאָר ס'האָט די שענסטע פֿון די דאַמעס,
די ווונדערלעכע פּיטערין שולמית,
מיט הייסער סטראָפֿע זיי אַ ריר געטאָן
און האָט די קלייניקע מחבלים — די שועלים קטנים
אין תּנ"ך באַזעצט אויף אייביק אויבן אָן.
אין נאָבעלער אַכסניא פֿון די ספֿרים
זײַנען זיי גוט און פֿרום געוואָרן,
און נוצן די געוווינהייט פֿון די רויבערשע שפּאַצירן
אין נעכט אין פֿינצטערע פּאָעטן צו פֿאַרפֿירן.
כ'בין שטאָלץ — זיי האָבן זיך פֿאַרנאַדעט אין מײַן ווײַנגאָרטן, מײַן כּרם,
דעם אָרעמען, אָן צאַם, אָן שויץ, דעם נאַקעטן אַרום,
און ברענגען מיר אין מיטן נאַכט, אין חושך און אין חרם
אַ טראָפּן ווײַן, אַ שטראַל פֿון העלער זון.

The Little Foxes, Little Foxes[201]

Into my wine garden, my vineyard,
Sneaked the little foxes, little foxes,
And at night they fill my house with ruddy light.
They carry in their muzzles radiant rhymes,
The little foxes—little foxes,
And without my say-so, stick them in my poems.

Indeed, they are minute, these small destroyers,
Who bit the blossoms in the vineyard very long ago.
For that, they have been rightly whipped in The Song of
  Songs:
Chapter, verse, and sermon will rebuke them evermore.

But the most beautiful of the ladies,
That wondrous grazier, Shulames,
With her ardent strophe stirred them up
And set those small destroyers, little foxes,
Forever in the Bible's seat of honor.
Within this grand hotel of books most holy,
They've become most pious and most good,
And use their thieving rambles, that old habit[202]
In the darkest of dark nights for seducing poets.
I'm proud—they wormed their way into my wine garden, my
  vineyard,
That poor vineyard, fenceless, no protection, naked all
  around,
And, in the middle of the night, in darkest excommunication
They bring me a drop of wine, a ray of the bright sun.

אויב ס'וויל אַ שלעכטע האַנט דעם וועג זיי צאַמען,
די קליינע פֿוקסעלעך – שועלים קטנים,
וואָס פֿאַלן אָן בײַ נאַכט מײַן שטוב מיט רויטן שײַן,
די שלעכטע האַנט ט'ניט קענען זייער קומען שטערן,
זיי האָבן זיך באַהאָפּטן מיט מײַן ווײַנגאָרטן, מײַן כּרם,
און וועלן ברענגען מיר נאָך לאָגלען פֿרישן ווײַן.

If a wicked hand desires to fence the road before them,
The little foxes, little foxes
Filling my house at night with ruddy light,
That wicked hand could never keep them from coming.
They have mated with my wine garden, my vineyard,
And will bring me yet more wineskins of fresh wine.

קנאת סופֿרים תּרבה חכמה

קנאת סופֿרים תּרבה חכמה —
כ׳וואָלט וועלן זען דעם תּנא פֿון דעם שפּרוך.
ער האָט מסתּם געשמייכלט מיט הנאה,
דער קלוגער תּנא פֿון נהרדעא,
אין שעה פֿון בדיחה —
האָט דאָרן זיסקייט פֿון אַ פֿרוכט.

נאָר כ׳קען ניט, קלוגער תּנא, אויפֿנעמען דײַן אמת,
און ס׳האָט אַ ביטערקייט מײַן האַרץ גענאָגט,
ווען ס׳האָבן זיך צעסקריפּעט בייזע פּענעס,
ווי איובֿ כ׳האָב פֿאַר גאָט געקלאָגט:

מײַן גאָט,
דו האָסט מיר ניט דערציילט, געלערנט,
אַז ס׳איז דײַן גרינע בלאַט אַפֿילו —
דורכגעווערעמט.

דו האָסט מיך ניט געוואָרנט,
אין ריינער קינדהייט-שעה,
אַז ס׳איז אין ווײַסן טלית אַפֿילו —
שעטנז דאָ.

דו האָסט מיר ניט פֿאַרטרויט, געזאָגט,
אַז אין דער ריינסטער פֿידל —
דעם סמיק דער שׂטן נאָגט.

מײַן גאָט,
אָט אין אַ וועלט אַזאַ,
דו זעסט איך בין פֿאַרלאָרן.
אָט פֿאַר אַ וועלט אַזאַ —
צו שוואַך מײַן קליינער אָרעם.

The Rivalry of Writers Increases Wisdom[203]

"The rivalry of writers increases wisdom"—
I would like to see the Tanna, the sage who wrote this
maxim.[204]
He probably smiled delightedly,
The clever Tanna of Neharda'i,
In the hour of jocularity—[205]
"And the thorn has the sweetness of fruit."

But, clever Tanna, I can't accept your truth,
And a bitterness gnaws at my heart
Whenever wicked pens have creaked.
Like Job, before God, I lament:

My God,
You never told or made me learn
That even your greenest leaf is
Devoured by a worm.

In childhood's purest hour,
You warned me not at all
That *shatnes*, forbidden cloth, is woven
Into the white prayer-shawl.[206]

Never did you confide or show
That the purest fiddle endures
The gnawing of that devil bow.

My God,
In such a world as this,
I cannot find my way.
Because, in such a world as this,
My arms are far too weak.

דײַן שולד — טאָ גײ אַראָפּ,
און מײַנע גלידער גיב אַ רוף.
דײַן שולד —
לײג דעם צוריקװעגס
פֿאַר מײַן דאַרן גוף.

ערשט איך פֿיל: ס'איז אַ געװיטער,
עס גיט די גאַנצע שטוב אַ ציטער.
אַ װאַנט איז אָפֿן —
און זיבן דורות באָבעס שטײען
און מיך שטראָפֿן:

„פֿע, טאָכטער, האָסט פֿאַרזען,
װער זײַנען דײַנע שׂונאים דען?
פֿאָדסקריבעס עפּעס זשלאָבעס,
דו האָב קײן מורא ניט,
פֿאַרלאָז זיך אויף די באָבעס.

דעם ליבן פֿידלער דוד —
מיר װעלן אים פֿאַר אַלע פּאָלעס ציִען,
און אויך די פֿיר אמהות,
פֿאַר דיר װעלן זיך מיִען.

אַ רוף טאָן דבֿורה, מרים —
די קאָלעגינס בײדן —
גלײב אונדז — מיר קענען
אויפֿעפֿענען דעם גן-עדן".

די טרײסט געזאָגט —
און שוין ניטאָ.
װי קײן מאָל ניט געװען
די העלע שעה.

עס שטײט די װאַנט —
אַלץ װי געװען,
נאָר כ'שװער, די זעונג
כ'האָב געזען.

It's all your fault, so now descend
And call out to my limbs.
Your fault,
So set down the way back
Before my withered flesh.

At first I feel a whirlwind
Shake the house: it trembles.
A wall opens, crumbles—
And grandmothers, seven generations deep,
Stand there scolding; thus they speak:

"Feh, daughter, you neglect to see
Exactly who's your enemy!
Riffraff, dregs, boors,[207]
Don't be afraid,
Depend upon these grandmothers of yours.

That dear fiddler, David,
We'll give his skirts a tug or two,
And also the four Matriarchs
Will intercede for you.

A call to Deborah, Miriam—
Dear colleagues, lovely, nice—
Believe us, we are able
To open Paradise."

This consolation uttered,
And then they are no more.
As if this brilliant hour
Never were.

The wall stands there
As before, it may seem,
But I swear, I saw
That vision, that dream.

די זעונג כ'האָב געזען —
אַ זוניקע, און קלאָר און צײַטיק.
בײַ טאָג איז דאָס געווען,
אין טאָג פֿון קורצן פֿרײַטיק.

און אפֿשר, קלוגער תּנא,
דו האָסט דאָס געזוכט —
דעם דאָרן זיס מאַכן פֿאַר מיר,
ווי זיסן פֿרוכט.
אַ דאַנק דיר, גוטער תּנא,
כ'האָב פֿאַרשטאַנען דיך ביז גרונט,
און איך בעט דיך, גוטער תּנא,
ס'זאָל זײַן אי מיר, אי אַלע צו געזונט.

I swear I saw the vision,
Sunny, clear, and ripe.
It was on the short Friday,
In the bright daylight.[208]

And maybe, clever Tanna,
Your purpose of pursuit
Was to sweeten the thorn for me[209]
Like sweet fruit.
Thank you, good Tanna,
I understand you to the core,
And I ask of you, good Tanna,
May I, may we all thrive evermore!

מײַן געשפּאַן

שפּאַן אײַן די אַלטע פֿעדער
און די אַלטע כאָדאַקעס שפּאַן אײַן.
אַ שמיר די טרוקענע רעדער —
מען לאָזט זיך אין וועג אַרײַן.

דער טאָג איז שוין פֿאַרענדיקט,
און דאָס איז דאָך אַ גליק.
דער טאָג מײַנער איז שטענדיק
אַ האַרטער, שווערער קריג.

פֿאַר נאַכט די לעצטע סטאַנציע
און דער לעצטער שטראַל.
עס כליפּעט אויפֿן שלאַכטפֿעלד
דער פֿאַרשפּילטער גענעראַל.

אַך, מײַן שיין כּלי-זיין
אין דעם בלוטיקן קריג,
אַ טײַטל פֿון אַ מלמד
אַנטקעגן אַן אײַזערנער פּיק.

און מײַנע פּאָר כאָדאַקעס,
ווי ס'וואָלט זיי אַ כּישוף געבויט —
זיי שטייען געשפּאַנטע און שטאַרקע,
ווי מענדעלעס אייביקע בויד.

זיי שטייען האַרטע און קאַראַווע
לעם מײַן צעשאָטענעם בעט,
זיי שטייען פֿאַרעקשנטע און בראַווע
ווי אַ נאַר אין פֿאַרשפּילטן געוועט.

נעם איך ווידער מײַן הילצערנע טײַטל,
און מײַן מאָדנער געשפּאַן איז געשפּאַנט.
צי אַ שפּרונג, צי אַ זכות, צי אַ רוח
פֿירט מיך אין וועג פֿאַר אַ האַנט.

My Harness

Put the old pen in harness
And hitch up the old clogs.
Give the dry wheels a smudge of grease
It's time to take to the road.

The day is already finished,
And that is fortunate.
Each of my days is always
A relentless, difficult fight.

At dusk, the final station
And the final ray of light.
Sobbing on the battlefield,
The general in defeat.

Ah, my lovely weapons
In the bloody fight,
A schoolteacher's pointer
Against an iron spade.[210]

This pair of clogs, my own, are
As if by witchcraft fashioned.
They stand, harnessed and strong,
Like Mendele's eternal wagon.[211]

They stand, soiled and solid,[212]
Near my shattered bed,
They stand stubborn and gallant
Like a fool who's lost a bet.

Again, I take up my wooden pointer
And hitch up my strange team.
I'm led by the hand to the roadway
By some merit, some phantom, some charm.[213]

אין שטאַל פֿון לעבן

מײַן אָרעמער פּעגאַז גייט צו פֿוס.
אי ער, אי איך — מיר האָבן ביידע שוין פֿאַרגעסן שוועבן.
די וועלט איז זייער קליין,
עס טריקנט אויס דער ים.
איך האָב דעם ווילדן סוסל אײַנגעשפּאַנט אין שטאַל פֿון לעבן.
שלעפּן מיר זיך ביידע שפּאַן נאָך שפּאַן.

און ווער האָט אָפּגעשאָסן פֿליגלען זײַנע?
און ווער האָט אָפּגעגריזשעט שפּיץ פֿון פּען?
די זון פֿאַרגייט, די שויבן בלוטיק שײַנען.
אָט ענדיקט זיך די זון. אָט ענדיקט זיך מײַן זען.

קומט, שורות, שטעלט זיך אויס, גיט מיך אַ הייב.
איר זײַט מײַן שוץ און אויך מײַנע באַפֿעלער.
איך קען ניט איבערגיין דעם צאַם פֿון שפּינוועבס און פֿון שטויב
און ס׳ווערט מײַן פֿעלד אַלץ טונקעלער און שמעלער.

וואָס טויג באַרימערײַ, וואָס טויג?
וואָס טויג אַ מעשׂה נאָך אַ מעשׂה קנעטן?
נישט שטיי, פּעגאַז, צו נאָנט לעם היי פֿון סטויג,
דו קענסט, חלילה, ווערן אַ חמור מיט עפּאָלעטן.

In the Stable of Life

My poor Pegasus goes on foot.
Both he and I have forgotten how to soar.
The world is very small,
The sea dries up.
I've harnessed this wild steed in the stable of life.
We both drag along, step by step.

And who has shot off his wings?
And who has gnawed off the tip of the pen?
The sun sets, the windowpanes glow bloodily.
So the sun ends. So my vision ends.

Come, verses, display yourselves, raise me up.
You are my protection and also my commanders.
I cannot scale the fence of spiderwebs and dust
And my field becomes ever darker, narrower.

What's the good of boasting, what's the good?
What's the good when one tale another tale begets?
Don't stand too near the haystack, Pegasus,
For, God forbid, you could become an ass in epaulets.

VIII

ליכט פֿון דאָרנבוים

בוענאָס-איירעס, 1965

VIII

Likht fun dornboym
(Light of the Thorn Bush)
Buenos Aires, 1965

אָן ווערטער

אָן ווערטער ברענג מײַן זאָג,
אָן רייד.
און אָן קלעזמאָרים-שפּיל —
דעם ניגון פֿון מײַן חתונה,
אָן פֿעדעם פֿלעכט —
מײַן חופּה-קלייד.

אָט אַזוי —
ווי דער קלאַנג פֿליט אַרויס
און אַנטלויפֿט פֿון זײַן פֿידל.
און איך מיט צעוואָרפֿענע הענט,
איך אַנטלויף פֿון מײַן זײַן.

אָ, גיס מיר אָן פֿאַר נאַכט
דעם כּוס פֿון מערבֿ-ווײַן,
דעם פֿלאַמיקן געטראַנק
פֿון געשטאָרבענעם טאָג.
לאָד מיך אָן מיט דעם ליכט,
וואָס עס זיפּט אויס דער הימל
נאָך איידער די זון
וואַרפֿט איר מעשענע וואָג.

1955

Without Words

Without words, bring forth my saying,
Without speech.
And without musicians' playing—
My wedding tune,
Without thread, weave
My wedding dress.

Just like this—
Like the music flying
And escaping from his fiddle.
And I, with arms akimbo,
Am escaping from my being.

Oh, at dusk pour out for me[214]
The cup of sunset wine,
The flaming drink
Of dying day.
Load me with the light
That the sky sifts out
Right before the sun
Casts down her brass weight.

1955

דאָס ליד פֿון דיאָגענוס

די שיינע בלעטער פֿאַלן,
און די חכמים קענען זיי נישט היילן.
די ווײַסע בלומען וועלקן,
און די חכמים קענען זיי נישט מאַכן ווײַס.
עס נייגט זיך דער צעדערבוים
צום ווילדגראָז,
און די חכמים קענען נישט אָוועקטרײַבן דעם ווינט.
עס וואַלגערט זיך דער האַרפֿנהאַר
בײַם מיסטגרוב,
און די וועכטער פּײַפֿן אויף אויף אים די הינט.

ס'איז אומעטיק מיר,
ווי ס'איז מײַן נאָמען דיאָגענוס.
די ווײַסע טאָגע ברענגט מיר נישט
קיין ליכט.
די ווײַסע טאָגע פֿאַלט אויף מײַנע אַקסלען
ווי אַ לאַסט.
דער פֿלאַם פֿון שטורקאַצן
פֿאַרבלענדט די אויגן —
האָב איך באַהאַלטן זיך אין שאָטן —
פֿון אַ פֿאַס.

אין קלענסטן ווינקל רוט די טיפֿסטע שטילקייט.
דאָרט קומט דער קראַנקער לייב,
און עס קומט די גריל.
דאָרט גלײַכט זיך אויס דער העכסטער באַרג
מיט טיפֿסטן טאָל.
דאָרט קומט די זון מיט פֿולן שײַטער ליכטן
און ס'איז דער קלענסטער ווינקל
פֿאַר דער פֿולסטער מאָס נישט שמאָל.

איז רו צו מיר געווען,
ווי ס'איז מײַן נאָמען דיאָגענוס,
ס'האָט אײַנגעדרימלט דער פֿאַרדראָס

The Song of Diogenes

The lovely leaves fall,
And the sages cannot heal them.
The white flowers wither,
And the sages cannot make them white.
The cedar bows
To the wild grass,
And the sages cannot drive away the wind.
The Master of the Harp lolls
Near the garbage pit
And the watchmen sic the dogs on him.

I am dejected,
As my name is Diogenes.
The white toga brings me
No light.
The white toga falls on my shoulders
Like a burden.
Because the flames of torches
Bedazzle my eyes,
I have hidden myself within
The shadow of a barrel.

The deepest silence resides in the smallest corner.
There comes the sickly lion
And there comes the cricket.
There, the highest mountain is the same
As the deepest valley.
The sun comes, its full pyre alight,
And the smallest corner
Contains its fullest measure.

Then peace descended on me,
As my name is Diogenes,
Resentment fell asleep

און ס'איז אַוועק דער האַס.
ביַי נאַכט זיַינען די שטערן,
די פֿוסגייער פֿון הימל,
געקומען, זיך געשטעלט —
ביַים איַינגאַנג פֿון מיַין פּאַס.

די ווערטער פֿון מיַין האַרץ
זענען געוואָרן פֿולע,
אָפּגערוט פֿון טומל,
אָפּגעשטויבט פֿון ווידעררוף פֿון גאַס.
די ווערטער פֿון מיַין האַרץ
זענען געוואָרן שטילע,
נאָך שטילער ווי די שאָטנס
פֿון מיַין פּאַס.

עס זענען געקומען
די פֿאַרלאָשענע זונען,
די פֿאַרשטומטע פֿון חרמס
מיט זיַידענע טריט.
זיי האָבן געטראָגן די וויַיסקייט
פֿון בלומען,
און דעם שיַין פֿון פֿאַרלאָשענע ליכטן
געהיט.

עס האָבן די שאָטנס פֿון נאַכט
זיך צעהעלט,
די ווענט און די ענגשאַפֿט צענומען, צענומען
און די פּאַס איז געוואָרן —
די גרויס פֿון דער וועלט.

ס'איז רו צו מיר געוועזן,
ווי ס'איז מיַין נאָמען דיאָגענוס,
ס'האָט די שטראַלונג פֿון נאַכט
געזאָגט איר געזאַנג.
ס'איז רו צו מיר געוועזן,
ווי ס'איז מיַין נאָמען דיאָגענוס,
און אין שטראַלונג פֿון נאַכט
פֿאַרזיי איך מיַין זאַנג.

1957

And hatred left.
At night, the stars,
Pedestrians of heaven,
Came and placed themselves
At the entrance to my vat.

The words of my heart
Grew full,
Rested from the din,
Dusted off the echo of the street.
The words of my heart
Grew quiet,
Even quieter than
The shadows of my tun.

Then, with silken footsteps,
Extinguished suns came,
Silenced by excommunication,
Carrying the whiteness
Of flowers, and guarding
Candles' extinguished light.

The shadows of night
Brightened,
Demolished the crush and the walls,
And the barrel became—
The size of the world.

Then peace descended on me,
As my name is Diogenes,
The radiance of night
Recited her song.
Then peace descended on me,
As my name is Diogenes,
And in the radiance of night
I sow my corn.

1957

מייַן שיף פֿון פּימסנהאָלץ

צי ס׳רעגנט, צי עס רעגנט ניט —
כ׳וועל אויסבויען אַ שיף פֿון פּימסנהאָלץ
און אָפּשווימען אין לאַנד לייליט.
ווו איז דאָס לאַנד לייליט?
ווער ווייס.
וואָס טוט מען אין דעם לאַנד לייליט?
ווער ווייס.
צי עס איז ווייַט? צי עס איז טיף
עס פֿעלט אַ מאַסט נאָך אין מייַן שיף
אַז איך זאָל גרייכן צו דעם לאַנד לייליט.

ווען איך בין קראַנק,
און ווען כ׳בין מיד —
ציט מיך צו דעם לאַנד לייליט.
דאָרט איז אַ ווייַסער פֿויגל דאָ,
דער רופֿא פֿון מייַן חולאַת.
ער וואָלט פֿאַרהערט מייַן האַרץ,
מייַן פּלייצע אויסגעקלאַפּט,
געפֿרעגט פֿאַר וואָס כ׳בין בלאַס.
און וואָלט אַ רפֿואה מיר פֿאַרשריבן
מיטן כּתבֿ פֿון לאַנד לייליט.
דאָס איז גענוג אויף אייביק לעבן,
נישט קראַנק, נישט אַלט, נישט מיד.
צי ס׳רעגנט, צי עס רעגנט ניט —
כ׳וועל אויסבויען אַ שיף פֿון פּימסנהאָלץ
און אפּשווימען אין לאַנד לייליט.
איך בוי די שיף סייַ טאָג, סייַ נאַכט,
אַפֿילו אין מייַן חלום שטענדיק זיך געמיט.
כ׳וועל אפֿשר מאָרגן ענדיקן,
אַרויפֿפּצ׳יען די העכסטע מאַסט
און אָפּשווימען אין לאַנד לייליט.

My Ship of Gopher Wood[215]

Whether or not it starts to rain—
I'll build a ship of gopher wood
And float away to Leylit Land.
Where on earth is this Leylit Land?
Who knows?
What's there to do in Leylit Land?
Who knows?
Whether it's far or whether it's deep,
There is still no mast upon my ship
For me to reach Leylit Land.

When I am sick
And when I'm tired—
Let me drift toward Leylit Land.
There, they have a pure white bird
The healer of my ailments.
It would listen to my heart,
Tap between my shoulder blades,
And ask me why my face is pale,
Then write me a prescription
In the script of Leylit Land.
It guarantees I'll live forever,
Never sick or old or tired.
Whether or not it starts to rain—
I'll build a ship of gopher wood
And float away to Leylit Land.
I build the ship all day, all night,
Even in dreams, it's never done.
Maybe tomorrow I'll finish it,
Raising high the tallest mast,
And float away to Leylit Land.

און וואָס וועט זײַן —

און וואָס וועט זײַן —
אַז צוריק וועלן קומען די פֿליִער
און זאָגן אַז עס איז קיין הימל נישטאָ?
איז ווו וועל איך ווענדן די בליקן,
אויב נישט העכער, נישט אויבן?

ווי וועל איך פֿאַרטראָגן די גרויקייט פֿון רעגן?
פֿון שטיינערנע גאַסן די שטויבן?
ווו וועל איך זיך רעטן פֿון שווערן דערווידער?
און ווער וועט מיר העלפֿן צו שרײַבן די לידער?
אויב ס'איז גאָרנישט מיט גאָרנישט דאָרט אויבן?

נאָר איך וועל די פֿליִער נישט גלייבן.
איך וועל זיי נישט גלייבן...

ווײַל איך האָב אַ מלאך געזען,
נישט איין מאָל, אַ סך מאָל,
און ער האָט מיך מציל געווען —
פֿון פּלאָגן וואָס דראָען.

און איך וועל די פֿליִער נישט טרויען,
איך וועל זיי נישט טרויען.

און וואָס וועט זײַן —
אַז צוריק וועלן קומען די פֿליִער
און אָפּלייקענען דעם גן-עדן?
די היים פֿון צדיקים?
איז ווי וועט מיר גליקן
אַריבער פֿאַפּירענע בריקן
אויב נישט מיט צדיקים?
אויב כ'וועל זיך בײַ זייערע פּאָלעס נישט האַלטן,
ווי וועל איך אַריבערגיין גריבער און שפּאַלטן?
ווער וועט מיר מײַן אָרעמען נפֿש דערהאַלטן?
און ווו וועל איך אויפֿלייזן טרערן?

And What Will Happen?

And what will happen
When the fliers return
And say there's no heaven out there?
Where will I turn my eyes
If not upward, not higher?

How will I bear rain's grayness?
The stony streets' dust?
Where will I hide from repulsion,
And who will help me write my poems
If there's absolutely nothing up there?

But I won't believe the fliers,
I will not believe them.

For I've seen an angel,
Not one time, but many,
And he rescued me
From threatening torments.

And I won't trust the fliers,
I will not trust them.

And what will happen
When the fliers come back
Denying Paradise,
The home of the pious?
How will I ever manage
To cross over paper bridges
If not with the pious?
How will I walk across fissures
Without holding their coat tails?
And who will sustain my poor soul?
And where will I let my tears flow?

נאָר איך וועל די פֿליִער נישט הערן.
איך וועל זיי נישט הערן.

ווײַל איך האָב צדיקים געזען,
נישט איין מאָל, אַ סך מאָל.
זיי זײַנען געגאַנגען אין יאָך און אין קלעם,
געטראָגן די וועלט אויפֿן רוקן.

וועל איך אויף די פֿליִער נישט קוקן.
נישט אומקוקן זיך און נישט קוקן.

עס קענען צום הימל דערגרייכן
די וואָס וועבן די הימלישע בלויען,
און האָבן אויף ניסים געשפּאַנט ווי אויף טרעפּ
און קענען די גענג פֿון נהרדעא.

But I won't hear the fliers.
I will not hear them.

For I've seen the pious,
Not one time, but many.
They were walking in yokes and in vises,
Bearing the world on their shoulders.

So I won't look at the fliers,
I won't turn and look.

Those who weave heavenly blue
Can reach heaven,
Who stride across stairways of wonders
And know Neharda'i's pathways.[216]

אײַזערנער חלום

אין דור פֿון קופּער און פֿון שטאָל
איך פֿיטער נאָך דאָס אייזעלע דעם ווײַסן פֿון אַמאָל.

פֿון פֿייגל אײַזערנע אין זייער רוישיקן געשאַל
איך הער נאָך אַלץ דאָס ליד פֿון זומערדיקן נאַכטיגאַל.

און דורך די וואָלקנס רויך, און שטויב, און קויט
איך זע דעם אַלטן בבֿל-טורעם ווי מען בויט.

עס צי׳ען טרעפּ פֿון אַ קאָנווייער ערגעץ מיך אַרויף.
און כ׳פֿיל אין חלום אײַזערנעם עס פּליט מײַן גוף.

וווהין? — שרײַ איך — וווהין? — איך שרײַ.
און ס׳ענטפֿערן מיר ליפּן צוויי געגאָסענע פֿון בלײַ:

איך ווייס נישט ווו.
איך בין אַ גולם נאָר, אָט פּונקט ווי דו.

און פֿון די גולם-ליפּן גיט אַ בליץ אַ בלענד,
און כ׳פֿיל ווי ס׳גולמען זיך מײַנע פֿיס און הענט.

פֿון חלום אײַזערנעם ס׳נעמט מיך אַרויס
דאָס ווײַסע אייזעלע וואָס פֿיטערט לעם מײַן הויז.

אַ בשׂורה אַ פֿאַרחתמעטע ער האָט פֿאַר מיר.
פֿאַרשריבן איז די בשׂורה אויף אַ זונפּאַפּיר:

„דער בבֿל-טורעם איז אַ חלום נאָר.
איך און דער נאַכטיגאַל זײַנען די וואָרע וואָר“.

Iron Dream

In this generation of copper and steel
I graze the white donkey of old times, still.

In the iron birds' clamor and clang
I still hear the summer nightingale's song.

And through the clouds of smoke, dust, and filth
I see how the old Tower of Babel was built.

An escalator pulls me somewhere up high,
In the iron dream, I feel myself fly.

Where to, where? I shout in dread.
And I'm answered by two lips flowing with lead:

"I do not know where to.
I am only a golem, just like you."

From the golem's lips, lightning, a ray,
And I feel my arms and legs turn into clay.[217]

Then I'm lifted out of the iron dream
By the white donkey grazing near my home.

He brings me a message, secret and sealed
And inscribed on sun-paper, to be revealed:

"The Tower of Babel is but an illusion.
The nightingale and I are the true conclusion."

דאָס געזאַנג פֿון שבת

מיט די זעקס קיסרים
פֿון די זעקס טעג פֿון דער וואָך
האָב איך זיך געקריגט ביז ערבֿ-שבת.
זונטיק האָבן זיי צוגענומען מײַן שלאָף.
מאָנטיק האָבן זיי מײַן זאַלץ צעשאָטן.
און אויפֿן דריטן טאָג, מײַן גאָט,
האָבן זיי פֿאַרשלײַדערט מײַן ברויט
און איבער מײַן פּנים מיט ריטער געפֿאָכטן.
זיי האָבן געכאַפּט מײַן פֿליִענדיקע טויב
און האָבן זי געשאָכטן.
און אַזוי ביז פֿרײַטיק אין דער פֿרי.
און דאָס איז דאָך מײַן גאַנצע וואָך,
ווען עס שטאַרבט מײַן טויבנפֿלי.

פֿאַר נאַכט האָב איך אָנגעצונדן פֿיר ליכט
און צו מיר איז געקומען די מלכּה שבת.
עס האָט אַ לויכט געטאָן איר געזיכט
און די גאַנצע וועלט איז געוואָרן שבת.
מײַן צעשאָטענער זאַלץ
האָט געפֿינקלט אין זעלצל,
און מײַן טויב, מײַן פֿליִענדיקע טויב,
האָט געפּאַטשט מיט די פֿליגל
און געריייניקט איר העלדזל.

די מלכּה שבת האָט געבענטשט מײַנע ליכט.
זיי האָבן געלויכטן מיט אַ פֿלאַם אַ קלאָרן.
די שײַן האָט פֿאַרדעקט די טעג פֿון דער וואָך
און דעם קריג מיט די זעקס קיסרים.
די גרינקייט פֿון בערג —
איז די גרינקייט פֿון שבת.
דער זילבער פֿון טײַך —
איז דער זילבער פֿון שבת.

The Sabbath Song

I fought until Sabbath eve
With the six emperors
Of the six days of the week.
Sunday they confiscated my sleep.
Monday they scattered my salt.
And on the third day, my God,
They flung away my bread
And, above my face, they fenced with knights.
They caught my flying dove
And slaughtered her.
And so forth, until Friday dawn.
And this, you see, ends my whole week,
With the dying of my dove-flying.

At dusk, I kindled four candles
And the Sabbath Queen came to me.
Her countenance shone
And the whole world became Sabbath.
My scattered salt
Glittered in the saltshaker,
And my dove, my flying dove,
Flapped her wings
And groomed her throat.

The Sabbath Queen blessed my candles.
They shone with a clear flame.
The light covered the days of the week
And the battle with the six emperors.
The greenness of mountains—
Is the greenness of Sabbath.
The silver of a river—
Is the silver of Sabbath.

דאָס געזאַנג פֿון דעם ווינט —
איז דאָס זינגען פֿון שבת.
און דאָס געזאַנג פֿון מײַן האַרץ —
איז דער אײביקער שבת.

The song of the wind—
Is the singing of Sabbath.
And the song of my heart
Is the eternal Sabbath.

מײַן שפּראַך

ס'איז נישט כּדאַי
אַזוי פֿיל צער
פֿאַר וואָרט געזאָגטן,
צי פֿאַרשוויגענעם.
עס לעבט אין מיר
אַ ווײַסע שפּראַך,
אַ וואָרט וואָס כ'האָב נישט
געזיגלט אים.
און כאָטש מײַן ווײַסע שפּראַך
איז שטום —
פֿון ווערטער נישט געפֿורעמטע,
איז זי מײַן אויסשפּראַך און מײַן שטים,
און מײַן נשמה שטורעמט זי.

מײַן ווײַסע שפּראַך
האָט נישט קיין כּתבֿ
און נישט קיין צונג
פֿאַר איר אַנטפּלעק.
זי לויטערט אויף מיט איר באַשאַף,
אין ווײַסער שטילקייט טויכט אַוועק.

ווען איך אַליין וועל ליגן שטום,
זיך וווּנדערן —
וואָס איך בין טויט.
מײַן ווײַסע שפּראַך
וועט צונטערן
און אויפֿזיגלען די שטומע רייד.

איך הער זיי אָפֿט
ווען כ'ווער פֿאַרשטויבט
פֿון בייזן שפּאָט,
פֿון חוצפּה-ברום.

My Language

For this much grief
The spoken word
Or silenced word
Will not suffice.
There lives in me
A language, white,
A word that I
Have never sealed.
Speechless, dumb,
Not formed from words,
My white language,
My utterance, voice,
Assaults my soul.

My white language
Has no script
And has no tongue
For its display.
With its creation, it purifies,
Then in white silence, sinks away.[218]

When the day comes that I lie dumb,
Marveling
That I am dead.
My white language,
Catching fire,
Will unseal the stifled words.[219]

I hear them often,
When I'm dusty from
Cruel ridicule
And insolent hum.

מײַן װײַסע שפּראַך
זי ענטפֿערט אָפּ,
װען מײַנע ליפּן זײַנען שטום.

It's my white language
That replies
When my lips are dumb.

דער ווינט איז אַלט געוואָרן

דער ווינט איז אַלט געוואָרן.
די מעשׂיות וואָס ער ברומט מיט הייזעריקער שטים —
זיי זײַנען אומעטיק.
זיי וואַרפֿן מיך אַראָפּ פֿון באַרג,
און איך ווער אַ בעטלערקע אין טאָל.
דאָס גאָלד פֿון מײַנע פּערל —
ווערט אַשקאָליר.
דאָס טוט דער אַלטער ווינט,
וואָס רירט זיך אָן אָן מיר.

דער ווינט איז אַלט געוואָרן.
דער ניגון וואָס ער ברומט מיט הוילער שטים —
ער איז שרעקנדיק.
ער זעגט אַראָפּ די גרינקייט פֿון דעם וואַלד,
די זינגענדיקע גרינקייט פֿון אַמאָל.
מײַן באַרגפֿויגל —
ער ווערט אַ פֿלעדערמויז.
דאָס טוט דער אַלטער ווינט,
וואָס עסט מײַן האַרץ מיר אויס.

דער ווינט איז אַלט געוואָרן.
די סודות וואָס ער ברומט מיט שעפּטשענדיקער שטים —
זיי זײַנען טויטנדיק.
זיי לייקענען די קלאָרקייט פֿון אַ טרער.
זיי לייקענען די שבֿועה פֿון אַ בליק.
דאָס טוט דער אַלטער ווינט
טויב און שעפּטשענדיק.

נאָר צווייען גלייבן נישט דעם אַלטן ווינט:
די בעטלערקע אין טאָל — אין אַש און שטויב,
און די לבֿנה אין דער הייך — די ווײַסע, שטומע טויב.

The Wind Has Grown Old

The wind has grown old.
The stories that it roars with a hoarse voice
Are melancholy.
They cast me down from the mountain,
And I become a beggar woman in the valley.
The gold of my pearls
Becomes the color of ash.
Thus the old wind
Violates me.[220]

The wind has grown old.
The melody that it roars with a hollow voice
Is frightening.
It saws the green from the forest,
The singing green of the past.
My mountain bird
Becomes a bat.
Thus the old wind
Eats out my heart.

The wind has grown old.
The secrets that it roars with a whispering voice
Are deadly.
They deny the clarity of a tear.
They deny the promise of a glance.
Thus the old wind,
Whispering and deaf.

Only two do not believe the old wind:
The beggar woman in the valley—in ash and dust,
And the moon on high—that white, mute dove.

פֿון מידקייט כ׳וואַרף אַראָפּ די שיך און זאָקן

פֿון מידקייט כ׳וואַרף אַראָפּ די שיך און זאָקן,
זיך אָפּרוען פֿון אַ פֿאַרטאַכליעוועטן טאָג.
עס הייבן אָן די פֿיס מײַנע צו קלאָגן
מיט טרויער נאַקעטן, מיט שטומען זאָג:
ווו-ווו? ווהין? נאָך וואָס?
די אויסדאַכטונג געיאָגט — איז זי צערונען.
די בלענדעניש געוויקלט ווי אויף שפּונען.
פֿון שטויב געוועבט פֿאַר העמד אַ פֿאָדעם.
ווי טוט אַזוינס אין עלטער דײַנעם אַ בן-אָדם?

כ׳פֿאַרמאַך די אויערן, נישט הערן פֿון די פֿיס דעם דיבור.
צעפּלאַמען זיך די אויערן מיט מוסרדיקן פֿיבער:
וואָס? וואָס? וואָס האָבן מיר געהערט?
געהערט אַ ברכה איבער אַ פּוסטן כּוס.
פֿאַרשוועכט די ערלעכקייט פֿון פּראָסטן שטיקל גלאָז,
געהערט דעם רויש פֿון שוים און האָפֿן,
דער ווײַן איז אויסגערונען ביזן לעצטן טראָפּן.
אין דײַן עלטער איז משונה
פֿאַרטויבן אין די אויערן די גאָט-געבענטשטע סטרונע.

כ׳וויל אויפֿהייבן די הענט, זיך שיצן קעגן צאָרן,
הענגען זיי ווי פֿרעמדע, ווי נישט מיט מיר געבאָרן.
זיי מורמלען מיט ברוגז:
צו וואָס איז אונדזער מי? וואָס טויג עס?
געגעבן שלום דעם און יענעם,
קיין שלום איז נישטאָ, די פֿינגער קלעמען.
און אין דײַן עלטער, שוין קרובֿ צו אַ מאה —
ווי פּאַסט פֿאַר דיר די בלאָנדזשעניש אין תּהו?

איך האָב אַ שוץ געזוכט בײַ מײַנע טרײַע אויגן
אין מײַן שפּיגל.
נאָר דאָרט געשטאַנען איז אַ מענטש אַ פֿרעמדער.
ער האָט געקוקט אויף מיר ווי אַ פֿאַרשעמטער —
ווי קומט אַ פֿרעמדער מענטש צו מיר אין שפּיגל?

I Kick Off My Shoes and Socks in Exhaustion

I kick off my shoes and socks in exhaustion
To recover from a wasted day.
My feet begin their complaining
With naked sorrow and mutely say:
"Where on earth? Going where? And for what?
Chase after an illusion, it disappears.
The dazzle's wrapped about a spool.
A thread of dust's woven in a shirt.
In old age, does a human being do this, you fool?"[221]

I block my ears, so not to hear my feet's conversation,
But my ears burst into the flames of moral conflagration:
"What? What? What have we heard?
Heard a blessing over an empty cup.
Desecrated the virtue of a simple piece of glass,
Heard the hiss of foam and hops,
The wine's all run out to the last drops.
It's wild and strange that in your old years
The God-blessed strings deafen your ears."

I want to lift my hands, to shield myself from wrath,
But they hang like strangers, as if not mine since birth.
They mutter in anger:
"What's the point? Why bother
Greeting him and her with '*Sholem*,' with a handshake?
We have no peace. Our fingers ache.[222]
And in your old age, nearly a century old—
How does it suit you, this wandering in the void?"

Seeking protection in my faithful eyes,
I looked into my mirror.
But there stood a stranger, an unknown face.
He gazed at me, as if in deep disgrace:
"How does a stranger come to *me* in the mirror?"

מבול

פֿון מײַן שוועל ביזן טיש איז אַ לאַנגער מהלך.
איך גיי און איך שטרויכל און אָפּט מאָל אָט פֿאַל איך.
איך קום צו צו מײַן בענקל און זעץ זיך אַנידער.
דאַנק דעם בורא — דער טאָג איז פֿאַרבײַ, איז אַריבער.

איך האָב ווערטער געהערט, איך פֿאַרשטיי נישט דאָס לשון
אַזעלכע ווערטער געפּוצטע ווי די פּרות הבשן.
איך דערמאָן זיך אויך מײַנע גערעדטע דיבורים
ווי אסתּר-המלכּה אין שפּיל פֿון אַ פּורים.

עס קומט אונטער מײַן קאַץ, גיט אַ מיאַו, אַ פּלאַפּל:
דו ווייסט נישט? עס זײַנען די טעג איצט פֿון מבול,
ס'האָט מיר נח אַ רעטונג באַזאָרגט אין זײַן תּבֿה,
גיב אַ שמיר דײַנע ליפּן און לאָמיר גיין ביידע.

אָט איז זי די תּבֿה... מײַן קאַץ איז דערשוווּמען,
נאָר מיר האָט געשטערט אויפֿן הוט מײַנע בלומען.
איך קען נישט דערשווימען, איך בין נישט קאַפּאַבל,
זעט אויס, ס'איז באַשערט מיר צו זינקען אין מבול.

1964

Flood

It's a long stretch from my door to the table.
Too often falling, I walk and I stumble.
I come to my chair and then I sit down.
Thank God, the Creator, this day is now done.

I have heard words, not understanding the tongue,
Such words, all dressed up like the kine of Bashan.[223]
I also recall all the speeches I'd say
Like Esther the Queen in a Purim play.

My cat comes around, with her prattling mew:
Now are the Flood Days. I thought you knew!
I've been offered salvation in Noah's Ark,
So smear on some lipstick, and let's both embark.

Right here is the Ark. She has swum there, my cat,
But I've been held back by the flowers on my hat.
I can't swim that far, not even for refuge,
It seems that I'm fated to sink in the Deluge.

1964

שולמית

די העכסטע בערג זײַנען נידעריק, נידעריק,
דער קלענסטער באַרג איז הויך.
אַזוי האָבן געזאָגט חכמים זיבעציק
און איך הקטנה אויך.

די העכסטע בערג זײַנען נידעריק, נידעריק,
איך שפּאַן זיי אַריבער מיט מײַן בליק.
אַזוי האָבן געזאָגט חכמים זיבעציק
מיט טויזנט יאָר צוריק.

דער קלענסטער באַרג איז הויך גאָר אָן אַ סוף,
הויך און העכער גאָר אָן אַ שיעור.
ס'האָט דאָרט שפּאַצירט שולמית מיט איר שאָף
און זיבעציק חכמים נאָך איר.

זיי האָבן פֿאַר איר די חכמה אויסגעטראַכט.
דאָס ליד פֿון לידער פֿאַרפֿאַסט.
זי האָט דעם קלײנעם באַרג אַזוי הויך געמאַכט,
ווי פֿאַר איר האָט געפּאַסט.

איך בין אַזוי מקנא איר,
איר שײנקייט פֿאַרגייט נישט און בליט.
און טאַקע דאָס, וואָס חכמים זיבעציק
זײַנען נאָכגעגאַנגען אירע טריט.

1959

Shulames

The highest mountains are lower than low,
The smallest mountain is high.
All the seventy sages said so,
And I, too, insignificant I.[224]

The highest mountains are lower than low,
I step over them with one look.
All the seventy sages said so,
A thousand years ago, in a book.

The smallest mountain is high without bound,
Greater than all the ages.
Shulames strolled there, with her sheep all around,
Followed by seventy sages.

Shulames's wisdom they contrived,
The Song of Songs composed.
She made that small mountain rise as high
As ever she supposed.

I am consumed with envy of her:
Her beauty blooms on, does not die.
And also because the seventy sages
Trailed after her with a sigh.

1959

אויף דער פּאַפּירענער בריק

איך גיי זיך היינט פֿאַרדינגען פֿאַר אַ דינסטמויד,
אויב מען וועט מיך וועלן אָנדינגען.
האָב איך אַ זײַדענעם שלייף אויף מײַן הויב —
און דאָס איז נישט קיין מעלה פֿאַר אַ דינסטמויד —
אויב מען וועט מיך וועלן אָנדינגען.

און דערצו טראָג איך לאַקירענע שיך —
און דאָס איז נישט קיין מעלה פֿאַר אַ מויד אין קיך —
אויב מען וועט מיך וועלן אָנדינגען.

האָט מען מיר געזאָגט מיט אַ ליבלעכער מינע:
גיי געזונט, זײַ אַ דינסט בײַ אַבֿרהם-אָבֿינו.

בין איך געגאַנגען צוריק
אויף דער פּאַפּירענער בריק
ווו צדיקים שטײַגן —
און ווי זיי קומען דאָרט, און ווי זיי גייען דאָרט
איז אַ סוד, און זיי שווײַגן.

גיי איך זיך פֿאַרדינגען פֿאַר אַ שנײַדערהאַנט,
אויב מען וועט מיך וועלן אָנדינגען.
איז מײַן בליק אַ ביסל צעשפּאַנט —
און דאָס איז נישט קיין מעלה פֿאַר אַ שנײַדערהאַנט —
אויב מען וועט מיך וועלן אָנדינגען.

און דערצו טראָג איך אַ בײַטשל פֿון אַלטע פּערל —
און דאָס איז נישט קיין מעלה פֿאַר נאָדל און שערל —
אויב מען וועט מיך וועלן אָנדינגען.

האָט מען מיר געענטפֿערט איידל, פֿאַמעלעך:
גיי ניי די בגדים בײַ דוד-המלך.

בין איך געגאַנגען צוריק
אויף דער פּאַפּירענער בריק

On the Paper Bridge

I'll hire myself out as a serving maid,
If anyone wants to hire me.
I've tied a silk bow on my bonnet—
And this is not fit for a serving maid—
If anyone wants to hire me.

I wear patent leather shoes, in addition,
And this is not fit for a maid in the kitchen,
If anyone wants to hire me.

Then I am told with an amiable face:
Go serve Abraham, Father of our race.

So back I walked
Across the paper bridge
Where the Righteous ascend—
And their comings and goings there
Are a secret, and they are silent without end.

I'll hire myself out as a tailor's hand,
If anyone wants to hire me.
But my eyes are somewhat strained
And this is not fit for a tailor's hand—
If anyone wants to hire me.

And, in addition I carry a string of old pearls,[225]
And this is not fit for needle and shears—
If anyone wants to hire me.

Then they answer me, ever polite and patient:
Go, sew up King David's royal garment.

So, back I walked
Across the paper bridge

ווו די צדיקים זינגען זמירות
און דאָס ציגעלע דאָס ווײַסע האָט אַ פּאָדעם געשטריקט
און געלייגט אויף מײַנע זאָקן די צירעס.

גיי איך זיך פֿאַרדינגען פֿאַר אַ שטערן־פּוצער —
אויב מען וועט מיך וועלן אָנדינגען —
קען איך נישט אַרויסריידן קוצעניו־מוצע —
און דאָס איז נישט קיין מעלה פֿאַר אַ שטערן־פּוצער —
אויב מען וועט מיך וועלן אָנדינגען.

און דערצו בין איך געראָטן אין מײַן באָבע
און קען נישט טאַנצן די לעצטע מאָדע —
אוי, אויב מען וועט מיך וועלן אָנדינגען.

האָט מען מיר געזאָגט דעם שיינע־מאַריינע
און אָפּגעשיקט וויינען מיט רחל־אמנו.

בין איך געגאַנגען צוריק
אויף דער פּאַפּירענער בריק
ווו עס שווײַגן די צדיקים.
און וואָס איך האָב געהערט, און וואָס איך האָב געזען
איז פֿאַרשריבן אין די נוטריקין.

Where the Righteous sing Sabbath tunes
And the little white goat knitted its yarn
And garnished my socks with small moons.

I'll hire myself out as a star-shiner,
If anyone wants to hire me.
I'm no good at sweet-talking[226]
And this is no advantage for a star-shiner,
If anyone wants to hire me.

And, in addition I take after my grandmother
And can't dance the latest style or any other—
Oy, if anyone wants to hire me.

So they gave me the title of Beautiful Teacher[227]
And sent me off to weep with Rachel our Mother.

So back I walked
Across the paper bridge
Where the Righteous remain silent.
And whatever I've heard and whatever I've seen
Are entered in the code of *Nutrikin.*[228]

צום מלך שלמה קומט די הערלעכע שולמית

צום מלך שלמה קומט די הערלעכע שולמית —
אַ רויז פֿון שרון אירע צעפּ באַצירן.
זאָגט דער מלך צו דער הערלעכער שולמית: —
ווי קומסטו דאָ אַהער פֿון שיר־השירים?

מיט טרערן וויינט די הערלעכע שולמית,
פֿון טרויער בײַטן זיך אין פּנים די קאָלירן: —
גרויסער מלך, נעם מיך דאָ אַהער,
איך קען נישט אייביק זיצן דאָרט אין שיר־השירים.

מען האָט מיך שוין באַזונגען ווו ס'איז נאָר אַ פֿידל דאָ,
בײַ אַלע טײַכן און בײַ אַלע ברעגן,
און צו דיר קומט שטילערהייט די מלכּה שבֿאָ
און טוט דיך אירע טריפֿה רעטענישן פֿרעגן.

לאַכט דער מלך שלמה: — הערלעכע, איך וויל דיך נישט פֿאַרפֿירן,
דו ביסט די שענסטע פֿיטערין אויף בערג און טאָלן,
און אייביק מוזסטו זײַן אין שיר־השירים.
דאָס איז דער פּרײַז וואָס דאַרפֿסט פֿאַר שיינקייט צאָלן.

Glorious Shulames Comes to Solomon the King

Glorious Shulames comes to Solomon the King,
A rose of Sharon braided in her hair.
Of glorious Shulames inquires Solomon the King:
From the Song of Songs, how did you get here?

Glorious Shulames weeps actual tears,
Her cheeks change color from her sorrowing pangs:
Your Eminence, great King, accept me here,
I cannot sit forever in the Song of Songs.

At the edge of every river and by myriad shores,
They've sung of me, wherever there are fiddles,
But to you, the Queen of Sheba quietly appears
To tease you with her *treyf*, seductive riddles.

King Solomon laughs: You glorious thing, don't get me
    wrong,
You're the loveliest shepherdess of hill and vale, I'd say,
But you must stay forever in the Songs' exalted Song.
This, for beauty, is the price you pay.

דאָס ליכט פֿון דײַן טיש

(בײַם טאַטנס מצבֿה)

כ'האָב געזינדיקט פֿאַר דיר.
כ'בין פֿאַרנומען,
פֿאַרשוומען
מיט געשלעג,
מיט געיעג,
מיט וויר-וואַר,
און מיט צער
און אָפֿט מאָל אַפֿילו מיט בלומען.

כ'האָב געזינדיקט פֿאַר דיר.
צו דײַן פֿאַרחתמעטער טיר
כ'בין שוין לאַנג, אַזוי לאַנג
נישט געקומען.
פֿון ווײַט, גאָר פֿון ווײַט,
לעם דײַן שטיין בײַ דער זײַט
כ'זע די ווערבע די קליינע.
זי גרינט. זי איז שטיל ווי דער שטיין.
ווי דער שטיין אַ געהיימע.

דאָרט רוט ווי אַ גרעזל מײַן בענקען.
אין געוויי,
אין פֿאַרדריי
פֿון צעטומלטן טאָל
איך פֿאַל יעדן טאָג
זיבן מאָל, נאָך אַ מאָל,
ווי אַ שיכּור לעבן אויסגעדאַכטע שענקען.

בײַ נאַכט,
גאָט קערט מיר אום מײַן נשמה,
כ'זע דאָס ליכט פֿון דײַן טיש,
דײַן האַנט אַ פֿאַרטראַכטע
אַ בלאַט גיט אַ מיש
אין ספֿר מיט אוראַלטע ראָגן.

The Light of Your Table
(At My Father's Grave)

I've sinned against you.
I've been too busy,
Flooded, dizzy
With the quarrels,
With the chasing,
With the chaos,
And with sorrow,
And often, even with flowers.

I've sinned against you.
For far too long
I have not come before
Your hermetic door.
From far away, even from afar
I see the willow, the small willow
Standing near your stone.
It grows green. It is quiet.
Like the stone, it is secret.

There, like a grass blade, my longing rests.
In convulsion,
In confusion
From the valley of delusion,
Every day, I fall
Seven times, and then again,
Like a drunk drawing near a tavern's illusion.

Nighttime,
God returns my soul to me.
I see the light of your table,
And your hand absentmindedly
Turning a page
In that holy book with its ancient binding.

כ׳שטיי לעם דײַן אַקסל געבויגן.
כ׳בין אַן אַנדערע איצט, כ׳בין אַ צווייטע.
אָט באַלד וועסטו זאָגן:
גיי שלאָפֿן, מײַן קינד, ס׳איז דײַן בעט אַ געגרייטע.

ס׳איז אַ רגע — כ׳בין אין רו פֿון אַ היים.
נאָר אָט איז דײַן נאָמען געקריצט אויף אַ שטיין.
ס׳שטייט די ווערבע די קליינע.
עס שײַנט נאָך דאָס ליכט פֿון דײַן טיש.
ס׳איז די שײַן אַ געהיימע.

1963

I stand, bent near your shoulder.
Now, I'm someone else, another,
And soon you will say:
Go, sleep, my child, your bed is waiting.

For a moment—I'm in the peace of a home.
But here is your name engraved on a stone.
The small willow is standing.
The light of your table is still shining.
It's a secretive shining.

1963

ליבשאַפּט

אַ ווײַסע נאַכט אַזאַ.
די ווײַסקייט איז די ליבשאַפּט —
פֿון גן-עדן.
איך בין דער קרוג
וואָס דאַרף די ליבשאַפּט שעפּן.

און זי איז שווער.
איך גיי אַ גאַנצן טאָג
די ליבשאַפּט צו פֿאַרטיילן
און זי איז צער.
איך פֿאַל —
און קען די אַנגסטן נישט פֿאַרהיילן.

אַ ווײַסע נאַכט אַזאַ.
אַ שטיקל וואָלקן
ווי אַן אָפּגעבראָכענער פֿליגל.
דאָס איז מײַן רײַטוואָגן,
געקומען נעמען מיך,
אין ליבשאַפּט זיך פֿאַרוויגן.

דער טאַטע רופֿט צו מיר
און זאָגט מיר: קינד.
און אַלע לאַסטן פֿאַלן אָפּ.
די ווײַסע נאַכט פֿון ליבשאַפּט
איז אין מיר —
איך בין בײַם טויער
פֿון גן-עדן.

1952

Love

Such a white night.
This whiteness is the love
Of Paradise.
I am the vessel
That must lade the love.

And love is heavy.
I walk all day long
To portion it out,
And love is sorrow.
I fall
And cannot heal the angst.

Such a white night.
A piece of cloud
Like a broken-off wing.
This is my chariot
Come to take me,
Rocking me to sleep in love.

My father calls to me
And says to me, Child.
And all the burdens fall away.
The white night of love
Is in me—
I am at the gate
Of Paradise.

איך בין אַ ווידערקול

איך בין אַ ווידערקול
פֿון אַ פֿאַרשוווּנדענעם אָרקעסטער.
ס'איז אַ וווּנדער מײַן שטים,
צי ס'איז תּפֿילה צי לעסטער.

עס באַווײַזט זיך אַ פֿידלער,
ער זאָגט: כ'בין פֿון נעכטן.
ער הייבט אויף זײַן פֿידל —
זײַנע פֿינגער די בלייכע:

אָט באַלד װעל איך שפּילן
דעם זמר געךעכטן —
וואָס מען האָט געשפּילט
בײַ די ווענט פֿון יריחו.

אָט באַלד וועל איך שפּילן
בײַ די ווענט פֿון יריחו.

כ'וויל אַ ריר טאָן זײַן פֿידל
און זען צי ס'איז וואָר.
נאָר ער איז נישטאָ,
זײַן ווידערקול ציטערט:

איך בין דאָ, איך בין דאָ,
דו דאַרפֿסט נישט קיין וואָר.
ס'וועט מײַן שטים דיך דערגרייכן.
איך בין דאָ, איך בין דאָ,
נעם מײַן ווידערקול מיט
צו די ווענט פֿון יריחו.

אָט באַלד וועל איך שפּילן
בײַ די ווענט פֿון יריחו.

1960

I Am an Echo

I am an echo
Of a vanished symphony.
My voice is a marvel,
Whether it's prayer or blasphemy.

A fiddler appears,
Saying, I've come from yesterday.
He raises his fiddle—
His pallid fingers:

Soon I will play
The prescribed melody
That they played long ago
By the walls of Jericho.

Soon I will play
By the walls of Jericho.

I want to touch his fiddle
To see if it's real.
But he is no more,
His echo trembles:

Here I am, here I am,
You don't need what is real.
My voice will reach you.
Here I am, here I am,
Take along my echo
To the walls of Jericho.

Soon I will play
By the walls of Jericho.

בלעטלעך

בלעטלעך. נישט-פֿאַרענדיקטע לידער.
בראָכוואַרג פֿון ליכט, און בראָכוואַרג פֿון נעכט.
כ'בין מיט קיינעם נישט גאַנץ, מיט אַלץ קידער-ווידער.
מיט צעריסענע בלעטלעך איך פֿיר אַ געפֿעכט.

איך צערײַס און איך וואַרף אויפֿן ווינט זיי מיט צאָרן.
זיי קומען צוריק און אין פּנים מיר שמײַסן:
דערצייל און נישט שעם זיך ווי דו ביסט פֿאַרלאָרן.
נעם אונדז צוריק און פֿאַרריכט דײַנע גרײַזן.

איך צערײַס זיי און וואַרף זיי אַרויס אויף די מיסטן.
זיי קומען צוריק און זיי בלענדן און שטעכן:
דערצייל און נישט שעם מיך — דײַן אומגליק פֿאַרוויסטן
דו קומסט מיט פּאַפּירענע ווערטער פֿאַרשוועכן.

איך צערײַס מײַנע בלעטלעך און וואַרף צום פֿאַרברענען
און קוק אויפֿן גיריקן פֿלאַמען-פֿאַרניכט.
נאָר די אותיות בלײַבן געשוואַרצטע און קלעמען:
נעם אונדז צוריק און דײַן טעות פֿאַרריכט.

בראָכוואַרג פֿון געשען, פֿון געווען, און געוועזן.
בראָכוואַרג — איך האָב נאָך פֿאַר דעם נישט קיין נאָמען.
קומט אַ מלאך פֿאַרגיביק און פֿאַרקערט מיט אַ בעזעם
מײַן געוויין און די גרײַזן און הייסט זאָגן: אָמן.

Pages

Pages. Scraps. Unfinished poems.
Splinters of light and splinters of night.
I agree with no one, am at odds with everyone.
With these scraps of pages, I start a fight.[229]

I tear them up in a rage and throw them to the wind.
They come right back and strike my face:
Just say that you're lost, and don't be ashamed.
Take us back again and correct your mistakes.

I tear them up and throw them out in the trash.
They come right back—how they dazzle and hurt:
Don't be ashamed, just say you've come to profane
Your pathetic misery with paper words.

I tear up my pages and throw them in the fire,
Watching the greedy flames' annihilation.
But the letters remain, blackened and grieving:
Take us back and correct your aberration.

Splinters of events, existence, the past[230]
Splinters—I still have no name for them.
Then comes a forgiving angel with a broom and sweeps out
All my cries, all the misprints, while saying: Amen.

משה און אַהרן

ווי אַ שאַרפֿער אַקער
דורך די וואָלקנדיקע שפּאַרן
אײַלט זיך די לבֿנה,
פֿירט משה-רבינו און אַהרן.

זיי וואַנדערן יאָרן.
זיי קענען צום סיני נישט קומען.
זיי פֿירן די אַלטע געבאָטן
פֿאַרקריצט אויף אַ שטיין אויף אַ שטומען.

זאָגט אַהרן צום ברודער:
פֿיר שטילער דעם רודער.
דורות קומען און דורות פֿאַרגייען.
זיי לערנען און לערנען,
זיי קענען סײַ ווי נאָך
דײַן עבֿרי נישט לייענען.

נאָר משה-רבינו — ער הערט נישט.
פֿאַרטראַכט אויף די הימלשע לאַנען
ער שנײַדט דורך די קרײַזן
פֿון שטערן-געשפּאַנען,

צום סיני, צום סיני דערגרייכן
און נאָך אַ מאָל ברענגען
אויף קריינדלעך פֿון אותיות
דעם געטלעכן צייכן.

זאָגט אַהרן צום ברודער:
פֿיר שטילער דעם רודער.
פֿעלקער לעבן און פֿעלקער פֿאַרשווינדן.
זיי קענען סײַ ווי
פֿון די אותיות געקרוינטע
דעם טראַף נישט דערפֿינדן.

Moses and Aaron

Like a sharp plow,
The moon hurries
Through a crack in the clouds,
Guiding Moses our Teacher and Aaron.

They wander for years.
They cannot reach Sinai.
They carry the old Commandments
Engraved on mute stone.

And Aaron says to his brother:
Steer the helm more quietly.
Generations come and generations go.
They study and study,
And even so, they still
Cannot read your Hebrew.

But Moses our Teacher does not hear.
Absorbed in his thoughts in the heavenly meadows,
He cuts through the circles
Of stars in harness,

Toward Sinai, to reach Sinai
And bring back again
On crownlets of letters
The godly sign.

And Aaron says to his brother:
Steer the helm more quietly.
Nations come, nations go.
And even so, they still
Cannot pronounce the syllables
Among those crowned letters.

נאָר משה-רבינו — ער הערט נישט.
ער קריצט די געבאָטן.
ער שלײַפֿט זיי מיט שטראַלן,
זיי זאָלן זײַן לויטער,
קיין שטויב זאָל נישט פֿאַלן.

זאָגט אַהרן צום ברודער:
פֿיר שטילער דעם רודער.
רו זיך אָפּ אויף אַ שטערן.
מען באַקט דאָרט אַ לעקעך
מיט האָניק מיט ברוינעם.
איך בין מיד שוין ביז טרערן
פֿון די עולמות-עליונים.

נאָר משה-רבינו — ער הערט נישט.
ער שרײַבט מיט זײַן פֿעדער.
עס פֿליִען די פֿונקען,
ווי שטראַליקע צעדער.
עס שטראָמען די פֿונקען
עס קומען מלאכים
די פֿליגל דאָרט טונקען.

זאָגט אַהרן צום ברודער:
פֿיר שטילער דעם רודער.
כ׳בין נישט משה--רבינו,
כ׳בין פּשוט דײַן ברודער,
כ׳בין אַהרן. ס׳איז שווער דײַן געבאָט.
און זע אונדזער שיף — די לבֿנה —
פֿינצטערט אָפּ יעדן חודש — באַנקראָט.

מען איז איין מאָל געשטאַנען בײַם סיני.
זע דעם עינוי, זע דעם וויי.
וואָס דאַרפֿסטו כּסדר און אייביק
זיך צווינגען אויף זיי?
איך צווייפֿל אין גאַנצן...
איך צווייפֿל... ס׳האָט משה דערהערט.

But Moses our Teacher does not hear.
He carves the Commandments.
He polishes them with sun-rays
To make them purer
So no dust shall fall.

And Aaron says to his brother:
Steer the helm more quietly.
Come on, take a rest on a star.
They're baking gingerbread
Made with brown honey.
I'm bored to tears
By the Higher Worlds.

But Moses our Teacher does not hear.
He writes with his pen.
The sparks are flying
Like streaming cedars.
The sparks are surging.
Angels are coming
To dip their wings there.

And Aaron says to his brother:
Steer the helm more quietly.
I'm not Moses our Teacher,
I'm simply your brother,
I'm Aaron. Your Commandments are heavy.
And, look, our ship, the moon,
Darkens every month—goes bankrupt.

Once they stood at Sinai.
Look at the torture, look at the pain.
Why do you need forever and ever
To force them again?
I really do doubt . . .
I doubt . . . Then Moses heard.

ער האָט אַ פֿאָרהאַנג געעפֿנט
פֿון הימל ביז דר'ערד.

ס'האָט אַהרן דעם סיני דערזען,
און אונטן דאָס פֿאָלק —
ווי עס וואַרט...
מען ליגט אויף די זאַמדן און שטיינער
פֿאַרריסן די קעפּ
צו דעם באַרג.

ס'האָט אַהרן די אויגן פֿאַרמאַכט,
די באָרד מיט דער דלאָניע געגלעט
אַ שעה נאָך אַנאַנד.
און ער האָט געזאָגט:
אוי, רבונא-דעלמא,
ווו האָסטו גענומען אַן אומה אַזאַ,
אַ בריליאַנט?
אַ געדולדיקע, פֿרומע —
אָ, רבונא-דעלמא,
ווו האָסטו גענומען די אומה?

He opened a curtain
From heaven to earth.

And Aaron espied Sinai,
And beneath it, the people—
Waiting and waiting . . .
They're lying on sand and on stones,
Craning their necks
Toward the mountain.

Then Aaron closed his eyes,
Stroking his beard with his palm
Nonstop for an hour.
And he said:
Oh, Lord of the Universe,
Where have you taken a people like this,
Such a gem?
So pious, so patient—
O, Lord of the Universe,
Where have you taken this people?

יונה

אַפֿילו זיבן מאָל וועסט ענדערן דײַן פֿורעם,
פֿאַרבאָרגן דײַן געביין און דײַן געבינד,
וועט גאָט דיך צייכענען און רופֿן דורכן שטורעם:
אין נינוה גיי,
און לײַטער זי פֿון זינד.

מיט פֿאַרשטעלטע אויגן און פֿאַרמעקטן נאָמען
אַנטרינען וועסט נאָך שטילקייט און נאָך רו.
וועט גאָט דיך צייכענען און רופֿן פֿון די תּהומען:
אין נינוה גיי,
און וואָס איך הייס דיר — טו.

דו וועסט דײַן לשון אויסבײַטן אויף אַנדערע לשונות,
און אויסבריִען אין צונג אַן אַנדער שפּראַך.
וועט גאָט דיך צייכענען און זאַלבן מיט גאונות:
אין נינוה גיי,
און וואָס איך הייס דיר — מאַך.

דו וועסט אין גריבער ליגן אַ פֿאַרוואָרפֿענער מיט שטיינער,
מיט וווּנד אויף לײַב, מיט בראַנד און פּלאָג.
וועט גאָט דיך צייכענען מיט פֿײַער אין די ביינער:
אין נינוה גיי,
און וואָס איך הייס דיר — זאָג.

ווּעסטו בײַ גאָט זיך בעטן אין געיאָמער:
פֿאַר וואָס בין איך פֿון דײַן געבאָט דער קרוג?
איך וויל אַן עפּלבוים פֿאַרפֿלאַנצן, צי אַ תּמר,
צי איז דאָס ניט גענוג פֿאַר יונהן
פֿאַר גאָר פֿון דײַן באַשאַף איז דאָס גענוג.

און ס'ענטפֿערט דיר אַ שטים פֿון שטורעם:
פֿאַרגעס דײַן עפּלבוים, דײַן הויז און רינד,
ביסט אויסדערוויילט פֿאַר רחמים און יסורים,

Jonah

Even if you change form seven times,
Conceal your ligaments and your skeleton,
Still, God will mark you and call through the storm:
Go to Nineveh,
And purify its sin.

With eyes disguised and name effaced,
You will abscond, seeking peace, quiet, too.
Still, God will mark you, calling from the abyss:
Go to Nineveh,
And what I command you,—do.

You will exchange your language for other tongues,
And on your tongue, hatch a new kind of word.[231]
Still, God will mark you and anoint you with genius:
Go to Nineveh,
And as I command you,—serve.

You will lie in the ditch, pelted with stones,
There, with flesh wounds, burns, plagues, you will stay.
Still, God will mark you with fire in your bones:
Go to Nineveh,
And what I command you,—say.

Lamenting, you will plead with God:
Why am I your vessel, why me?
I want to plant a date palm, an apple tree,
Shouldn't that be enough for your Jonah?
It suffices your creation's entirety.

And a voice answers you from the storm:
Forget your apple tree, your house and your kine,
You are chosen for mercy and for pain,

אין נינוה גיי,
און לײַטער זי פֿון זינד.

Go to Nineveh,
And purify its sin.

באַהאַלט מיך אין אַ בלאַט

באַהאַלט מיך אין אַ בלאַט,
באַהאַלט מיך אין א שטיין,
זייערע זיכערע רו איך בין זיי מקנא.
באַהאַלט מיך, גאָט,
אין דײַן שוץ און באַהעלטעניש
און צאַם מיך אַרום מיט דײַנע צאַמען.

הייב מיך אַרויס פֿון דער שטויביקייט.
דער שטויב מאַכט מיך גרויען.
נעם מיך אַרום מיט דײַן אייביקייט
ווי אַ בלאַט און אַ שטיין —
דערנערטע מיט טויען.

מאַך אַ וועג מיר פֿון שטענדיקייט,
מײַן האַרץ איז פֿאַרשאָטנט.
זאַלב מיך אָפּ מיט דײַן בלענדיקייט
וואָס איך פֿיל אין מײַן אָטעם.

וואַש אָפּ דעם ציטער פֿון מיר.
וואַש אָפּ דעם צווייפֿל.
די נעכט זײַנען פֿאַרגייִקייט
און די טעג זײַנען ווייפֿול.

מײַן וואָרט פֿאַרלירט די שטים
און דעם חלל דעם האַרבן.
שיק דײַן הילף, אלהים,
אַז מײַן קול זאָל נישט שטאַרבן.
ווײַל איך פֿאַל,
ווײַל איך פֿאַל
אין דעם חלל דעם האַרבן.

און פֿאַרגיב מיר די תּפֿילה
אַזאַ צעבראָכענע

Shelter Me in a Leaf

Shelter me in a leaf,
Shelter me in a stone,
I envy them their sure peace.
Shelter me, God,
Protect and conceal me.
Enclose me in your fences.

Pick me up from the dust
That turns me gray.
Embrace me with your eternity
Like a leaf and a stone
Nourished with dew.

Make me a path of permanence,
My heart is shadowed.
Anoint me with your dazzle[232]
Which I feel in my breath.

Wash away my trembling.
Wash away doubt.
The nights are ephemeral,
The days, filled with pain.

My word loses its utterance
In the baffling void.
Send your help, God,
So my voice shall not die.
Because I fall,
Because I fall
In the baffling void.

And forgive me this prayer,
Broken

ווי מיט בײַטשן געשלאָגן.
מען שלאָגט מיך און מײַן תּפֿילה,
אונדז ביידן צוזאַמען.
צאַם מיך אַרום מיט דײַן שטראַליקייט
און זײַ דו — מײַנע צאַמען.

As if beaten, whipped.
My prayer and I are
Both beaten.
Enclose me in your radiance
And you, be my fences.

אונטערגאַנג סתּם

כ'האָב געזען אַן אַלטן קאַפּיטאַן
ער האָט שוין קיין שיף נישט געפֿירט,
נאָר געטראָגן זײַן היטל מיט גאָלדענע ברעגן.
אין די אויגן די כמורנע —
אַ פֿאַרגליווערטער ים איז געלעגן.

די שיפֿן וואָס ער האָט געפֿירט זײַנען אונטערגעגאַנגען
נישט אין שטורעם, נישט אין תּהומען פֿון ים.
עס האָט זיי פֿאַרשלונגען דער תּהום פֿון זכּרון
אַ ברעג אָן אַ נאָמען,
אַן אונטערגאַנג סתּם.

ווען דער ווינט גיט אַ ריס זײַן באַגילדעטן היטל,
וואַכט אויף זײַן זכּרון,
ער דערמאָנט זיך די אינדזלען, די שטיינערנע ריפֿן,
ער שמייכלט מיט ביטול:
נאָך שטאַרקער פֿון שטורעם איז דער ברעג אָן אַ נאָמען —
דער אונטערגאַנג סתּם.

דאָרט זײַנען צעקלאַפּט זײַנע שיפֿן.

1963

Random Sinking[233]

I saw an old captain
Who no longer steered a ship
But still wore his cap with its golden brim.
In his clouded eyes
Lay a frozen sea.

The ships that he steered have sunk
Not in storms, not in oceans' abysses.
The abyss of memory has swallowed them,
A nameless coast,
A random sinking.

When the wind tears at his gilded cap,
His memory awakens,
He remembers the islands, the stony reefs,
He smiles with scorn:
Even stronger than storms is that nameless coast—
That random sinking.

There, his ships are pounded to pieces.

1963

אין ירושלים קומען מלאכים

אין ירושלים קומען מלאכים
און עפֿענען טירן פֿון ייִדישע הײַזער.
זיי לערנען די קינדער צו ליב האָבן תּורה,
צו שווײַגן אין חכמה,
צו ווערן די שפּײַזער.

ס'קומט יעדן טאָג איינער,
ס'קומט יעדן טאָג איינער,
ביז ס'וועלן דערוואַכן די טרוקענע ביינער.

אין ירושלים קומען מלאכים
און גייען אויף גאַסן נאָך נישט קיין ברוקירטע.
זיי פֿירן די זאַמדן,
זיי שלעפּן די שטיינער,
מיט אָרעמע ייִדן, מיט געטלעך באַרירטע.

ס'קומט יעדן טאָג איינער,
ס'קומט יעדן טאָג איינער,
ביז ס'וועלן דערוואַכן די טרוקענע ביינער.

אין ירושלים קומען מלאכים
נאָך איידער די זון קומט,
נאָך איידער, נאָך איידער.

זיי טראָגן כאַלאַטלעך,
געקירצט און גענעטלט —
די שכינה זאָל לויכטן
אויף געלאַטעטע קליידער.

ס'קומט יעדן טאָג איינער,
ס'קומט יעדן טאָג איינער,
ביז ס'וועלן דערוואַכן די טרוקענע ביינער.

In Jerusalem, Angels Come

In Jerusalem, angels come
And open the doors of Jewish homes.
They teach the children to love Torah,
To stay silent in wisdom,
To become bread-winners.

Every day, an angel comes,
Every day, another comes,
Until the awakening of dry bones.

In Jerusalem, angels come
And walk upon the unpaved streets.
They carry sand,
They drag the stones
Alongside poor Jews touched by the divine.

Every day, an angel comes,
Every day, another comes,
Until the awakening of dry bones.

In Jerusalem, angels come
Before the sun comes up,
Before the sun has risen.

They're wearing such garments—
Robes shortened and mended—[234]
The *Shekhinah* illumines[235]
Their patched-up clothing.

Every day, an angel comes,
Every day, another comes,
Until the awakening of dry bones.

אין לאַנד ישׂראל

כ'בין געקומען אין דעם לאַנד ישׂראל,
האָט אַ פֿאַסטעכל אַ מתּנה מיר געגעבן —
אַ שאַלעכל אַ הימל-בלויעם
כ'זאָל אים טראָגן דאָס גאַנצע לעבן.

און ער זאָגט: מײַן אייגן שאָף געשאָרן,
און ער זאָגט: מײַן אייגן וואָל געוועבן —
אַ מתּנה, פֿאַר אַ בת-ישׂראל,
זי זאָל עס טראָגן אויפֿן גאַנצן לעבן.

כ'וויל אים דאַנקען. כ'בלײַב אין שרעק,
מײַן אָטעם אַ דערשעפּטער —
עס שטייט אַנטקעגן מיר אַ מלך
און אין האַנט האַלט ער אַ סצעפּטער.

וויל איך פֿאַלן אין געבוקונג,
ווי מען מוז דאָך פֿאַלן פֿאַר אַ מלך,
שמייכלט ער צו מיר אַ וווּנדערלעכן שמייכל,
און ער זאָגט דערהויבן און פֿאַמעלעך:

כ'האָב לאַנג אויף דיר געוואַרט,
געוואָלט דיך זען, דײַן שטים דערהערן.
ניט וווּנדער זיך — דער פֿאַסטעך-שטעקן אין מײַן האַנט,
קאָן יעדן טאָג אַ סצעפּטער ווערן.

דאָס איז געווען לעם שטעטעלע רחובֿות
אַ סימן — דער פֿאַסטעך איז לעם מיר פֿאַרבײַגעגאַנגען,
אויף אַ גראָען שנירל דער פֿאַסטעך-שטעקן
אויף זײַן הויכן אַקסל איז געהאַנגען.

און נאָך אַ סימן: דאָס שטעטעלע רחובֿות,
און אַרום אַ ייִדיש לאַנד,
און דאָס שאַלעכל דאָס הימל-בלויע
וואָס ליגט נאָך איצטער אויף מײַן האַנט.

In the Land of Israel

When I came to the Land of Israel,
A shepherd gave me a gift—
A scarf as blue as the sky;
I shall wear it my whole life.

And he said: Shorn from my own sheep,
And he said: Woven from my own wool—
For a daughter of Israel, a gift;
May she wear it her whole life.

I want to thank him. I freeze in fear,
My breath, a shudder:
There stands a king,
His hand holding a scepter.

I want to fall prostrate to the ground,
As one must fall before a king,
When he smiles a wonderful smile,
And his words are exalted and slow:

I've long awaited you, wanting
To see you, hear you. You've come!
Don't be surprised, this shepherd's staff
Can transform into a scepter.

This happened near the town of Rehovot.
A sign—that near me, the shepherd passed,
And from a gray cord on his tall shoulder,
Hung the shepherd's staff.

And another sign: the town of Rehovot
And all around it, a Jewish land,
And the scarf as blue as the sky,
That, even now, lies in my hand.

גאָטס קינדער

כ׳בין געקומען צו דעם מלך שלמה
שוין אַן אַלטע און ניט מער קיין שיינע,
האָט ער נישט געוואָלט מיך אַפילו פֿאַר דער טויזנט-איינסטע,
האָב איך בײַ זײַן טויער זיך געזעצט מיט די געמיינסטע.

דאָרט דערציילט מען די שיינע, שיינע מעשׂיות,
ווי פֿון פֿונקען זײַנען אויסגעשאָסן שטערן,
און גאָטס קינדער די באָרוועסע און די געטרײַסטע
זיצן ליכטיקע און הערן, הערן, הערן.

ווי אַ נאַר דער שופֿט איז געוואָרן
און האָט זיך אָנגעטאָן אין סאַמעטענע זאַכן,
און גאָטס קינדער די באָרוועסע און די געטרײַסטע
זיצן ליכטיקע און לאַכן, לאַכן, לאַכן.

דאָרט דערציילט מען די האַרציק ליבע וווּנדער,
ווי די טויטע שטייען אויף תּחית-המתים,
און גאָטס קינדער די באָרוועסע און די געטרײַסטע
ווי צו אויפֿשטיין ווייסן, ווייסן, ווייסן.

ווי מלאכים האָבן אײַנגעהילט די פֿליגל
און באַוויזן זיך צו גוטע, פֿרומע מענטשן,
און גאָטס קינדער די באָרוועסע און די געטרײַסטע
זיצן הערלעכע און בענטשן ,בענטשן, בענטשן.

דאָרט דערציילט מען די פֿײַערדיקע נסים,
ווי אין מידבר האָבן אויפֿגעשלאָגן קוואַלן,
און גאָטס קינדער די באָרוועסע און די געטרײַסטע
זיצן שיכּורע און שאַלן, שאַלן, שאַלן.

נאָכן זונפֿאַרגאַנג קומט אַרויס דער מלך,
וואָס זײַן חכמה איז ניט אָפּצושאַצן.
צווישן גאָטס קינדער זעצט ער זיך דער מלך,
און הערט דעם וווּנדער פֿון זײַנע פּאַלאַצן.

God's Children

I came to the great King Solomon,
An old woman, no longer lovely,
He wouldn't want me as number one-thousand-and-one,
So I sat down at his gate with the lowly.

At the king's gate, they tell stories:
How a star shoots out from a spark,
And God's children, the barefoot, the faithful,
The luminous, hark and hark.

How the judge has become such a fool,
Dressing up in velvet clothing,
And God's children, the barefoot and faithful,
Sit in brightness, laughing, laughing.

There they tell of their favorite wonders,
How the dead are brought back to life,
And God's children, the barefoot and faithful,
Know full well how to come back to life.

How sometimes the angels, folding their wings,
Show themselves to the good and the pious.
And God's children, the barefoot and faithful,
Sit in splendor, and bless and bless.

There they tell of the fiery miracles:
How wellsprings broke through desert land.
And God's children, the barefoot, the faithful,
The drunken sit, and their voices resound.

The king comes out after sunset,
His wisdom has no measure.
The king sits among God's children
And hears of his palaces' treasure:

ווי דער שפּילפֿויגל זינגט און טאַנצט בײַ זײַן שויב,
און בײַם טראָן ברומען גאָלדענע בערן.
קיין מאָל, קיין מאָל האָט ער אַזאַ פּאַלאַץ ניט געזען,
און ער וויינט מיט שווערע און עלנטע טרערן.

The mechanical bird at his window,
Golden bears that growl by his throne.
Never has he seen such a palace,
And he weeps heavy tears, alone.

אונדזער שיף

אַ שיף — אַ מולטער — אין פײַנען געגליטע
פּירט אַ זכר פֿון פוילן, אַ רעשטל פֿון ליטע.
אַ געפּרוּווטער דער רודער, קען ברעכן אַ קריעה,
עס לײַכט אים פֿון ווײַטן דער באַרג פֿון מוריה.

אם אין אני לי —
מי לי?
זינגט דער רודער,
אַ ייִד פֿון קאָוונע
זאָגט אים נאָך.
„איך האָב אַ טרער
אַן איינציקע באַהאַלטן —
חצי לי, וחצי לך".

עס שווימט ווײַ און ווינד פֿון וואַרשע און באַרדיטשעוו,
עס וואַרפֿט דער שוים אַ תּליה אויף אַ תּליה,
מען גנבֿעט דעם ים. דאָס ליכט איז אויסגעלאָשן,
עס לויכט פֿון ווײַטן דער באַרג פֿון מוריה.

אם אין אני לי —
מי לי?
זינגט דער רודער,
אַ קינד אַ יתום
זאָגט אים נאָך.
„איך האָב אַ תּפֿילה
אַן איינציקע באַהאַלטן —
חצי לי, וחצי לך".

ווי פֿרעמדע זעלנער, געלערנט אויף רציחה
באַפֿאַלן כוואַליעס די מולטער, ווי אַ שטאָט.
ס'איז קריג. די שיף איז אויסגעלאָשן,
עס לויכט פֿון ווײַטן איר אַ לעמפּעלע פֿון עין חרוד.

Our Ship

A ship—a trough—glowing in anguish
Carries a trace from Poland, a remnant from Lithuania.
The helm is experienced at rending clothes in mourning,
Far away, shines Mount Moriah.

If I am not for myself,
Who will be for me?[236]
Sings the helm.
A Jew from Kovno
Repeats after him,
"I have hidden a tear
A single tear—
Half for me, half for you."

Woe and wound swim from Berdichev and Warsaw,
The foam throws up gallows and gallows,
They steal through the sea. The light is extinguished,
Far away, shines Mount Moriah.

If I am not for myself,
Who will be for me?
Sings the helm.
A orphan child
Repeats after him,
"I have hidden a prayer,
A single prayer—
Half for me, half for you."

Like foreign soldiers, schooled in violence,
Waves attack the trough like a city.
A battle rages. The ship is extinguished,
Far away, shines a lamp from Ein Harod.

אם אין אני לי —
מי לי?
זינגט דער רודער,
אַ האַרץ אַ מידע
זאָגט אים נאָך.
„איך האָב אַ האָפֿענונג
אַן איינציקע באַהאַלטן —
חצי לי, וחצי לך".

1952

If I am not for myself
Who is for me?
Sings the helm.
A heart, a tired heart
Repeats after him,
"I have hidden a hope
One single hope,
Half for me, and half for you."

1952

אַ פּליט

אויף אַ וועג אַ שמאָלן —
שטיינער, גריבער, דערנער,
אַ בחור גייט אַ פּליט,
אַ כּשר קינד, אַ לערנער.

אחת, שתים,
אחת, שתים,
ווײַט דער וועג ביז ירושלים.
אחת, שתים,
אחת, שתים,
גרינג דער וועג קיין ירושלים.

אויסגעהונגערט, אָן אַ העמד,
באָרוועס און דערפֿראָרן,
וויל זיך אָפּרוען דער פּליט,
איז שטיין, און גרוב, און דאָרן.

קומט אַנטקעגן אים משיח
אויף אַן אייזעלע געריטן,
— איך וועל דיר אויסבאָרגן מײַן רײַטער
בלײַב נישט שטיין אין מיטן.

אחת, שתים,
אחת, שתים,
ווײַט דער וועג ביז ירושלים.
אחת, שתים,
אחת, שתים,
גרינג דער וועג קיין ירושלים.

אָן דעם אייזעלע משיח,
צי וועט ער נישט פֿאַרזאַמען?
עס וואַרט אויף אים אַ פֿאָלק פֿאַרמאַטערט,
אויף אומגליקוועגן, ימען.

A Refugee

On a narrow path—
Stones, ditches, thorns,
A lad walks, a refugee,
A proper child, a student of Talmud.

One, two,[237]
One, two,
It's a long way to Jerusalem.
One, two,
One, two,
The road is easy to Jerusalem.

Hollowed by hunger, without a shirt,
Barefoot and frost-bitten,
The refugee longs to rest
Among the stones, ditches, and thorns.

The Messiah approaches him,
Riding on a donkey,
—I will lend you my steed,
Don't stand in the middle of the road.

One, two,
One, two,
It's a long way to Jerusalem.
One, two,
One, two,
The road is easy to Jerusalem.

But without his donkey, won't the Messiah
Be somewhat delayed?
An exhausted people waits for him
On the roads and seas of misery.

ער וועט נישט גיין צו פֿוס, חלילה,
מען דאַרף פֿאַר אים נישט זאָרגן,
ער וועט דעם פֿײַערדיקן וואָגן
בײַ אליהו באָרגן.

אחת, שתים,
אחת, שתים,
ווײַט דער וועג ביז ירושלים.
אחת, שתים,
אחת, שתים,
גרינג דער וועג קיין ירושלים.

וואָס זשע וועט אליהו טאָן
אָן פֿײַערדיקן וואָגן?
ער האָט שליחותן אַ סך
ווי וועט ער זיך דערשלאָגן?

ער וועט נישט גיין צו פֿוס, חלילה,
ער האָט אייניקלעך, די אמתע בחורים,
ער וועט אויסבאָרגן אַ רעדל
בײַ אַ חלוץ פֿון בית-אורים.

אחת, שתים,
אחת, שתים,
ווײַט דער וועג ביז ירושלים.
אחת, שתים,
אחת, שתים,
גרינג דער וועג קיין ירושלים.

וואָס זשע וועט דער חלוץ טאָן
מיט נאַקעטע ידים?
ווי וועט ער קענען ברויט און תּורה
קיין תּל-אָבֿיבֿ דערסטײַען?

ער וועט נישט גיין צו פֿוס, חלילה,
ער וועט זיך אַן עצה טאָן בערך.

He won't go on foot, God forbid,
Don't worry about him,
He will borrow the fiery wagon
Of Elijah the Prophet.

One, two,
One, two,
It's a long way to Jerusalem.
One, two,
One, two,
The road is easy to Jerusalem.

What, then, will Elijah do
Without his fiery wagon?
He has so many missions.
How will he attain them?

He will not go on foot, God forbid,
He has grandsons, those strong lads,
He will borrow a wheel
From a settler in Beit-Orim.

One, two,
One, two,
It's a long way to Jerusalem.
One, two,
One, two,
The road is easy to Jerusalem.

What then will the settler do
With empty hands?
How will he be able to supply
Tel Aviv with bread and Torah?

He will not go on foot, God forbid,
He will manage, somehow.

ער ווייס די גענג פֿון ארץ־ישׂראל,
ער שפּאַנט קפֿיצת־הדרך.

אחת, שתים,
אחת, שתים,
וויַט דער וועג ביז ירושלים.
אחת, שתים,
אחת, שתים,
גרינג דער וועג קיין ירושלים.

1950

He knows the paths of the Land of Israel,
He will find a shortcut.

One, two,
One, two,
It's a long way to Jerusalem.
One, two,
One, two,
The road is easy to Jerusalem.

1950

Endnotes

The endnotes intend to remind the reader of the connotations of language that are necessarily changed in or absent from the English translation. The notes define culture-specific words or concepts, such as Hebraic words or phrases that denote Jewish custom or law, Slavic words that connote the interaction between Jewish and Christian cultures, and archaic Yiddish terms that allude to Jewish folkways. The notes also point out where the poet draws on literary sources.

The following dictionaries were consulted: Reuben Alcalay, *The Complete Hebrew-English Dictionary* (Jerusalem: Massada, 1975); Alexander Harkavy, *Yiddish-English-Hebrew Dictionary* (New York: YIVO and Schocken, 1988), reprint of 1928 expanded second edition; Uriel Weinreich, *Modern English-Yiddish/Yiddish-English Dictionary* (New York: YIVO and McGraw-Hill, 1968); Yitskhok Niborski and Simon Neuberg, *Verterbukh fun loshn-kodesh-shtamike verter in Yidish* (Paris: Bibliothèque Medem, 1997); Yudah A. Yofe and Yudl Mark, *Groyser verterbukh fun der yidisher shprakh*, 4 vols. (New York: Yiddish Dictionary Committee, 1961–80); and Yehoash (Sh. Bloomgarden) and C. D. Spivak, *Yidish verterbukh* (New York: Farlag Veker, 1926).

1. Two alternate translations of the entire sequence: Kathryn Hellerstein, "Songs of Women," *Yiddish* 7, nos. 2–3 (1988): 182–87, and F. Pecznik, "Women's Songs," *Yiddish* 7, nos. 2–3 (1988): 174–80. Alternate translations of individual poems from the sequence: Adrienne Rich, "Women Songs" (I

and VII), *A Treasury of Yiddish Poetry*, ed. Irving Howe and Eliezer Greenberg (New York: Holt, Rinehart and Winston, 1969), 284–85. Irving Feldman, "Women's Songs" (II and VI), *Penguin Book of Modern Yiddish Verse*, ed. Irving Howe, Ruth R. Wisse, and Khone Shmeruk (New York: Viking, 1987), 320–22.

2. The Hebraic word *agune* denotes the Jewish legal category of an abandoned or deserted wife who cannot remarry until her husband is either proven dead or grants her a divorce. The word *agune* derives from the Hebrew verb *agon*, meaning, "to shut oneself in or off, especially from marriage, to imprison, to anchor." Thus the *agune*, literally "anchored" by law to a husband whose very existence is ambiguous, is the epitome of a woman caught in a bind.

3. The Hebraic word *tumah* denotes Levitical uncleanliness or ritual impurity. Marcus Jastrow, *Sefer Milim: A Dictionary of the Targum, Talmud Babli and Yerushalim, and the Midrashic Literature*, vol. 1 (Israel: Reissue, 1970), 524. Reissued by Rabbi Salomon Alter Halpern.

4. The Yiddish participle *farrisn* can denote "smudged" (Weinreich), "torn up," or "haughty" (Harkavy). Another translator, F. Peczenik, defines the word as "blotted out." *Yiddish* 7, nos. 2–3 (1988): 174.

5. Tammuz is the tenth month and Av is the eleventh month in the Jewish calendar, corresponding respectively to June and July, July and August.

6. *Hamapil* is the benediction, "who maketh bands of sleep to fall" in *Kri'at shema 'al hamittah* (*Krishme*, in Yiddish), and is recited before the *Shema*, the prayer of the central tenets of the Jewish faith, before going to bed.

7. The Yiddish syntax is ambiguous here, for the second sentence is a threat, leading the translator to ask whether the lips of the mother are dried out because they did not fear God or because they did fear God.

8. Ambiguous Yiddish syntax and punctuation. The following lines could read:

And now that I am a woman,
And wear brown silk decollete
With my head bare[,]
And my own life's misfortune has hunted me down[.]
[And] like a crow falling upon a chick,
My room is lit up all night

9. The Yiddish line reads: "un kh'halt di hent iber mayn kop farvorfn." *farvorfn* are *oyfvorf(n)*, reproach(es), reproof(s).

10. Molodowsky plays on two meanings of the word *bleter*—the leaves of a tree and the leaves or pages of a book.

11. Alternate translation: Aaron Kramer, *A Century of Yiddish Poetry* (New York: Cornwall Books, 1989), 171.

12. I have translated as "prayerbook" (lines 1, 13, 18) Molodowsky's

term *sider* (Hebrew *siddur*) and as "women's prayers" and "a prayer") (lines 3 and 8), her term *tkhine(s)* (Hebrew *tehinah; tehinot*). *Sider* here serves as a generic term for any prayerbook, although it usually refers specifically to a volume containing the traditional Hebrew liturgy. *Tkhine* denotes a genre of supplicatory prayers in Yiddish, composed for women's private devotions. The *sider* Molodowsky describes here also contains two stories from the *Tsenerene* (Hebrew *Tse'enah U're'enah*), the so-called Women's Bible, a sixteenth-century Yiddish selection, translation, summary, and annotation of the Hebrew Bible and some rabbinical commentaries, by Rabbi Josef Ashkenazi. The story of the Binding of Isaac is told in Genesis 22, as well as in rabbinic literature, such as *Sefer ha-Yashar, Wa-Yera; Pirqes de Rabbi Eliezer*, 32. The story of Abraham and Nimrod's lime-kiln is retold in Louis Ginzberg, *The Legends of the Jews*, vol. 1, trans. Henrietta Szold (1909; reprint, Philadelphia: Jewish Publication Society, 1968), 175–76, as well as in *Sefer ha-Yashar, Noah. Bere'shit Rabba* 38:13. For more about the Yiddish adaptations of these legends, see Chava Weissler, "The Traditional Piety of Ashkenazic Women," in *Jewish Spirituality: From the Sixteenth Century Revival to the Present*, ed. Arthur Green (New York: Crossroads, 1987), 245–75.

13. Pesach (Passover) is the spring festival that commemorates the exodus of the Israelites from Egypt. During the Seder, the holiday meal, a wine goblet is filled for the prophet Elijah, who, according to legend, enters every home. Elijah's appearance is associated with messianic redemption.

14. It is very hard to convey the subtle play in this poem on *umgeyn* which means "to keep company, to go around with, to haunt" and *geyn* (to walk). The feeling of urgent expectation and hope that pervades the Yiddish poem is conveyed in the repeated words but varied word order of lines 4 and 12. English allows for less flexibility in the order of a sentence.

15. Otwock (pronounced *otvotsk*): A popular Polish resort twenty-six kilometers east southeast of Warsaw. Around 1923, Molodowsky, diagnosed with a spot on her lung, spent several months recuperating in Otwock. See her autobiography, "Mayn elterzeydns yerushe," in *Sviva* 35 (December 1971): 60–61.

16. The Yiddish word is *agunes.*

17. *Blat:* denotes both the leaf of a tree and the leaf or page of a book.

18. "Proszę mnie" is printed here as the original Polish, meaning "please, do it for my sake."

19. The syntax are faulty in the Yiddish; there is a dangling modifier:

> in tikher ayngehilt, mit fiberdike oygn,
> ver darf unz nokh?
> . . .
> Wrapped around in shawls, with feverish eyes,
> Who needs us still?

20. "In bloyen baginens III" seems to be both a) a radical version of a *tkhine* that women recited upon visiting the cemetery to consult with the

graves of their dead ancestors, and b) an imitation of Moyshe Leyb Halpern's 1919 poem "Portret: mayn zeyde," part IV (in *In nyu york*, 1919); Molodowsky's speaker, like Halpern's, resurrects the dead.

21. The rhyme scheme and repetitions make the nonsense make sense in Yiddish. The poet plays on *bet* (to beg) and *bet* (bed), and she repeats *oygn* (eyes). She also creates a mirror-like consonant pattern in line 2.

22. This poem imitates Halpern's poems of cataclysm in *In nyu york*. Its meter and rhyme are irregular.

23. This poem imitates Halpern's and Mani Leyb's art folk ballads. The Yiddish version depends on its metrical and rhyming pattern: three trochaic dimeter lines and one trochaic tetrameter line, rhymed mnaa.

24. The folk image of the white kid or goat (usually *vayse tsigele*, but here in the plural *vayse tsign*) is best known from the folk lullaby, "Roshinkes mit mandlen," adapted for the theater play *Shulames* by Avraham Goldfaden.

25. The Yiddish word *keytn* (chains) suggests "di goldene keyt," "the golden chain," of Jewish tradition, another folk symbol.

26. This is a poem of female strength, a radically secular version of a *tkhine* for lighting the Sabbath candles. The speaker celebrates her emergence from the folk-bound female storyteller, the women by the well who weave white threads and traditional stories. But she celebrates it in the terms of the traditions. Her small, female hands and feet have the physical power of the male. She does not cover her eyes when she says the blessing over the candles, but she stares at the sun, as if the sun were the prototype for her candles. She is not pious, and thus is different from the long generations of the past. Yet she is still a blesser, a lighter, and a weaver.

27. *Shtetl*, Yiddish for "town," specifically a predominately Jewish town in eastern Europe.

28. "Gevendt tsu mir" means, literally, "turned to me." I translated *opkern* as "turned" in lines 4 and 29.

29. I want to maintain in the English a trace of the variants—*gebet* (prayer); *betn* (to pray, to entreat, to ask); and *tfile* (prayer) in the Yiddish.

30. The Yiddish says *goyish* (gentile).

31. The Yiddish says *shikses* (gentile girls, uncomplimentary).

32. The Yiddish uses the adjective *akoredike* from *akore*, a Hebraic term for a barren woman.

33. The line is unclear. *Opvuen* may be a typographical mistake in the Yiddish. The word *fartsukte* (or *fartugte*) means "to devour."

34. The Yiddish plays on the variants *opdaygn* (to worry away) and *oysgedaygetn* (either "freed from worries" or "saturated with worries").

35. The Hebraism *shure* denotes in Yiddish both a "line" and a "line of verse."

36. I kept the ellipticism of the curse. It could be rendered more explicitly: "Child, banish your fear and misery to wasted villages," or "My child, may your fear and misery fall on desolate villages."

37. The meaning of the Yiddish is not clear. The adjective *oysgeblakevetn* is a variant of *oysgeblakevet* and *oysgeblakirt* from the verbs *oysblakeven*

and *oysblakirn*, which refer to cleansing from a defect, a mark, or speck; making something whiter; or drying pelts into leather.

38. The word *vesh* denotes wash, underclothes, underwear, undergarments, linens, which it implies, belong to her trousseau (see "Froyen-lider VI").

39. Note the rhythm and placement of adjectives: "mit negl oysgeshtshurbete far oysgehorevete yorn."

40. Ambiguous syntax without punctuation: "un alte blaybn in vinklen nisht baloykhtene in ergets lign." It can be translated as: a) "and old (people) stay, lying in unlit corners somewhere" (emphasizing the arbitrary places they find to lie) or b) "and old (ones) remain behind somewhere in unlit corners, to do nothing but lie there."

41. In 1846, Sir Moses Haim Montefiore (1784–1885), the British, Orthodox Jewish philanthropist, made a famous tour of the Pale of Settlement. He was received by the czar and attempted (unsuccessfully) to plead for a mitigation of harsh laws and a restoration of Jewish communal autonomy. To Jews like Molodowsky's father, living in the small towns of White Russia, Moses Montefiore represented a kind of redeemer—a worldly and Enlightened western Jew with the desire and power to help his beleaguered brethren in Russia. The father in this poem hangs Montefiore's portrait on the eastern wall of his home, where traditionally a *mizrakh* was placed, a design that reminded the observant Jew to face east, toward Jerusalem, while praying.

42. In the Yiddish, there is consonance: "bloye/blaykhe/baroybte/oysgebrente."

43. Molodowsky added the diminutive suffix *-ke* to the Yiddish word *parasol* for the rhyme with "Olke." Although it is possible to bring the protagonist's name into the target language (such as "Marisol with her blue parasol" or "Bella with her blue umbrella"), as Lea Goldberg did in her famous Hebrew translation of this poem, I chose to import Molodowsky's choice of the name and the rhyme in order to keep the sense of the Warsaw setting.

44. The Yiddish word *moyd* means "maid" or "servant," as well as "hussy" or "brazen woman." Here, Molodowsky wants to convey that "dos meydele olke" (line 13), "the girl Olke," is both quite grown up for her age and is also being used by her parents as a servant.

45. The Yiddish reads: "geyt di ganz gure / un di genzelekh in shure." *Gure*, a modifier characterizing either the goose or the way she walks, appears to be an invented word, for it is not in the Yiddish dictionaries and none of my informants, all native speakers of Yiddish, whom I asked during the summer of 1985, recognized it.

46. The Yiddish word, *shoyte*, means "fool, blockhead."

47. The verbs denoting women's work are *tsireven* (to darn, to mend), *kireven* or *kereven* (to steer or guide), *dreyen* (to twist, rotate, turn), *farneyen* (to sew up).

48. The Yiddish reads, "men darf kniplekh dreyen," literally, "knots need to be turned or twisted." It is not clear that this phrase denotes a real task.

49. The Yiddish word *karahod* denotes a circle dance.

50. The golem is a legendary human figure made of clay, brought alive upon command. The most famous of the Jewish legends tells how in the sixteenth century, the Maharal (Rabbi Loeb of Prague) molded a golem and breathed life into it in order to defend the Jewish community against pogromists. This poem resembles both the European tale of "The Sorcerer's Apprentice" and the Jewish Passover song, "Khad gadya" ("One Kid").

51. These last three lines are very hard to translate. The Hebraic word *vayhi* means, literally, "and it came to pass," and more figuratively, "an evil occurrence, trouble, a calamity." The phrase "in eyn vayhi" is an idiom, meaning "in a jiffy." The literal meaning and literary reference of *vayhi* are essential here to set up the last line of the poem, which draws attention to the act of storytelling: "punkt vi s'volt a meysele geven" means, literally, "exactly as if it were a story." *Maysele* can also mean "good deed."

52. In the Yiddish, Feyge-beyle really wears "mansbilshe kamashn" ("men's low-laced boots"), but there aren't such shoes in English that suit the rhyme.

53. I have added "carrots" for the sake of the rhyme.

54. The Yiddish rhyme scheme in this apparently simple poem is complex and beautifully intertwines the lines, especially in the second half of the poem.

55. The Yiddish "goldene keyt" ("golden chain") is a symbol in Jewish lore of the continuity of traditional beliefs and values. I. L. Peretz wrote a famous play called *Di goldene keyt*, of which Molodowsky was certainly aware.

56. The Yiddish name is Khane, with the English equivalents being Hannah or Ann. I chose the latter for the rhyme. The Yiddish word that characterizes her is the noun *oystrakhterke*, which denotes a fastidious person. The appellation suggests that perhaps while Khane is particular or picky, she also has discriminating taste. The meaning of the root verb *oystrakhtn* (to invent), intimates that the girl is also inventive and imaginative, although maybe not in an entirely good way.

57. The word *pritsim* means "landowners" and is understood to refer to Gentiles, for Jews were generally not allowed to own land in Poland and Russia. The *pritsim* in this couplet contrast with Rothschild, the famous Jewish millionaire and philanthropist who lived in France, mentioned in the following couplet.

58. These lines contain an idiom: "un s'voynen dortn leydikgeyer shpaser, / vos tuen nisht arayn a hant in kaltn vaser." Literally: "And idle jokers live there, / Who don't [even] put a hand in cold water."

59. The Yiddish lines read: "di mame hot geheysn shraybn keyn amerike a brivele / tsu der mume khana-sheyne-sore-tsivele." Literally: "Mother commanded to write to America a letter / To Aunt Khana-Sheyne-Sore-Tsivele." "Erica" is an addition, for the sake of the rhyme.

60. *Shin*, *mem*, *alef*, *beys*, *lamed*, and *khaf* are letters of the Yiddish alphabet which correspond to the English letters or clusters "sh," "m," "a," "b," "l," and "kh."

61. The actual place Dzshike Street was notorious among Warsaw Jews for its terrible jail, which held political prisoners. The poem is dedicated to Joseph Opatoshu (1886–1954), a Yiddish novelist in New York City whose realist works depict the gritty underside of shtetl life.

62. *Iyar* is a spring month on the Hebrew calendar. Because each Hebrew month commences at the new moon, the fifteenth day coincides with the full moon. Most Jewish holidays, including Sukkot, Purim, Pesach, and Shevuot, fall on the full moon. Molodowsky has chosen to set this poem on the fifteenth of *Iyar*, exactly one month after Pesach, precisely because there is no Jewish holiday attached to this date.

63. The Yiddish phrase is *feygl-milkh*, literally, "bird-milk." Harkavy defines it as "anything delicious; starflower." The starflower is a star-shaped flower and is used to describe either a type of lily also known as the Star-of-Bethlehem or a flower in the primrose family. One informant, Professor Wolf Moskovich of the Hebrew University, insisted that *feygl-milkh* is an idiom for the impossible, what cannot exist, and that the denotation of starflower would be less known by the Yiddish reader. However, in this poem, both the literal and figurative meanings are relevant.

64. The Yiddish phrase *pervi sort* ("first-rate") derives from the Russian and may well allude ironically to the vanguard Communists as excessively self-righteous in their moral consistency.

65. The Yiddish word *tshobotes* (translated here as "clodhoppers") derives from the Lithuanian *cebetas* (great boots).

66. The Yiddish word *laptshes* means "bast shoes," shoes made from the strong, woody fiber obtained from the phloem of plants.

67. In the Yiddish, the end rhyme *mir/papir* (me/paper) strengthens the extended metaphor of blood and ink, poet and poem.

68. *Elul* is an early autumn month on the Hebrew calendar; *Tebeth* is a winter month. Pesach (Passover), the holiday of liberation, falls in the spring month of *Nissan*.

69. Pawiak was the infamous prison in Warsaw, located between Dzielna and Pawia Streets used by the Poles against political prisoners and later by the Nazis. There was a special building for women prisoners. David Rosenthal, interview with the author, September 15, 1997, quoting from *Encyclopedia of Warsaw* (Polish). (Warsaw: Panstwowe Wydawnictwo Naukowe, 1975), 8471.

70. Three lines of dashes in the Yiddish text may indicate that three lines of verse were omitted from the published poem. The reason is unknown.

71. As well as "chronicle," the Yiddish word *khronik* means current events or local news. The genre of the Polish *kronika*—a type of witty, gossipy article that alluded to censored topics by describing everyday details—was introduced by the novelist Boleslaw Prus (1845–1912), who also defined the newspaper as "the history of the day."

72. According to Jewish legend, when the Messiah comes, the Jews will cross into Paradise over a miraculously strengthened bridge of paper. The poem is dedicated to the Russian Yiddish writer David Bergelson (1884–

1952), one of Molodowsky's mentors, who introduced the impressionist style to Yiddish fiction between 1905 and 1917 but, after the Bolshevik Revolution, abruptly made his work conform to socialist realism.

73. The Yiddish verb in the preceding stanzas is *fartrakhtn zikh*, which means "to contemplate, to ponder, to sink into thought." The verb in the last stanza is *fartrakhtn* (without the reflexive pronoun *zikh*), which means "to conceive, to contrive."

74. The Yiddish word here is *treyf*, meaning "illegitimate, nefarious, impure, contaminated."

75. The Yiddish line reads: "vi a kleynike goye," literally, "Like a small Gentile girl."

76. The Yiddish line is ambiguous: "vos makht mir vays mayn trakhtn." It could also be read, "vos makht mir veys mayn trakhtn" or "vos makht mayn trakhtn mir veys," meaning "that makes my thoughts known to me."

77. These lines echo the diction of Moyshe-Leyb Halpern's 1919 elegy, "I. L. Peretz," and Molodowsky's poem, written in 1932, appears to be a tribute to Halpern, who died that year.

78. The essence of this poem is all in the rhymes: *gas* (street)/ *Montparnasse; fremd* (foreign)/ *hemd* (shirt). The street name, Montparnasse, is foreign, Parisian, while the rhyme with *fremd* (foreign) is that most familiar item of clothing, *hemd* (shirt). The subsequent couplet about not wanting to rhyme, which is also repeated and varied in the concluding lines, depends on a half rhyme, of *nit* (not) and *lib* (love). These two words sum up the speaker's problem: her beloved does *not love* her anymore!

79. Throughout the poem, Molodowsky plays on half rhymes, like *duner/getrunken* and on alliteration in the verb prefixes, like *farvoglt/fartrogn/farbrenter* and *tseefnt/tseblien.*

80. In Jeremiah 27:1–15, God instructs Jeremiah to place a yoke on his neck as a symbol of the divinely decreed servitude of the Jews under King Nebuchadnezzar.

81. The Yiddish word *moreshkhoyre* (melancholy, gloom) is a Hebraism.

82. Another Hebraism *mehume* (turmoil, riot, stampede, tumult).

83. The Yiddish reads: "un tsinger, vi gleker fun tume." *Tume* is another Hebraism, meaning "ritual impurity."

84. More Hebraisms: *matbeyes* (coins) and *sokhrishe* (merchantly).

85. A Slavicism, *sinyakes* (bruises, livid spots).

86. In Jeremiah 28:1–17, Hananiah ben Azzur, a prophet from Gibeon, falsely prophesies the restoration of the Temple, the end of exile, and the coming of peace. To make his point, Hananiah breaks the yoke that Jeremiah wears. Jeremiah argues against this prediction and accuses Hananiah of misleading the people with his lies.

87. More Hebraisms: *nevue* (prophecy) and *geule* (redemption).

88. Anathoth, Jeremiah's native city, in the region of tribe of Benjamin (Jeremiah 1:1).

89. The Slavicism *katsaveyke* denotes a quilted peasant jacket.

90. The irony in this couplet depends upon an untranslatable rhyme,

between the Hebraism *deveykes* (religious ecstasy, excessive devoutness) and the Slavicism *katsaveyke* (quilted peasant jacket).

91. Shloyminke the Blacksmith is a figure upon whom Molodowsky focused in her memoirs, "Mayn elterzeydns yerushe" ("My Great-Grandfather's Legacy"), in *Svive* 21 (December 1966): 25–27.

In her account, Molodowsky notes that as a girl, she was fond of Shloyminke the Blacksmith, the owner of the two rooms and kitchen the Molodowsky family rented every autumn. She tells that his name came from his affinity for wine, even in the middle of the week, and from his youthful profession as a horse dealer. Now he was

> an old man, worked very little in the smithy, but all day he would walk around in a waistcoat with turned up sleeves as if he were indeed working. Occasionally he still used to nail a horseshoe on a horse, straighten a wheel on a wagon, and returning from the smithy would boast: Thanks be to God, my hands still serve! And he would show the various coins that he had earned. . .
>
> In the evenings he loved to tell us, the children, about his past years how he used to travel to the fairs and deal in horses. Above all he used to tell about demons that he himself had met on the road and the remedy he had against them, Hear O Israel.

92. The Yiddish lines read: un kh'hob tsu zikh aleyn pretenzye— / vos darf ikh hern M—skes bekemekene retsenzye / as kh'hob dayn goldenem oytser far a shpigl zikh gemakht.

Molodowsky rhymes *pretenzye* (claim, pretense, false show, pretext, pretension) with *retsenzye* (review).

93. Although the Yiddish poem rhymes, I was unable to rhyme this translation.

94. Molodowsky uses the French word *lunette* for "telescope."

95. Lermontov, Russia's great nineteenth-century romantic poet, spent much time in the Caucasus. One of his most famous poems is a ballad, "Tamara," first published in 1843, which is based on a Georgian legend about Queen Daria, who lived in an ancient tower overlooking the Terek River. The legend has it that she was like a siren, tempting wanderers to spend the night with her and then cutting off their heads in the morning and throwing them in the river.

96. Note the Hebraisms, especially the two-word phrase at the end: "di torbe fun *sam*. . . / farpakte af loyfn *ley'ver hayam*" ("the sacks of poison. . . / packed up for escaping over the sea").

97. *Tevye der milkhiker*, by Sholem Aleichem (Sh. Rabinovits). A collection of Sholem Aleichem's best-known monologues. *Penek*, a novel by David Bergelson (Warsaw: Literarishe Bleter, 1937). "Penek" is also the name of the hero of Bergelson's two volume novel *Baym dnieper*. Penek, as a middle-class boy, spouts Communist ideology in volume 1 and becomes a revolutionary in volume 2. Volume 1 was published in Germany in 1932, and volume 2 was

published in the Soviet Union in 1936. With these two titles, Molodowsky characterizes Freydke as a reader of Yiddish literature ranging from the popular classic to the latest political writer.

98. The Yiddish reads: "foroys—es traybt dos grine rod, / der vint, vos glet, der hunger, vos badrot." Weinreich defines the verb *badrotn* as "to wire, to provide with wires." Given the puzzling phrase, "der hunger, vos badrot" ("the hunger that wires"), Molodowsky probably chose *badrot* for the sake of the rhyme with *rod* (wheel).

99. *Ha Shilo'aḥ* (pronounced in Yiddish *Hashaloyakh*) (The Messenger) was one of the most important Zionist journals, published in Hebrew by Aḥad Ha'Am and then by Dr. Joseph Gedaliah Klausner (Kloyzner) (1874–1958). Klausner published the journal first in Warsaw (until 1904), then in Odessa (1907–19), and later in Eretz Yisroel (1921–26).

100. The Yiddish reads: "hot lib gehat a posek zogn un a pshat." The Hebraic words *posek* and *pshat* denote respectively "verse of a sacred book" and "literal interpretation" (usually of a sacred text).

101. The woman's name Sheyndl Kanarey means roughly "pretty canary." *Sheyn* is an adjective meaning "pretty"; *shayndl* denotes an ornament; *kanarik* means "canary."

102. Katovitz (Polish: Katowice) is an industrial city in Silesia (southwest Poland).

103. Aḥad Ha'am (pseudonym of Asher Ginzberg) (1856–1927), edited the Zionist Hebrew newspaper *Ha shilo'aḥ* (*The Messenger*) from 1896–1902, and was an important Zionist thinker, whose nationalist ideology focused on a collective Jewish will to live and a national cultural and moral revival to emanate from the hoped-for Jewish state in Palestine. Source: Lucy Dawidowicz, *The Golden Tradition: Jewish Life and Thought in Eastern Europe.* (Boston: Beacon Press, 1967), 367.

104. The Yiddish reads: "yidn zenen take an am hab'khire." The Hebraism here, *am hab'khire* (people of free will) connotes Zionism rather than religiosity.

105. Joseph Klausner (Kloyzner), who succeeded Aḥad Ha'am as editor of the Zionist Hebrew newspaper *Ha Shilo'aḥ* (Hashaloyakh) (The Messenger), wrote the book *Yahadut v'enoshiut* (Judaism and Humanism) (Warsaw: Yavneh, 1904–5; Hebrew year 5665). Molodowsky's narrator reverses the title to *Anushes Vyehoydes* and renders it in the Ashkenazi pronunciation for the sake of rhyme and irony.

106. A *gildn* was a coin worth fifteen *kopeks.*

107. Mrs. Pshenytsa is referred to disrespectfully here as *di pshenitsikhe* (the female Pshenytsa).

108. Text note: The 1935 edition has "fokhet zi zikh op" ("fans herself"), while the 1936 edition has reversed the letters and printed "khopet zi zikh op."

109. Mrs. Pshenytsykhe speaks in a dialect with an affectation:

kokhanye, zogt zi, kh'bet inen, mayn dinstmeydl tsu alde shlek,
iz ergets-vu avek,

un ikh muz opnemen a vlokhke palme,
nisht vayt fun danen, af krokhmolne.
ikh bet inen—

For example: *kokhanye* (dearie), is the inflected form of the Polish word for "dear" (*kochana*). The personal pronoun *inen* is an archaic or dialect form of *aykh* (accusative, dative second person plural or formal). The adjective *vloske* comes from the Polish *włoskie* (Italian).

110. The Yiddish reads: "mayn man—hot zi geshtikt zikh, staytsh. . ." ("My husband, she choked, that is. . ."). Note that seven lines above, Sheyndl's machine "hot geton a varg" ("did or gave a choke").

111. Molodowsky transliterates the Polish phrase "Do wynajecia" ("for rent") in Yiddish characters. (Compare with "Otvotsk I," note 15.)

112. Łodz is a city to the south of Warsaw. Nałęczów is a town approximately thirty kilometers west of Lublin, noted since the nineteenth century for its sanatorium and spa and frequented by residents of Lublin and Warsaw.

113. The Yiddish reads: "mit tseoderter fon." The adjective *tseodert* (from the verb *tseodern*) is very difficult to translate. The transitive verb *odern* means, literally, "to cut or pull veins from meat; to porge meat, removing the forbidden fat and veins to make it kosher"; and figuratively, often humorously, "to tear pieces out of someone," to harry someone to death. The prefix *tse-* denotes the undoing, the negative act. Thus, the tattered flag is one that has been made unkosher, like a piece of meat that, once properly stripped of its veins, now has had the impure veins reimplanted, perhaps sewn in again with a bloody thread.

114. *Alef, beys, giml* are the letters of the Yiddish alphabet (a, b, and g) that correspond to "abc" in English.

115. The Yiddish reads: "fun verter der treyfener shatnez." *Shatnez* is a cloth made of mixed linen and wool, forbidden by Jewish law to Orthodox Jews. *Treyf* denotes that which is ritually unclean, according to Jewish law.

116. Molodowsky has made a verb, *soloveyen* out of the noun *solovey* (nightengale).

117. Molodowsky has made a verb, *farzumern*, out of the noun *zumer* (summer).

118. The Yiddish reads: "ot shteyen di kulbakishe bronzene yungen"; the adjective *kulbakishe* refers to the characters in the works of the Soviet Yiddish writer Moyshe Kulbak.

119. The Aramaic phrase "khad-gadya" literally means "one kid," and is the title and refrain of a counting song about divine retribution, sung at the end of the first Passover Seder. Idiomatically in Yiddish, "khad-gadye" means "an idle story."

120. Molodowsky chooses the Hebraism *drokhim* (ways, paths) in the phrase "hoykhe drokhim" ("high paths") rather than the more common *vegn* (ways, paths) for the sake of the half rhyme of *drokhim* and *farkrokhn* (crawled into/under).

121. The Yiddish reads: "es zol mayn kolirter stragan / zikh vaklen, vi a

kreml mit shnit" ("May my colorful market-stall /Shake/Wobble like a fabric shop"). Molodowsky included a footnote on the Bereze localism *stragan*, defining it as *mark-geshtel* (market-stall).

122. The Yiddish reads: "ot itst, ven finger unzere zaynen in klem," literally, "just now, when our fingers are in a fix."

123. Adam Mickiewicz (1798–1855), the great Polish nationalist and poet.

124. *Felker-libe* (literally, nations' love), translated here as "Brotherhood between peoples."

125. *Tsimes* is a vegetable or fruit stew.

126. *Hemdl* can denote both the diminutive of *hemd* (shirt) and "book jacket."

127. Molodowksy transliterates the Americanism "Okay" (*o-key*) into Yiddish here.

128. The Yiddish idiom, "es toyg af a kapore," literally translates, "it is fitting for a scapegoat." The *kapore* or scapegoat referred to here is a chicken used in a pre-Yom Kippur atonement ceremony popular in Eastern Europe, in which the chicken served as a scapegoat.

129. The New York Yiddish poet H. Leyvik (1888–1962) (originally Leyvik Halpern) was well known for his modernist, visionary poetry and, indeed, had very light hair. The adjective *vays* (white) here means "blond" or "tow headed," but also connotes a quality of light and passion surrounding this poet. In one of his poems, "Do voynt dos yidishe folk" ("Here Lives the Jewish People"), trans. in Howe and Greenberg, *A Treasury of Yiddish Poems*, he writes of the *vayse fayern* (white fires) of New York City.

The Parisian poet, Moyshe Valdman, wrote a poem similar to Molodowsky's in 1966, "Vayser man," in *Fun ale vaytn* (Tel Aviv: H. Leyvik Farlag, 1980), 184.

130. The Yiddish reads: "an ukrayner hot zayn sokol dershtikt." Molodowsky has used *sokol*, a Russian and Ukrainian word for "falcon," which symbolizes freedom and Ukrainian independence. Here, the falcon may allude to the short-lived Ukrainian Republic, the fall of which at the end of World War I the world blamed on the Ukrainians themselves; their pogroms choked their freedom. The only other translation of this poem in English omits this line. "A Tow-headed Poet," trans. Jehiel B. Cooperman and Sarah H. Cooperman, *America in Yiddish Poetry* (New York: Exposition Press, 1967), 269–71.

131. The Yiddish transliterates the English: "meks, dzshaz!"

132. Birobidzhan is a province in the Amur district of the far eastern part of the USSR, which the Soviet government designated as an autonomous "Jewish State" in 1934. An agricultural settlement with Yiddish as its official language, Birobidzhan was settled by about 20,000 Jews in 1928, of whom over 60 percent later left. By 1934, Jews comprised only 20 percent of the region's population. The "Jewish State" was not a great success, due to the difficulties of life and farming in the region and to the increasing Stalinist persecution of Jews and of increasing nationalism during the 1930s. (Max Raisin, *A*

History of the Jews in Modern Times. Revised edition, vol. 6 [New York: Hebrew Publishing Company, 1949], 447–48; also *A History of the Jewish People*, ed. H. H. Ben-Sasson [Cambridge: Harvard University Press, 1976], 972–73, 977.)

133. The phrase "a finfer-lempl" means something like "a size-five lamp" or "a five-penny lamp" and refers either to the fixed measure of the lamp's glass shade or to its cost.

134. The English word "store" appears transliterated in the Yiddish line.

135. The Yiddish reads: khotsh s'klingt dos vort fazan / tsu fremd, tsu eydl. / s'iz nisht vi mamzer-gonoruk, / un shoyn avade nisht vi katshke-dreydl.

As discussed in the introduction, the phrases "mamzer-gonoruk" and "katshke-dreydl" are untranslatable. "Mamzer-gonoruk" may mean "gonorrheal bastard," for the Hebraic *mamzer* denotes "bastard." However, not one of the several informants I consulted (native Yiddish speakers from various regions) understood or recognized the word *gonoruk* in this phrase. Dr. Mordkhe Schaechter hypothesized that it means "gonorrheal," for *-uk* is a pejorative suffix and there is another phrase that ends in *-uk* that means syphilitic. He stated in a 1987 conversation with the author in New York that this phrase may be a Warsaw insult, not part of provincial diction. According to Dr. Schaechter, one might also call a person with venereal disease, "a frantsivate moyd" (or *yung*). On the other hand, the late Yiddish translator and poet M. Littwin told me in a 1988 conversation in Jerusalem that he thought the phrase somewhat stilted for a curse. To his Lithuanian ear, *gonor* was medical terminology. He thought the crass, common term for gonorrhea, from the Russian, *triper*, was more likely to be used in a curse. He speculated that Molodowsky chose *gonor* because it sounds like *goner* (gander, male goose). This wordplay would connote the same family of associations as *katshke* (duck) in the next line. In another conversation, the scholars Dr. Avraham Nowershtern and Dr. Anita Norich expressed doubts that Molodowsky would even have known the difference between syphilis and gonorrhea.

In the second phrase, *katshke* denotes "duck" and *dreydl*, "chicanery, scheme [hum.], as well as top, teetotum," according to Weinreich. But the literal translation, "duck chicanery," makes no sense. Both Dr. Itzik Gottesman (who is American-born, but speaks Rumanian Yiddish from home) and Dr. Mordkhe Schaechter (Itzik's uncle, from Rumania) thought that "katshke-dreydl" is a nonsense rhyme in a children's counting or game song, like "eenie meenie minie mo." Gottesman recited a line, "eli melekh katshke dreydl. . ." M. Littwin did not recognize "katshke-dreydl." He speculated that is was a *zidl-vertl* or localism. Yet another pair of informants, Dr. Joshua Fishman and Gella Schweid Fishman, supplied me with, "odem a mentsh / un katshke dreydl" ("Adam a person and duck chicanery"), which is an expression that pokes fun at a person's self-importance and exaggerated seriousness.

Because both these phrases are impenetrable and connotative, I've left them in the Yiddish. Molodowsky's point seems to be that these are two extremes of diction, to her ear—the insulting sexual curse of the city street and the intimate rhyme of a childhood in a specific locality. In contrast to these, the word *fazan* (pheasant) sounds "too foreign, too delicate," but still has something in common with the names of the supposedly utopian Jewish state in the USSR.

136. Bire is the river running through Birebidzhan. Tiga is a region in that area.

137. Molodowsky quotes the Hebrew here, "vegar zeeiv im keves," from Isaiah 11:6.

138. *Mem*, *alef*, and *lamed* are the Yiddish letters corresponding to "m," "a" (or here, "o"), and "l," the first three letters in Molodowsky's name.

139. I've kept the Yiddish expression, "keyn ayen hore" ("no evil eye"), in the translation for the sake of the rhyme.

140. Molodowsky imports the Americanism "Boy Scouts" into her Yiddish line, along with the American names of the cousins.

141. *Badkhn* denotes generally a joker and specifically the traditional joke-maker or professional jester hired to appear at a wedding to compose rhymed satires and sentimental songs about the bride and bridegroom. *Oriman* denotes a pauper.

142. The Yiddish reads: "in farblondzsheter bet." The adjective *farblondzsheter* denotes "wandering, maverick, misguided, lost; meandering, bewildered, aimless."

143. The Yiddish reads: "in praysn geven, un abisl fartshadet." The Yiddish verb *fartshaden zikh* means, according to Harkavy, "to be stupified by the fumes of charcoal." Gella Fishman defined it as, "to be confused, perplexed."

144. The Yiddish is ambiguous. The word can be read as either the adverb *dervayl* (variant of *dervayle*, "meanwhile, for the time being"), as Irving Howe has done in his translation, or as the familiar imperative of the verb *derveyln* (to elect). The second reading, which makes the poem starker, was suggested to me by Professor Avraham Novershtern and the poet Avraham Sutzkever.

145. The Yiddish reads: "nem tsu fun undz di shekhine fun gaones." The phrase "shekhine fun gaones" is ambiguous. *Gaones* denotes "scholarship, brilliance, ingenuity, genius," and *shekhine* denotes "Divine Presence," or "Divine Manifestation."

146. The Hebraic word *megile* denotes in Yiddish the Book of Esther, a scroll, and, in this context, figuratively, a very long letter.

147. The Yiddish line reads: "nit ayngeshlogn ergets nit far zikh keyn slup" ("[I did] not drive in a post anywhere for myself"). This line is important primarily for the end rhyme with: "vi eydl du flegst ton fun kos a zup" ("as delicately, you used to take a sip from your cup").

148. "Ikh bin gefaln un tsetrotn." This line echoes the opening line of David Edelstat's popular 1889 lyric, "In kamf" ("In Struggle"): "Mir vern gehast un getribn."

149. In the phrase "khometsdikn vayn" ("mundane wine"), the Hebraic adjective *khometsdik* denotes a food containing or contaminated by leavened dough or bread, and thus forbidden during Passover.

150. Molodowsky uses a Hebrew expression, "b'kfitsat derekh," meaning "short cut, miraculous abridgement of journey," according to the *Alkeley Hebrew Dictionary*, p. 2322.

151. The Yiddish line reads: "gevolt meshadekh zayn zikh mitn himl. . ." The Hebraism "meshadekh zayn zikh" means, according to Weinreich (and Yehoash, 174), "to be come connected by marriage, marry one's children into the family (of)."

152. *Beys* and *giml* are the second and third letters in the Yiddish alphabet, corresponding to the English "b" and "g."

153. In Slavic folklore, especially Polish, the witch *baba jaga* controls bad weather.

154. The Hebraic *mes-lesn* denotes a solar day, the twenty- four hour period of a day and a night.

155. This line seems to echo the verse from the popular song "Shpil Balalayka" ("Play the Balalaika"):

vos ken brenen un nisht oyfhern?
vos ken benken, veynen on trern?
. . .
Libe ken brenen un nisht oyfhern,
A harts ken benken, veynen on trern.
. . .
What can burn and not be consumed?
What can yearn, cry without tears?
. . .
Love can burn and not be consumed,
A heart can yearn, cry without tears.

156. The Hebraic word *khoyshekh* denotes utter darkness, especially the primordial darkness of Genesis 1:1.

157. The Hebrew instructions for blowing the shofar during the Rosh Hashanah service: *Teki'ah* denotes the blowing of the shofar; *teru'ah* denotes the succession of tremulous notes sounded on the shofar; *shebarim* denotes the tremolo or broken, disconnected sounds of shofar.

158. The Germanic word *fintsterkayt* has a very different feel than the Hebraic *khoyshekh*.

159. The Yiddish lines read: "nor s'iz nisht mafsik, / es shalt nisht der horn." The Hebraic periphrastic verb *mafsik zayn* means "to interrupt, especially a prayer."

160. The Hebraic *shorabor* denotes the legendary wild ox or bison which, according to Jewish lore, will be eaten by the righteous when the Messiah comes.

161. The Yiddish *mitvokh* denotes the weekday Wednesday and means literally, "midweek." The footstool alludes to the folk belief that a woman will serve as a footstool in heaven for her husband.

162. The Hebraic word *khurbm*, denoting "ruin, destruction, catastrophe, devastation, havoc," is used in the phrases "khurbm-bayes-rishn" and "khurbm-bayes-sheyni," which name the Destructions of the First and Second Temples in Jerusalem, by the Babylonians (586 B.C.E.) and by the Romans (70 C.E.). In modern Yiddish, *khurbm* has come to refer to the destruction of European Jewry by the Nazis during the Second World War.

163. The Hebraic word *heykhl* denotes the Jewish Temple.

164. The Yiddish lines read: "khotsh koyheles hot a svore, / az zi toyg af a kapore." The Hebraic *koyheles* is the name of the Book of Ecclesiastes. The Hebraic *svore* denotes "guess, hypothesis"; the phrase "es iz a svore az" means "it is likely that, probably." The idiom "zi toyg af a kapore" translates literally as "it is fitting for a scapegoat," and means here, "it is worthless." See note 126.

165. The Yiddish letters *hey* and *khes* correspond to the English "h" and the sound "kh."

166. The Yiddish line reads: "dem payn fun shtumloshn vet emitser derleyzn." The Germanic and Hebraic components of the compound noun *shtumloshn* (sign language) mean literally "mute language/tongue."

167. It is worth noting the many verbs in this poem that begin with the prefix *der-*: *dervaremen* (to warm up) [stanza 2]; *dergeyn* (to arrive) [4]; *dershraybn* (to finish writing), *derblikn* (to discern), and *dershtikt* (to choke) [7]; *derleyzn* (to rescue) [8]; *dermonen* (to remember) and *derkonen* (to recognize) [9]. Also, note the variations on verbs beginning with *far-* in [7]: *farkrimen* (to distort), *fartempn* (to dull), *farendikn* (to finish). These features, and also the play on the roots *-shraybn* and *-geyen* and *-leyzen* and *-loykhtn* throughout the poem are characteristic of Molodowsky's style.

168. This poem echoes Moyshe-Leyb Halpern's poem, "Der foygl" ("The Bird"), from *Di goldene pave* (The Golden Peacock) (Cleveland: Farlag Grupe Yidish, 1924).

169. The Yiddish line reads: "kum arayn, foygl-fidl, guter klezmer fun mayn yugnt-lid." The compound *foygl-fidl* (bird-violin) is a playful invention. The Hebraic *klezmer* means "musician," especially the traditional Jewish shtetl musician who performed in groups at weddings and other celebrations.

170. The Yiddish line reads: "kum arayn, kitsl-katsl, fun mayn kindhayt strashner vizltir"; the word *vizltir* means "bison, ure-ox, aurochs," the latter of which is the nearly extinct European bison.

171. The Yiddish line reads: "ikh hob nit eyn mol dem bezim farzukht tsulib dir." ("Not once did I sample / taste the broom on your account," or "I never sampled the broom because of you.") *Farzukhn* means "to taste, to sample." The line can mean either "I never had a taste of the broom on your account," meaning "I never was beaten by the broom on your account" or "I never had to look for the broom in order to clean up after you or to chase you out of the house."

172. This compound, *tsigl-migl,* means "literally, goat-nauseau/disgust."

173. The phrase "dayn lid" ("your song") refers to the famous Yiddish lullaby, "Rozshinkes mit mandlen" ("Raisins and Almonds"), which Avraham Goldfaden adapted from a folksong, with the opening stanza's reference to a "klor vays tsigele" ("pure white goat").

174. "Khad gadya": [Aramaic], "One Kid." The title of the counting song in the Hagaddah, sung at the Passover Seder. The song is one of consequences—from one small kid comes a chain of destructions resulting at last

in the intervention of God. In Yiddish idiom, the phrase "khad gadya" can also mean both "an idle story" and "a prison."

175. The Hebraic word *sefer*, used here, means holy book, important or sacred book, in contrast to the Germanic *bukh*, denoting any volume, and especially a secular book. In English, "book" derives from the Anglo Saxon, while "volume" and "tome" are from the Greek; none of these words are as specifically value-laden as in the Yiddish.

176. *Shebat* (pronounced in Yiddish *shvat*) is the fifth month of the Jewish calendar, usually corresponding with January and February.

177. The Hebrew phrase "ki tov" is quoted from Genesis 1:4, "vayar elohim et haor ki tov" ("and God saw the light that it was good").

178. The Yiddish line reads: "un mir taytshn es—s'iz gut." The Germanic *taytshn* means "to interpret, to translate into Yiddish."

179. The Hebrew "Shir ha-Ma'alot" (pronounced in Yiddish *shir hamales*) denotes "a song or psalm of degrees or ascents." This phrase opens a cluster of fifteen Psalms (Ps. 120–134), although the meaning of the phrase is not clear: it may refer to a gradational style of musical execution, to the return (or ascent) from Babylon, to "pilgrim psalms," or to fifteen actual steps in the Second Temple, where levitical musicians used to stand during a Sukkot ceremony. Source: *Encyclopedia Judaica*, vol. 13, 1319–320.

180. *Badekns* denotes the custom of veiling the bride, prior to the traditional Jewish wedding ceremony.

181. The image of the shadows folding their arms in order to observe the Dead Sabbath is a bitterly ironic version of ritual purity among observant Jews, combining in the figure the separation of Sabbath from the week and the separation of a devout person from ritual impurities, such as those embodied in a menstruating woman, a diseased person, a corpse or carcass, or bodily emissions.

182. *Minḥah* (pronounced in Yiddish *minkhe*) is the daily afternoon prayer service.

183. Vistula, a river flowing through Poland, from the Carpathian Mountains north into the Gulf of Danzig.

184. Note the wordplay and allusion here between the literal and figurative meanings of *dude*, which literally denotes "a fife, a pipe, a bag-pipe," and figuratively means (according to Harkavy) "a burden," as in the phrase "haltn zikh mit der dude" ("to bear the burden"). Sodom is the city of evil men that God destroys (Genesis 19:1–28) despite Abraham's bargaining to save it if ten righteous men could be found there (Genesis 18:20–33).

185. *Ma'ariv* (pronounced in Yiddish *mayrev*) is the evening prayer service; *Shaḥarit* (pronounced in Yiddish *shakhris*) is the morning prayer service.

186. The *Khidekl* (Tigris) and the *Pras* (Euphrates) Rivers are mentioned in Genesis 2:14 as the eastern and western rivers in the Garden of Eden. The Vistula River runs through Poland (see note 183).

187. The Hebraic *krie* denotes a rent made in a garment as a sign of mourning.

188. Note, in the refrain, the word Germanic *kroyn* (crown) is used, while in lines 3 and 5 of this stanza, the Hebraic word *keter* (crown) is used. *Keter* is a much "higher" word, suggests divine or unearthly majesty, contrasting David's *kroyn* with Messiah's *keter.* The higher tone of *keter* underlines the bitter irony in the tone here—King David is the only survivor of the Jews to reach the Messiah and pass on the crown, all that's left of the Jewish people and nation that David's monarchy represented.

189. The Hebraic *Havdalah*, literally, "the dividing," is the ceremony with which observant Jews mark the end of the Sabbath and the beginning of the week, by reciting blessings over a lighted, braided, multiwicked candle, wine, and sweet-smelling spices. The first line of this poem, "Got fun avrom" ("God of Abraham"), is taken from the Yiddish *tkhine* (supplicatory prayer) that women recite at the beginning of the Havdalah ceremony.

190. *Bereishit* (pronounced in Yiddish *Bereyshis*) (in the beginning) is the first word in the Hebrew Bible (Genesis 1:1).

191. The Hebraic and Germanic components of *shkhite-varshtatn* literally denote "slaughter, Jewish ritual slaughter; massacre" and "workshop, shop; workbench."

192. The components of the Hebraic *khokhmes-hadomim* mean, literally "wisdom of the bloods." Following the pattern of *khokhmes-hanefesh* (psychology), perhaps Molodowsky means here "the science of the blood," meaning either racism or the science of murder.

193. Jewish legend has it that when the Messiah comes, the Jews will cross over into Paradise upon a miraculously strengthened bridge of paper, while the Gentiles will walk upon a bridge made from iron, a substance lowly regarded in Jewish folklore. Significantly, Molodowsky uses this image in other poems, especially notable by contrast to this Zionist application of the figure is her 1933 poem, "Di papirene brik," in *Dzshike gas* (see note 72).

194. The *sukkah* is a booth, a temporary shelter with an open roof, covered with branches, in which meals are eaten during the eight days of Sukkot, the autumn Festival of Booths.

195. Molodowsky uses the Hebraic *sneh* (thorn bush), in contrast with the Germanic *dornboym* of the title of her last book, *Likht fun dornboym.*

196. "My Children" is Molodowsky's only poem that directly addresses her childlessness. The rhymes, which in the Yiddish occur in irregular couplets, lighten the tone.

197. The Hebraic word *negine* denotes Jewish music, especially vocal. It is impossible to convey in English the effect of the high Hebraic diction of this poem—*negine* for "music," *yesurim* for "pain, agony," several lines above, *rayen* for "thought (idea); thought (imagination)" in the following line, *in gezer zayn* for "to be sentenced to," several lines later. Molodowsky chose these words for their rhymes, and perhaps, too, because she speaks of aborted or miscarried children, the dead who never had a chance to live in this world. Perhaps she gives them a more elevated, abstract diction because they can speak only hypothetically of earthly life and experience.

198. It is worth noting that the poet also strains her diction toward the

German in this poem, with *vimlen* (from the German *Wimmeln*), meaning "to swarm, to team" in line 28: "az hinter zey nishomes unzere farvelkte vimlen?"

199. The Hebraic *kafakele* denotes, according to Weinreich, limbo or purgatory and, according to Harkavy, the sling (one of the tortures of hell).

200. The Yiddish line reads: "un kh'bin dos gantse glik dir moykhl" ("And you may keep your entire happiness! And never mind all that happiness!"), in line with the idiom in Weinreich, "ikh bin dir moykhl di vetshere" ("you may keep your supper! never mind the supper!").

201. The title of this poem consists of a repetition of the phrase "the little foxes," first in Yiddish, then in Hebrew: "di kleyne fukselekh—shu'olim k'tanim," quoting from Song of Songs 2:15, "Catch us the foxes, the little foxes, that ruin the vineyards—For our vineyard is in blossom." (*Tanakh: A New Translation of The Holy Scriptures According to the Traditional Hebrew Text* [Philadelphia: Jewish Publication Society, 1985], 1408). The pattern of bilingual repetition recurs throughout the poem, also with the phrase, "mayn vayngortn, mayn kerem" ("my vineyard"). Such bilingual repetition is untranslatable, because the Hebrew is at once "high" or Biblical (but not foreign) and recognizable in Yiddish, due to the innate Hebraic component in the language. By deliberately weaving the biblical Hebrew words into the Yiddish rhyme scheme, Molodowsky "canonizes" in her poem the wicked and seductive influences that she refuses to renounce, as the biblical verse brings the wicked and the seductive into the canon of the Bible.

202. Note Molodowsky's strongly German diction here: *nobeler*, from the German *nobel* (grand, noble, distinguished) and *gevoynhayt*, from the German *Gewohnheit* (habit, custom, practice).

203. The title is a Hebrew phrase: "kinat sofrim tarbeh khokhme" ("the rivalry of writers increases wisdom"), a quote from Proverbs.

204. The Aramaic word *Tanna* denotes a sage of the Mishnah, one of the first doctors of Talmud.

205. Neharda'i was a famous yeshivah in Babylonia. The Hebraic *bedikhe* means "joke," but because Molodowsky chose this and not the common Yiddish word for "joke," *vits*, the line calls for a higher translation.

206. The Hebraic *shatnes* denotes the forbidden interweaving of linen and wool.

207. The Yiddish line reads: "podskribes epes zshlobes." The Byelorussian word *podskribes* (riffraff) (the Ukranian is *podskrobkes*) refers, like the more common Yiddish *zhlobes* (boors), to the lowest stratum of society. According to the lexicographer David Guralnik (in a letter, October 20, 1990), the Yiddish noun is derived from a Slavic verb meaning "to scrape clean," which was used to refer to the youngest children in a family, who had the last crack at the dinner pot and would clean up every last morsel, thus the meaning of the low one on the totem pole.

208. The Yiddish reads: "in tog fun kurtsn fraytik." "Short Friday" refers to the Friday at the winter solstice, before the Sabbath.

209. There may be a typographical error in the Yiddish text: *den darn* (the withered one) was printed perhaps mistakenly for *dorn* (thorn).

210. The Yiddish lines read: "a teytl fun a melamed / antkegn an ayzerner pik." The dictionaries (Harkavy and Weinreich) define *pik* as "spade in cards." The gardening tool "spade" is "der ridl," "di lopete," "di shpodl." Molodowsky uses *pik* here for the rhyme with *krig*, literalizing the card suite as the tool, for the weapons in the battle she fights are the teacher's pointer and the peasant's tool of labor.

211. "Mendeles eybike boyd" ("Mendele's eternal wagon") refers to the legendary, half-covered wagon, driven by Mendele the Bookseller, the author's pseudonymous persona, in the fiction of Sh. Abramovich, the so-called grandfather of modern Yiddish literature.

212. The Yiddish reads: "zey shteyen harte un skarave." *Skarave* is not in the dictionary, but perhaps it is a misprint for the adjective *skarbove* which Harkavy defines as "of a landowner, of a treasury; old, traditional"; "skarbove nigunem" means "traditional tunes." Or *karave*, meaning "soiled, dirty."

213. The Yiddish reads: "tsi a shprukh, tsi a zkhus, tsi a ruakh / firt mikh in veg far a hant." The Germanic *shprukh* is a charm or an incantation; the Hebraic *zkhus* denotes "merit, rare privilege, justification, accumulation of merit in the divine reckoning"; the Hebraic *ruakh* means "ghost, phantom, spirit."

214. The poem relies on the play upon the preposition *on* (without) and the verb prefix *on. . .* , as in *ongisn* (to pour) and *onlodn* (to load).

215. In Genesis 6:14, God commands Noah, "Make yourself an ark of gopher wood . . ."

216. Neharda'i was a famous yeshiva in Babylonia.

217. The Yiddish lines read: "un fun di goylem-lipn git a blits a blend, / un kh'fil vi s'goylemen zikh mayne fis un hent." The invented verb, *goylemen zikh*, means "turn into a golem." The legendary golem was a mannikin made of clay.

218. The Yiddish lines read: "Zi loytert oyf mit ir bashaf, / in vayser shtilkayt toykht avek." *Oyfloytern* and *avektoykhn* are not in the dictionaries, although *loytern* means "to purify, to refine," and *oystoykhn* means "to come to the forefront or resurface," as in "zikhroynes toykhn oys" ("memories resurface"). *Avektoykn*, apparently an invented word, then means "to disappear beneath the surface." The verb prefixes *oyf* and *avek* dramatize the movement toward and away. *Oyfloytern*, then, is understood to denote a process of purifying or extracting an essence or an ore out of an impure medium.

219. *Shtume reyd* (mute speech/words), contrast to *shtumloshn* (sign-language) in "Leavetaking," note 173.

220. The Yiddish lines read: "dos tut der alter vint, / vos rirt zikh on on mir." The verb *onrirn* means "to touch, to lay hands on, to violate; affect, injure, ruffle, move (emotionally)." Followed by the preposition *on*, the meaning of *onrirn* seems to emphasize the negative connotations of touching. (The phrase "onshparn zikh on der tir" means "to lean against the door.")

221. The Yiddish line reads: "vi tut azoyns in elter daynem a ben odem?" Literally: "How does a human being do this in your old age?"

222. The Yiddish lines read: "gegebn sholem dem un yenem, / keyn

sholem iz nishto, di finger klemen" ("Greeting this one and that, / There is no peace, the fingers grieve"). The pun in these two lines is difficult to translate. "Gebn sholem" means "to greet" (with a "sholem aleykhem," a hello, literally, "peace onto you"). "Keyn sholem iz nishto" means "there's no peace at all."

223. The Yiddish pronunciation *pores haboshen* of the Hebrew *parot habashan* (the cows or kine of Bashan, in Amos 4:1) rhymes with *loshn* (language) in the preceding line. In colloquial modern Hebrew, "parot habashan" means "a very fat woman" (Alcalay, *The Complete Hebrew-English Dictionary*).

224. The Yiddish line reads: "un ikh haktane oykh." The Hebrew *hakatana* (the minor, the insignificant) is an epithet of modesty used by rabbis before their signature.

225. The Yiddish line reads: "un dertsu trog ikh a baytshl fun alte perl." *Baytshl* means, literally, "little whip."

226. The Yiddish line reads: "ken ikh nisht aroysreydn kutsenyu-mutse." The full expression is "kutsenyu-mutsenyu," a nonsense phrase which denotes fondling, flattery, cajoling, or sweet-talk, and appears to have been altered for the sake of the rhyme.

227. The Yiddish-Hebrew phrase "sheyne-mareyne" ("beautiful teacher") denotes a Talmudic scholar who has been honored with the title *Morenu* (Our Teacher). Molodowsky uses the term ironically in reference to a woman of questionable reputation when she quotes a gossipy neighbor in her autobiography, "Mayn elterzeydns yerushe," *Suive* 28 (May 1969): 62–63.

228. *Nutrikin* (or *Nutrikon*) is the mystical technique of interpreting letters of one word as initials of other words.

229. The Yiddish line reads: "mit tserene bletlekh ikh fir a gefekht." *gefekht* is not in the dictionaries; *fokhn* means "to fan"; *fekhtn* means "to fence" (as in the martial art).

230. The Yiddish line reads: "brukhvarg fun geshen, fun geven, un gevezn."

231. The Yiddish lines read: "du vest dayn loshn oysbaytn af andere leshoynes, / un oysbrien in tsung an ander shprakh." Note the play on *loshn* (language/tongue), *tsung* (tongue), and *shprakh* (language).

232. The Yiddish line reads: "zalb mikh op mit dayn blendikayt." Although *zalbn* means "to anoint" and the prefix *op-* indicates the negating or undoing of an action (un-), so that *opzalbn* would mean "to un-anoint" or "to desecrate," this meaning does not follow in the logic of the poem.

233. The title, "untergang stam" means something like, "sinking for no reason; just sinking; random sinking."

The movement of this poem depends on shifts in the phrase: "untergang stam," as it is in title; "an untergang stam" ("a random sinking") in line 10; and "der untergang stam" ("that random sinking") in line 16. There is also a pun on the word *breg*, meaning "border, coast, edge, brim." First it refers to the captain's hat—the gold edge of the hat—"nor getrogn zayn hitl mit goldene bregn" ("brim") in line 3. Then it alludes to the edge of the ocean as a figure of speech, while referring to the captain's memory: "es hot zey farshlungen der tom fun zikorn / a breg on a nomen" ("a coast without a name") in lines 8–9, and again in line 15: "nokh shtarker fun shturem iz der breg on a nomen" ("the nameless coast").

234. The Yiddish lines read: "zey trogn khalatlekh / gekirtst un genetlt." The word *genetlt* is not in the dictionaries.

235. *Shekhinah* is the Divine Presence, the glory of God.

236. Famous saying attributed to Hillel, the legendary Jewish sage and biblical commentator of first century Babylonia and Palestine.

237. Throughout the poem, this refrain is in Hebrew: "aḥat shtayim" ("one, two").

Bibliography

Works by Molodowsky

Kheshvendike nekht: lider (poems). Vilna: B. Kletskin, 1927.

"Meydlekh, froyen, vayber, un . . . nevue." *Literarishe bleter* 4, no. 22 (June 3, 1927): 416.

Mayselekh (children's poems). Warsaw: Yidishe Shul Organizatsye in Poyln, 1931.

Dzshike gas (poems). Warsaw: Literarishe Bleter, 1933, 1936.

Freydke (poems). Warsaw: Literarishe Bleter, 1935, 1936.

In land fun mayn gebeyn: lider (poems). Chicago: Farlag L. M. Shteyn, 1937.

Oyfn barg (poems). New York: Yungvarg Bibliotek, 1938.

Ale fentster tsu der zun: shpil in elef bilder. Warsaw, Literarishe Bleter, 1938.

Fun lublin biz nyu-york: togbukh fun rivke zilberg (novel). New York: Farlag Papirene Brik, 1942.

Pitḥu et hasha'ar: shirei yeladim (children's poems). Hebrew translations by Fanya Bergshteyn, Natan Alterman, Lea Goldberg, Avraham Levinson, Yankev Fikhman. With a story about the poet by Yankev Fikhman. Illustrated by Tirtsa. Israel: Hakibbutz Hameuchad Publishing House, 1945; 2d. ed., 1979.

Yidishe kinder: mayselekh (children's poems). New York: Tsentral-Komitet fun di Yidishe Folks-Shuln in di Fareynikte Shtatn un Kanade, 1945.

Der melekh dovid aleyn iz geblibn (poems). New York: Farlag Papirene Brik, 1946.

Nokhn got fun midbar: drame (play). New York: Farlag Papierene Brik, 1949.

In yerusalayim kumen malokhim (poems) New York: Farlag Papirene Brik, 1952.

A hoyz oyf grand strit (play). New York, 1953.

A shtub mit zibn fentster (short stories). New York: Farlag Mantones, 1957.

Oyf di vegn fun tsion. (essays for youth). New York: Pinchas Gingold Farlag of the National Committee of the Jewish Folk Schools, 1957.

Lider fun khurbn: antologye (anthology of Holocaust poems). (editor). Tel Aviv: Farlag I. L. Peretz, 1962.

Likht fun dornboym: lider un poeme (poems). Buenos Aires, Farlag Poaley Tsion Histadrut, 1965.

"Mayn elterzeydns yerushe." *Svive* (March 1965–April 1974). Serial autobiography.

Baym toyer: roman fun dem lebn in yisroel (novel). New York: CYCO, 1967.

Martsepanes: mayselekh un lider far kinder (children's poems). New York: Bildungs-Komitet fun Arbeter-Ring and Farlag CYCO, 1970.

Shirei Yirushalayim (poems). Hebrew translations by Mordehai Saber. Israel: Hakibbutz Hameuchad, 1971.

Molodowsky was also the editor of the literary journal *Svive*, which she founded, from 1943 to 1944, and from 1960 to 1974.

Works about Molodowsky and Yiddish Literature

Glatshteyn, Yankev. "In tokh genumen: Kadya Molodowsky's nay bukh lider" ("The Essence of Things: Kadya Molodowsky's New Book of Poems"). *Yidisher kemfer* (New York) 28, no. 678 (November 29, 1946): 14–15.

Hellerstein, Kathryn. "'A Word for My Blood': A Reading of Kadya Molodowsky's 'Froyen-lider' (Vilna, 1927)." *AJS Review* 13, nos. 1–2 (1988): 47–79.

———. "A Question of Tradition: Women Poets in Yiddish." In *Handbook of American-Jewish Literature: An Analytical Guide to Topics, Themes, and Sources*, 195–237. Edited by Lewis Fried. New York: Greenwood, 1988.

———. "The Subordination of Prayer to Narrative in Modern Yiddish Poems." In *Parable and Story in Judaism and Christianity*, 205–36. Edited by Clemen Thoma and Michael Wyschogrod. New York: Paulist Press, 1989.

———. "Hebraisms as Metaphor in Kadya Molodowsky's Froyen-Lider, I." In *The Uses of Adversity: Failure and Accomodation in Reader Response*, 143–52. Edited by Ellen Spolsky. Lewisburg: Bucknell University Press; Toronto: Associated University Presses, 1990.

———. "In Exile in the Mother Tongue: Yiddish and the Woman Poet." In *Borders, Boundaries, and Frames: Essays in Cultural Criticism and Cultural Studies (Essays from the English Institute)*, 64–106. Edited by Mae G. Henderson. New York: Routledge, 1995.

———. "Tigvuat meshorreret idish b'amerike: kadye molodovski—al nokheha hashoah." Translated into Hebrew by Professor Shalom Luria, *Chulyiot* 3 (spring 1996): 235–53.

Howe, Irving, Ruth R. Wisse, and Khone Shmeruk, eds. *The Penguin Book of Modern Yiddish Verse.* New York: Viking, 1987.

Kazdan, Kh. Sh. "Di dikhterin af der dzshike gas" ("The Poetess on Dzshike Street"). *Vokhnshrift far literatur, kunst, un kultur* (Weekly for Literature, Art, and Culture) 22, no. 122 (June 9, 1933): 2.

Klepfisz, Irena. "*Di mames, dos loshn*/The Mothers, the Language: Feminism, *Yidishkayt*, and the Politics of Memory." *Bridges* 4, no. 1 (winter/spring 1994): 12–47.

Korn, Rokhl H. "Dzshike gas un ir dikhterin" ("Dzshike Street and Its Poetess"). *Literarishe bleter*, 11th year of publication, 10, no. 506 (3), Warsaw (January 19, 1934): 36–37.

Leyvik, H. "Kadya Molodowsky—Dikhterin fun *unzer* dzshike gas" ("Kadya Molodowsky—Poetess of *Our* Dzshike Street"). *Fraye arbeter shtime*, New York, October 11, 1935, 5.

Niger, Sh. "Shver tsu zayn a poet" ("It's Hard to be a Poet"). *Der tog*, February 10, [1933].

Peczenik, F. "Encountering the Matriarchy: Kadya Molodowsky's *Women Songs.*" *Yiddish* 7, nos. 2–3 (1988): 170–73.

Pratt, Norma Fain. "Culture and Radical Politics: Yiddish Women Writers in America, 1890–1940." In *Women of the Word: Jewish Women and Jewish Writing*, 111–35. Edited by Judith R. Baskin. Detroit: Wayne State University Press, 1994.

Ravitsh, Melekh. "Kadya Molodowsky." In *Mayn leksikon: Yidishe dikhter, dertseyler, dramaturgn in poyln tsvishn di tsvey groyse velt-milkhomes*, 122–24. Montreal: A Committee in Montreal, 1945.

Zucker, Sheva. "Kadya Molodowsky's 'Froyen-Lider.'" *Yiddish* 9, no. 2 (1994): 44–51.

www.ingramcontent.com/pod-product-compliance
Lightning Source LLC
LaVergne TN
LVHW020430080826
844660LV00034B/1377